Story, Formation, and Culture

Story, Formation, and Culture

From Theory to Practice in Ministry with Children

EDITED BY
Benjamin D. Espinoza
James Riley Estep Jr.
Shirley Morgenthaler

FOREWORD BY
Holly Allen

☙PICKWICK *Publications* • Eugene, Oregon

STORY, FORMATION, AND CULTURE
From Theory to Practice in Ministry with Children

Copyright © 2018 Wipf and Stock Publishers. All rights reserved. Except for brief quotations in critical publications or reviews, no part of this book may be reproduced in any manner without prior written permission from the publisher. Write: Permissions, Wipf and Stock Publishers, 199 W. 8th Ave., Suite 3, Eugene, OR 97401.

Pickwick Publications
An Imprint of Wipf and Stock Publishers
199 W. 8th Ave., Suite 3
Eugene, OR 97401

www.wipfandstock.com

PAPERBACK ISBN: 978-1-5326-4685-0
HARDCOVER ISBN: 978-1-5326-4686-7
EBOOK ISBN: 978-1-5326-4687-4

Cataloguing-in-Publication data:

Names: Espinoza, Benjamin D., editor. | Estep, James Riley, Jr., editor. | Morgenthaler, Shirley, editor. | Allen, Holly, foreword.

Title: Story, formation, and culture : from theory to practice in ministry with children / edited by Benjamin D. Espinoza, James Riley Estep Jr., and Shirley Morgenthaler; foreword by Holly Allen.

Description: Eugene, OR: Pickwick Publications, 2018 | Includes bibliographical references.

Identifiers: ISBN 978-1-5326-4685-0 (paperback) | ISBN 978-1-5326-4686-7 (hardcover) | ISBN 978-1-5326-4687-4 (ebook)

Subjects: LCSH: Church work with children. | Christian education of children.

Classification: LCC BV639.C4 S8 2018 (print) | LCC BV639.C4 (ebook)

The chapter, "Nurturing the Infant Soul: Spiritual Formation and Very Young Children" was originally published as "Nurturing the Infant Soul: The Importance of Community and Memories in the Spiritual Formation of Young Children." It is republished here with permission of the *Christian Education Journal* (www.biola.edu/cej).

Sections of the chapter, "What's God Got to Do with It? Nurturing Spirituality and the Ability to Thrive," borrow from "An Invitation to Thrive: Helping Young People Find Their Coordinates," *Fuller* magazine, Issue 7 (Fall 2016), pp. 60–61, available at https://fullerstudio.fuller.edu/invitation-thrive-helping-young-people-find-coordinates/). Used with permission from FULLER studio, "providing resources for a deeply formed spiritual life. For more, visit fuller.edu/studio."

Manufactured in the U.S.A.   10/12/18

Ben

To my family, friends, mentors, and co-laborers who have impacted my journey in profound ways. *Gracias por todo.*

Jim

To all those who have works with and for children over the decades to pass on faith in Christ to the next generation.

Shirley

To my eight grandchildren, ranging in age from 3 to 33, who represent a generation of exploration on how a grandparent's story shapes a child's faith formation.

Contents

Foreword | xi
—Holly Allen

Acknowledgments | xv

Introduction: Story, Formation, and Culture | xvii
—Benjamin D. Espinoza, James Riley Estep Jr.,
& Shirley Morgenthaler

Part I: Story

1. The Power of Story in the Spiritual Development of Children | 3
   —Marva Hoopes

2. Children's Ministry and Narrative Theology: An Exploration | 17
   —Taryn Cleaves

3. Deconstructing Bible Storytelling with 3-5 Year-Olds | 26
   —Sandra Ludlow

4. Faith Formation and Bible Stories: A Biblical Framework for Nurturing Faith Formation through the Study of Biblical Narratives | 38
   —Barbara Fisher

5. The Role of Theology in the Definitions of Spirituality, Spiritual Maturity, and Measuring Spiritual Development | 53
—Karissa Glanville

Part II: Formation

6. An Invitation to Worship & Wonder: An Overview of Contemplative Models of Spiritual Formation | 65
—Trevecca Okholm

7. Making Space: Attending to the Spiritual Wisdom of Children | 76
—Erin Minta Maxfield-Steele

8. Making Meaning of God: The Faith Experiences of Preschool Children | 86
—Mimi L. Larson

9. Moral Formation of Children, Ages 0-12 | 99
—Catherine Maresca

10. Nurturing the Infant Soul: Spiritual Formation and Very Young Children | 108
—Shirley K. Morgenthaler, Jeffrey B. Keiser, & Mimi L. Larson

11. The Intersection of Intellectual Giftedness and Faith Development in Children | 123
—Amy Boone

12. The Experience of Conversion in the Lives of Those Nurtured in Faith | 136
—Edyta Jankiewicz

13. Communally Discerning the Legitimacy of Children's Revelatory Experiences with God | 147
—Karissa Glanville

14. Spiritually Coping with the Bind between Trauma and Ambiguous Loss Experienced by Foster Children | 159
—Ron Bruner & Chad Thompson

15. Nurturing Spiritual Development in Children Whose Parents are Incarcerated: A Holistic Approach | 170
    —Holly Allen, Carly Brandvold, Alana Lauck,
      & Erin Trageser

16. Intergenerational Community Service as a Means toward the Spiritual Formation of Children | 184
    —Joseph P. Conway

Part III: Culture

17. A Faith Worth Making: Understanding the Cultural Nature of Children's Theology—and Why it Matters | 195
    —David M. Csinos

18. The Gentle Art of Moving Your Church's Family Ministry from Programs to Process | 208
    —Trevecca Okholm

19. Embodied Faith Formation | 216
    —Rebecca Chaffee

20. God & Digital Natives: Tweens' High-Tech Habits Relate to Their Spiritual Lives | 227
    —Pamela Caudill Ovwigho & Arnold R. Cole

21. What Do Kindergarteners' Spiritual Experiences and Expressions Look Like in a Secular Classroom? | 235
    —Jennifer Mata-McMahon

22. Religious and Spiritual Struggles Among Adolescents: Implications for Youth Workers and Research | 253
    —Steffany J. Homolka, Julie J. Exline, Joshua A. Wilt,
      & Kenneth I. Pargament

23. Connecting Children with God through Nature: Why We Should and How We Can | 272
    —Beverly J. Christian

24. The Building Blocks of Faith: A Model for Integrating Children's Ministry into the Congregation's Vision for Faith Formation | 284
—Robert J. Keeley & Laura Keeley

25. What's God Got to Do with It? Nurturing Spirituality and the Ability to Thrive | 296
—Pamela Ebstyne King

Contributors | 307

Foreword

IN THE SUMMER OF 2000 several children's ministry professors from North America participated in a new conference held in Chichester, England; it was the first *International* Conference on Children's Spirituality. Following that experience, a half dozen of those who attended this international conference met informally to explore the possibility of a North American gathering for academics and practitioners interested in children's spirituality in Christian settings.

With the help of a planning grant from The Louisville Institute, the first Children's Spirituality Conference: Christian Perspectives was held in June 2003 at Concordia University in River Forest, Illinois under the leadership of Kevin Lawson of Talbot School of Theology, La Mirada, California. The conference met three more times at Concordia University in 2006, 2009, and 2012.

On June 12-14, 2016, the Children's Spirituality Conference: Christian Perspectives convened once again, but for the first time at Lipscomb University in Nashville, Tennessee. Approximately 150 academics and thoughtful practitioners gathered around the children's spirituality table and discussed child theology, best practices, sociological research, and ministry implications for nurturing children's spiritual growth and development.

Men and women from around the globe—from Canada, Nigeria, Albania, Australia, and from twenty-five states—shared their current research, their innovative ministry models, and their stimulating workshops with spiritual formation leaders, children's ministers, developmental psychologists, Christian educators, sociologists, youth ministers, and theologians from a wide spectrum of Christian faith traditions. The planning team members for the 2016 conference are listed below:

- Holly Catterton Allen, *Chair*; Lipscomb University, Nashville, Tennessee
- Kathie Amidei, St. Anthony on the Lake Parish, Pewaukee, Wisconsin
- Chris Boyatzis, Bucknell University, Lewisburg, Pennsylvania
- Ben Espinoza, *Vice-President*; PhD student at Michigan State University
- Jim Estep, *Secretary*; Heritage Christian Church, Fayetteville, Georgia
- Bob Keeley, *Treasurer*; Calvin College, Grand Rapids, Michigan
- Mimi Larson, Wheaton College, Illinois
- Shirley Morgenthaler, Concordia University, River Forest, Illinois
- Trevecca Okholm, Azusa Pacific University, Azusa, California
- La Verne Tolbert, Urban Ministries, Chicago, Illinois

This book, *Story, Formation, and Culture: Current Approaches to Children's Spirituality and Ministry*, represents the best of the plenary, workshop, and paper/seminar presentations from the 2016 conference. Chapters from two of our plenary speakers, Dave Csinos and Pamela Ebstyne King, open our eyes to new ways to welcome children, bless children, nurture children, and join children on their spiritual journeys. Several chapters derive from conference workshops and seminars that addressed the impact of divorce, parental incarceration, and foster care on the spiritual lives of children. Other chapters describe spiritual disciplines with children, the importance of narrative and story for children's spiritual growth and development, and the spiritual significance of intergenerational Christian experiences for children.

Now, as this fifth conference book goes to press, plans for the sixth Children's Spirituality Conference are coalescing; we are now known as the *Children's Spirituality Summit*, but with the same commitment to bring together scholars and practitioners to

- Network Christians who are doing research and writing on children's spiritual development and formation,
- Provide a forum for integration of biblical, theological, and social science perspectives on children's spiritual experiences and formation, and

- Explore innovative approaches in children's ministry and provide encouragement to those in this vital area of ministry.

We invite you to join the conversation at the 2018 Children's Spirituality Summit and future conferences. You can find information about the 2018 Summit on our website, childrensspirit.org.

Holly Catterton Allen
Chair, Children's Spirituality Summit
November 2017

Acknowledgments

VOLUMES OF THIS MAGNITUDE require sincere efforts from a myriad of people. We would like to briefly acknowledge the people who have shaped this book and have brought it to fruition.

We first would like to thank the board of the Society for Children's Spirituality: Christian Perspectives (now Children's Spirituality Summit). Without the incredible help of the many people who comprise the board, the chapters before you would not have been possible. Additionally, we would like to thank the many authors who graciously submitted their work for inclusion in this volume. Between the many back-and-forths about formatting, citation and reference style, and other items, you have all been so gracious with us during this process. We also want to thank the team at Pickwick that has shepherded us through this process: Matthew Wimer, Chris Spinks, and Rae Harris. Thank you so much for generously and patiently working with us to bring this book to fruition. Finally, we thank our family, friends, and co-laborers who have journeyed with us during this process. All of your support has made this volume a reality, and we are so appreciative. Thank you for believing in us every step of the way, and supporting our efforts to strengthen and sharpen the church's ministry with children. Above all, *Soli Deo Gloria*.

Benjamin D. Espinoza,
James Riley Estep Jr.,
Shirley Morgenthaler,
Editors

Introduction

Story, Formation, and Culture

In 2016, the Society for Children's Spirituality: Christian Perspectives convened the fifth Children's Spirituality Conference, a multidenominational and multicultural gathering bringing together those with a deep interest in helping children grow spiritually. Scholars, pastors, ministry leaders, educators, non-profit leaders, and parents from a broad array of Christian traditions all came together around a desire to deepen our understanding of what contributes to the holistic, spiritual development of children. We shared in engaging conversations, explored cutting-edge research in children's spirituality, and debated a myriad of theological, cultural, and practical issues. Many of us left the conference energized from pondering the possibilities of how the field of children's spirituality will grow in the coming years.

One of the great traditions of our organization (now known as the Children's Spirituality Summit) is to compile a collection of the best plenary sessions, presentations, workshops from our conferences. These volumes give readers a snapshot of how the field of children's spirituality is growing and changing. The books have served as textbooks for courses on children's spirituality and ministry, and guidebooks to understanding and developing ministry practices based on cutting-edge research.

The book before you is one such collection. The 2016 conference yielded a feast of rich resources that conference participants quickly devoured. What you have in your hands represents the best of current thinking on children's spirituality and ministry with children. You will notice from the compilation of biographies toward the end of the volume that the authors come from a variety of backgrounds. This diversity strengthens the field, as we learn to converse with each other in ways that lead to productive partnerships and new, rich insights. Some authors are working in local church ministry, while others are teaching in college or seminary settings. Some work in the non-profit sector, while others are ministry leaders sharing what has worked for them in their contexts. These authors are driven by a passion to understand how children grow and develop spiritually, in addition to a deep love for the body of Christ. We are pleased with the caliber of these chapters, and we believe that you will be too.

We have divided this volume into three distinct sections: *Story, Formation,* and *Culture.* As we worked with conference presenters to produce this volume, we noticed that these three themes kept popping up in our conversations. Several presenters spoke on the importance of engaging the story of God in Christ when ministering to and with children. Other presenters emphasized how children grow in faith and pondered *our* role in this formation. A final category of presenters discussed the unique cultural and contextual factors that influence our ministry with children. Together, these themes provide a holistic picture of the various ways we understand children's spirituality and ministry. Moreover, they provide a snapshot of current thought and practice in our field. We hope that these chapters serve as a springboard for further conversations in children's spirituality that center the lives and experiences of children and look to the future.

We begin our volume by exploring the role of story in children's spirituality. Marva Hoopes discusses several ways that ministry practitioners can use stories as a means of helping children grow spiritually. Taryn Cleaves explores the role of narrative theology in formulating children's ministry practices. Sandra Ludlow offers an overview of Bible story-telling methods while reflecting on her own work ministering to and with 3-5 year olds. Similarly, Barbara Fisher explores Bible-story-telling methods based on the Four-H model, with which Ludlow engages. We close this section with a piece from Karissa Glanville on how we understand, define, and measure spiritual development in theological perspective. Together, these chapters inform our understanding of how the grand narrative of God and our own narratives play a part in children's spiritual formation.

In Part II, we explore the formative influences on children's spiritual development. Trevecca Okholm encourages us to ponder contemplative models for children's spiritual formation, and how we can implement these models into our ministries. Coming from a perspective similar to Okholm, Erin Minta Maxfield-Steele reflects on the importance of making space for children to reflect on their experiences theologically and spiritually. Mimi Larson examines preschool children (who are often ignored in the literature on children's spirituality) and their faith development. Offering a Montessorian perspective, Catherine Maresca explores how children are formed morally, from birth to age 12. Shirley Morgenthaler, Jeffrey Keiser, and Mimi Larson all explore the spiritual formation of very young children. Amy Boone (the 2016 recipient of the Stonehouse and May Research Scholarship) shares the results of her study on the connections between intellectual giftedness and children's faith development. Edyta Jankiewicz shares the results of her study that explores the conversion experiences of those who have grown up in the Christian faith. Once again, we hear from Karissa Glanville, who describes a model that emerged from her research on children's revelatory experiences with God. Ron Bruner and Chad Thompson give needed attention to the experiences of foster children, explaining how the powerful bind in which PTSD and ambiguous loss can overwhelm children in foster care. They describe ways in which the church can step in and aid these children. Holly Allen, Carly Brandvold, Alana Lauck, and Erin Trageser describe findings from their study on the spiritual development of children whose parents have been incarcerated. Closing out this section is J.P. Conway, who describes how intergenerational community service can enhance the spiritual formation of children. Together, all these chapters address important aspects of children's spiritual formation and faith development. To be fully enjoyed and understood, we encourage you to read this section as a *conversation*.

Our final section explores several aspects related to engaging societal and ecclesial cultural trends, with special attention to developing ministry practices across several contexts. David M. Csinos, one our plenary speakers from the 2016 conference, discusses the cultural nature of children's theology. Once again, we hear from Trevecca Okholm, who helps us understand how we create a family ministry culture in our local churches. Rebecca Chaffee discusses what embodied faith formation looks like in the local church. Pamela Caudill Ovwigho and Arnold R. Cole describe the impact of social media and technology on the spiritual lives of tweens. Jennifer Mata-McMahon examines how kindergarteners' spiritual experiences manifest in secular classrooms. In a fine example of rigorous scholarly research, Steffany J. Homolka, Julie J. Exline, Joshua A. Wilt, and Kenneth Pargament describe the religious and spiritual struggles of adolescents with special attention to how youth workers can effectively minister to struggling youth. Beverly J. Christian describes why and how we should encourage children to connect with God through interaction with the created order. Robert and Laura Keeley describe an approach known as the Building Blocks of Faith that integrates children's ministry into the broader context of the church's vision for discipleship and faith formation. Finally,

Pamela Ebstyne King, another one of our plenary speakers for the 2016 conference, closes out our volume by discussing the connections between spirituality and thriving in today's society.

These chapters are only a sampling of the rich, interdisciplinary field that is children's spirituality. The question we are left with is "where do we go from here?" Our field is ever-growing, ever-changing, and always eager to explore new theories, frameworks, and perspectives. As a reader, we invite you to ponder how you will build on this rich tapestry. Will you incorporate the insights you gain from this volume into your own thinking? Will these essays cause you to rethink your approach to ministry with children? We hope that this volume will serve as a source of refreshment and encouragement in your ministry with children.

Benjamin D. Espinoza,
James Riley Estep, Jr.,
Shirley Morgenthaler,
Editors

PART I
Story

We all have a story, even children, and especially children. Especially children in the church. This section explores the significance of story in ministering to and with children as a part of the body of Christ. Listening to children tell their own faith story, sharing The Story of God's Word with children for their formation in Christ, and even forming a narrative theology for children's ministry . . . all affirm the place of story in the context of ministering to children.

The Story of God is the metanarrative for the life of the Christian, and, as such, becomes the metanarrative that must be communicated to the children with whom we minister.

The chapters in this section represent the full spectrum of story's engagement with children and of those serving in children's ministry. Whether it is children's stories, our stories, the church's story or the Story of God . . . our ministries are, at least in part, driven by story. We can listen to children's stories, they can listen to ours, and we can all listen to His Story. In doing these things, we form a context for growing in Christ. While this section will not read like a story, it is about story. Through this, it calls us to become good storytellers, as well as good story listeners.

Chapter 1

The Power of Story in the Spiritual Development of Children

# Marva L. Hoopes

STORIES HAVE LONG BEEN included in Christian education, but is the practice of telling stories something that is continued merely because "we've always done it this way," or is there merit in continuing their use? Is there more to a story than amusement? This research attempts to address the importance of story in the spiritual lives of children by investigating empirical, theoretical, and theological literature related to how story can be used by Christian educators and parents to benefit the child's instruction and spiritual growth. It will show how story affects the whole person, rendering it a very powerful medium for ministry with children.

Using Luke 10:27 as an organizing principle, story is analyzed as to how it affects the *heart*, the affective realm; the *soul*, the spiritual realm; *strength*, the behavioral realm; the *mind*, the cognitive realm; and *loving neighbor as oneself*, the social realm. These realms, together, comprise a faith that involves a totality of commitment. We will then make recommendations as to how Christian educators and parents can use the power of story to benefit the instruction and the spiritual growth of children. The use of story can be a spark for children's spiritual growth and holds great potential benefit for the church and for the children who are a part of the community of faith.

Questions

It was a ministry staff retreat. The lead pastor asked us to list things in ministry that most demanded our time and then to evaluate the expenditure of that time. I jotted down, "*Preparing and telling the Wednesday night chapel story.*" Looking back over two decades in children's ministry I realized much of my time involved telling stories to children. That retreat time of reflection and evaluation of ministry led to this study. I asked questions such as: Was all that time spent in telling stories, time well spent? Did all those stories really make a difference in children's spiritual lives, or were they just entertaining? Was there truly power in a simple story? I suspected that there was indeed great power in this medium of story, but I still needed to ask further questions. I wondered if we continued the practice of telling stories merely because "we've always done it this way" or whether there is there real merit in continuing their use.

Story is a wildly popular theme in Christian education today. Children love stories. They ask for stories and are entertained by them. But does a story have transformative power? If so, what gives story its power and how can that power best be used by Christian educators to help children grow spiritually? An extensive research followed. A summary of current empirical and theoretical literature regarding the use of story is included here. Conclusions are then proposed on how story can be better utilized by Christian educators and parents to benefit and strengthen the spiritual growth of children.

Definition of Story

Story is understood here as an account of the experiences of a certain character or characters in a chain of events moving through time and space, facing conflict and reaching resolution (Steffen 2005; Fackre 1984). In the church setting, stories told are usually from the Bible, but may also include mission stories, modern day dilemmas, heroes of the faith, and even classic stories from children's literature (May et al. 2005). In popular culture, a story is often viewed as fictitious, and in many instances this may be the case. Biblical stories, however, are held as true historical events that took place with genuine people, in actual places, as real, past experiences (Fee & Stuart 1993).

A story may also be an historical account of a person's life experience, such as that of a missionary or a person in church history. By the same token, contemporary stories of people in each community of faith tell of their significant experiences. A person may tell his or her own story, and thus derive meaning and significance in the sharing (May et al. 2005).

A story can be oral, written, visual, or dramatized as it is communicated. The term "God's Story" can be used to describe the metanarrative, or "the entire collective story found in the Bible" (Novelli 2008, 7). Although many findings can be generalized globally, the focus of this research applies to children who are between the ages of 5–11, and is primarily directed to Christian, evangelical families and churches in North America.

From this research it is clear that children do have valid spiritual lives and they need the caring help and guidance of invested adults to nurture them. Although there are certainly many factors affecting children's spirituality, the focus here will be on the power of story, and how it potentially impacts children's spiritual growth.

How Can Story be Better Used to Benefit the Instruction and Spiritual Growth of Children?

Empirical and theoretical literature was reviewed and organized into main themes utilizing Jesus' conversation with an expert in the law regarding the inheritance of eternal life in Luke 10:27: Love the Lord your God with all your heart and with all your soul and with all your strength and with all your mind;" and, "Love your neighbor as yourself."

Jesus directed the love of God and our faith to the whole person. This love of God "indicates the totality of one's commitment in the purest and noblest intentions of trust and obedience toward God. The words taken together mean that the people are to love God with their whole selves" (Barker & Kohlenberger 1994, 247). In loving the Lord with all your *heart*, the affective realm is addressed. In loving the Lord with all your *soul*, the spiritual realm is acknowledged. In loving the Lord with all your *strength*, the behavioral realm is included. Loving the Lord with all your *mind* refers to the cognitive realm. In loving your *neighbor as yourself*, the social realm is drawn in as well. Each of the points in the following realms summarizes the findings in empirical research and theoretical literature investigated in this project.

The Affective Realm. To "love the Lord your God with all your heart" involves the affective realm, or the emotional area, involving values, attitudes, or convictions. The review of social-science literature showed the influence of story in the affective realm in some heartening ways.

- Stories can help people face difficult times (Coles 1989).
- Stories support children dealing with loss, grief, and illness (Scaletti & Hocking 2010; Edgar-Bailey & Kress 2010; Crogan, Evans, & Bendel 2008).

- Stories help children develop values and moral reasoning (Sanchez 2007).

The Spiritual Realm. To "love the Lord your God with all your soul" involves the spiritual realm, or that part of mankind in relationahip to God. It involves the vertical relationship we have with God. The review of social-science literature showed the meaningful influence of story in the spiritual realm.

- Stories from the mission field can give inspiration and play a part in the formation of a child's worldview and direction for life (Schoepflin 2001; Wimberly 1996).
- Stories can be used to encourage forgiveness and healing (Haitch & Miller 2006).
- Stories of physical healing can be used to affirm faith and belief in the reality and power of God (Singleton 2001).
- Stories from Scripture help draw meaning for life (Worsley 2004).
- Biblical stories help children know God, as they experience God with awe, wonder, and mystery (Stewart 1989).

The Behavioral Realm. To "love the Lord your God with all your strength" involves the behavioral realm, sometimes called the psychomotor domain. This involves actions and skills, or competence. The review of social science literature showed evidence for the influence of story in the behavioral realm.

- As Bible stories are heard and internalized, children's behavior is affected (Hauerwas 1985).
- Stories told in a Christian education setting have lasting effects in the behavioral realm (Hoopes 2010).

The Cognitive Realm. To "love the Lord your God with all your mind" involves the cognitive realm. This domain describes the area of thinking and knowing, or cognition. The review of social-science literature showed the influence of story is apparent in the cognitive realm.

- Storytelling enhances the learning of history (Mills & Sanchez 2005).
- Life narratives help students connect pedagogic moments, providing space for knowing as learning (Goodson & Crick 2009).
- Reading stories aloud together helps students extend their knowledge (Wiseman 2011).

- Stories have power in helping children learn the tenets of the faith (Nolan 2007).

The Social Realm. To "love your neighbor as yourself" involves the social realm. This is the part of mankind that relates to people. As the spiritual dimension refers to the vertical relationship we have with God, the social dimension involves the horizontal relationships we have with others, thus using the cross as a metaphor for the relationships of every Christian. Another power of story is to help us see through the eyes of others.

- Story helps children understand and identify with people in cultures and environments quite different from their own (Lenox 2000).
- Stories can help children change their perceptions of others who may have physical or mental disabilities (Johnson 2010).
- Stories can help in understanding the need for justice in our society (Cascante-Gómez 2007).

So what can we conclude from this broad empirical and theoretical research? What gives story its power? Story can be seen as having an effect on the whole person! Because it has an influence on the affective, spiritual, behavioral, cognitive, and social dimensions of children's development, it has an amazing potential for transformation. The benefits of story are important, and the wise leader and parent will utilize this vital method for the children's benefit.

Recommendations for Leaders to Observe in the Transmission of Stories

The research uncovered good practices for Christian educators and parents as stories are used to nurture the spiritual development of children:

- Bible stories must be faithful to the biblical account. Children should not be taught something they will have to "unlearn" later (Copley 2007; Dalton 2007; Boomershine 1988).
- Bible stories told in chronological order appeals to people of varied ages, worldviews, learning styles and dispositions, and can move students through a spiritual formation process (McIlwain 2005; Novelli 2008).
- As we see the larger *story* that "stories" are a part of, we place ourselves in "God's Story" (Short 2012).

Implications for Ministry—Using the Power of Story

How can those who work with children in church and parachurch ministry contexts employ the power of story to enhance the spiritual development of children? Twenty recommendations (although there are actually many more) were selected from this research.

Share Faith Stories. Since children draw heavily on what parents, extended family members, and religious leaders have told them (Coles 1990; Wuthnow 1999), we must share our faith stories with children. Ways that we trust in God. Personal faith practices; Spiritual disciplines we employ. These stories can help children find how God might be leading them in these areas. Invite older Christians to come and tell their stories to children (Wimberly 1996). One church devoted a time each week for someone to share "My Story for God's Glory." Individual people shared a story of how God had worked in the past, and how that impacted them. The stories were transcribed and put into an album for all to read and to receive inspiration as evidence of God's power to bring transformation.

Tell Stories from the Bible to Help Children Gain an Understanding of Who God is and What He is Like. God's character is revealed through the stories in the Bible. Parables and historical narratives in Scripture show God's nature and character, helping children to know him better (James 2002). When telling a Bible story, ask the children to listen for what they might learn about God, even if the story is about another character. For example, in telling the story of Moses and the parting of the Red Sea, ask, "What does this story tell us about God?" Through the story of Moses, insight into God's character can be gained.

Provide Times for Children to Respond to God with Wonder and Awe. Point out how God is the hero of the story. Ask how our hearts are drawn to him through this story. Stories have significant value in the affective realm to shape attitudes and values. The use of Bible stories will help children learn to "know, love and worship God, not just learn *about* God" (Stewart 1989, 350). Telling biblical stories with a sense of reverence can lead children to follow our lead and experience awe and wonder as they catch the sense of God's grandeur.

Present the Bible as One Grand Story Rather than a Compilation of Many Isolated Stories. Bible stories told in chronological order can help children understand God's grand story and can help move students through a spiritual formation process (McIlwain 2005; Novelli 2008). Children need to see the overarching story of God's great plan for mankind (Short 2012). As particular Bible stories are told, they can be identified on a timeline or graphic, demonstrating the big picture of Scripture. Teachers can tell children that within the large story of God, this particular story falls in this place and fits perfectly into God's plan. As children learn the story of God, they can put themselves into God's story as well (Stonehouse & May 2010).

Read Scripture Stories Directly from the Bible. Help children know the Word of God by not diluting or changing the words (Cavalletti 2002). Explain difficult words or concepts before or afterwards or both. Children who can read can look up the passage and read it for themselves.

When Telling Bible Stories, Make Them True to the Biblical Account. Sometimes Bible stories can be told in child-friendly language, translating the Scripture into language they can understand (Dalton 2007). A good storyteller edits material in order to effectively reach the audience (Boomershine 1988). If editing is done for biblical stories, the storyteller should communicate this to the children (Copley 2007; Dalton 2007). A wise practice could be to read the story directly from Scripture, and then tell it, act it out, use puppets, or yet another method, but tell the children, "We don't know for sure, but this Bible story *could have* gone something like this . . ." Let them know this is your interpretation of the story, not the words from the Bible.

This also applies to Bible story videos. I had just finished telling the story of Joshua and the fall of Jericho, and felt it had gone well. I had used an engaging method, had followed the biblical account closely, had added emotion and drama, and made God the hero. As I was putting materials away, a child approached me and said, "That was a good story, but that's not the way it really goes. I have the video at home, and you didn't tell it quite right!" I realized that the video had taken great liberties with the story and had inserted possible scenes not in the biblical account. After that encounter, whenever I show a Bible story video I preface it with: "As we watch this Bible story video, think about what the Bible actually says. What part of the video really happened, and what parts have been added by the producers to make it an exciting and fun story for children?" After the showing, it is critical to include a discussion of the above question. This helps children develop viewer discernment.

Provide Times when Children Reflect on and Respond to the Actual Bible Story. Instead of pre-determining a particular point for every Bible story, lead the children in a discussion using reflective engagement (Stonehouse &

May 2010). Explore how the characters in the story might have felt, and what the story could mean to people back then, and to children today. Let children reenact the story using concrete materials. Provide times for children to reflect and respond to God with wonder and awe (Dalton 2007). Allow children to engage with the story itself and leave room for the Holy Spirit to speak to them. Give time for children to think deeply about the story (Short 2011). Ask open-ended questions. Use activities that relate directly to the story.

Use Bible Stories as a Source of Encouragement and Comfort when Facing Difficult Times (Coles 1989). The story of Joseph demonstrates that God had a plan and worked for the good for Joseph and his family, even though there were difficult circumstances. The point: while God's plan for our lives is different than it was for Joseph's, God works in our lives for his purposes, just as he worked in Joseph's life. He will help us through difficult times. Likewise the stories in the book of Daniel show that God gives courage to be faithful and is with his children during times of trial. Many Psalms are evidence of how David turned to God in times of discouragement and when he was feeling threatened. Help children find Bible stories that will bring them encouragement and comfort in times of need.

Use Story to Help Children Deal with Loss, Grief, and Illness. Forms of story such as creative writing, journaling, bibliotherapy, or drawing a narrative to express and work through feelings can help children process a difficult event. Bible stories of those who suffered and found help in the Lord can be of great encouragement. Jeremiah, Elijah, Nehemiah, and the Apostle Paul all found help in God's strengthening and comforting power. As children find comfort in the Lord, they can use their own story to encourage others through verbal sharing or through stories they write (Scaletti & Hocking 2010; Edgar-Bailey & Kress 2010; Crogan, Evans, & Bendel 2008).

Use Story to Help Children Develop Values and Moral Reasoning (Sanchez 2007). The use of Bible stories can help children develop in character, attitudes, and values. Stories of prophets such as Elijah or Jeremiah, who stood up to evil and godlessness, can help develop boldness in children today. The stories of God's people listed in Hebrews 11 are excellent examples of God's faithfulness (James 2002). Stories of missionaries, martyrs, and heroes of church history, such as Amy Carmichael, Jim Elliott, and George Mueller, can inspire children to follow their faithful examples.

Tell Stories from the Mission Field to Give Inspiration and Play a Part in the Formation of a Child's Worldview and Direction for Life. Many missionaries affirm that they first thought God might be "calling" them to the mission field when, as children, they listened to mission stories and listened to visiting missionaries' tales (Schoepflin 2005). There are many choices of inspiring mission stories. Dave and Neta Jackson have written several series of books (*Trailblazer Books*, and *Hero Tales*, Bethany House) that present stories adapted for children on the lives of missionaries and other heroes in church history. Janet and Geoff Benge have written a series on the lives of Christian heroes (*Christian Heroes: Then and Now*, YWAM Publishing). How can Christian educators promote these books and encourage children to actually read them? One way is to offer activities such as Book Clubs, in which children can read books for a friendly contest. Promoting books, telling children about them, and even reading a brief section of a book with enthusiasm will also spark interest. Develop a lending system so that children can easily and readily have access to books.

Read Aloud to Children. Read books to the children in class time. A chapter read each week will build interest and keep them looking forward to the next portion. Leaders can extend biblical knowledge and godly ways of thinking as they guide the children to think about and respond to the story (Wiseman 2011).

Use Stories to Encourage Forgiveness and Healing (Haitch & Miller 2006). When stories are told illustrating the necessity and power of forgiveness, children can be challenged to take the step to forgive, if and when necessary. Bible stories expressing God's view of forgiveness include Jesus' parable of the unforgiving servant, Jesus on the cross, and the martyrdom of Steven. There are many stories from history that also can be used, such as Maskepetoon, a Native chief who after his conversion became known as a peacemaker, even forgiving the murderer of his father. Forgiveness as an issue, should not limited to heinous wrongs; sometimes even small actions require an attitude check and the application of forgiveness. A personal story by a leader could be a brief, simple, and powerful witness to the power of God, as an example that will empower children to also forgive.

Use Stories of Physical Healing to Affirm Faith and Belief in the Reality and Power of God. Stories of healings often bring confirmation of faith in our amazing and powerful God. They can be a powerful catalyst to bring the unbelieving to faith (Singleton 2001). The Bible abounds with healing stories giving honor and testimony to a God who hears and answers prayer. It is important to point to God's sovereignty and power in these stories, and not glibly promise children that God will heal everyone at all times. God assures us that he hears and cares about our suffering. God does answer prayers for healing and these stories remind us of his power.

Use Stories to Help Children Learn the Tenets of the Faith. The story of salvation told through biblical narrative and related to a specific doctrine, followed by the application of that doctrine to daily life, was practiced first by Augustine. It was the best and most effective way to pass on the faith to the next generation, and still can be used today (Nolan 2007). For example, when teaching the Ten Commandments, utilize stories that illustrate someone following (or not following) each of the commandments. Children will more likely remember the commandments by associating them with the stories they have heard.

Tell Stories that Have Settings and Characters in Other Places and Cultures. As children listen to people's struggles and situations in cultures different from their own, they can learn to be more accepting and identify with people of other races, nationalities, and cultures (Lenox 2000). Carefully choosing those stories is important, as we do not want to encourage following a false religion or belief, but instead to value all people as created by God and therefore precious. Missionary stories can be particularly influential when they affirm the value of people and do not represent the other cultures as somehow inferior or cast them in a negative light (Schoepflin 2005). Good stories will portray characters in other cultures that share godly values and find redeeming elements of that culture.

Tell Stories that Feature a Child with a Physical or Mental Disability. Understanding what children with disabilities face can be augmented by a well written story (Johnson 2010). Children can sympathize with and relate to others through a story. The next step would be to encourage Christ-like ways that will be caring and kind to others, as treating others as we would want to be treated. Viewing others through the eyes of Jesus and valuing and befriending those "others" will lead children to "love your neighbor as yourself."

Use Biographies and Autobiographies to Help Children Understand the Need for Justice. True, personal stories can bring injustice to light and help children respect and care for others (Cascante-Gómez 2007). Stories of Harriet Tubman and the Underground Railroad, Elizabeth Fry fighting for prison reform, or Mary Slessor battling twin killing are all fine examples of people who were moved to action to stand up for justice. Find stories of people who are engaged in current struggles to eliminate injustice such as homelessness, hunger, and the care for prisoners and their families. A local soup kitchen or homeless shelter may have some good resources and stories of courageous people right in your own community. They may also encourage field trips for children to see their work in action and even provide help to that work.

Wise Storytellers Prepare Well to Tell Bible Stories. As stories are prepared, identify the episodes of action within the larger story. Draw out insights into the characters to create identification with those characters. Suspense and surprise in a story's development can take place through verbal threads of repeated words and phrases and clear delivery. Analyze the text in order to translate it into the spoken word. Study the story, pray the story, tell the story, and then help someone else learn the story (Boomershine 1988).

Storytellers Play an Important Role in How Children Receive Stories. Establishing a caring relationship is an important step in ministry with children. A storyteller's voice is a tool which can capture children's attention and make imaginations soar. As a storyteller enjoys the story, children will find pleasure in it as well. Children have preferences for a variety of learning modalities, and it is essential to reach every child by using different methods along the way. Creative techniques and unique presentations can create memorable experiences which can then lead to thoughtful processing and life changes. The leader must remain faithful to tell the stories as the Holy Spirit guides, and then pray and trust God for the results (Hoopes 2011).

Implications for Ministry and Recommendations for Christian Education Directors and Curriculum Developers

What about implications for ministry for those who are Directors of Christian Education and for curriculum developers? Should stories from the Bible be presented exclusively in chronological order, or should thematic units be employed? What about open storying versus telling stories with pre-determined points? Is there a time for leader-directed stories, or should there always be student participation?

The answer: it is not a matter of either/or, but rather both/and. All are needed! Using both chronologically ordered stories and thematic units will provide a proper biblical perspective for children. Open storying can be very beneficial to allow the Holy Spirit to move in a child's heart, but pre-determined points will also give appropriate hermeneutical structure and guidance. Both are needed. Using leader-directed teaching along with student participation can achieve different goals. With both methods, different kinds of learning can take place to make a significant impact in a child's spiritual development.

Conclusions

Story has great power because of its effect on the whole person through the affective, spiritual, behavioral, cognitive, and social dimensions. As faith grows holistically, it is transforming in all areas of life. An important conclusion of this research is the call for Christian educators to be intentional about their use of story with children. The question is not *whether* there will be an influence, but to what end that influence will take place. How will children be changed through each story? The power of story has significant value in shaping attitudes and values, faith and spiritual development, actions and behavior, ways of thinking and knowing, and in relating to others.

The church and the family must work together to help children develop spiritually. It is not an either/or affair—the church must support and encourage the family and the family must participate in and embrace the church.

It must be noted that the Christian faith is more than story. There are great portions of Scripture that are not encompassed through story, and should not be neglected in the life of a disciple, including children as disciples. These include propositions, laws, poetry, epistles, and visions. The rational must not be neglected while the imaginative is set in its rightful place. However, there is power in story to transform lives in a way that a cognitive, rational proclamation cannot.

The power of story is available to all — to people of all ages, social or economic status, educational level, or experience. Story must be used prudently and with purpose for the spiritual development of children. God has given this method through which his very character and design for life can be understood. The church is wise to use this providential method for the spiritual development of children as faith is passed on from one generation to the next.

Perhaps most important is the realization that through story, children, parents, and teachers become part of God's never-ending story. As we each tell our own story and connect it with the Biblical perspective, we find our place in God's grand story.

References

Allen, Holly Catterton. 2012. "How Parents Nurture the Spiritual Development of Their Children: Insights from Recent Qualitative Research." In *Understanding Children's Spirituality: Theology, Research, and Practice*, edited by K. E. Lawson, 197–222. Eugene, OR: Cascade.

Barker, Kenneth. L., and John Kohlenberger III, eds. 1994. *Zondervan NIV Bible Commentary* Vol. 2, *New Testament*. Grand Rapids: Zondervan.

Berryman, Jerome. 1991. *Godly Play: A Way of Religious Education*. San Francisco: HarperSanFrancisco.

Boomershine, Thomas. 1988. *Story Journey: An Invitation to the Gospel as Storytelling*. Nashville: Abingdon.

Cascante-Gómez, Fernando. 2007. "Countercultural Autobiography: Stories from the Underside and Education for Justice." *Religious Education* 102, pp. 279–87.

Cavalletti, Sofia. 2002. *The Religious Potential of the Child: 6 to 12 Years Old*. Oak Park, IL: Catechism of the Good Shepherd.

Coles, Robert. 1990. *The Spiritual Life of Children*. Boston: Houghton Mifflin.

Copley, Terence. 2007. "The Power of the Storyteller in Religious Education." *Religious Education* 102, no. 3, pp. 288–97.

Crogan, Neva, Bronwynne Evans, and Robert Bendel. 2008. "Storytelling Intervention for Patients with Cancer: Part 2—Pilot Testing." *Oncology Nursing Forum* 35, no. 2, pp. 265–72.

Dalton, Russell. 2007. "Perfect Prophets, Helpful Hippos, and Happy Endings: Noah and Jonah in Children's Bible Storybooks in the United States." *Religious Education* 102, pp. 298–313.

Edgar-Bailey, Meredith, and Victoria Kress. 2010. "Resolving Child and Adolescent Traumatic Grief: Creative Techniques and Interventions." *Journal of Creativity in Mental Health* 5, no. 2, pp. 158–76.

Fackre, Gabriel. 1984. *The Christian Story: A Narrative Interpretation of Basic Christian Doctrine*. Rev. ed. Grand Rapids: Eerdmans.

Fee, Gordon D., and Douglas Stuart. 1993. *How to Read the Bible for All Its Worth: A Guide to Understanding the Bible*. 2nd ed. Grand Rapids: Zondervan.

George, Annie. 2010. "Children's Perceptions of the Role of Biblical Narratives in Their Spiritual Formation." PhD diss., Talbot School of Theology, Biola University, La Mirada, CA.

Hay, David, and Rebecca Nye. 2006. *The Spirit of the Child*. Rev. ed. London: Kingsley.

Hoopes, Marva L. 2011. *Exploring the Perceived Effects of Memorable Stories Presented to Children in a Christian Education Setting*. Unpublished Manuscript, Christian Education Department, Talbot School of Theology, Biola University, La Mirada, CA.

James, Steven. 2002. *The Creative Storytelling Guide for Children's Ministry: When All Your Brain Wants to Do is Fly*. Cincinnati: Standard.

Johnson, Jonathon. 2010. "Addressing Physical and Emotional Issues in Children's Literature." *Community & Junior College Libraries* 16, pp. 225–28.

Lenox, Mary. 2000. "Storytelling for Young Children in a Multicultural World." *Early Childhood Education Journal* 28, pp. 97–103.

May, Scottie, et al. 2005. *Children Matter: Celebrating their Place in the Church, Family, and Community*. Grand Rapids: Eerdmans.

McIlwain, Trevor. 2005. *Building on Firm Foundations*. Vol. 1, *Guidelines for Evangelism and Teaching Believers*. Rev. ed. Sanford, FL: New Tribes Mission.

Nolan, Lucinda. 2005. "Scaling the Heights of Heaven: Sister M Rosalia Walsh and the Use of Story in the Adaptive Way." *Religious Education* 102, pp. 314–27.

Novelli, Michael. 2008. *Shaped by the Story: Helping Students Encounter God in a New Way*. Grand Rapids: Zondervan.

Scaletti, Rowena, and Clare Hocking. 2010. "Healing through Story Telling: An Integrated Approach for Children Experiencing Grief and Loss." *New Zealand Journal of Occupational Therapy* 57, pp. 66–71.

Schoepflin, Rennie. 2005. "Making Doctors and Nurses for Jesus: Medical Missionary Stories and American Children." *Church History* 74, pp. 557–90.

Short, Sharon. 2011. "A Case Study of Children's Responses to Bible Stories." *Christian Education Journal* 8, pp. 306–25.

Short, Sharon. 2012. "Formed by Story: The Metanarrative of the Bible as Doctrine." *Christian Education Journal* 9, no. 3, pp. S-110–23.

Singleton, Andrew. 2011. "Your Faith has Made You Well: The Role of Storytelling in the Experience of Miraculous Healing." *Review of Religious Research* 43, pp. 121–38.

Steffen, Tom. 2005. *Cross-Cultural Storytelling at Home and Abroad: Reconnecting God's Story to Ministry*. Waynesboro, GA: Authentic Media.

Stewart, Sonja. 1989. "Children and Worship." *Religious Education* 84, pp. 350–66.

Stonehouse, Catherine, and Scottie May. 2010. *Listening to Children on the Spiritual Journey: Guidance for Those who Teach and Nurture*. Grand Rapids: Baker Academic.

Wuthnow, Robert. 1999. *Growing up Religious: Christians and Jews and Their Journeys of Faith*. Boston: Beacon.

Yust, Karen. 2012. "Being Faithful Together: Families and Congregations as Intergenerational Christian Communities." In *Understanding Children's Spirituality: Theology, Research, and Practice*, edited by K. E. Lawson, 223–37. Eugene, OR: Cascade.

Chapter 2

Children's Ministry and Narrative Theology

An Exploration

───── Taryn Cleaves ─────

Narrative theology is a term that you may or may not have heard during your tenure in children's ministry. When I first encountered the term (sitting in my very first seminary class) I remember feeling that I finally had an official label for an unofficial goal I had been attempting to achieve with the children under my tutelage. That first encounter was a turning point; narrative theology became the means to my end goal.

Begin at the End

With any project that I begin, I like to start at the end. Sounds a little odd, but for me, it's the only way I can really sink my teeth into a new project or program. As I begin my sixth year in children's ministry, I find myself wondering about success. What does an individual's success really look like throughout their time in ministry and at the end of their time in ministry? To me, if I can answer that question I feel that I can make a solid plan in order to move forward. So I ask you, what is *your* end goal? Picture yourself at your retirement party. You've served faithfully in ministry for fifty years. You gather together with familiar friends and family from throughout all of these years. There are even generations of families that grew up underneath your teaching and leadership. They are all there to reminisce and to wish you well in your old age. Stories are told from a handful of people of the ways you've impacted, taught, led, and walked through the many seasons of life alongside them. They call your service a success. What would that mean at that time? How would you define success at the end of your calling? What factors would determine whether or not you achieved success in ministry? Yes, even in my mere beginnings in ministry, it is here at my make-believe retirement party that I begin.

My end-goal (i.e., success) is to showcase God the Father, Son, and Holy Spirit in such an accurate, understandable, and engaging way that children come to desire and grow (be transformed by) a head-heart-hands relationship with him. To be clear, this isn't some type of magical formula. My end-goal was developed over a number of years and after many experiences that have shaped both my personal understanding and my specific ministry context. Your end-goal may be worded differently. But however yours is worded, it is where we all begin, whether we realize it or not.

What is Narrative Theology?

I prefer to use Stanley Grenz, David Guretzis, and Cherith Nordling's (1999) definition of narrative theology: "a theological approach that utilizes the concept of story and the human person as storyteller to provide the central motif for theological reflection" (82). They further state that "narrative theologians claim that we construct our personal identity as our individual stories are joined with the transcendent story of the religious community and ultimately with the overarching narrative of salvation history" (82). Narrative theology with children is the foundation we should be laying in children's ministries today. Rather than force feeding them truth, or even interpreting the Bible for them, I believe narrative theology, taught correctly, is the answer to the staggering number of biblically illiterate adults who have seemingly "grown up" in the church.

I like to use the following visual definition of narrative theology to offer more clarity:

A Visual Representation of Narrative Theology

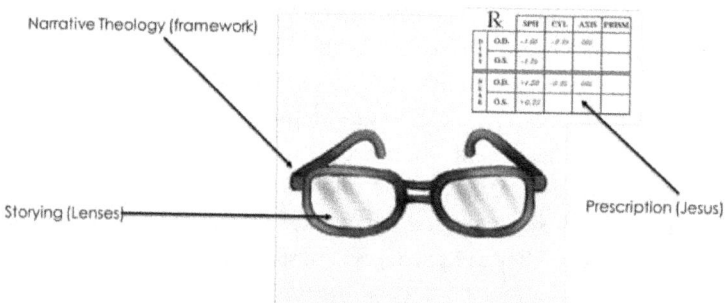

Picture narrative theology as the frames of a pair of glasses. Narrative theology connects all of the pieces and parts. The lenses however, are the method of "storying." Storying and narrative theology go hand-in-hand. Narrative theology can stand alone, however, storying as a method to children's ministry must be inside the framework of narrative theology to be successful (i.e., achieve the end-goal). However, just like any pair of glasses, the prescription must be accurately and precisely tuned to be of any use to the wearer! For illustrative purposes, our prescription is Jesus. Without the proper prescription our stories can force children to be focused on the wrong things (like good behavior) rather than on the ultimate end: Jesus!

May, Posterski, Stonehouse, and Cannell (2005) write, "we tell stories for multiple reasons. In particular, we tell the stories of Scripture because through them children comprehend the deep truths about God and the world. Through stories they understand realities that they would not grasp through abstract explanations, propositional statements, or theological concepts" (176). How does this concept relate to Children's Ministry? How does narrative theology differ from simply telling stories? Why use this approach with children? And how do children's ministry leaders implement a narrative theological approach in their ministries? It is my intent to answer these questions in the following paragraphs.

What's Happening Now? The Current State of Children's Ministry

I believe that the most troubling issue in children's ministry today is the lack of sound, biblical theology and hermeneutical education for children. Rather than focusing on the varied reasons for this, let us consider the results. Children no longer come to church seeking to learn more about God and the overarching story that he has begun and continues in us. Instead, today's children expect to be taught moral lessons and good behavior. Parents, too, assume children will come away from Sunday school with practical life lessons, rather than a driving desire to understand and know the Creator of the universe. Beckwith (2004) summarizes it well: "Unfortunately, the 20th-century modern church's method of biblical interpretation has caused its people to lose a sense of the awe, mystery, scope, and majesty of the ancient texts by turning the Bible into God's answer book" (124). Post-modernism has not only tainted how we think and interpret the Bible as adults, it has polluted the way we are teaching our children. Beckwith continues "When we use the Bible with children simply to teach doctrinal tenets, moral absolutes, tips for better living, or stories of heroes to be emulated, we stunt the spiritual formation of our children and deprive them of the valuable spiritual story of God" (Beckwith 2004, 126). Unfortunately, this is exactly what is happening in many children's ministries and Sunday school classes across the nation every week.

What Does Narrative Theology Look Like in Children's Ministry?

It is my firm belief that narrative theology is essential to effective children's ministry. We, as ministers, should not wait until our church members are adults to begin building a theological and hermeneutical foundation. It is imperative that we start building the community and teaching the narrative as early as possible. May et al. (2005) write:

> The faith community has the privilege of leading children into the stories of Scripture, where they meet God and begin to discover God's character and God's ways. In those stories they also hear God's call to live a life of love, purity, and obedience to God, a life that makes a difference in the world. Children grasp the meaning of stories and their experiences first intuitively and affectively. (142)

No matter what denomination, no matter what background, narrative theology transcends religious backgrounds, beliefs, and politics. Narrative theology isn't something for a specific Christian denomination. I believe that too many children's ministers and leaders underestimate children's abilities to understand the more difficult characteristics of God. Instead of accurately portraying his decrees of justice, his disgust at human sin, and his wrath poured out on people groups who continually and repeatedly ignore his invitation to mercy and grace, we have made the truth more palpable by telling only the positive side of the story, and in doing so, watering it down so that it is no longer hermeneutically accurate. While it is tempting, especially with toddlers and pre-K children, to read to them from a children's story Bible, we should tread lightly and choose our resources wisely. Many children's story Bibles are guilty of telling sanitized versions of biblical narratives. In her article, *Alternative Bible Stories for Young Children*, Jewish author Lifsa Schachter writes, "Because the Bible is not written for children, its stories are rewritten in simplified form in order to make them accessible to them. But the biblical narratives cannot be reduced to simple tales without doing great damage to their meaning. This meaning is totally lost when the Bible is reduced to a simple tale. Young children's difficulties with biblical narratives are further complicated because they lack knowledge of the social and cultural context of the Bible" (as cited in Stroup 1991).

Beckwith (2004) summarizes it well in the following,

> Are we afraid that God will lose face in the eyes of the children if we tell the whole story? Are we worried that children will become scared of God if we tell the whole story? We cheat children out of their knowledge of God when we are willing to only show them part of God's character. We give children a false view of God when we sentimentalize the Bible's stories of God for them. We sell short a child's ability to love and understand all of God's character when we shield them from the parts of God that don't seem so loving and graceful. (129)

However, it's important to keep in mind that narrative theology is more than just telling stories. Narrative theology is a strategy. A strategy is intentional. A strategy has a plan and must be implemented and maintained to be effective. By committing to a narrative theological foundation for children's ministry, we are effectively saying "no" to a lot of popular ideas and easier methods. We have all seen the advertisements for "no prep-work necessary" curricula. They make life in the ministry easy for the busy children's pastor and leader (i.e., all of us)! However, when we begin with our end-goal in mind we see and are able to say "no" to a method that doesn't get us there. Like a marathon runner who sacrifices personal time to train each day, we say "yes" to giving lesson prep extra time. This doesn't necessarily mean that we need to write our own curriculum from scratch; it means that we understand that a curriculum is just a baseline and springboard that we can tweak to fit within our narrative theology framework.

Implementing narrative theology as a foundation also means saying "no" to instantaneous behavior changes (we are no longer just teaching moral stories), neat and tidy Bible lessons that end in happy-ever-after each week, and the need to strictly adhere to our lesson plans.

Practical Steps for Implementation

"Faithful ministry requires that we engage resources with well-thought-through theological, educational, and developmental foundations," states Cheryl Magrini (2005) in her article on children's ministry resources. Earlier, I stated the importance of building a community in which children are valued. How does that relate to the narrative and story of the Bible? May and her colleagues answer, "As children come to know the stories of the Bible, they develop their identity as part of the Christian community" (2005, 176).

The two work hand in hand. Stories and community are both essential and must co-exist to truly be effective.

I propose the following methods for implementing the foundation of narrative theology and education into children's ministries. Certainly these are not the only solutions, but I believe they provide a launching pad to facilitate growth and confidence in this approach. As with any change of philosophy or group leadership, adaption should be gradual and accompanied by proper goal setting. We would do well to remember that with effective and lasting transformation, it may take years to begin to see the fruits of our labor.

While there are many factors to consider when implementing a narrative theological foundation in your children's ministry, I offer a handful of universal tips rather than an exhaustive list of directives.

1. Choose Resources and Curriculum Wisely

Many children's Story Bibles are guilty of telling sanitized versions of biblical narratives. Biblical narratives can be simplified only so much before they become sterile and inaccurate. Along the same principle, we need to help educate parents and families with reliable resources for home use. The reality is that children's Bibles are a mixed bag. A great Bible for kids will put an emphasis on God as the central character in the story rather than on the human Bible characters or even our (the reader's) behavior. When a story is completed, does the conclusion turn the reader's focus on what God has done for his people? Or does it focus on the Bible character's behavior and how we (the reader) can emulate them? These differences are great but often largely missed by parents and ministry leaders as we focus on the "extras" beyond the biblical text, i.e. color pictures, cool graphics, teaching points on the side of the text, front cover design, etc.

2. Build a Community in which both Children and Story are Valued and Meaningful

Narrative theology plays a major role in the spiritual formation of children. It allows them (and us) to develop their identity as children of God and understand their role in the Story through the lens of their communal uniqueness. "Faith is not something that develops in a vacuum. Having faith, understanding faith, exploring faith, and questioning faith are not solo activities" writes Beckwith on the role of community (2004, 74). John Westerhoff wisely states, "If our children are to have faith, we need to make sure that the church becomes a significant community of faith" (1976, 54).

In the same way that children learn by watching and imitating their parents, they also learn by watching and being a part of the faith community around them. "When children are present, experiencing life in the faith community, they sense the joy, wonder, and awe of those around them as they worship together . . . And they watch and imitate the adults and teenagers they see worshipping, relating to others in the community, and serving. Experiencing the faith community is crucial to the faith formation of children" (May et al. 2005, 142). Marva Dawn best expresses my personal feelings on the subject: "Scriptures cannot be known unless there is a genuine Christian community in which to study, memorize, and obey them" (1997, 32).

3. Maintain Healthy Balance

Because our end-goal is for children to be transformed in a growing head-heart-hands relationship with Christ, we can't focus solely on the academic side of narrative theology. We must balance narrative theology foundation with learning styles, child development, the need for play, reflection, and interpersonal relationships with peers. We can easily over-develop the mind and under-develop the heart if we are not mindful of the need for balance. Likewise, over-developing the heart and under-developing the mind is just as problematic, producing overly-sensitive believers who can be swayed by any contemporary and trendy doctrine out of a desire to "love others" like Jesus commanded. Yes, Jesus did command us to "love others" but not at the expense of truth.

4. Become a Great Storyteller

One of the roles of the church in regard to narrative theology is to intentionally continue telling and teaching the narratives of the Bible in ways that capture the attention of children. As our children are increasingly exposed to the commercialization of television and other forms of media, it is our task to discover techniques that will keep them equally engaged when teaching the life-changing narratives of the Bible.

While we tend to think that stories are generally reserved for children, adults are also exposed to stories on a daily basis–whether it be through television, songs, magazines, movies, or other sources. If you've ever watched a movie and found yourself pulling for the underdog or sympathizing with a character who is reaping the effects of bad choices, you are able to understand, as May and her colleagues write that "we relate to stories because they embody themes that resonated with us. Bible stories are rooted in reality and have the ring of truth" (2005, 174). And just as stories in movies that move us the most can pique our imaginations and become a part of us, so too can the Scriptures as story, "the imagination of the child is honored and the child's story becomes part of the Scripture story," (Magrini 2005).

5. **Get the Whole Family Involved**

In my experience, one of the most important steps to take when implementing change in children's ministry is to inform and equip the parents and/or caretakers. Even a full-time children's pastor or ministry leader has a maximum of approximately four or five hours a week with a child. This is a small morsel of time when compared to the average child's weekly schedule of school, team practice, and family time. Children's pastors must do everything within their power to effectively equip and train parents on how to lead and oversee their children's spiritual lives and formation. "Children's ministry at its most effective is ministry with the entire family, in whatever shape or form of family the child lives within, and so family systems theory and congregational systems frameworks become tools for effective, life-giving ministry with children-and their families" (Magrini 2005).

Conclusion

As a wise proverb states, "It is easier to build boys than to mend men," so too it is easier to construct a sound theological and hermeneutical foundation on which to build than to deconstruct inaccuracy and error that results from American pragmatism, relativism, and post-modernism. These missteps eat away at our ability to see the Bible and the story of God as anything more than an answer book for moral and ethical dilemmas. I conclude with a powerful reminder of the importance of biblical narrative to God's people—including children: "When biblical narrative falls silent, the people of God have nothing to remember, and with nothing to remember they soon forget who they are. Their untutored imaginations turn to other narratives and other gods. It is a familiar story" (Stroup 1991).

References

Beckwith, Ivy. 2004. *Postmodern Children's Ministry*. Grand Rapids, Michigan. Zondervan,

Carroll, John T. 2001. "Children in the Bible." *Interpretation* 55, pp. 121–34.

Dawn, Marva. 1997. *Is It a Lost Cause? Having the Heart of God for the Church's Children*. Grand Rapids. Eerdmans.

Grenz, Stanley, David Guretzki, and Cherith Fee Nordling. 1999. *Pocket Dictionary of Theological Terms*. Downers Grove, IL: InterVarsity.

Magrini, Cheryl. 2005. "The Top Five Resources in Children's Ministries." *Religious Education* 100, pp. 448–52.
May, Scottie, et al. 2005. *Children Matter: Celebrating their Place in the Church, Family, and Community.* Grand Rapids: Eerdmans.
Schachter, Lifsa. 1985. "Alternative to Bible Stories for Young Children." *Religious Education* 80, pp. 308–13.
Stroup, George W. 1991. "Theology of Narrative or Narrative Theology: A Response to Why Narrative?" *Theology Today* 47, pp. 424–32.
Westerhoff, John M. 1976. *Will Our Children Have Faith?* New York: Harper & Row.
Worsley, Howard. 2004. "How Children Aged 9–10 Understand Bible Stories: A Study of Children at a Church-Aided and a State Primary School in the Midlands." *International Journal of Children's Spirituality* 9, pp. 203–17.

Chapter 3

Deconstructing Bible Storytelling with Three-to-Five Year Olds

Sandra Ludlow

Three-to-five-year-old children's spiritual awareness, biblical knowledge, faith, and values formation is grounded in the process of meaning making as they listen to and reflect on Bible stories. As Christian early childhood teachers research, pray, prepare props, tell, and reflect on the Bible-story time, they consciously and unconsciously apply theoretical, and pedagogical constructs to the process of intentionally nurturing young children's spiritual awareness, biblical knowledge, faith, and values formation. This paper unpacks auto-ethnographically the lived experience of the teacher researcher's application of early childhood theoretical, and pedagogical constructs to the telling of Bible stories through the lenses of attention to detail, context, and experience, together with four metaphors for children's lives, theories of child development, and their associated pedagogical strategies. It reflects upon and teases out the storyteller's metacognition before, during, and after storytelling, and pays attention to the reciprocity of the relationship between the storyteller and listener as a catalyst for scaffolding children's spiritual awareness, biblical knowledge, faith, and values formation.

Theoretical Constructs Informing the Research

Bible storytelling is a process that actively connects the teller with the listener, through language, imagination, and shared understanding (Morgenthaler, Keiser, & Larson 2014). When used effectively, it is uniquely placed to be a powerful medium for communicating meaning, faith, spiritual awareness, biblical knowledge, and values to young children aged three to five years. It invites the listeners to use their head, heart, and hands in the development of their spiritual awareness and faith formation. Storytelling is a process that is enabled and enriched by the presence and work of the Holy Spirit at all stages of the storytelling process. Storytellers need to be aware of their role in this process, bathing the session in prayer, thorough preparation, and active metacognition.

Bible storytelling has the potential to become a passive experience for the young listener; one that may, in fact, lead to disinterest, and misunderstanding (McNaughton & Williams 2009). In order to avoid this pitfall and to maximize the possibility of nurturing faith and spiritual awareness, Christian early childhood teachers need to combine good storytelling techniques and active self-reflection with a deep understanding of contemporary early childhood pedagogies and theories. The reflective practices of auto-ethnography are useful as a means of maximizing the full potential of the Bible storytelling session. This research began by reviewing contemporary theoretical and pedagogical understandings, and used the findings of the literature review to inform practice.

Preschool children's spiritual awareness, biblical knowledge, and faith formation occur through an overarching framework of four interwoven metaphors for children's lives: belonging, being, becoming, and believing. "Belonging is integral to human existence," (Grajczonek 2009, 7). Children belong to a family, culture, and to groups within communities. Bible storytelling sessions, through shared attention, scaffold children's sense of connectedness and belonging to the family of God. These sessions enable children to share ideas and practices with the Christian community, and to experience a sense of the rights and responsibilities of group membership within this community. Through engaging with, and thinking about the plot, and characters of many Bible stories, children begin to develop an understanding of the "security, love, protection, and mystery of God," (Stewart 1989b, as cited in Jonkers 2015, 308). This further supports the development of their sense of belonging.

"Being recognizes, and respects the importance of the here and now in children's lives" (Grajczonek 2009, 7). It recognizes the necessity for the storyteller and the children to take the time to ask questions, express and explore ideas, and tease out understandings together, right now, in the middle of the storytelling process (Government of South Australia, Department Education & Children's Services 2008; Millikan & Giamminuti 2014). It recognizes, celebrates, and intentionally nurtures each other's experiences, alternative perspectives, felt senses, and expressions of wonder, awe, and joy (Grajczonek 2012). The experiences children have during repeated Bible storytelling sessions build on each other to help children "see patterns, and connection," (Government of South Australia Department Education & Children's Services 2008), which shape their continually evolving spiritual awareness, biblical knowledge, and faith in God and Jesus.

The metaphor of becoming recognizes the events and experiences young children encounter, and shapes their identities, knowledge, understandings, capacities, skills, and relationships (Millikan & Giamminuti 2014), as well as their dispositions. The becoming process is rapid, and constantly changing. It gives attention and respect to the notion of development. Participation in any one Bible storytelling session is but one step in the development of these capacities in relation to a child's developing spiritual awareness, biblical knowledge, and faith formation. It is through these three metaphors that the final metaphor begins to occur—believing through faith in God's existence, understanding of His character, and unconditionally trusting in His word. Three to five year old's believing is scaffolded through their interest in the notions of God's love and care, and his superhuman powers (Barratt 2012). Their faith, whether intuitive (Fowler, as cited in Straker, n.d.), borrowed (Gillespie et al. 2001), or experienced (Westerhoff III 1976), has the potential to engender a sense of courage, trust, and a willingness to obey (Habernicht & Burton 2004). Keeping the above four metaphors for children's learning at the forefront of their thinking helps storytellers holistically and skillfully approach the craft of Bible storytelling.

Theories that appear to be highly relevant to the storytelling process are: cognitive–maturational theory, socio-cultural theory, transactional theory, and feminist post-structural theory. Cognitive-maturational theory posits the child as an active constructor of their own understanding, intuitively and reflectively using theory of mind (thoughts, perceptions, wants, and feelings) to sort out what they see and hear during the storytelling process (Barratt 2012). Proponents of this theory tell us that three-to-four-year-old children view God in "anthromorphic terms," (applying the characteristics of people to God) (Boyatzis 2013, 500; Barrett 2012, 79). Maturationally, three-four-year-olds are just beginning to develop an awareness of other people's perspectives and feelings; therefore they need opportunities to label and discuss characters' feelings during Bible stories. Interestingly, Barrett's research uncovered another characteristic of young children's thinking about God. He found that children intuitively develop ideas about "nonhuman agents" who have creative powers and other superhuman properties (2012, 79–80). This has implications for children's spiritual awareness and faith formation in an omnipotent, omnipresent, creative God.

Sociocultural theorists recognize the importance of language and the relationship between the child and adult in scaffolding the child to a higher level of knowledge, skills, attitudes, and values. Adults identify and work within the child's zone of proximal development. Using the sociocultural notion of cognition, the storyteller's role is to "guide children to more advanced levels of spiritual connectedness to the sacred" (Boyatzis 2013, 502), through conversations that are truly reciprocal and use visual imagery.

Transactional theorists endorse this notion of reciprocity by focusing on the bi-directional nature of this adult/child relationship within the zone of proximal development; advocating for sustained shared thinking (SST), as a highly important pedagogy. Teachers can sustain a three-five-year-old child's thinking by asking such question as "I wonder what will happen next; why do you think he did that?; do you think that was a good thing to do?" (Fellowes & Oakley 2014, 518). Other behaviors that support SST are listening, pausing, reacting, responding, extending, and provoking alternative perspectives. During SST, teachers should also encourage children to make connections between the plot of the story and their own prior experience and knowledge.

Post-structuralist theorists add to the notion of SST by using discourse, i.e., ways of talking, valuing, and behaving, to problematize, critique, and scaffold children's reflexive competence (Damber 2015). Storytellers need to listen for and elicit the child's comments during the storytelling process, and to use these comments as triggers for discussion during and at the end of the story in order to negotiate, build, and monitor children's construction of meaning intellectually, affectively, and aesthetically (Soundy 2007). Ignoring children's comments during the story and leaving discussion of the story until the end is age-inappropriate for three-to-five-year-olds. Children of this age find it difficult to wait until the end of a story to express their thoughts or to ask questions. The storyteller needs to address questions immediately within the flow of the story. These questions are vital comprehension and metacognition cues. Wise teachers use them to shape the story as it continues to unfold.

Pedagogical Strategies Informing the Research

Nye's (2011) SPIRIT checklist highlights optimal conditions for scaffolding children's spirituality. It positions the storyteller as an agent in the process of stimulating children's spiritual awareness, and faith formation. The checklist indicates the need for a special intimate, physical, emotional, and auditory space for the story to occur in and leads the researcher to provide a story mat and storyteller's chair in her classroom. Nye's checklist also highlights the need for the storyteller to form a respectful, reciprocal relationship with the listeners during all storytelling sessions. This relationship helps children view the storytelling session with anticipation and scaffolds their spontaneous participation, comments, and questions during the story; helping them to tease out the meaning of events, characters' feelings, and God's role in each story.

The SPIRIT checklist, together with Fisher's (2010) *Four H Biblical Framework Model*, reminds the researcher of the importance of using rich description, props and action to stimulate imagination and children's comments during the session. The active learning environment scale (Government of South Australia Department. Education & Children's Services 2008), reinforces the importance of environment and props as collaborative scaffolds for meaning-making. It reminds the researcher of the importance of posing open-ended questions and waiting for answers, of finding out what children already know and have experienced, and using this knowledge to scaffold understanding of the plot, story setting, and characters' feelings. When used in conjunction with the *Four H Biblical Framework Model*, children become deeply involved in the story, developed empathy with the characters, and begin to understand the story at a deeper level. The *Four H Biblical Framework Model* draws attention to the need to make explicit historical information during the storytelling as a means of scaffolding children's meaning-making. The fact that Abram, when leaving Ur, would have only been able to take items with him that would fit onto a camel or donkey built awareness of all that Abram his family gave up, and of the slowness of their journey. The fact that Galilean fishermen usually fished at night because fish swim in deeper water during daylight helped the children comprehend the miraculous in the story of Jesus and his breakfast on the beach.

In this manner, combining all of the above strategies, the researcher and the children engage in sustained shared thinking, scaffolded and co-constructed children's personal meaning-making, as well as comprehension of the plot, setting, characters feelings, and of God's role in the story. These strategies act as important precursors to the development of spiritual awareness, biblical knowledge, and faith formation.

The 2016 *Transformational Planning Framework*, (used by Adventist Schools Australia to inform their Early Encounters Bible Curriculum), also informs the researcher's storytelling practices. This framework considers the Bible story through four lenses:

- Hook: what is this story about—engaging the child's curiosity;

- Head: I wonder what the Bible says—scaffolding knowledge and understanding;
- Heart: what does this mean for me—experiencing the love of God, and how He works in our lives;
- Hand: what is God asking me to do—responding to the Bible message.

The children and researcher consider head, heart and hand concepts over time, as they experience, and unpack the story together, (often during multiple revisits).

The hand phase of the transformational planning framework (ASA 2016) occurs during play, prayer, praise, and service, enabling children to use metacognitive reflective analysis, and schema to revisit the Bible story, actively constructing and re-constructing meaning for themselves. While engaged in these types of events children move through the various levels of Bloom's Taxonomy: remembering, understanding, applying, analyzing, evaluating, and creating (Anderson & Krathwohl 2001).

Every time a Christian early childhood teacher prepares to tell a Bible story, this transformational planning framework, together with the theory of multiple intelligences, can be used as a scaffold for metacognition about where to begin and what to include in the storytelling session. The theory of multiple intelligences alerts the researcher to the need to incorporate props, actions, and questions across as many intelligences as is practical each time she tells a Bible story. Song, rhyme, role play, and visual, and auditory props became regular features of the storytelling session. Musical instruments are used to create sound effects for the storm, a song becomes a means of concluding and revisiting the story of Jesus and the storm. Magnet experiments are used to explore the power of the Holy Spirit during Elijah's trip to heaven. Role play is incorporated into many Bible stories.

Table 1. Multiple Intelligences Experiences

Bible Story	Head Concept	Multiple Intelligence Experience
Jarius' Daughter	Jesus heals	Thank you Lord—action rhyme
Mustard seed	God's love helps us to grow more like Him	- Seeds—what do seeds need to grow? - Seed match game, set sorting (big little seeds) - Song *Read your Bible pray every day*

Bible Story	Head Concept	Multiple Intelligence Experience
Daniel and his 3 friends	God loves to see us make good choices	• Paper bag food sort • Blindfold—smell food • Mother may I? game—good bad food choices

Incorporating these types of experiences as a part of the storytelling session appears to achieve one of three purposes: either preparing the children to understand the plot or head concept before the storytelling begins, or enabling them to think more deeply about the story during the storytelling, or enabling their revisiting of its concepts at the end of the story.

Most stories begin with a story box or story bag containing props for the story. This box becomes a powerful hook, engaging the children's curiosity and interest before the story begins. There is always one child who asks, "what's in the bag (or box), today?" Sometimes we look at all of the props before we begin and wonder together about what the story could be about, and sometimes we unveil them as the story unfolded.

Stonehouse and May's (2010) reflective engagement approach to Bible storytelling, spiritual awareness and faith formation reminds us to harness the value of time, "to slow down, become quiet, and take the time" (71), to allow children to "meet God in the story" (84). To wonder together and to question so that children are able to celebrate and to unpack the wonder and mystery of God's love and plan for their lives. When Bible storytellers do this, they allow space for the Holy Spirit to speak to the heart of each listening child. All of the above pedagogical strategies, when informed by the listed theories and metaphors of children's learning and development serve to shape the researcher's thinking, and informed her decisions and actions before and during the Bible storytelling sessions.

Discoveries Made During Current Research: The Role of Metacognition and Reciprocity

For three years this teacher-researcher auto-ethnographically reflected on her metacognition, and application of early childhood theoretical and pedagogical constructs before, during, and after Bible storytelling sessions with three to five year olds. This section of the paper gives the reader a glimpse into her metacognitive processes.

When Reflecting on This Transformational Planning Framework, She Wrote the Following in Her Journal...

In my experience, it is the relationship with the storyteller that often provides a powerful initial hook into the story for the children. If they know you, and know that you always have interesting things to do and say, then they will be eager to settle and begin the story.

I often begin with a question e.g. when talking about Naaman when he decided to visit Elisha to say thank you—I asked them "have you ever been ecstatic? The man in our story today was ecstatic! He was jumping for joy, and yelling yahoo," (naturally we talked about what ecstatic meant). Then we pretended to be ecstatic. Lots of children commented about what made them very happy, and so the story began. I think that the term hook should be plural because a storyteller uses many hooks continuously throughout the story. Hooks may be the objects or the questions you bring into the story, as it progresses, or the variations in your tone of voice. Hook, and head should be a rolling, continuous part of the story.

I always try to help the children think about the characters' decisions throughout the story, and to apply it to their lives. For example, when talking about Abraham leaving Ur, we had a discussion about what he should pack and take with him if he was loading a camel or a cart. The children had many practical suggestions. We even managed to talk about the best type of sleeping bags! We also wondered together about how Abram heard God's voice telling him where to go. One child told me that every morning God looked down from heaven, and yelled out "Go that way!" We explored the concept of God putting ideas into our minds. One boy told me that he knew what ideas were. He had many ideas in his mind. Many of the children told me they had never heard God talk to them, and we wondered together about how he might talk to us. I think a number of them, (particularly the four and five year olds), went away wanting to listen for God's ideas in their mind. All of this discussion occurred as the story unfolded.

Hook, head, and heart interwove together throughout this 15-min story. During the action the children were thinking and becoming aware of how God interacts with us. This is the power of talking with *children rather than* at *children. Throughout this story the children, and I discoursed together, employing metacognition and reciprocity, to carefully scaffold spiritual awareness, faith formation, and biblical knowledge,* (Author's Reflective Journal, 21/3/16).

Despite this occurrence of reciprocity; my experience of telling Bible stories to three-to-five year olds has led me to the conclusion that a storyteller has only a brief window of opportunity (probably no more than 2 minutes) in which to engage the child's reflection on the heart, and head concept (the "felt sense,") (Hyde 2008, 84), as they apply to the story, (what does this mean for me/what is God asking me to do). Ideally, the storyteller's statements and eliciting of dialogue during and at the end of the story subtly led the child to consider the head concept. It is important to keep the message simple, just one concept for each story. Build awareness of this message through wondering and action. Explore the concept further during each revisit of the story and in follow-up Godly-play experiences, (Author's Reflective Journal, 25/4/16).

Table 2. Head & Heart Concepts

Bible Story	Head concept	Heart Concept
10 Lepers Healed	Jesus heals	I can ask Jesus God for help if I am sick
Jesus Stills the Storm	Jesus has special powers	Jesus will use His special powers to help me
Naaman	No other Gods are more powerful than God / Jesus	Jesus will use His special powers to help me

Table 3. Sample Notes for Evidence of Children Displaying *Hand* Concepts

Bible Story	Hand concept
Noah's Ark	2 boys building, re-building the ark from junk construction—deciding that God must have thoughtfully placed the heavy animals at the bottom of the boat, and Noah his family at the top of the boat to avoid the smell.
Lost Coin & Lost Sheep	Playing over and over again losing the coins and the sheep. Empathetically helping the *woman*, and the *shepherd* to find the lost, and joyously celebrating the finding of that which was lost.

Bible Story	Hand concept
Jairus' Daughter	Reverently thanking Jesus for his care and blessings while holding the flashing scrunchy ball or engaging in a stepping-stone prayer game
Widow's Mite	Bringing money every week to put in the offering so a child in India can attend school

When Reflecting on the Storyteller's Metacognition during the Storytelling Session for Jesus and the Storm, the Researcher Wrote...

Keep the action well-paced, and those sound effects coming. I'll need to talk louder over the sound effects so the children can hear me. Connect the action with the children's experience of storms. Don't make it too scary. Listen for the children's comments. That's a good one to bounce off of. Keep rowing, and bailing. Unpack the disciple's feelings even more. I need to prompt Oscar to do his storm calming. Praise the drum player, and the rest of the sound effects team. Praise the bailers and rowers, spur them on.

Time to ask—why was Jesus able to stop the storm? Relate it to their power—can you stop a storm? Wow, that girl is a deep thinker! She is right! Jesus is mighty! She's connecting it to the song we sang before (My God is so Big). He does have special power. I need to capitalize on this concept as we bring the story to a close. It is time for the reflective question, and the application to their experience of God and Jesus. Pace this well. Elicit, wonder, elicit again, and praise good thinking.

Thoughts like this constantly run through a storytellers mind, in parallel to the storytelling activity, and show that good storytellers always remain alert to their audience, using all their senses to weave the threads of the story together so that the listening child can not only hear the story, but can also experience and respond to the story through their emotions, senses, and imagination (Fellowes & Oakley 2014) as the setting comes alive, and the children begin to empathize with the characters.

What these journal reflections show is that fostering spiritual awareness, biblical knowledge, faith, and values formation through storytelling appears is be best described as a process of metacognition and reciprocity on the part of both the children and the storyteller. It is fostered in moments of time (in partnership with the Holy Spirit) with individual children who display behaviors of belonging, being, becoming and believing. Storytellers catch the teachable moments through the dynamic interaction of metacognition and reciprocity as they scaffold the child's meaning-making. This process is best envisioned as the metaphorical "tossing of a ball," (Rinaldi 2001, 78), backward and forward between the storyteller and the children throughout the story. In this manner children become active participants in the story, actively building their spiritual awareness, biblical knowledge, faith, and values through the metacognitive process of mindful sense-making, deepening their understanding of the setting, plot, characters feelings, and God's and Jesus' role in the story. They also begin to apply the head concept of the story to their own lives.

The Bible storyteller's use of pedagogical strategies (such as those found in the theory of multiple intelligences, the reflective engagement model, the *Four H Biblical Framework Model*, and sustained shared thinking), to initiate metacognitive and reciprocal dialogue with three to five year olds throughout the storytelling appears to be an important catalyst to children's formation of spiritual awareness, biblical knowledge, faith, and values.

References

Adventist Schools Australia. 2016. "Adventist Early Childhood Education, and Care: Communities of Faith and Learning." *Early Encounters Bible Curriculum*. Ringwood, VIC.

Anderson, L., and David. R. Krathwold, eds. 2001. *A Taxonomy for Learning, Teaching Assessing: A Revision of Bloom's Taxonomy of Educational Objectives*. New York: Longman.

Australian Government Department of Education, Employment & Workplace Relations. 2009. *Belonging Being & Becoming: The early years learning framework for Australia*. Barton, ACT.

Barrett, Justin. L. 2012. *Born Believers: The Science of Children's Religious Belief*. New York: Free.

Berkowitz, Doriet. 2011. "Oral Storytelling: Building Community through Dialogue, Engagement, and Problem Solving." *YC Young Children* 66, pp. 36–40.

Boyatzis, Chris. J. 2013. "The Nature, and Functions of Religion and Spirituality in Children." In *APA Handbook of Psychology, Religion, and Spirituality*, ed. Pargament, K. no. 1, 497–511. Washington, DC: APA.

Damber, Ulla. 2015. "Read-Alouds in Preschool: A Matter of Discipline?" *Journal of Early Childhood Literacy* 15, no. 2, 256–80.

Fellowes, J., and Grace Oakley. 2014. *Language, Literacy, and Early Childhood Education*. South Melbourne, VIC: Oxford University.

Fisher, Barbara. 2010. *Developing a Faith-Based Education: A Teacher's Manual*. Terrigal, NSW: Barlow.

Habenicht, D., and Larry Burton. 2004. *Teaching the Faith: An Essential Guide for Building Faith-Shaped Kids*. Hagerstown, MD: Review & Herald.

Gardner, Howard. 2003. *Making Teaching Visible: Documenting Individual, and Group Learning as Professional Development: A Making Learning Visible Monograph.* Cambridge, MA: Project Zero, Harvard University Graduate School of Education.

Gillespie, V. Bailey, et al. 2001. *Keeping the Faith: A Guidebook for Spiritual Parenting.* Riverside, CA: Hancock Center.

Grajczonek, Jan. 2012. "The Spiritual Dimensions of the EYLF Document: Implications for Educators in Religiously Affiliated Early Years Settings." *Schoolink*, 18, no. 3, pp. 8–9.

Government of South Australia, Department of Education & Children's Services. 2008. *Assessing for Learning, and Development in the Early Years Using Observation Scales: Reflect, Respect, Relate.* Hindmarsh, SA: DECS.

Hyde, Brendan. 2008. *Children, and Spirituality: Searching for Meaning, and Connectedness.* London: Kingsley.

McNaughton, G., and Gillian Williams. 2009. *Techniques for Teaching Young Children: Choices in Theory & Practice.* Frenchs Forest, NSW: Pearson Education Australia.

Milikan, J., and Stephania Giamminuti. 2014. *Documentation, and the Early Years Learning Framework: Researching in Reggio Emilia, and Australia.* Castle Hill, NSW: Pademelon.

Morgenthaler, Shirley, Jeffrey Keiser, and Mimi Larson. 2014. "Nurturing the Infant Soul: The Importance of Community and Memories in the Spiritual Formation of Young Children." *Christian Education Journal* 3, pp. 244–58.

Nye, Rebecca. 2011. *Children's Spirituality: What It Is, and Why It Matters.* London: Church House.

Rinaldi, Carla. 2001. "Documentation, and Assessment: What Is the Relationship?" In *Making Learning Visible: Children as Individual, and Group Learners*, edited by Claudia Giudici et al., 78–89. Reggio Emilia: Reggio Children.

Saraj-Blatchford, Iram. 2009. "Effective Pre-School, and Primary Education Project EPPE 3–11 an Associate ESRC TLRP Project." Paper presented at ACER Conference Frameworks, and Foundations: "When only the BEST will do." Sydney, NSW, March 26.

Soundy, Cathleen, Smita Guha, and Yun Qiu. 2007. "Picture Power: Placing Artistry & Literacy on the Same Page." *YC Young Children* 62, no. 3, pp. 82–88.

Stonehouse, Catherine, and Scottie May. 2010. *Listening to Children on the Spiritual Journey: Guidance for Those Who Teach, and Nurture.* Grand Rapids: Baker.

Straker, D. n.d. "Fowler's Faith Stage Theory." ChangingMinds.org. http://changingminds.org/explanations/learning/fowler_stage.htm.

Westerhoff III, John. H. 1976. *Will Our Children Have Faith?* San Francisco: Harper SanFrancisco.

Chapter 4

Faith Formation and Bible Stories
A Biblical Framework for Nurturing Faith Formation through the Study of Biblical Narratives

——— Barbara J. Fisher ———

As Scripture Teachers, we may unintentionally reduce biblical narratives to a values-education program, making them engaging entertainment, self-help stories, cautionary tales or a collection of 'good' stories. An essential aspect of faith formation involves nurturing the personal love of, knowledge about, and interactive engagement with biblical narratives (Bible stories) on both an intellectual and a relational level, so the following *Four H's Biblical Framework* (four- phase process) was designed to assist Scripture Teachers as they nurture a student's faith formation through an engaging and interactive 21st century transformational approach to studying biblical narratives.

Bible Stories and Narrative Schema

Everyone relates to stories. Stories have universal appeal. They connect people, present them with new ideas, motivate them, and challenge their thinking (Fisher 2014). Beck (2008) states that, "Perhaps it is these characteristics of the story that led an all-knowing God to introduce the divine Person to us by using this literary tool" (3). Chronicled in a library of sixty-six books (Old and New Testament), the sacred story is told through a variety of literary genres with the main literary genres, according to Crain (2010), being poetry, prose (narrative), and drama. However, Barton (2010), Beck (2008), Fee & Stuart (1993), Harrison (2015), and Ryken

(1984) all point out the dominance of the narrative genre evidenced in twenty-two of the sixty-six Bible books.

Crain (2010) suggests that by using literary genre conventions to study the Bible, the reader can dig deeper into the story; discover the themes, setting, characters; and points of view while illuminating the biblical writer's message. In the narrative classification or genre, writers use the terms *story* and *narrative* interchangeably because, as Fee & Stuart (1993) indicate, "narratives are stories" (78). Bratcher (2013) reasons that the two terms are synonymous since they have identical literary forms, i.e., structure, style, narrative elements and language features (Lee 2001); both forms have a linear story line; and both have identical key elements of plot structure, characters, setting, theme, and conflict (Trischitta 2008; Walch 2015). Interestingly, the narrative's plot structure can likewise be defined using synonymous terminology (Barwick 1999; Trischitta 2008).

A biblical narrative, Fee & Stuart (1993) state, is their term of preference when referring to Bible stories because:

1. they believe that the contemporary understanding of stories "has come to mean something that is fictional";
2. the term, "narrative" is a technical term that is more objective and less prejudicial; and
3. stories usually mean a single or individual story that stands alone with its "single set of characters and single plot." (79)

For these outlined reasons the term "biblical narrative" is the author's term of choice for this chapter.

The Biblical Metanarrative

Christians believe the Bible contains the true story of the world; therefore we embrace the biblical story as our metanarrative or grand story (Stonehouse & May 2008). The Bible, according to Gibson (2016), is a grand narrative "rich with interesting characters in an unfolding saga of infinite love, horrific loss and glorious restoration at last. It tells of a God who loves each of us more than His own existence; one who would rather die forever than live without us" (12). Walch (2015) sees the metanarrative as a unifying story that helps us understand the details of the individual stories. White (1952) further suggests that, "the central theme of the Bible, the theme about which every other in the whole book clusters, is the redemption plan, the restoration in the human soul of the image of God" (125).

Without the entire story as the overarching backdrop, individual narratives and episodes may lead to incorrect assumptions or misinterpretations. It is important to remember, says Ryken (1984), that, "the episodes relate to each other in the unfolding progress of the story" (49). Described as an epic, overarching, explanatory story (that provides objective reasoning and justification for Christian beliefs, morality, and identity), the Christian metanarrative employs a typical narrative form or schema (Table 1) that incorporates many of the various forms of narrative (poetry, allegory, parables, biography, etc.) to showcase and explain this grand story (Fisher 2014).

Table 1. The biblical metanarrative schema (Fisher, 2010)

Biblical Metanarrative	Narrative Episodes	Biblical Roots
The Orientation	1. Triune Godhead	Old Testament stories point to the Cross and the promise of salvation.
Setting, Characters	2. Creation	
Complication	3. The Fall	
The Resolution	4. The Rescue	
	5. Waiting and Living	New Testament stories look back to the Cross and claim salvation has come.
Conclusion	6. Redemption and Re-creation	

The Christian metanarrative, as found in the Bible, is a progressive, linear narrative (Figure 1), not cyclic as in Hinduism, and tells the story of the great cosmic conflict set in typical narrative structure (Fisher 2010). This supernatural cosmic power struggle has been described by the contemporary theologian Boyd (2016), as a "Warfare Worldview," while Eldredge's (2004) book, *Epic: The story God is telling*, outlines God's role and our human role in this universal conflict. The interaction between the two opposing forces in the cosmic conflict is highlighted in the following comment by Rasi (1995):

> It centres on two conflicting views of God's character and principles: one that considers God as loving, gracious and just; the other that considers God as arbitrary, unjust, and unfair. Our world has become a battle-ground for these opposing forces of good and evil, and the battle is played out principally through human lives. (E8)

Figure 1. The Linear Biblical Metanarrative Condensed into a Timeline (Fisher, 2010, p. 120)

GOD	CREATION	FALL	RESCUE	WAITING & LIVING	REDEMPTION & RE-CREATION
1	2	3	4	5	6
New World			Jesus' Death	ME	New Earth

Following is an explanation of the numbered chapters (1–6) on Fisher's (2010) condensed linear biblical metanarrative timeline in Figure 1.

1. **God:** The Trinity (God, Christ and Holy Spirit) exists in a perfect world (Genesis 1:1, John 1:1). Lucifer, a created being, leads a rebellion against God (Isaiah 14:12–14, Revelation 12:7). Lucifer is cast out of God's kingdom and becomes the devil (Satan) (Revelation 12:8–9).

2. **Creation:** God creates His earthly kingdom in six days. On the seventh-day God creates the Sabbath, a God-relational space, says Gibson (2016), where God receives "reciprocated love from His creation" (p. 40). God creates man and woman in His image with a free will (Genesis 1 & 2).

3. **The Fall:** Satan introduces the spirit of rebellion (Genesis 3) on Earth through Adam and Eve's rebellious choice (Roy 1999). Satan now claims to be the ruler of the earthly kingdom. Roy (1999) writes, "He questions God's character, the fairness of His law, His right to rule and Jesus' right to save sinners from eternal death" (E4). Satan is in daily conflict with God concerning who will control people's lives and to whose kingdom they will show allegiance (Ephesians 6:12).

4. **Rescue:** This confirms Christ's right to be the ruler of the earthly kingdom and guarantees the eventual destruction of evil and Satan (Romans 5:19). Roy (1999) says that:

   > Through Christ's life of perfect obedience to God's will, His suffering, death and resurrection, God provided the only means of paying for, and escaping from, sin. The resurrection of Jesus Christ proclaims God's victory over sin. (E4)

5. **Waiting and Living:** God is now waiting before He reclaims His earthly kingdom because He wants everyone to (a) see the results and

consequences of giving allegiance to Satan; and (b) have the opportunity (John 3:16) to know God as King and Lord because He does not want anyone to perish (2 Peter 3:9). Each person has a choice to either accept or reject God's offer of love and liberation, by way of salvation, and eternity. He sends the Holy Spirit and the angels to comfort and protect His followers (Hebrews 1:14) during the waiting time.

6. **Redemption and Re-Creation:** Christ returns as promised. The devil and evil are finally destroyed, and those who have chosen God's offer of redemption and salvation change from mortality to immortality, just as it was before the *Fall*. God's character has been vindicated before the entire universe. A perfect re-created world has returned (Revelation 21:1–7).

To be effective nurturers in the faith formation of their students, Scripture Teachers need to be able to identify their part in this grand story before they can assist any child to identify his/her personal role in this ongoing daily spiritual drama.

Biblical Narratives: Their Role and Function in the Bible

The biblical narrative's role, state Fee and Stuart (2014), is to "*demonstrate* God's involvement in this world and *illustrate* his principles and calling" (110). Fee and Stuart further point out that the Old Testament narratives are used to illustrate doctrines that are "taught propositionally elsewhere" in the Bible (111) and demonstrate conflicts and tensions that need to be resolved. For Corcoran (2007), biblical narratives "depict the universals in human existence" (41) and tell us about life as a part of salvation history. Ryken (1984) adds that the biblical narratives also reveal that people still behave the way they did in Bible times "and with the same dire results" (73). White (1952) further argues that: "As an educator no part of the Bible is of greater value than are its biographies. These biographies differ from all others in that they are absolutely true to life" (146). It is important to note that these biographies are not just true to life, they are *true*.

When the Bible is regarded as having hierarchical narrative order, then individual stories can be placed in their contextual framework (as illustrated in Figure 2). Beck (2008) points out that biblical narratives are designed to be interdependent because: "A Bible story never stands alone, but is always placed within the literary context where it interacts within a larger family of stories" (14).

Figure 2. The Relationship between the Metanarrative, Episodes, Bible Characters and Individual Narratives

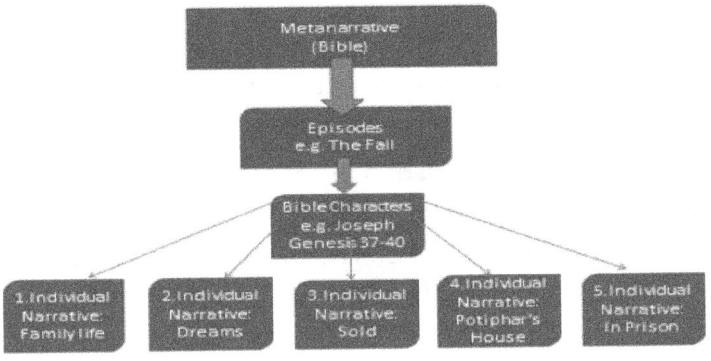

A Framework for Interpreting and Applying Biblical Narratives

The *Four H's Biblical Framework (Four H's)* is a four-phase process *(History, Head, Heart, and Hand)* that can support the interpretation of, reflection upon, and engagement with biblical narratives in the 21st century. It aims to connect the students with God through thoughtful interactions with the Christian biblical grand epic and its individual narrative episodes on a personal and relational level. This framework highlights the fact that we are not spectators in God's Big Drama of the Ages but players, or actors, with a specific charter.

When studying biblical narratives, the *Four H's (History, Head, Heart, and Hand)* are designed to place equal emphasis on each of the four phases, ensuring a balance is given to both biblical knowledge and life-application. Knowledge of narrative genre is beneficial when implementing the *Four H's* because:

1. understanding narrative plot structure can assist Scripture Teachers when portraying and interpreting a biblical narrative because: setting, characters, and action, and the interaction between these three elements, are the building blocks of stories (Ryken 1984);

2. Harrison (2015) points out that, "Recognising (sic) the genre of each passage helps us to know how it was intended to be understood" (1660); and

3. individual biblical narratives can be placed and understood within the context of the Christian metanarrative.

When teaching a Scripture Lesson, teachers generally divide the experience into three main sections: **Introduction; Narration and Discussion;** and **Conclusion**. The *Four H's* can be applied in all three sections of Scripture Lessons. For example:

(a) During the Lesson **Introduction**, *History, Head or Heart* phases can be utilized to HOOK students, or gain their attention;

(b) Next, the **Narration** of the biblical narrative and its **Discussion** can incorporate the *Head and History* phases to provide the setting, essential background information and a knowledge base for studying and interpreting the biblical narrative;

(c) Once the biblical knowledge base has been established and developed, then spiritual engagement and a commitment response from the *Heart* phase becomes appropriate;

(d) A **Discussion** of how the Cosmic Conflict is evident in this biblical narrative, along with our personal role in the Cosmic Conflict, is appropriate during the *Head* and *Heart* stage of the lesson; and

(e) Finally, during the **Conclusion** section of the Scripture Lesson the *Hand* and *Heart* phases can initiate discussions about applying the lesson to the student's life and discovering ways to engage in personal outreach (Fisher, 2016).

The *Four H's Biblical Framework* Defined and Explained

*1. **History:** listening and discovering. An overview of where the biblical narrative fits into the biblical metanarrative. It includes Bible reading, biblical history, world history, cultural information, maps, and timelines (Fisher 2010).*

All biblical narratives are about actual people and places set in Jewish, Middle Eastern cultures and times. The *History* phase sets the scene for the biblical narrative as it considers the historical setting and context of the biblical narrative while also identifying its biblical reference and location. Including background information provides an opportunity for students to meet Bible characters as real people in a real world (who slept, ate, cried, laughed, and had the same temptations and problems as they do).

By placing the biblical narrative in the larger context of the cosmic conflict metanarrative, it shows an epic saga already in progress that involves historical, biblical, and contemporary individuals. By providing a sense of the narrative's context, Walch (2015) argues that Scripture Teachers can assist students to understand their part and place in this grand narrative. Bratcher (2013) further adds that "while the story itself may be studied on its own for its own message, the surrounding stories, the flow of thought of the larger work, as well as its historical and cultural setting, affect how the individual story is to be heard (1). Scripture Teachers need to be aware of inadvertently teaching biblical narratives as history lessons, with little or no relevance to the 21st century, so the interplay of world history, biblical history, and the cosmic conflict needs to be addressed. Figure 3 is an example of how to demonstrate the interrelationship of these historical timeframes.

Figure 3. The Relationship between Biblical History, World History, and Contemporary History (Fisher, 2010, p. 168)

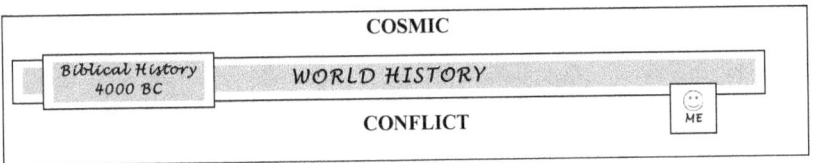

Commercially prepared time charts can be helpful to illustrate how Biblical history is a cultural subset of the larger context of world history. One example of a comprehensive biblical and world history time chart is: *The Timechart History of the World: 6000 Years of World History Unfolded* (Gibbons, 2004). It provides students and Scripture Teachers with an opportunity to see how biblical characters and historical figures fit into the larger picture of a cosmic conflict (Fisher 2010).

> *2. Head: learning and knowing (Fisher 2010). Knowledge of God evident in biblical narratives; familiarity with narrative genre; relationships between episodes and individual narrative plot structure (orientation, complication, resolution, and conclusion); and the metanarrative.*

The *Head* phase builds on the contextual knowledge gained in the *History* phase. Students need the opportunity to observe God's extravagant, forgiving love, to see His power to change people's lives, to witness a Bible character's active faith, and to comprehend the consequences and results of personal choices (Fisher 2014). Narrative genre structure has the potential to assist teachers and students in reaching this goal. During the *Head* phase, therefore, students need personal access to an appropriate version of the Bible so that they can individually read the biblical narrative being studied and become familiar with God's written word through regular interaction and engagement.

Table 2 demonstrates how, using the story of Joseph (and his multicolored coat), a narrative plot structure can highlight the main points of the narrative.

Table 2. An example of a biblical narrative plot structure

Narrative Plot Structure Outline	**EXAMPLE:** An Old Testament Biblical Narrative Joseph: his multicolored coat and family interactions
Orientation	Joseph lives in a dysfunctional family in the Middle Eastern desert
Complication	Joseph's father is perceived to favor Joseph above his brothers by giving Joseph a multicolored coat
Resolution	Joseph's brothers sell him to the Ishmaelite traders from Gilead who are on their way to Egypt, thus ridding themselves of the troublemaker
Conclusion	Joseph lives as a slave in Egypt. Many years later God's loving foreknowledge is demonstrated when Joseph saves his family

The narrative plot structure, states Bratcher (2013), reminds the Scripture Teacher that the plot of the individual biblical narrative is specifically "related to the point (message) of the story" (1) and the students are assisted to help remember the major points of the narrative while also gaining an understanding and knowledge of "how the conflict is resolved (or not)" (1). Bratcher further states that "biblical narratives do not tell us everything about an event; they are selective and focused on those elements that contribute to the plot, and cannot be made to address every question we might want to ask of the story (1).

Once the biblical narrative has been placed in its historical and cultural context, then the "freezer dried" narrative is brought to life using multisensory and modality-based experiences (visual, auditory, kinesthetic and tactile) and resources as demonstrated by the examples in Table 3.

Table 3. Biblical narrative multisensory and modality-based ideas

• Touching thorns	• Listening to music
• Smelling perfume	• Feeling lamb's wool
• Making unleavened bread	• Holding sand
• Imagining that you are a bystander in the Bible story and then describing the scene	• Using puppets
	• 'Stepping-out' the size of Noah's ark

Multisensory questions, according to Ryan (2001), can engage the students in the narrative through creative imagination (See examples in Table 4). Engaging the imagination when reading a biblical narrative, Ryken (1984) states, "is the first requirement for reading biblical narrative" (34) because it involves personal interaction.

Table 4. Examples of multisensory questions

Sounds: What sounds can you hear around you in this narrative?

Sights: In this narrative what can you see happening around you?

Smells: What are the dominant odors you are experiencing as you witness this narrative?

Touch: What textures can you feel and touch during this biblical narrative?

Taste: What possible tastes might you encounter in this biblical narrative?

A biblical narrative can be perceived as a good moral story unless it is brought to life by the Scripture Teacher and the power of the Holy Spirit (Fisher 2016). Stonehouse (1998) observed: "If the stories have become real to us, the children will sense our excitement and join us, through their imaginations, in the story" (161). Bringing the biblical narrative to life is the goal of the *Head* phase.

> **3. Heart:** *loving and responding (Fisher 2010). Opportunity for spiritual (emotional) engagement; heartfelt commitment and a reflective response to the biblical narrative.*

The *Heart* phase is where engagement with and response to the narrative at an emotional and reflective level is encouraged. For the *Heart* phase to be an effective internalization phase it is essential that previous interaction and engagement with the *History* and *Head* phases has occurred. Without these introductory phases (*History* and *Head*) it is possible that a *Heart* response may lack the intellectual information that supports transformational faith formation, conviction, and personal commitment. Rice's (2014) words summarize the goal of the *Heart* phase: to create a heartfelt longing and to provide the opportunity for an "intellectual decision to act on God's Word" (1).

During the *Heart* phase students are encouraged to enter the grand narrative and create their own faithful versions (Wright 1991). With spiritual wisdom and insight being vicariously experienced through biblical narrative, this opportunity can provide unique, age-appropriate transformational learning and faith formation opportunities for all students. Barwick (1999) states that a narrative portrays a theme or message that the listener responds to in "a reflective, imaginative or emotional manner" (4). While DeVries (2015) argues that, "well-crafted stories feed our imaginations to step beyond the factual limits of our own particular lives" (1). Beckwith (2004) reminds Scripture Teachers that students need to be given the opportunity to interact with the Bible as a way of seeing God's overarching story and purpose in the world. So identifying with and discussing a biblical character's actions, as demonstrated in a biblical narrative, is one way that students can engage in reflection and response to further their faith formation.

Reflective questions, (see Table 5), also have the potential to provide students with an opportunity to internalize, reflect upon, interpret and emotionally engage with the biblical narrative. A simple 'Yes/No' question can become a reflective question when 'Why? or Why not?' is included (see Question 3 in Table 5 below). Scripture Teachers can design rhetorical questions for personal and private reflection while a variety of group reflective questions can be planned for small group interactions (Fisher 2016).

Table 5. Examples of *Heart* Reflective Questions and Discussion Starters (Fisher, 2016)

1. McNabb & Mabry (1990) suggest the following questions: "How would your life be different if you really took this Bible passage seriously?" and "What is God saying to me through this biblical narrative?" (27).

2. Explain which character in the biblical narrative would remind you of Jesus. Why?

3. Are you like or unlike any of the characters in the biblical narrative? Why/Why not?

4. What is the Good News for you in this biblical narrative? Why?

5. How can learning about Bible characters help you to be more like Jesus?

6. What attributes of God's character are demonstrated in this biblical narrative? Why and how?

7. What have you learned about God's 'extravagant' love from this biblical narrative?

8. How has this narrative impacted your life? Why?

9. If you had been part of or witnessed this biblical narrative, how do you think you would have reacted? Why?

10. What have you learned about the 21st century cosmic conflict from studying this biblical narrative? Why?

Developing discernment and problem-solving skills are imperative in the 21st century because Christian students are constantly bombarded by the values and attitudes portrayed via the media. So applying God's word to the *Heart* and becoming reflective thinkers, rather than echoing the thoughts of others, can be encouraged through engaging, interactive, non-judgmental question and discussion opportunities provided in the *Heart* phase.

> *4. Hand: living and giving (Fisher 2010). This phase explores how students can apply and implement the metanarrative in their lives and ways of sharing it with others in their community.*

The fourth phase of the *Four H's* involves an acknowledgment that Christian students, committed to a relationship with God (*Heart*) can share God's love to a needy world (*Hand*). Once a person steps into God's story and begins to create his or her story, then, according to Shortt (2014), he or she has a responsibility to invite others to step into the story with him or her so they can experience it together. This external action validates a genuine *Heart* internal response because as Rice (2014) comments: "Without an authentic external action our internal response may prove ineffective" (1).

To assist teachers in applying the *Hand* phase of the *Four H's* a selection of suggested questions and application ideas are listed in Table 6.

Table 6. Examples of *Hand* Questions (Fisher, 2016)

1. How can you share with others the biblical narrative's message about God's love?

(As a class group, develop a list of ways to share the special message from the current Bible story about God's love that is non-confrontational)

2. Why is it important to learn about Bible people and their stories?

    (Compare a well-known current local "Hero" and his or her lifestyle choices with those of a Bible character)

3. What is the difference between "being" and "acting as" a Christian?

    (Ask the students to form small groups and discuss the role that 21st century social media plays in influencing personal Christianity. With student collaboration, create a set of media viewing guidelines for Christians)

4. What is your role in the cosmic conflict?

    (Create a collage of all the events in the newspaper for one day that illustrate the cosmic conflict. Identity how the cosmic conflict is evident in the classroom)

Four H's Implementation

It should be noted that the four phases of the *Four H's* framework are not necessarily used in chronological order, often overlap, and may occur several times during the lesson. *History* and *Head* knowledge are powerless without a *Heart* response and a *Heart* response provides the impetus for *Hands* to demonstrate a personal and committed relationship to Jesus Christ (Fisher 2016).

While each phase of the *Four H Biblical Framework* is necessary, if this transformational, interactive, and engaging biblical study approach is to be realized then a positive and affirming interaction between the Scripture Teacher and students is paramount. According to McNabb and Mabry (1990), "Our job as Bible storytellers is more than getting our students to understand what the Bible says about a particular issue; we must help them understand what God is saying to them personally" (21). This is the specific and all-encompassing goal of the *Four H's Biblical Framework*.

Conclusion

Over 60 years ago, White (1952) wrote that: "The teaching of the Bible should have our freshest thought, our best methods, and our most earnest effort" (186). This statement, written in the 20th century, is still relevant in the 21st century. However, we cannot rely on the previous generation's methodology to reach today's contemporary student. In this generation, young people and children live in a constantly-changing society; have unique life-style issues, and experience the world differently. So Scripture Teachers need to constantly seek for the "best methods" and ideas to meet these contemporary challenges while also ensuring that Bible teaching "has our freshest thought." Students will see that Scripture Lessons are relevant, appropriate and meaningful for all age groups and learning abilities when it engages the teacher's "most earnest effort." The *Four H's* can support teachers as they strive to reach this goal. God has asked teachers to sow the seed. He has promised that He will look after the harvest (Fisher 2016).

References

Barton, John. 2010. *The Bible: The Basics*. London: Routledge.
Barwick, John. 1999. *Targeting Text: Narrative, Poetry, Drama (Upper Level)*.Glebe, NSW: Blake Education.
Beck, John. 2008. *God as Storyteller: Seeking Meaning in Biblical Narrative*. St Louis: Chalice.
Beckwith, Ivy. 2004. *Postmodern Children's Ministry: Ministry to Children in the 21st Century*. Grand Rapids: Zondervan.
Boyd, Greg. 2016. *What is the Warfare Worldview?* http://reknew.org/2008/01/intro-to-warfare-worldview/.
Bratcher, Dennis. 2013. *Guidelines for Interpreting Biblical Narrative*. http://www.crivoice.org/narrguide.html.
Corcoran, Henry Andrew. 2007. "Biblical Narratives and Life Transformation: An Apology for the Narrative Teaching of Bible Stories." *Christian Education Journal* 4, pp. 34–49.
Crain, Jeanie C. 2010. *Reading the Bible as Literature: An Introduction*. 1st ed. Cambridge, UK: Polity.
DeVries, Paul. 2015. *The Power of Bible Stories as Teaching Tools of Impartiality*. http://www.christianpost.com/news/the-power-of-bible-stories-as-teaching-tools-of-impartiality-139879/#IzIGTRGyym37welr.99.
Eldredge, John. 2004. *Epic: The Story God is Telling*. Nashville: Nelson.
Fee, Gordon D., and Douglas Stuart. 1993. *How to Read the Bible for All its Worth*. 2nd ed. Grand Rapids: Zondervan.
———. 2014. *How to Read the Bible for all its Worth*. 4th ed. Grand Rapids: Zondervan.
Fisher, Barbara J. 2014. "Bible stories in the classroom: The why and the how." *The Journal of Adventist Education* 77, pp. 24–31.
———. 2010. *Developing a Faith-based Education: A teacher's manual*. Terrigal, NSW: David Barlow.
———. 2016. "The Four H Teaching Strategy: An Interactive, Multisensory Approach to Teaching Bible." *The Journal of Adventist Education* 78, pp. 16–28.
Gibbons, David, ed. 2004. *The Timechart History of the World: 6000 Years of World History Unfolded* 2nd ed. New York: Metro.

Gibson, Ty. 2016. *Refresh! Jesus The Essence of our Faith*. Nampa, ID: Pacific.

———. "A Story to Tell." 2016. *Adventist World, South Pacific Edition*, pp. 12–14.

Harrison, Sean A. 2015. *Holy Bible, New Living Translation*. Cold Stream, IL: Tyndale House.

Lee, David Y. W. 2001. "Genres, Registers, Text Types, Domains and Styles: Clarifying the Concepts and Navigating a Path through the BNC jungle." *Learning Language and Technology* 5, 37–72.

McNabb, Bill, and Steve Mabry. 1990. *Teaching the Bible Creatively: How to Awaken Your Kids to Scripture*. Grand Rapids: Zondervan.

Rasi, Humberto. 1995. "Christians versus Culture." *Dialogue* 7, pp. 5–8.

Rice, Jonathon. 2014. *How to Apply Biblical Truth to Our Daily Lives*. http://intervarsity.org/blog/how-apply-biblical-truth-our-daily-lives.

Roy, Don. 1999. *Growing in Faith: Religious Education for Seventh-Day Adventist Primary Schools in the South Pacific Division*. Wahroonga, NSW: South Pacific Division of Seventh-day Adventist Church.

Ryan, Maurice. 2001. *Teaching the Bible: A Manual of Teaching Activities, Commentary and Blackline Masters*. Katoomba, NSW: Social Science.

Ryken, Leland. 1984. *How to Read the Bible as Literature*. Grand Rapids: Zondervan.

Shortt, John. 2014. *Bible-Shaped Teaching*. Eugene, OR: Wipf and Stock.

Stonehouse, Catherine. 1998. *Joining Children on the Spiritual Journey: Nurturing a Life of Faith*. Grand Rapids: Baker.

Stonehouse, Catherine, and Scottie May. 2008. "The Story and the Spiritual Formation of Children in the Church and in the Home." In *Nurturing Children's Spirituality: Christian Perspectives and Best Practices*, edited by Holly Catterton Allen, 366–379. Eugene, OR: Cascade.

Trischitta, Andrea. 2008. *Narrative Writing, Years 3-6*. Heatherton, VIC: Hawker Brownlow Education.

Walch, Jason. 2015. "Nested Narratives: Interpersonal Neurobiology and Christian Formation." *Christian Education Journal* 3, pp. 151–61.

White, Ellen G. 1952. *Education*. Mountain View, CA: Pacific.

Wright, N. T. 1991. *How Can the Bible be Authoritative?* http://ntwrightpage.com/Wright_Bible_Authoritative.htm.

Chapter 5

The Role of Theology in the Definitions of Spirituality, Spiritual Maturity, and Measuring Spiritual Development

 Karissa Glanville

THIS CHAPTER IS AN attempt to spur the discussion for a more theologically-based and broadly-applicable definition of spirituality and the subsequent understandings of spiritual maturity and spiritual formation/development, all with the field of children's spirituality in mind.

The Need

At the very foundation of research about children's spirituality is the need to define spirituality itself. Most authors writing on the topic of children's spirituality, if they do not start out by specifically defining their definition of spirituality, their definition quickly becomes evident in how they say spirituality relates to children. In general, an agreed-upon definition of spirituality has yet to be settled upon in the field, and probably won't be any time soon (Anthony 2006).

As it stands, definitions of spirituality, given by Christian scholars in the field of children's spirituality, often fall into one of the following categories:

1. The definition *may largely fall along the lines of developing a relationship with God* within the context of a community of relationships, and may or may not include mention of the Holy Spirit or Jesus.

2. The definition *may not necessarily address the spirituality of all human beings*, but rather focus only on the potential of a child once one becomes a Christian or is raised in a Christian setting. These types of definitions are either separating the science of human development from theology or not allowing theology to fully impact the definition from the foundation. Perhaps this is done because it is easier to define Christian children's spirituality that applies only to people within one's own faith, versus defining spirituality from a perspective that may cause disagreement in discussion with those of other faiths.

3. Parallel to the previous point, there is a *tendency for Christians to jump right into attempting to answer the question, "What is Christian spiritual growth or development?"* instead of first defining spirituality. At the 2016 Children's Spirituality Conference, Holly Allen submitted to the attendees a "working definition" of spirituality—written by herself and Ryan Porche—which ended up actually being titled "Spiritual Formation" (Allen 2016). Even though she discussed needing to define spirituality, what she submitted was actually a definition for spiritual formation. Allen's definition:

> Spiritual Formation is a lifelong, intentional, and communal process of growing in our ability to attend and relate to God, submitting ourselves to His transforming power through the Holy Spirit in order to become increasingly more like Jesus in every aspect of our lives—practicing restored relationship with God, ourselves, and others. (Allen 2016)

This definition gives a wonderful aim and direction for human spirituality, but it does not address how it applies universally, to all people. It has skipped over a broadly applicable, theological understanding of spirituality and jumped directly into a description of the ideal Christian life. This tendency is putting the cart before the horse.

Theology needs to provide the basis for understanding human development and enlightening a definition of spirituality that addresses children with and without Christ. This chapter is meant to spark a conversation in hopes that we will dive deeper together, looking to understand *all* that God made children (and us, and humanity at large) to be. We are holistic beings, and, as Christians, believe that God created us. However much we try to isolate a definition of spirituality from theology, it would only succeed in giving a partial understanding of a definition that will not be fully helpful for Christian practitioners or researchers.

Theological Understanding of Spirituality

Even in the broader and longer-established field of Christian Spirituality scholars have not settled upon a definition (Jensen 2009). It is impossible to dive deeply into centuries of theology and in-depth Bible study on the whole of spirituality in just one chapter, however, this chapter will be an attempt to move the conversation further along in the field of Children's Spirituality. Below are some theological perspectives and Biblical passages to take into consideration.

Evan B. Howard makes the case that "Nearly all of the literature published on Christian spirituality . . . to some degree" or other, "refers specifically to relationship with God through Jesus Christ" (2008, 16). John R. Tyson says, "'Christian Spirituality' describes the relationship, union, and conformity with God that a Christian experiences through his or her reception of the grace of God, and a corresponding willingness to turn from sin and (to use a Pauline phrase) 'to walk according to the Spirit'" (1999, 1). Right away these understandings, though focusing on relationship with the Triune God, do not include a spirituality that encompasses non-Christians. How should or can non-Christians be included in a Christian perspective or definition of spirituality? Are we saying that spirituality is only for Christians?

According to the *Dictionary of Christian Spirituality*, "spirituality is seen to be a *universal human attribute*" (Scorgie et al. 2011, 27–28). The Bible verifies this through the following passages. James 2:26 states that without a spirit a body is dead. It can thus be assumed that every living being has a spirit. 1 Corinthians 5:5 points out that people have a spirit and that part of the goal is for that spirit to be eternally saved. *All people have the potential and were created to be eternally saved.*

Romans 8:11–16 makes a contribution regarding relationship, showing that a person's spirit can relate with the Holy Spirit and be brought into a relationship with God through Christ, as a child of God. And Acts 2:42 lists fellowship with other believers as part of a list of important activities in the same category as prayer, communion, and continuing in the doctrine of the apostles. This taps into the idea of relationality that David Hay and Rebecca Nye's work popularized (2006). *People were created for relationship with God and with each other.* 1 Corinthians 6:17 shows the result of relationship with God saying the one "who is joined to the Lord is one spirit with Him," and it is through this oneness, this abiding in him, and he abiding reciprocally, that fruit is born (John 15:5). *People were made to become one with God through Christ and produce resulting fruit.*

With only this cursory glance at Scripture, if I were to make an initial attempt at a broad theological understanding of spirituality that encompasses Christians and non-Christians, from a Christian perspective, it could be:

> *Human spirituality is the relational aspect of each human being that includes the capacity to relate to God and others, and was designed to be complete and come into the maturity of eternal union with God, through Christ, by the power of the Holy Spirit.*

Spiritual Maturity

With this preliminary working definition of spirituality that is theologically based, an understanding of spiritual maturity and ultimately spiritual formation/development can be built. Before looking at how development or formation happens, there must be an understanding of what we are meant to develop or form into. What would it look like to be spiritually mature from a theological perspective?

First of all, when Jesus was asked what the most important commandment was, he answered, "'You shall love the LORD your God with all your heart, with all your soul, and with all your mind.' This is [the] first and great commandment. And [the] second [is] like it: 'You shall love your neighbor as yourself.' On these two commandments hang all the Law and the Prophets" (Matthew 22:37–40, NKJV). Everything God has asked of us relates to first loving God, and second, loving others. *Love and unity, the epitome of relationality, is the most important of all that God made people to be.* Jesus prayed that his followers would be one with him in the Father (John 17:21), and in verse 26, finishes his prayer with "And I have declared to them Your name, and will declare [it], that the love with which You loved Me may be in them, and I in them" (NKJV).

Secondly, looking at how "maturity" is used in the New Testament gives a few more hints at what spiritual maturity may look like. In Philippians 3:8–15, perfection is said to be knowing Jesus, and, in the process, becoming like him. Though people may not fully attain that in this life, also according to Philippians 3:8–15, knowing Jesus and becoming more like him is what the mature continue to pursue. Ephesians 4:11–16 speaks of maturity only attainable in the context of the Body of Christ. The church is to be a loving unity that is joined together in submission to Jesus, with each person growing to be more of who God made them to be until they reach what is said in verse 13 to be "the whole measure of the fullness of Christ" (NIV). 2 Corinthians 3:18 expands on becoming more like Jesus, saying God is at work to transform those who follow Jesus into the image of his Son by the power of his Spirit. Then yet other passages give us clues as to what this transforming work the Spirit of God looks like in people. Galatians 5:22–23 speaks of the fruit of the Spirit, and 1 Corinthians 12:8–10 discusses the gifts of the Spirit. Hebrews 5:14 also says that the mature can "distinguish good from evil" (NIV).

From these passages it could be said that,

> Maturity is the pursuit ofe knowing Jesus, and in the process, becoming more like him. It is bound by love for God and each other, includes being able to distinguish good from evil, and is ultimately attained only as part of the Body of Christ and by the power of the Holy Spirit.

But how do we get to this point? How do we pursue knowing God with the result of becoming more like Christ? That is where spiritual formation/development can finally come in. It is necessary to know the goal of spirituality before figuring out how to attain it. Otherwise, it is like shooting aimlessly in the dark, hoping to hit a target by chance.

Spiritual Formation/Development

Catherine Stonehouse (1998) writes, "The spiritual life is formed through practices that help to open the person to God and break down barriers that hinder his or her perception of God" (21). I am not arguing that practices can't play a part to "help to open" people "to God and break down barriers that hinder" our perceptions. Indeed, I believe they can. However, good counseling, or other self-help/coaching tools and religious rituals may also be able to do some of this. "Practices" alone could become a self-empowered pursuit, and at worst, lead to the kind of legalism Paul was escaping in Philippians 3.

Scorgie et al. (2011) say, "Whenever formation is dislocated from its proper relational context and neglect of necessary divine impulses, it becomes a mere portfolio of spiritual disciplines and another grinding self-improvement project" (28). Scorgie et al.'s admonition highlights a few important keys in this one sentence; 1) the importance of keeping relationality with Jesus central to an understanding of spiritual formation, 2) the role of divine empowerment, and 3) the danger of turning spiritual formation into a human-strength-powered, self-improvement exercise.

So how are people to be transformed or matured? Scripture tells us that it is actually the power of the Holy Spirit that transforms us into the image of

Christ (2 Corinthians 2:18) and that both God and people have roles to play. John Wimber and Kevin Springer (1991) said, "Spiritual growth . . . is a product of the initiating, empowering work of the Holy Spirit *and* of our active cooperation . . . If *either* divine initiative *or* human response is missing, we will not grow" (p. 140, emphasis in original). Based on Galatians 2:20; 5:22–23, Wimber and Springer (1991) make it clear that even though our cooperation is needed, the spiritual maturity discussed in the Bible, becoming like Christ, can only be achieved by the power of the Holy Spirit and is the fruit of the Holy Spirit. It is the Spirit of Christ who brings the transformation. 1 Corinthians 6:17 says the one ". . . who is joined to the Lord is one spirit with Him" (NKJV). This joining increases the potential of a human spirit. It is only through "abiding" in Christ that we can produce fruit (John 15). Philippians 2:12–13 speaks of both; people needing to work out their own salvation, and God who works in his people to do what he desires. Ephesians 1:17–19 speaks of knowledge of God coming through revelation.

Without the Spirit of Christ, a person is limited to the potential of the human spirit and will only get as far as their human efforts can take them. Without the Holy Spirit, people can develop and "improve," but into what? What is their goal? If knowing Jesus and becoming more like him is the goal, people need the Holy Spirit, the Spirit of Jesus, to attain that. Non-Christian and non-theological beliefs regarding spirituality and spiritual maturity will have different goals and different, less-empowered ways to attain them; ways that are possible through human strength alone. On the other hand, Christians have access to empowerment beyond the strength and limits of the human spirit.

To be clear, I am not saying the Holy Spirit is only working among those who are followers of Jesus. The Holy Spirit is at work throughout the world (John 16:8). Yet there is a transformative power done from the inside out, within those in whom the Holy Spirit dwells. In John 14:16–17 Jesus says, "I will pray the Father, and He will give you another Helper, that He may abide with you forever—the Spirit of truth, whom the world cannot receive, because it neither sees Him nor knows Him; but you know Him, for He dwells with you and will be in you" (NKJV). If spiritual development is considered growing in and through relationship with Jesus through the indwelling Spirit of God, which results in being transformed by the Holy Spirit into the image of Jesus, this is a type of development only accomplishable within the lives of those who have received the Spirit of Christ in them.

What exactly is the evidence of this transformative work of the Holy Spirit that should be seen in the lives of those who have the Spirit of Christ in them? There is knowing Jesus mentioned in 1 John 14, and there is the resulting transformation to be like him. Some of the scriptures that describe what being like Jesus looks like are the beatitudes in Matthew 5 (King, 2016). Wimber and Springer (1991) cite various passages from 1 Peter to describe what they believe is an accurate description of a mature life. Wimber and Springer (1991) also mention Galatians 5:22 which lists the fruit of the Spirit. And 1 Corinthians 12:7–12 describes the gifts of the Holy Spirit. The Spirit produces both fruit and gifts, growing people more completely into the image of Jesus. Yet, according to 1 Corinthians 12:7–12, all people are not given the same or all of the gifts. And Ephesians 4:11–16 says God gave the various roles in the church (apostles, prophets, teachers, etc.)

> ... for the equipping of the saints for the work of ministry, for the edifying of the body of Christ, till we all come to the unity of the faith and of the knowledge of the Son of God, to a perfect man, to the measure of the stature of the fullness of Christ ... from whom the whole body, joined and knit together by what every joint supplies, according to the effective working by which every part does its share, causes growth of the body for the edifying of itself in love.(NKJV)

So then how is spiritual growth to be measured or compared? Is it even possible to measure spiritual growth in any uniform way? This passage in Ephesians above makes it clear the Body of Christ's relational edification of itself in love described is not attainable on an individual basis, but rather in the Body of Christ as a whole. Each person has a role to play, and together, people become the fullness of Christ. In the field of children's spirituality, it has been an elusive holy grail to discover what the possible progression of spiritual development might look like. Building on what 1 Corinthians 12:7–12 and Ephesians 4:11–16 say about the diversity of gifts and that spiritual maturity is accomplished as and within the Body of Christ, then each person is given different gifts with the purpose of being transformed uniquely, and relationally, into the image of Christ. Christ's Body is being corporately transformed, with individuals having different gifts as different parts of the Body. This implies that each individual's spiritual gifts will grow uniquely toward a different-looking role. Because each person's growth is unique, that person's relationship with God, and the growth of that relationship with God and others will also be unique. Someone's growth into becoming a mature "arm," per se, and how the person will relate to God and others, will not look like another's development into a full grown "eye," nor with the relationship that that person has with God and others. Evidence of growth can be seen outwardly through increase in the fruit of the Spirit and increase in mature usage of the gifts of the Spirit, but with each individual's spiritual journey being completely unique. Each person's relationship with

God and with others, and development of the fruit and gifts of the Spirit in their lives, will be as unique as each person's love story, and journey of growth into their selected career.

Based on the brief and preliminary points above, I offer an expanded working definition of spirituality. It starts out with a theologically based, universally applicable definition of spirituality, and includes elaboration on the goal of maturity and how the process of spiritual growth is accomplished.

> *Human spirituality is a relational aspect of each human being that includes the capacity to relate to God and others, and was designed to be complete and come into the maturity of eternal union with God, through Christ, by the power of the Holy Spirit with the resulting Christ-like fruit and gifts of the Holy Spirit, all within the context of being unique individuals within the Body of Christ.*

This definition addresses spirituality, maturity and spiritual development, the latter two enabled by the theological grounding of the first.

This definition creates a challenge in that it is not one that is easily used as a foundational place to dialogue with those studying children's spirituality from a non-Christian perspective. The capacity of the human spirit without God or without the context of community can be explored without a theological foundation or even with only one member of the dialogue having a theological foundation. However, if a person's understanding of spirituality is theologically based, the ultimate goal of spirituality and the way it is accomplished will be different from the goals and means of any other approach. The Scriptures speak of oneness with Christ and being transformed into the image of Christ, with the Holy Spirit and our response, as the means. But someone not using the Scriptures could decide the goal of spirituality is whatever they believe is the highest potential of the human spirit. Surely there are spiritual aspects of the human spirit that can be cultivated without God, but as James Loder (1998) said, "the answer to 'What is a lifetime?' and 'Why do I live it?' must finally be bestowed by the Creator Spirit" (32–33). Trying to understand the goal and purpose of life using the human spirit alone will end in futility.

References

Allen, Holly, and Ryan Porche. 2016. "A Working Definition of Children's Spirituality." In *Children's Spirituality Conference—Christian Perspectives 2016*. Lipscomb University.

Anthony, Michael J. 2006. *Perspectives on Children's Spiritual Formation: Four Views.* Nashville: B & H Academic.

Hay, David, and Rebecca Nye. 2006. *The Spirit of the Child*. Rev. ed. London: Kingsley.
Howard, Evan B. 2008. *The Brazos Introduction to Christian Spirituality*. Grand Rapids: Brazos.
Jensen, Paul L. 2009. *Subversive Spirituality: Transforming Mission through the Collapse of Space and Time*. Princeton Theological Monograph Series. Eugene, OR: Pickwick.
King, Pamela Ebstyne. 2016. "Kids and God: Nurturing Spirituality and the Ability to Thrive." In *Children's Spirituality Conference—Christian Perspectives 2016*. Lipscomb University.
Loder, James E. 1998. *The Logic of the Spirit: Human Development in Theological Perspective* 1st ed. San Francisco: Jossey-Bass.
Scorgie, Glen G, et al. 2011. *Dictionary of Christian Spirituality*. Grand Rapids: Zondervan.
Stonehouse, Catherine. 1998. *Joining Children on the Spiritual Journey: Nurturing a Life of Faith*. Grand Rapids: BridgePoint.
Tyson, John R. 1999. *Invitation to Christian Spirituality: An Ecumenical Anthology*. New York: Oxford University Press,
Wimber, John, and Kevin Springer. 1991. *Power Points: Your Action Plan to Hear God's Voice, Believe God's Word, Seek the Father, Submit to Christ, Take up the Cross, Depend on the Holy Spirit, Fulfill the Great Commission*. 1st ed. San Fancisco: HarperSanFrancisco.

PART II

Formation

Children grow, develop, and change. This formative process, whether regarded as moral or spiritual, is part of being a child, as well as a child of God. The processes of formation are distinctively human. Formation occurs within children themselves. Each child's own humanity is the initial context for moral and spiritual formation.

The chapters assembled in this section focus on the context of formation in the lives of children. Families and homes of all kinds provide the foundational relational context in which formation happens. Parents engage the formative process of their children, whether they are birth, adoptive, or foster parents, just as do those parents who are absent due to incarceration. The church as a community of faith, providing worship and intergenerational experiences, is another influential context in which formation occurs, giving children a context beyond themselves or their families in which to grow, develop, and change.

As one reads these chapters, the spectrum of formative events and processes at work in the life of children will be explored, and our part as children's pastors and educators will be affirmed and informed. As you explore the chapters in this section, you may find yourself engaging in a type of conversation with each author. You may also find yourself wanting to discuss these ideas with a colleague. Act on that good idea. It is through the discussion of new ideas and concepts that our own ideas and concepts will be expanded, revised, changed completely, or corroborated

Chapter 6

An Invitation to Worship & Wonder

An Overview of Contemplative Models of Spiritual Formation

Trevecca Okholm

This is a place where we walk more s-l-o-w-l-y, talk more softly, and have all the time we need to worship God. Thus begins the invitation to enter into a worship-and-wonder model of faith formation. At a time in our North American culture when entertainment and activity are often seen as the default mode for ministry with children, the appeal of a more contemplative model for spiritual formation may seem foreign and yet, at the same time, so inviting to our souls. But how will our children respond to such contemplative opportunities? Will they think it boring? Will they embrace the uncommon opportunity to be quiet and reflect? Will they respond in awe and feel the holy-otherness of such models? Ironically the appeal of contemplative models of spiritual formation is taking hold in church ministries within a spectrum of denominations and non-denominations across North America and has, in the past few decades, already found a footing in churches and homes in many parts of Europe and Australia. This chapter will introduce a brief history of contemplative models (often referred to as worship-and-wonder models) as well as a theology of and objectives for these models.

A Brief History of Worship and Wonder

For the most part, this model began mid-twentieth century through the work of Maria Montessori and her research with children in Italy. The goal of her research has been summed up as the desire to educate the human potential by developing natural interests in children as opposed to more formal teaching methods. With the blessings of Maria Montessori, one of her students, Sofia Cavalletti, along with the support of another of Montessori's students, Gianna Gobbi, began exploring the religious potential for Montessori's work. Cavalletti developed a model referred to as *Catechesis of the Good Shepherd* in the 1950s followed with her books, *History's Golden Thread: The History of Salvation* (1966) and *Religious Potential of the Child: Experiencing Scripture and Liturgy with Young Children* (1992).

In the 1960s, Jerome Berryman, a student at Princeton Theological Seminary, had a request for his professor. He asked professor D. Campbell Wyckoff if, instead of taking the then required seminary course in Christian education, he might substitute an independent study with Wyckoff. His assignment was to write a theory of Christian education. This assignment led him to Italy to study under Cavalletti in a year-long program at The Center for Advanced Montessori Studies in Bergamo, Italy. From there he returned home to the United States where he continues to develop his theory some fifty years later. Jerome Berryman is, at the time of this writing, the director of the Center for the Theology of Childhood, a part of the Godly Play Foundation, established in late 2007. He continues to speak widely on his theory and his *Godly Play* model, a model that also, along with Cavalletti's *Catechesis of the Good Shepherd*, falls within the definition of a contemplative worship and wonder for spiritual formation. Berryman's works include *Children and the Theologians: Clearing the Way for Grace* (2009) and *The Spiritual Guidance of Children: Montessori, Godly Play, and the Future* (2013), as well as a volume co-authored with Sonja Stewart, *Young Children and Worship* (1988) and his eight-volume series of *Godly Play* (2002–2012).

After leaving the Presbyterian Church where he had served as an ordained minister since 1962, Berryman was ordained as an Episcopal priest in 1984 and served to 1994. Berryman served as Canon Educator at Christ Church Cathedral in downtown Houston until 1994.

It was during the early 1980s that a professor of Christian Education from Western Reformed Theological Seminary in Grand Rapids, Michigan arranged a field trip with a few of her students to travel to Texas and observe the work being done by Berryman at Christ Church Cathedral. Following that trip with her students, Sonja Stewart and Jerome Berryman co-authored the first published collection of lessons using a worship-and-wonder model, entitled *Young Children and Worship* (1988). Berryman's eight-volume series of *Godly Play* would not begin to be published for another decade (2002–2012) and the term *Godly Play* would not be coined until the mid-1990s. Stewart, without the co-authorship of Berryman, went on to author a second book of lessons, *Following Jesus* (2000).

A Matter of Theology

More so than many of the Christian educational curricula currently marketed to churches, contemplative models of spiritual formation are intentionally grounded in theology and liturgy and not associated with any particular denominational entity. These models incorporate intentional use of sacred language (parable, sacred story, contemplation, liturgical actions). They are rooted in the four-fold order of historic Christian worship (see below), and also follow the cyclical, Christological flow and rich tradition of the liturgical church year calendar. They are rooted in ancient storytelling and worship practices, taking on a narrative approach to theology and faith formation. The very heart of such a model is the invitation for children to *experience God*—not just learn about God. Rather than simply Christian morality and behavior modification, the goal is to create space for children to enter into *holy otherness* with awe, mystery, and wonder. Children have an innate sense of the presence of God and an innate potential for worship that the church has too often, and usually unintentionally, bred out of them.

To expand on this, the intentional use of sacred language forms the basis and flow of a worship-and-wonder model. The use of the *languages of faith*—religious, liturgical and sacred—theologically ground the lessons, filling them with wonder and mystery of our ancient and future Christian faith. The intentional use of sacred story, based on the cyclical rhythm of the church year calendar, opens space for silence and contemplation. The rehearsing of liturgical actions, and the mystery of parables create wonder and give depth to our spiritual capacity.

The rhythmic and cyclical nature in the order of worship and the unfolding of the lessons invites all ages to remember who we are as an historic people of God as well as why we exist and find our meaning and place in God's story. We are a people created to belong to a story. Eugene Peterson, the well-known author and the translator of *The Message*, tells of an episode in which his four-year-old grandson jumped onto his lap and demanded, "Grandpa, tell me a story, and put me in it." (Kang & Parrett 2009, 17). This is precisely what faith formation is all about. God is unfolding the great Story of God's purpose and faithfulness, and God has invited us to take our places in that story. Our children long not for facts and arguments alone. At the heart of who we are created to be is an innate desire to belong to a bigger story that defines us and gives us place and purpose.

In the cycle of lessons that make up worship-and-wonder models is the church's historical faith story, beginning with the ebbing of the light in *Advent*, waiting for the new born King to again enter our reality at *Christmas*, and his entrance to enter into our world with the increasing light of *Epiphany*.

PART II: FORMATION

The story then weaves into the cycle of love as the church turns toward the leanness of *Lent,* the depth of *Paschal Triduum* and the hope of *Eastertide* moving us with grace to the season of *Pentecost* and the birth of the church. The story then flows into what is often referred to as *Ordinary time*—sometimes called *Growing season.* As the story is rehearsed again and again with each turning year, we are invited to enter more deeply into our place in the story—God's story. As the church cycles down into each new calendar year, the children of God are invited to cycle up into a new reality of belonging and purpose. This is the cycle of the lessons in worship-and-wonder models of faith formation forming us into an alternative reality of hope.

Figure 1. The Church Year Calendar

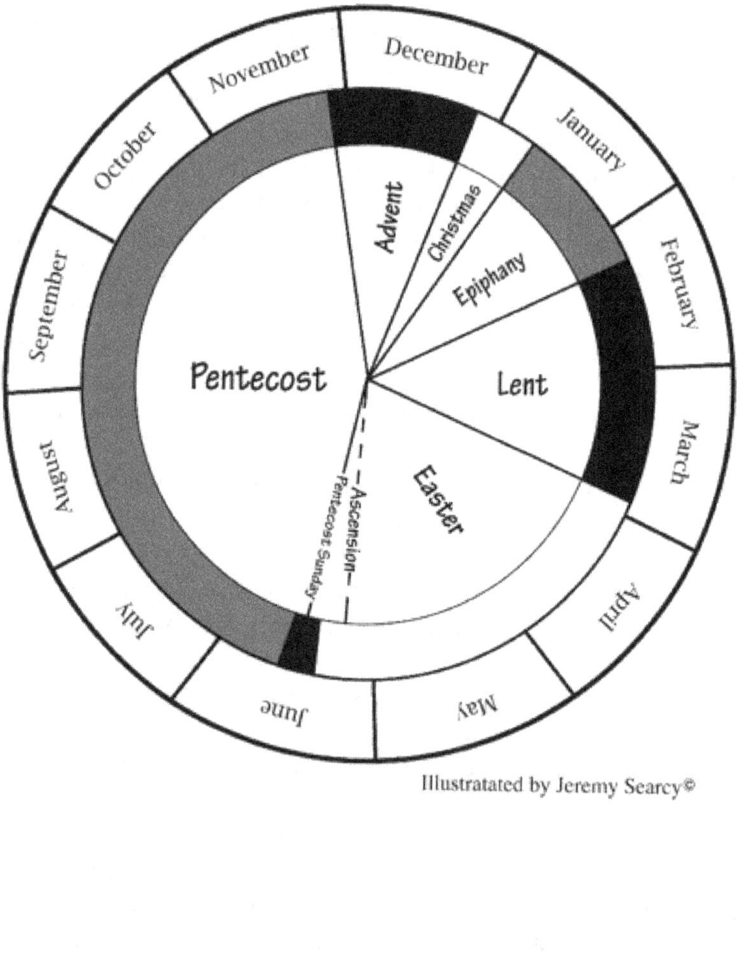

Illustratated by Jeremy Searcy©

The Fourfold Order of Christian Worship

Matthew Price (2013) reminds us of an old adage typically used by educators: *external order organizes internal experience.* Traditionally in Christian worship, there is a proper use of order that facilitates how the church communicates and acts out the story of salvation so that the congregation's internal experience of encountering the story is maximized. This ancient order of worship, still practiced by liturgical churches around the world, has become unified into a four-fold action of:

1. preparation to worship (call to worship, opening, inviting, gathering in);
2. proclamation and celebration of the Word along with a time for response (listening to the story of God and allowing space for response to God's holy Word);
3. sacramental celebrations around the baptismal font and the Lord's Table along with response (welcoming in and sharing a meal together with the people of God);
4. dismissal (benediction, sending out, the charge).

Through this intentional ordering of worship the participants: (a) enter into the presence of God and into a sense of *holy space*; (b) listen to God speak to them through God's Word, creating an opportunity for praxis between God's *Story* and our own stories and life experiences—a breaking into our ordinary and infusing it with wonder and meaning; (c) receive Christ through the sacramental and sacred acts of our communal faith; and (d) are sent out with blessing into the world in Christ's name.

Child development research shows us that children respond best to an environment with order and a familiar, predictable routine, giving them a sense of belonging, a sense of security and opportunity to develop self-discipline. Structure combined with the opportunity to explore and wonder begin to create a safe opportunity for children to engage with the holy-otherness and mystery of God. Rather than simplifying God to our children's developmental level, we invite our children to embrace the mystery along with us that lifts us all up to the activity of the Holy Spirit (something that too often gets squelched out of traditional children's Christian education curricula). As each step in the order of worship unfolds, a meaningful encounter with God becomes more fully realized.

In a worship-and-wonder model, this fourfold order plays out as:

The Gathering (Entering into the Circle)

Children are invited to join the circle where there is *always room for more*. Sitting in a circle on the floor rather than in desks or chairs around tables begins to create and reveal the intentionality of this model. While each child is greeted at the entrance (sometimes a door, other times a curtain opening into a tent or alcove or an atrium) they decide when they are internally ready to join the circle—an invitation to personally prepare their hearts for worship and wonder. When the circle is ready, the storyteller may speak a *call to worship*, moving from ordinary time to sacred time (in which we move more slowly and talk more softly and have all the time we need to worship God). This entering in may include praise singing, an opening prayer, and possibly a time of sharing or greeting each person right where they are.

Hearing the Word of God Proclaimed

As the storyteller transitions into the Word of God spoken through story and use of manipulatives, they may invite children into *liturgical actions* such as saying The Lord's Prayer together, reciting all or a small portion of one of the creeds of our common faith heritage such as The Apostles' Creed or the Nicene Creed. There might be a time of observing the Church Year Calendar on the wall and moving the arrow to the next story while remembering the earlier stories and anticipating the stories yet to come. When the time is right, the storyteller may invite the children to sing a song of preparation for the anticipated story. One that is often used is *"Good News, Good News."* Worship-and-wonder models are rooted in a sensorimotor approach which means that children learn via all their senses: the sight and tactile nature of the manipulatives, the smell of candles, hearing the story told with invitation to imagine, the tastes of the feast, all of which create s-p-a-c-e for the action of the Holy Spirit.

Thanksgiving and Response

"Let us give thanks to God. It is right to give Him thanks and praise." The use of listening and wondering questions in *Response Time* does not ask nor expect pat answers but rather invites the profoundly simple act of wondering. For example, rather than asking children *how many animals of each kind entered the ark or, how many days it rained,* the teacher might say, *I wonder how Noah felt when he saw all the animals. I wonder how he fed them all.* Or perhaps, *I wonder why God allowed the flood to happen,* or *I wonder what*

it must have been like to finally walk out on dry land again. And with older children or adults, *I wonder which other of God's stories are like this one. I wonder if there is a place like the ark where we can go and know we can be safe. I wonder what 'safe' feels like.*

The sacred acts of communal faith—the ritual lighting of the Christ candle, the words that are used and re-used each time we gather, the reading of God's holy Word (honoring the holy Scripture rather than tagging on a memory verse at the end or beginning of our curriculum), the rituals of eating the feast together—all become the rhythm and rituals that form meaning.

Benediction, Blessings, and Sending Out

The ending is equally as intentional as the beginning and the storytelling. Many worship-and-wonder models invite the children to come, one by one, to stand before the storyteller and receive a personal blessing as parents arrive for pick-up. One church I know asks each child to take up their *carpet circle* and return it to a large basket after which the child stands before the storyteller for a blessing before lining up at the door and returning in an orderly fashion to sit with their parents in worship as the Eucharistic table is being set.

Gathering Together

Another church I have worked alongside invites all the children to sing a benediction song entitled *"Go Now in Peace"* as they end their time together. It is this intentionality and seriousness from beginning to sending out that engages children and becomes more meaningful than an announcement that it is time to clean up before parents arrive followed by a free-for-all race to the door.

Objectives for a Worship-and-Wonder Model

Jerome Berryman lays out six objectives in the beginning of his *Godly Play* volumes, explaining that "the goal of *Godly Play* is for children to move through the spiral curriculum during early, middle, and late childhood in such a way that they will enter adolescence with an inner working model of the classical Christian language system to root them deeply in the tradition and at the same time allow them to be open to the future." Berryman's six objectives (2009) for meeting the above goal are:

1. to model how to wonder;
2. to show children how to create meaning with *wondering* questions;
3. to invite children to choose their own work;
4. to organize the mentoring time around the deep structure of Christian worship;
5. to support the community of children by respecting and challenging them to participate constructively;
6. to clarify the whole Christian language system by the organization of the meeting space.

Another way of explaining the objectives for a worship-and-wonder model is to pay close attention with intentionality to the following goals:

Engagement with Christian Liturgy

This liturgical engagement is sometimes referred to as a *playful orthodoxy* using the theological understanding of the word *play* as meaning any activity that engages humans into the creative process in communion with God's work of creativity in the world. And *orthodoxy* simply means *straight doctrine*. So one could say that worship-and-wonder models engage us in the creative work of getting our doctrine straight. This meaning goes deeper than getting biblical and theological information into our heads. It is a holistic engagement with our hearts as well as our heads.

Contemplative Silence

The goal here is simply to create that space for contemplation on God and self in relationship with God. There is something so utterly *un-cultural* in inviting our children into silence. Too often our churches seem to avoid it at all costs and yet it is a state in which our spiritual nature longs to dwell.

Creating Order vs. Chaos

This goal seems to go without saying that the world we create for our children is too often filled with chaos and busyness. A still, quiet, orderly place with the routine that our children yearn for is simply an amazing opportunity that the church can model and provide for our children and their families.

Cyclical / Spiral Nature of Faith Development

In C. S. Lewis's *The Last Battle* (1956), as the children and creatures begin to enter the next realm, one exclaims, "I have come home at last! This is my real country! I belong here. This is the land I have been looking for all my life, though I never knew it till now . . . Come further up, come further in!" I tend to associate the cyclical nature of following the church year calendar to going further up and further in to where God has created me to dwell. By flowing into and through the church year over and over again our children find themselves living into an alternative reality of God's working in this world. Rather than providing theological information only that our children can take into their already-established daily routines, this intentional weaving into and out of the church's ordering of time allows a transformational way of understanding themselves and the surrounding world.

And Finally . . . A Few Practical Ideas for Getting Started

What do worship-and-wonder rooms and materials look like and how can it fit in your church—or home—situation? With so many churches using non-traditional meeting spaces and times, the thought of having a place dedicated to such a model may seem unrealistic and next to impossible.

Here are a couple of solutions I have observed. One example is a church in Southern California that calls itself *the pizza church* (it has a real name; however, this describes their meeting space. They are officially known as Restoration Abbey). They move in and set up and tear down each week. There is the restaurant space used for worship but seemingly nowhere to create a dedicated space for the children. They have, however, discovered a grassy area in the strip mall that is in view of the restaurant. Their solution has been to use a pop-up tent in this grassy area. It is draped with colorful scarves on the outside, an unrolled round rug on the inside, and a small, portable altar to hold the Christ candle and Bible. As the children enter they feel the transition into a holy space.

Another church meets in a host church where the host church's children's space is boldly decorated with lots of colorfully attractive distractions. Their solution is to put up PVC pipes draped with curtains where, as with *the pizza church*, children are invited to enter into a quiet space free of distractions. Of course, as Berryman describes in his *Godly Play* volumes, in an ideal situation the space is one that can be permanently set up to look like a *visual Bible* with materials around the room arranged to communicate visually and silently the language system of the Christian faith: the sacred stories of the Old and New Testaments, the parables and liturgical action materials, enrichment presentations each identified with *story icon* image that invites the child to wonder about the story a container might hold. Each lesson includes an *underlay* and teaching manipulatives for telling the narrative. Shelves for supplemental materials such as books, maps, and other resources, as well as shelves to hold supplies for art and reflection, add to the intentionality of the visual space. Stories for Christmastide and the Easter season have their own location on either side of the *focal* shelf located in constant view just behind the storyteller.

Because our worship spaces and timing changes from congregation to congregation, the time allotted for children's education might vary widely. One question to ask as you consider this model for your congregation is *when, where, and how much time you have*. Most worship-and-wonder models are designed to last for 60–90 minutes with the children, giving space for lots of varied response time, including the feast; however, many churches give only 20–30 minutes for the children to leave corporate worship during the preached sermon before the children return to corporate worship for the Eucharist / communion with their families.

A wealth of pictures and ideas can be found online at various websites, blogs and Pinterest. Materials can easily be home-made with patterns included in many curricula such as Sonja Stewart's *Young Children* (1989) *and Worship, Following Jesus* (2000), and if you can locate it, Janet Schreuder's *iWonder* (1998); however, complete sets of materials are also available for purchase from sites such as *Godly Play Foundation* and *Worship Woodworks*. (On both these sites the materials cost about the same and I encourage you to explore the differences. For example, he Worship Woodworks figures are thicker and stand on their own much better, while some of Godly Play Foundation materials offer unique advantages in design.) Many of the blogs and websites are created by parents who do an *at home* form of worship and wonder. My hope is that you will explore all the wealth of ideas and materials and settings in which this model has been incorporated.

As I said at the beginning of this chapter, worship and wonder is used in churches and homes around the world and is surprisingly easy to translate between various cultures. I have transported it on mission trips from Mexico to Africa to Romania and find it a fresh, inviting, child-engaging, and translatable means for communicating the Gospel message.

And thus continues an invitation to children of all ages and ethnicities to enter into a sacred space where time moves as an alternative rhythm to our cultural rush and hurry, an invitation to enter in and become centered in the old, old story of God's reality.

References

Berryman, Jerome. 1995. *Godly Play: An Imaginative Approach to Religious Education*. Minneapolis: Augsburg.

Berryman, Jerome. 2009. *Teaching Godly Play: How to Mentor the Spiritual development of Children*. Rev. and expanded ed. Denver: Morehouse.

Cavalletti, Sofia. 1992. *The Religious Potential of the Child: Experiencing Scripture and Liturgy with Young Children*. 2nd ed. Chicago: Liturgy Training.

Gibson, Richard. n.d. *Biblical Lessons*. Protection, KS: Worship Woodworks.

Kang, S. Steve, and Gary Parrett. 2009. *Teaching the Faith, Forming the Faithful: A Biblical Vision for Education in the Church*. Downers Grove, IL: InterVarsity.

Montessori, Maria. 1989. *To Educate the Human Potential*. 1st paperback ed. ABC-CLIO.

Price, Matthew. 2013. *The Fourfold Order of Christian Worship*. Worship Library blog. www.worshiplibrary.com/blog/the-four-fold-pattern-of-worship/.

Schreuder, Janet. 1998. *iWonder . . . More Bible Stories for Children and Worship*. New York: Reformed Church.

Stewart, Sonja. 2000. *Following Jesus: More about Young Children and Worship*. Louisville: Geneva.

Stewart, Sonja, and Jerome Berryman. 1989. *Young Children and Worship*. Louisville: Westminster John Knox.

Chapter 7

Making Space

*Attending to the Spiritual
Wisdom of Children*

— Erin Minta Maxfield-Steele —

I.

*"Childhood is when the mouth tastes earth.
When the body is the body's sign."*

—Ned O'Gorman (2006, 242–43).

Shaken and moved by the world and by the internal stretch and pull of growth and development, the bodies of children are in the midst of constant change. They have agency, but little power. Agility, but limited strength. They have intuition, curiosity, and ideas, but they grow in communities where adult voices are listened to more carefully than theirs. Though they grow and change like all living beings, they are often seen as unformed or unfinished—waiting to become adults. The belief that children are incomplete can be theologically and pastorally problematic. It can lead to the neglect of children's spiritual lives and to inadequate responses to their emotional and spiritual needs. This belief and my response to it form the basis of this project.

In a culture that applauds the strength and independence of the "able-bodied," the fragility and dependence of early and late life are often dismissed or denied or hidden. This tendency to overlook the spiritual needs and the spiritual wisdom of the young and the old sends a damaging theological message about who belongs in the body of Christ.

In order to more effectively honor the wisdom of children, both children and adults in the church need resources that help them acknowledge the young body as a place of encounter with the Divine. I believe that spiritual practices can allow the practitioner to rest in their own *being* and to step away, for a moment, from the shifting of the external world and to seek God's presence.

II.

> *"To ask, to remember, to lament, to complain, to seek one's own self and that which is beyond the self. Prayer is the trajectory and the perspective, enabling you to locate your own sense of self in this trajectory."*
>
> —Chaim Potok (1998, 65).

Human life can be thought of in terms of milestones, progress, or stages of development. We are constantly *becoming*: becoming educated, socialized, professional, mature, etc. And though *becoming* is central to all life, spirituality can punctuate the process of growing and changing by creating space for simply *being*, for, as Chaim Potok (1998) puts it, "locat[ing] your own sense of self in this trajectory" (1998, 65). Many caregivers and parents of children can attest to the tension between being and becoming; to care for a child in a way that only strives to equip them for the future does a disservice to the joys and challenges of their present. But since change and growth are such visible elements of childhood, adults can forget the importance of the *being* in the overwhelming rush of a child's *becoming*. Put another way, in focusing on a child's continuing formation adults can overlook the wholeness of children.

Seeing *Becoming*: Barriers to Acknowledging Wholeness

In addition to the development and change that mark childhood, children deviate from many of the cultural norms that determine human value. Children have differing levels of physical, linguistic, and cognitive ability. Our culture's frequently-unchallenged Ableism values individuals based these abilities or, as is often the case with children, by the potential to acquire them. A child's ability to articulate spiritual experience is expressed in words they have learned and may be limited by their cognitive development. This may lead some adults to assume the absence of such experiences or to dismiss them as inauthentic (Champagne 2010).

Children often—intentionally or unintentionally—challenge social mores of niceness and respectability. Children sometimes disrupt adult ways of expressing spirituality. Children's spirituality can also challenge fundamental assumptions about theological authority. Who decides how we talk about God? What beliefs are acceptable? Though children are highly valued by our society, Ableism, objectification, and natural boundaries such as developing self-expression often prevent adults from honoring the wisdom of children. Though many parents and caregivers do recognize this, I believe we still must listen more attentively for and to the spiritual lives of children.

For many adults, the idea that a child could be considered—at least for themselves—the religious authority of their own spirituality makes no sense. This is, however, the claim that I hope to convince the reader of: that finding ways to allow children to make and to enter into their own spiritual space (allowing the *being* of their spiritual body) is an important spiritual practice.

Seeing *Being*: Acknowledging Children's Wisdom

Our epistemology often favors rational ways of knowing, making us vulnerable to overlooking truth claims that are intangible or illogical, such as a six-year-old's claim that, "Jesus wants me to tell you to tell all the other children only to listen to adults with soft eyes" (Stairs 2000, 167). Recognizing the value of other epistemologies, such as ones that affirm revelation or intuition as valid ways of knowing, may allow us to listen to children more carefully. Doing this requires that adults let go of their assumptions that *their* wisdom is needed to temper and shape the strange ideas that children have. The impulse to educate, correct, and lead children is not *bad*, but it is not always needed. Jean Stairs claims that, "whether we admit it or not, we probably have . . . clung to the assumption that children must become like us . . . . Rather than coming between a child and God, I am suggesting that we stand back and allow such contact to occur" (170–71).

What, if any, is the role of an adult in acknowledging children's expressions of spirituality? Caregivers often *do* weave time for *being* into the movement of everyday life. Reading aloud to children, for example, while recognized as important for the development of a child's reading skills and vocabulary, can be a luxurious and "non-productive" time. The space created when adult caregivers and children snuggle up together to share a story that the adult gives voice to is a time when little is required of the child. The voice does more than soothe the child toward naptime or bedtime, it connects them to a story beyond their own life while it also connects them to the reader's voice and body.

For those of us rooted in the Christian tradition, we may have spiritual practices developed at an early age that have helped us through difficult times. Since adults shape much of a child's unstructured time, we are in a unique position to make time for the child. Making space for children's spiritual practice, then, requires a step back, an invitation, or a commitment to co-create (whether the practice is regular or irregular, private or communal, silent or noisy or both). Encouraging children to take time to pray or to engage in a spiritual practice that the *child* ultimately shapes offers them a way to seek connection with the Divine, to *be* with a "Love that stretches beyond [even] their immediate parental figures" (Stairs 2000, 162). Spiritual practice is a work of leaning toward connectedness, or of simply recognizing connection. This is true as much for adults as it is for children.

Overcoming some of the barriers that prevent us from seeing children as fully-formed spiritual beings can help us place ourselves along the trajectory of our lives. In creating space for children to express their embodied wisdom, to step away from their becoming in order to simply be, to seek time with the sacred, and connection with the Divine, we allow children to be the agents of their practice and to find a place of rest.

III.

Called into *Being*

I once cared for two small children while their parents were in English classes. Both under the age of one, they took turns cutting teeth with all the feverish foul tempers and floods of tears that new teeth bring. Being bumped along in a stroller often resulted in more crying, but one day I decided to try again in hopes of sparing my neck and back the strain of carrying them around. Only when we were well on our way down the gravel road through the woods did I realize that this simply would not work. In my frustration I pulled the double stroller to the side of the road, flipped on the breaks, and gathered each little one up in my arms. The wailing stopped and the two of them looked around, dazed and sniffing.

We were in north Georgia woods, grown up from terraced cotton fields into pines and sweetgum. Unsure of what to do I stepped into the woods, a warm, recovering baby firmly pressed against each side. I was struck by how beautiful the woods were in this new space that the babies' silence had created. They each held on tightly as I walked, and we came upon a huge pine with deeply notched bark, tinged rust-red in the cracks and stippled with glazed pearls of sap.

The babies stared at the tree as we drew near. Soon we stood inches from the bark—close enough to see little ants moving carefully and quickly along its ridges and cracks. The three of us watched in rapt attention as the ants worked. One baby reached out a hand, not to touch the ants, but to be closer. I shifted my hip toward the tree a bit so the little hand could reach the ancient bark. We continued watching for what felt like a long time until my arms became tired.

Prayer and contemplative spiritual practice require the work of *attending* to something inside of our bodies and beyond them. The place the three of us were drawn to seemed to breathe *"pay attention."* For a moment, I forgot my frustration. The children forgot their aching gums and distant parents. For a moment, we stepped out of the movement of life's *becoming* and rested in simply *being*, together, caught up in our wonder.

Drawn by *Beauty*

Approaching God involves recognizing ourselves at our point of connection. Through spiritual practice we realize both the other that draws us in and the self that is being drawn. Like the umbilical cord, our very connection to the other quickens our awareness of ourselves. Feminist theologian Wendy Farley writes, "the great beauty that is ourself is drawn to the great beauty that is God" (2005, 17). In Farley's reckoning, it is the elemental self, our "beauty," that is drawn to God. Farley holds the tension of paradox in her claim that "This beauty beyond all knowing and naming pulls us out of ourselves and toward ourselves" (17). Rather than transcending the self in order to encounter God, we discover ourselves as we respond to the pull of the Divine. To be drawn toward God and self in one motion is to feel again the scarred skin of our connective tissue. In allowing ourselves to be drawn toward the *beauty* within us and beyond us we let ourselves rest in simply *being*.

In Farley's understanding, we come into contact with the Divine as wounded beings. As the great beauty pulls us, it is as our broken, mysterious selves that we are called—not as whom-we-will-become or as who-we-have-been, nor as perfect, fully-formed and fully-healed beings. Rather, we are called as the image of a God who, through Christ, is wounded and yet whole. This has profound implications for children, since it posits that the self is whole while still broken, formed while still being formed, complete while still healing, wondering, or uncertain. Christ's invitation is to come as those who are "weary and heavy laden" (Matthew 11:28), or, for us that day, to come as those who are swollen-gummed and sad, who carry in our small bodies the inarticulate memories of war and birth and hunger. Welcomed as wounded and burdened, we are invited to rest in our very beings.

Attending to God's Voice

The stories of Moses and Samuel are examples of attending to mystery. In the book of Exodus, Moses sees something curious and decides to go closer to try to understand. He slips his sandals from his feet and stands on holy ground, overwhelmed and frightened, yet present to hear God's words. Attending to a mystery in the desert results in Moses hearing God's unsettling and ultimately liberating words. One theological claim in this story is that God seeks our attention. Still, only "when God recognizes that Moses has 'turned aside to see' does God call out to him" (Miller-McLemore 2007, 42).

Prayer may take shape in *our* seeking, like Bartimaeus who yells out to Jesus as he passes on the road, or it may take the shape of *being called*. Isaiah writes, "Listen to me, O coastlands, pay attention, you peoples far away! The Lord called me before I was born, while I was in my mother's womb he had named me" (Isaiah 49:1). God may take shape in beauty or strangeness and call to us. In such cases what is required of us is that we "stop and notice."

God's presence in the Bible is not restricted to the quiet internal spaces that we tend to associate with spiritual encounter. God speaks from whirlwinds, in a flurry of languages, and, for Moses, from the crackling fire of a burning bush, not far from a flock of sheep! Encountering the divine does not require silence, solemnity, or solitude. Bonnie Miller-McLemore writes, "God bestows peace not as a promise of perfect serenity or an end to chaos, anxiety, and strife but as a source of strength in turmoil" (Miller-McLemore, 2007, p. 18). Encountering God, then, is a source of strength not reserved only for the silent and the still.

We do not always recognize God's voice or presence. Young Samuel clearly hears a voice but does not *recognize* it. As we are born within communities, we often need the help of others as we strive to attend to the pull of the divine. When Eli realizes that Samuel is being called by God, he says "Go, lie down. If you are called again, say, 'Speak, *Adonai;* your servant is listening'" (1 Samuel 3:9). Samuel needs Eli's *help* but, as Eli seems to know, he does not need Eli's *mediation*. Eli's response to Samuel is to help him recognize God's voice, and to send him back to his room on his own to wait and to listen.

Surrendering Control

Though adults are rich resources for children in their being and becoming, we cannot control or dictate who they are or who they become. Admitting this may be uncomfortable, and admitting our lack of control over their spiritual lives may be less comfortable still. While the complicated questions that accompany religious life baffle adults and children alike, it may still be tempting to claim that we understand, especially if we think that adults are responsible for teaching their children to be Christians. Claiming that something is simple when it is anything but simple forecloses on the possibility to listen with the child for unfolding revelation of truth that transcends human knowledge. However, confessing mystery requires adults to surrender control—or at least to admit that we do not have it.

The amount of mystery I have experienced in my own journey has almost always been disquieting. I *like* to feel like I understand, like I am in control. However, Elaine Champagne writes that "Children can remind adults that chaos is a place where the goodness of creation can emerge" (Champagne 2010, 393). If prayer requires the work of attending to that which is beyond and within us, then being with children in a way that creates space for their own spiritual practice requires us to let go of any illusion that we are in control of how "the goodness of creation" will be revealed to them. Courage is required to step out of our familiar place, to surrender our expectations, and to release ourselves from our illusions of certainty.

IV.

"We are each other's harvest:
we are each other's business:
we are each other's magnitude and bond."

—Gwendolyn Brooks (2005, 113).

From Theory to Practice

In this final section I will move from theory to practice, and I will examine just a few of the myriad ways we may invite ourselves and others to *turn* and attend. I will explore some aspects of the practice of *being* and will offer up a few questions.

What is lost in attending to the body's experience is *in*attention. Inattention can serve an important role in protecting the body. Since the body is marked with past experiences, attending to the body may mean connecting with painful or traumatic experiences. Acknowledging and affirming the *goodness* of the body/self may or may *not* feel good when the body holds harmful memories. Respecting the boundaries that have formed is as important as affirming the body. Only the individual can sense where these lines have been drawn. If connecting with the body feels unsafe, then rest will not be possible. Safety is a necessary prerequisite to true, free, and liberative connection. Resting in being may bring greater awareness of what the body has been through. It may feel like the volume has been turned up and that a person "hears" the emotions, sensations, and memories in ways that are difficult to avoid.

Like turning toward mystery and accepting unknowing, taking time to be, to attend to the self, is likely to make a person more aware of the complexity of who they are and what they have experienced. Ask, *How do I talk about myself? How does this child talk about himself or herself? Does he/she carry the embodied experiences of physical, verbal, or sexual abuse or bullying? Has he/she been through significant illnesses, or periods of physical pain?*

Setting aside holy places, such as a certain part of the house, yard, or garden, is another concrete way of inviting children into space that has been *marked* as a place of attending. This is something that could be done as a family, as a Sunday school community, a class, or a daycare. Making sure that such spaces are always voluntary (in other words, not places where a child is told to go in order to calm down) is important. Designating such places may be a helpful way of communicating to children that they have access to a spiritual "time out" where they can rest and center themselves when they need to. They may have special things they want to take there or leave there. If the place is outside or near a window, it could be a place to attend to the changing beauty of the natural world. Ask, *Do I ever see this child comforting themselves? Do I ever see this child attending, spending time experiencing awe? Do I interrupt or encourage him or her? How do I expect the child's spirituality to look and does that really fit with the things I know about this child? Do I respect him/her as a source of spiritual wisdom, as a unique point of connection with God?*

After spending some time reflecting on your own or a child's spiritual practice, broadly defined, there may be ways to make your spiritual practice an invitation to others. For example, if you engage in traditional prayer, you may consider praying aloud what you might normally pray in silence, or you may incorporate traditional physical expressions of prayer such as kneeling, crossing yourself, or holding out your hands. Without telling a child what to do, letting a child know that they are welcome to join in will create the space for them to be a part of your spiritual practice—or not. Being careful to express *your own prayer* (even if tailored to be appropriate to the child or changed so that the child understands) is the best invitation to the child for *his or her own way of praying*.

"Help me listen" can be a tool for attending. Similar to a technique used in Cognitive Behavioral Therapy, ask the young person to help you listen by closing your eyes and asking them to name all the things they can hear starting with the loudest/closest things, down to the quietest. Be careful not to correct the child, even if they are "wrong" about what a sound is—just *listen* with them. This is a very simple way to stop and attend with a child. If you both enjoy it, you may find the child asking you to help them listen.

Finally, some adaptation of *lectio divina*, or divine reading, could help you and/or a child to rest in being. In *lectio divina*, a passage of Scripture is read aloud multiple times and is meditated on. The Trappists describe this ancient practice as like reading a love letter. Whatever words you choose (a poem, a psalm, a song, a mantra), the words are spoken and then spoken again. In being spoken, the words become prayer and are "tasted" by the speaker, "'in the mouth of the heart'" (Robertson 2011, p. xv). Repetition allows both speaker and listener to attend to the words, to taste them. Meditation (or *meditatio*) "carr[ies] the living word of God from the mind down into the heart where it awakens in us a loving response" (2011, xv).

Conclusion

With the body as the locus of awareness of God's presence, as well as the locus of *all* experience—including pain, trauma, abuse, and self-directed oppression—the practice of connecting lovingly with one's body must strive to root itself in liberative self-acceptance and love. The theological claim here is that God meets us, drawing us more deeply into ourselves and outside of ourselves toward one another, the world, and the divine. To choose to find rest in our being and attend to our points of connection with God is to accept God's invitation to live more fully, deeply, and mysteriously.

References

Brooks, Gwendolyn. 2005. "Paul Robeson." In *The Essential Gwendolyn Brooks*, edited by Elizabeth Alexander, p. 113. Chicago: American Poets Project.

Champagne, Elaine. 2010. "Children's Inner Voice: Exploring Children's Contribution to Spirituality." In *Children's Voices: Children's Perspectives in Ethics, Theology and Religious Education*, edited by Annemie Dillen and Didier Pollefeyts, 373–96. Louvain: Uitgeverij Peeters.

Farley, Wendy. 2005. *The Wounding and Healing of Desire: Weaving Heaven and Earth*. Louisville: Westminster John Knox.

Miller-McLemore, Bonnie. 2007. *In the Midst of Chaos*. San Francisco: Jossey-Bass.

O'Gorman, Ned. 2006. Childhood. In *The Other Side of Loneliness: A Spiritual Journey*. New York: Arcade.

Potok, Chaim. 1997. "Giving Shape to Turmoil: A Conversation with Chaim Potok." Interview by Michael Cusick. *Mars Hill Review*, Winter-Spring.

Robertson, Duncan. 2011. *Lectio Divina: the Medieval Experience of Reading*. Collegeville, MN: Cistercian.

Stairs, Jean. 2000. *Listening for the Soul: Pastoral Care and Spiritual Direction*. Minneapolis: Fortress.

Chapter 8

Making Meaning of God
The Faith Experiences of Preschool Children

Mimi L. Larson

PART OF BEING HUMAN is to make meaning of our experiences. We question why things happen. We seek to understand new ideas. We look for meaning in the stories we hear. Children are no different as they make meaning of the world they encounter. But their ability to make meaning comes through the common experiences of childhood. Through discovery and play, wonder and stories, reflection and language, young children are able to make meaning of their lives and experiences. Children are capable to create understandings and form knowledge through language, stories, play, and relationships. This research aimed to understand how these common experiences of childhood help young children engage and make meaning of faith. Is it possible for preschool children to engage in the biblical story and understand abstract spiritual ideas? We will discover that faith for young children is fostered through exploration and intentional experiences, all within a strong atmosphere of faith.

Exploring the Literature

Christian education has been highly influenced by developmental theorists. Piagetian theorists believe that basic theological concepts are difficult for a child to understand, for a child's religious development is intricately connected to their cognitive development. Within this train of thought, a young child does not have the cognitive ability to understand faith. These ideas, along with the stage-based theory of cognitive development, have affected the church's understanding of moral development (see Fowler 1981; and Kohlberg 1984, for extended discussion).

John Westerhoff and Lev Vygotsky emphasized the importance of community and social experiences that form the context for children's understanding and learning (Vygotsky 1978; Westerhoff 2000). For Vygotsky, it is the social relationship with others, containing interaction, language, and thought, that forms a foundation for an individual's learning (Court 2010). Children are capable of knowing things before they can verbalize or articulate them. For Westerhoff, it is not the words that create a place for meaning and understanding for the child. Instead, it is the child's experiences, the experiences connected with words that truly matter for the child and his or her faith development. Faith "is an action which includes thinking, feeling and willing and it is transmitted, sustained and expanded through our interactions with other faithing selves in a community of faith" (Westerhoff 2000, 89).

Traditionally, education is thought of as one person imparting knowledge to another person with the goal of producing a specific learning outcome in that individual. Westerhoff challenged that view, believing in an enculturation model that emphasizes «what one person has to bring to another and the dialogical relationship between equals» (Westerhoff 2000, 80). This idea of interaction, not instruction, undergirds his theory of faith development. Faith requires the interaction between "faithing selves" in order to emerge, to make meaning, to expand and develop in character and content. This is a relational faith, and it is in the intersection between these experiences, these interactions, these sharings, where faith is nurtured and grows.

The Means of Making Meaning

Experiences provide the context for young children's ability to make meaning where they explore, play, discover, and wonder. They experience enormous growth in their physical, emotional, cognitive, and social development. Through language, stories, play, relationships, and experiences, young children are able to grasp information and create understanding.

Language is a means for children to express their understandings and is more than words. Language also encompasses actions, emotions, and attitudes (Cavaletti et al. 1994). Drawing is also a form of language (Cox 2005). Since drawing is a communicative form of language and meaning-making (Tay-Lim & Lim 2013), it is through their art where children are able to express their ideas and understandings (Chang 2012; Pahl 1999). This research contained a drawing activity following the biblical storytelling where children drew pictures and then engaged in a dialogical relationship where they were invited to share their understandings.

Play is a common childhood experience and it is through everyday lived experiences such as play where children make meaning. Play enables a child's ability to make meaning (Yust 2004). Elkind (2007) contends that for early childhood, play is "the dominant and directing mode of learning" (7). When children play, they have the opportunity to experience and try out new ideas which bear no consequences since it is only play (Eaude, 2005). Vygotsky (1978) asserts that in real life, action overrules meaning. Yet, it is in play where "action is subordinated to meaning" (Vygotsky 1978, 101). As children engage in play and make meaning through these experiences, they are equipped to integrate these new ideas into both their family and community life (Paradise & Rogoff 2009).

Stories provide a narrative framework for children to interpret meaning (Hall 2007). Robert Coles (1989) contends that storytelling provides a better and richer sense of ourselves and our experiences. He states: "Novels and stories are renderings of life; they cannot only keep us company, but admonish us, point us in new directions, or give us the courage to stay a given course. They can offer us kinsmen, kinswomen, comrades, advisers—offer us other eyes through which we might see, other ears with which we might make soundings" (Coles 1989, 159–60). In terms of a child's spirituality, it is within stories and rituals where children are encouraged to explore, question, and wonder about spiritual and sacred understandings. Spiritual stories can encourage a sacred space for children to wonder and awe, a natural quality that is nurtured and developed through exploration.

Because of the connection between cognitive and social learning (Ainsworth 1969; Rogoff 1990), relationships contribute to a child's meaning making. "Children's spirituality involves living, exploring, and belonging by building close relationships with peers" (Harris 2007, 271). Social relationships help children respond to and make sense of significant moments and nurture the inner realm of the child. Through the everyday tasks of living, parents, caretakers, and other significant adults can nurture this inner spirituality.

Implications of Making Meaning in Terms of a Child's Spirituality

Current research on children's spirituality rarely discusses early childhood or preschool children, and little data are available on what meanings young children can actually make of their spiritual experiences. One reason for this might be the belief that faith and the verbal articulation of faith must be linked. This belief is disconcerting since it means that several populations may not be able to possess faith such as those with dementia, the intellectually disabled, and the young. Research shows that children are capable of being deeply spiritual (Stonehouse & May 2010). They are capable of reflecting on spiritual questions (Gersch et al. 2008). They are even able to make spiritual meanings (Lipscomb & Gersch 2012).

The Present Study

With these understandings from the literature, this qualitative study explored how preschool children make meaning of their faith experiences. This study was set in a full-day preschool classroom in a Midwestern Christian early childhood center, and the purposeful and information-rich sampling contained a total of twenty-six three-, four-, and five-year-old children in which approximately fourteen to eighteen children participated in the research activity each day.

For four consecutive weeks, the children engaged in their regular Christian education time three times a week. The first experience was a storytelling experience where the teacher read a children's storybook based on a biblical story. The second experience utilized *Young Children and Worship* (Stewart & Berryman 1989), a form of godly play storytelling that encourages children to engage the biblical story through words, questions, silence, movement, and wooden figures. While the third faith experience was not originally included in the research design, it emerged from the lead teacher's desire to continue exploring the week's biblical story and contained music, stories and dialogue between the teacher and children. The biblical stories chosen for this research included the story of the Good Shepherd (based on Ps 23), the Good Shepherd and the lost sheep (based on Ps 23 and John 10), the Good Shepherd and the wolf (based on Ps 23, John 10, and Matt 18), and Jesus and the little children (based on Matt 18, Mark 10, and Luke 18).

After the first and second experiences, children were encouraged to participate in a drawing activity, creating a meaningful picture from the story or an expression of what the story meant to them. Both the researcher and lead teacher were present at the table to ask questions of the children, encouraging their dialogue and expression of thoughts. Following the drawing, children were interviewed and asked to share their pictures and thoughts. The storybooks and story figures were available throughout the week for children to use and engage with.

In terms of data collection, observations were founded on the children's actions and behaviors, dialogue and questions, and non-verbal interactions. Similar to photo elicitation, the children's drawings were used to facilitate the interview questioning, gaining insight to the children's understandings and meaning-making. The discussions at the drawing table included a combination of group talk, self-talk, and specific dialogue between the adults and children.

Documents were also gathered and consisted of the children's drawings and weekly teacher reflective journals. Since children create meaning though a variety of means such as non-formalized play, informal conversations, and other behaviors, the teacher journals were utilized to capture any meaningful behaviors, dialogue, comments, or questions that occurred throughout the week from the children that related to the faith experiences.

Data were analyzed based on what Westerhoff (2000) describes as *Experienced Faith* where faith is experienced enactively and children have the freedom to explore, wonder, question, try, imagine, create, observe, copy, play, experience, and react. The eight individual coding categories were defined and any additional codes that emerged through further reading and analysis of the data were added. Further understanding regarding a child's demonstration of meaning-making was assessed based on language, actions and behaviors, and interaction with others.

How Children Make Meaning of God

Children approached meaning-making through a combination of verbal communication, play, story, art, and mirroring behaviors in which relationships were a critical link between engagement and articulation of understanding.

Meaning Making through Verbal and Non-Verbal Behaviors

In their faith experience, children utilized both verbal and non-verbal behaviors when making meaning of faith. For example, after hearing the story of Jesus and the children through the *Young Children and Worship* storytelling technique, a four-year-old girl mimicked the storyteller's movements as she walked the little children figures out of the city toward the Jesus figure, placing the disciple in between Jesus and the children. Looking at the story figures on the floor, she exclaimed: "Stop! Jesus is too busy for you!" She then picked up the Jesus figure and stated: "Let the little children come to me."

Placing the disciple off to the side, she holds the Jesus figure in one hand, bringing the children one by one to Jesus, having him kiss each child.

Later, that morning, this same four-year-old demonstrated the combination of verbal and non-verbal behavior in her drawings and interview. While she was drawing, she non-verbally represented the story with the familiar characters of Jesus, the disciples, and the children. She drew quietly, stopping at one point to verbally explain to herself, "I'm drawing another one because so there are two disciples." In describing the picture to the interviewer, she stated: "It's the disciples who said S-T-O-O-P . . . that means 'stop' . . . Jesus is too busy for you!" When asked what she understood of Jesus, she shouted, "Let the little children come to *me*!" and shared that Jesus loves the children and kisses them on the cheek. This verbal description resembles the previous non-verbal behavior that occurred during play where she held Jesus and had him kiss the children.

This young girl demonstrated how young children are able to integrate and flow between the verbal and the nonverbal as they seek to make meaning and articulate understandings. Relationships also have an impact on the child's verbal and non-verbal behaviors. A skilled teacher is able to draw out verbal explanations, helping children articulate the meanings and understandings. As educators, it is important for us to learn to listen to both children's verbal and non-verbal behavior in order to understand how young children make meaning of their faith.

Meaning Making through Language and Images

As children spoke, they utilized various forms of language to articulate their faith, and these various forms of language reflect the creative and varied way children are able to make meaning. These forms of language include a descriptive and concrete language, a symbolic language, a theological language, a fairy tale or fantasy language, and a private or inner language.

Meaning Described with Descriptive and Concrete Language.

The children utilized descriptive and concrete language to express their understandings of faith. For example, when asked who the Good Shepherd is, a child replied: "That's Jesus." When the teacher explored by further asking "Who is Jesus?," the child, unable to articulate the connection between Jesus and the Good Shepherd, physically pointed to the Bible and said "that you're reading" and then pointed to the wooden shepherd figure in her hand and stated: "Him."

In an interview with a three-year-old child, she also used descriptive and concrete language when describing her picture with these words:

Girl: (pointing to a line on the side of her page) This is God.

Researcher: That's God? And what is this?

Girl: Those are the sheep that go blah blah.

Researcher: They go blah blah?

Girl: Uh-huh. Blah blah.

Researcher: They what?

Girl: They look like babies that play?

Researcher: They look like babies that play? Does Jesus play with the sheep?

Girl: No. He only watches . . . .

Researcher: He what . . . .

Girl: He's big and his heart still beats because he is so big.

This three-year-old girl described the lambs as babies and Jesus as big with a heart that still beats. In drawings, she used images such as a vertical line to demonstrate God. These concrete and descriptive images express her understanding of the meanings she has ascribed to the biblical story and are rooted in her experience. Another child demonstrated this concrete and descriptive language when he explained that Jesus "cares for the sheep and eats breakfast with them every day." This breakfast experience, one in which the child has partaken, was utilized to concretely describe his understanding of the caring relationship between Jesus as the Good Shepherd and the sheep. Just like children eat breakfast with their parents, the sheep eat breakfast with Jesus.

Meaning Described with Symbolic Language.

The data also demonstrated the children's use of symbolic thought and language in describing meaning. They exhibited this by stating that we are all sheep, or as one child exclaimed "the lambs are us!" Whether by words or created drawings or objects, the young children used a symbol, such as a sheep, to form a representation of a real object or person, all of which aids their making meaning.

In particular, there was one five-year-old girl who demonstrated this interplay between the verbal and creative thinking. Upon hearing the story in the first week, she exclaimed that she understood who the sheep were in the story. During the second week, she spoke of "sheep-people" and in her drawings, called the sheep "people." The third week, looking at a picture of Jesus with children, she shouted out "Look at all the sheep!" After being told that there were no sheep in that specific picture, she mimicked the picture and illustrated the people following Jesus as sheep who were following Jesus, the Good Shepherd. In the fourth week, she continued drawing pictures of sheep. When asked why she was drawing sheep since there no sheep in the biblical story for that day, she explained, "The sheep are the people." When questioned what that might have to do with the story, she responded by stating: "The sheep are them, the people . . . kids."

This interplay of symbolic and imaginative understanding was also demonstrated in her drawings. When the story told of parents bringing their children to see Jesus, she drew a picture of grandma and grandpa sheep with a kid sheep at the feet of the shepherd, who she verbally described as Jesus. She continued to demonstrate her ability to make meaning through imaginative and symbolic thinking by describing Jesus leading his sheep to the door, initially described as a city, then clarified to be the sheepfold, and later identified as a church. On the last day of data collection, she created the story of the Good Shepherd out of clay. Engaging in symbolic language, she explained her creation, describing Jesus as the one who "takes care of the sheep." Her symbolic meaning-making was captured even past the completion of formal research when she was able to expand this symbolic thinking to other biblical stories. When hearing the biblical parable of the prodigal son, the little girl "burst out" and exclaimed that the story was just "like the Good Shepherd!" She went on to explain that "the daddy was like the shepherd and he loved the son, even though he went and was lost, they still had a party." This young child demonstrated the ability to make meaning of symbolic language within the biblical stories.

Meaning Described with Theological Language.

Whether it was a form of imitation or mirroring behavior, the young children also utilized a form of theological language to describe meanings of their experiences. Upon seeing an illustration of three crosses, a child described it as "the sign of the cross," a phrase used in the classroom as well as in the church to describe a crossing motion that the children made to signify the cross of Jesus Christ. Children also utilized typical "Jesus" answers, in which a child quickly responds to any spiritual question by answering "Jesus." The teacher or storyteller would ask additional questions to push past the surface "Jesus" answer, which would engage the children in deeper thought and understanding.

For the children, theological language was simple and concrete, yet it demonstrated significant meaning-making. For example, a four-year-old girl simply described salvation and Jesus as the "door to heaven." She expanded this meaning by illustrating Jesus with sheep following him to heaven. While her simple description might have mirrored or replicated a phrase both seen and heard in an earlier story, she explained that "Jesus is leading . . . is leading the sheep home" where Jesus is opening the door to heaven and the sheep willingly follow Jesus because he knows their names.

Meaning Described with Fairy Tale and Fantasy Language.

In understanding their experiences, preschool children utilized what could be described as a fairy tale or fantasy language to express meanings. They described the protagonist in the story (in this case, the Good Shepherd) as "the good guy" and antagonists (the thief or the disciples) as the "bad guys." They described the disciples as mean and the wolf as harmful. They talked about the Good Shepherd who saves and of the sheepfold as being safe. They knew there were scary and dark places in which the Good Shepherd would rescue the lost sheep.

In the play activity, children utilized this language as well to demonstrate meaning making. As a three-year-old boy played with the wooden figures, he made Jesus the hero whose adversaries in the story were the disciples. He described the Jerusalem city as "the church" and placed Jesus "at the top of the church." With the children looking up to Jesus, he said, "they are learning about God" while singing to himself "The B-I-B-L-E" song. Later, he has the disciple figures trying to enter the church (Jerusalem city) and placed Jesus in their way. As he attempts to have the disciples knock Jesus down, he did not let Jesus fall. Holding Jesus to face the disciples, he said: "You are not the boss of me," and then brings the protected children figures to the hero Jesus, quietly whispering, "thank you." He then proclaimed to himself: "Jesus loves the children."

Meaning Described with Private or Inner Language.

Private speech is a process where children talk to themselves, describing their actions, asking themselves questions, or repeating phrases, attempting to utilize language "as an instrument of thought" (Frauenglass & Diaz 1985, 357). In this research, children demonstrated the use of private or inner speech usually during an authentic and personal activity such as drawing pictures or playing with wooden figures. As mentioned earlier, the three-year-old boy and four-year-old girl talked to themselves while playing with the wooden figures. This is a demonstration of private speech. During drawing time, a little boy drew a picture of Jesus welcoming the children and the disciples trying to stop them. While drawing, he kept repeating to himself, "little children come to me." Another boy drew a picture of Jesus with people, telling himself: "Remember . . . remember Jesus died on Easter."

Children demonstrated various different types of language and images to express their faith understandings. As educators, we must remember these various ways of articulation, and while there are similarities, each child is different. It is important to learn each child's unique and personal faith language in order to understand what meanings they are attributing to the biblical story.

Meaning Making through Storytelling

The way a story is told matters. In this research, children engaged in a variety of storytelling activities, each unique in presentation and style. Different types of storytelling encouraged different ways that children could make meaning.

The Importance of Exploration.

Meaning-making was demonstrated through exploration in both the *Young Children and Worship* activity as well as the teacher-led activity. Children led the meaningful exploration, usually, by asking questions as they searched for further understandings. Sometimes, the adult (either the lead teacher or storyteller) was needed to encourage deeper exploration by asking clarifying questions and challenging children to better articulate their understanding, making connections with prior understandings.

The Importance of Relationships.

While different in style, each of the storytelling activities incorporated relational interactions, and these relationships were important to a child's meaning-making ability. Children were more responsive in the storybook and teacher-led activity, dependent on the teacher's initiation of the discussion and questions. This style of interaction exposed a separation between the adult and child where the adult was more learned and the children were recipients of that knowledge. In order for the children to make meaning, the adult was needed to scaffold them to higher understandings. The *Young Children and Worship* activity exhibited a different type of interaction—a more relational and participatory experience. Here, there was cooperation between the adult and child where they participated as co-learners, exploring individual understandings that were then shared in a collaborative meaning-making process. In each of these situations, the meaning-making process was based within relationships, where learning is a co-constructional process involving both child and teacher (Bodrova & Leong 1996).

The Importance of Repetition.

The repetition of the stories facilitated the children's ability to make meaning. The children demonstrated deeper understandings as the story was told in different ways. It was the repetition of the story that provided the space for children to engage *with*, make associations *within*, and ultimately demonstrate deeper meaning and understandings *about* the story. On the first day, children experienced the story for the first time, making observations and asking clarifying questions. As the children continued with the story throughout the week, their engagement deepened and language improved. Children began to state deeper associations in comparison to the earlier descriptive observations, and their questions prompted deeper discussions and explorations. Westerhoff (2000) described a similar process when discussing how children learn: Children learn first through experience, then by imaging and stories, followed by use of signs such as conceptual language. The data here demonstrated this movement from experience to story to language.

The Childlike Ways of Meaning Making

In order to understand how children make meaning, adults must pay close attention or risk overlooking a serious and purposeful activity. While this appears to be child's play, young children are engaging in a serious activity of meaning making that occurs through play, reading a storybook, drawing, or mimicking behavior—all activities that appear to be childish and inconsequential. Yet, it is here that children engage in a serious activity that helps them understand what they have experienced.

This research demonstrated that for children, meaning making is an integrative process. Young children combine verbal and non-verbal behavior and utilize a variety of language and images. Activity, including repetitive activity, facilitates their ability to personally respond, react, and make meaning of the biblical story. In this study, children played with the story figures, drew pictures, and dialogued with others to make meaning of what they experienced. And it is here, in these multiple means of knowing, where children wrestled with faith and theological understandings.

How does this, then, impact our work with young children in the church? Educators can shape an atmosphere for spiritual meaning-making by creating intentional experiences for children to engage in. Through a variety of different and repetitive activities, children can explore, engage, and express their faith in their own unique ways. These experiences engage emotions as well as cognitive facilities where children can respond both physically and intellectually. Nestled within relationships with adults and other children, young children have the ability to engage with biblical story in a holistic and integrative manner. For those who pay careful attention, they are privileged to view a young child's faith develop through a mosaic of meaningful channels.

References

Ainsworth, Mary D. Salter. 1969. "Object Relations, Dependency, and Attachment: A Theoretical Review of the Infant-Mother Relationship." *Child Development* 40, no. 4, pp. 969–1025.

Bodrova, Elena, and Deborah J. Leong. 1996. *Tools of the Mind: The Vygotskian Approach to Early Childhood Education*. Englewood Cliffs, NJ: Merrill.

Cavalletti, Sofia, et al. 1994. *The Good Shepherd & the Child: A Joyful Journey*. New Rochelle, NY: Don Bosco Multimedia.

Chang, Ni. 2012. "The Role of Drawing in Young Children's Construction of Science Concepts." *Early Childhood Education Journal* 40, no. 3, pp. 187–93.

Coles, Robert. 1989. *The Call of Stories: Teaching and the Moral Imagination*. Boston: Houghton Mifflin.

Court, Deborah. 2010. "What Happens to Children's Faith in the Zone of Proximal Development, and What Can Religious Educators Do About It?" *Religious Education* 105, no. 5, pp. 491–503.

Cox, Sue. 2005. "Intention and Meaning in Young Children's Drawing." *International Journal Of Art & Design Education* 24, no. 2, pp. 115–25.

Eaude, Tony. 2005. "Strangely Familiar?—Teachers Making Sense of Young Children's Spiritual Development." *Early Years: Journal Of International Research & Development* 25, no. 3, pp. 237–48.

Elkind, David. 2007. *The Power of Play: Learning What Comes Naturally*. Philadelphia: Da Capo.

Fowler, James W. 1981. *Stages of Faith: The Psychology of Human Development and the Quest for Meaning*. San Francisco: HarperSanFrancisco.

Frauenglass, Marni H., and Rafael M. Diaz. 1985. "Self-Regulatory Functions of Children's Private Speech: A Critical Analysis of Recent Challenges to Vygotsky's Theory." *Developmental Psychology* 21, no. 2, pp. 357–64.

Gersch, Irvine, et al. 2008. "Listening to Children's Views of Spiritual and Metaphysical Concepts: A New Dimension to Educational Psychology Practice?" *Educational Psychology in Practice* 24, no. 3, pp. 225–36.

Hall, Todd. W. 2007. "Psychoanalysis, Attachment, and Spirituality Part II: The Spiritual Stories We Live By." *Journal of Psychology and Theology* 35, no. 1, pp. 29–42.

Harris, Kathleen. I. 2007. "Re-Conceptualizing Spirituality in the Light of Educating Young Children." *International Journal of Children's Spirituality* 12, no. 3, pp. 263–75.

Kohlberg, Lawrence. 1984. *The Psychology of Moral Development: The Nature and Validity of Moral Stages*. San Francisco: HarperSanFrancisco.

Lipscomb, Anna, and Irvine Gersch. 2012. "Using a 'Spiritual Listening Tool' to Investigate How Children Describe Spiritual and Philosophical Meaning in their Lives." *International Journal of Children's Spirituality* 17, no. 1, pp. 5–23.

Pahl, Kate. 1999. "Making Models as a Communicative Practice—Observing Meaning Making in a Nursery." *Reading* 33, no. 3, pp. 114–19.

Paradise, Ruth, and Barbara Rogoff. 2009. "Side by Side: Learning by Observing and Pitching In." *Ethos: Journal of the Society for Psychological Anthropology* 37, no. 1, pp. 102–38.

Rogoff, Barbara. 1990. *Apprenticeship in Thinking: Cognitive Development in Social Context*. New York: Oxford University Press.

Stewart, Sonja M., and Jerome W. Berryman. 1989. *Young Children and Worship*. Louisville: Westminster John Knox.

Stonehouse, Catherine, and Scottie May. 2010. *Listening to Children on the Spiritual Journey: Guidance for Those who Teach and Nurture*. Grand Rapids: Baker Academic.

Tay-Lim, Joanna, and Sirene Lim. 2013. "Privileging Younger Children's Voices in Research: Use of Drawings and a Co-Construction Process." *International Journal of Qualitative Methods* 12, no. 1, pp. 65–83.

Vygotsky, Lev S. 1978. *Mind in Society: The Development of Higher Psychological Processes*. Edited by M. Cole et al. Cambridge, MA: Harvard University Press.

Westerhoff, John. 2000. *Will Our Children Have Faith?* Harrisburg, PA: Morehouse.

Yust, Karen M. 2004. "The Toddler and the Community." In *Human Development and Faith: Life-cycle Stages of Body, Mind and Soul*, edited by F. B. Kelcourse, 147–64. St. Louis: Chalice.

Chapter 9

The Moral Formation of Children, ages 0–12

Catherine Maresca

I'd like to begin with an account of an act of moral courage. My son, Kevin, at age eighteen, went to a basketball tournament at his old high school with a friend, Tom. During the award ceremonies Tom called out a derogatory comment to one of his friends. Kevin thought this was directed at a player from another team. A minute later a man unknown to Kevin charged up to Tom, pushed him against the wall with his forearm across Tom's neck, and began to yell at him. Kevin laid his hand on the man's shoulder, pulled him away from Tom, and stepped between them. The man continued to yell for another minute, then stomped away saying, "I'll see you in my office." Kevin asked, "Who was that?" and was surprised to learn that the man was on the faculty of the high school. While his friends who attended the school were unable to confront his misuse of power, Kevin was freer to identify it and respond with action.

Kevin's response was the fruit of three kinds of preparation: preparation of the heart, preparation of the body, and preparation of the mind. Kohlberg's seminal work on moral development has focused primarily on children's cognitive skills. Yet scholars now recognize that this is not the only component of a moral response. We will use the understanding of children portrayed by the work of Maria Montessori and of Sofia Cavalletti to explore these three areas of moral formation.

Maria Montessori was an Italian medical doctor and educator whose method of education is based almost exclusively on observation of young children. She believed that children revealed their educational needs and potential through their responses to and interaction with the environment around them, not only through their words, but, more significantly, their actions and behavior. From her we have a developmental model of children through age twenty-four that is divided into four equal stages, or planes of development. (See diagram). This chapter deals with children in the first two planes of development. Moral formation must take into account the needs and abilities of these two stages or planes.

From a moral-development perspective, the most important difference between the two planes is that children do not begin to judge right from wrong (conscience) until the second plane of development. This does not mean moral formation cannot begin until age six. Rather, the focus is on the preparation of the heart and body instead of on the conscience during the first six years. Montessori's methodology can be applied to every aspect of moral formation. In addition, her work on self-discipline guides our approach to preparation of the body.

Sofia Cavalletti was also Italian. Her work began a year after Montessori's death and focused on religious formation. Her method of observing and learning from the children was the same as Montessori's. From that observation has grown a Christian-formation approach called the *Catechesis of the Good Shepherd*, which I have used with children since 1981. Cavalletti observed that the planes of development are also operative in the spiritual life of the child. It is from her work that we draw guidelines for the preparation of the heart and mind.

Preparation of the Heart

Sofia Cavalletti (1964) wrote, "To teach morality the [adult] must be convinced that at its root is love, and then proceed from that principle. Morality emerges from love" (110). Montessori (1966) writes eloquently of the love of the young child,

> Who will love us as this child loves us now? Who will call us when he goes to bed, saying affectionately: 'Stay with me!' . . . What drives a child to go in search of his parents as soon as he gets up if it is not love? When a child bounces from his bed early, at the break of day, he goes to find his still sleeping parents as if to say: 'Learn to live holily! It is already light! It is morning!' But a child goes to his parents not to teach them but only to see again those whom he loves." (128)

The preparation of this loving heart begins with the experience of God's love, and the characteristics of empathy and communion present in young children. Before age six the child is unencumbered with moral decisions. The foundation is laid for a moral life in the relationships of love in the child's life, including the mysterious but rich relationship with God. "Early childhood is the time for the peaceful presence of God in our life . . ." Cavalletti said, "Therefore, our task with young children is above all to let the child know that someone loves him or her with an everlasting love." (Cavalletti n.d., 14).

In my Christian tradition, using the *Catechesis of the Good Shepherd*, this announcement is made primarily through the image of the Good Shepherd. The children are given a small two-dimensional model of a shepherd and ten sheep with a sheepfold. With these materials they are able to reflect on the words of the Scripture about the care of the Good Shepherd for his sheep, and internalize their message. The parable of the Good Shepherd seems to affirm and articulate their relationship with God, a relationship that God initiates at the beginning of the child's life.

That God reaches for relationship with the child is only part of the connection, however. Buber (1970) writes of the new human being, "In the beginning is relation as the category of being, as readiness, as a form that reaches out to be filled . . . The development of the child's soul is connected indissolubly with his craving for the You." (77–79) The child is born reaching for the Other, and finds in God a true match. Cavalletti (1983) writes, "In the contact with God the child finds the nourishment his being requires, nourishment the child needs in order to grow in harmony. God—who is love—and the child, who asks for love more than his mother's milk, thus meet one another in a particular correspondence of nature" (45).

Howard Thurman (1976), in his book *Jesus and the Disinherited*, states, "The socially disadvantaged man is constantly given a negative answer to the most important personal questions . . . 'Who am I? What am I?' . . . The awareness of being a child of God tends to stabilize the ego and results in a new courage, fearlessness, and power" (49–50). Regardless of one's human circumstances, the relationship with God is formative for the person, and empowers him or her to take moral action.

Moral formation is also rooted in relationship with other people, particularly through the gift of empathy, or compassion. A *US News and World Report* article on moral development stated, "Empathy develops naturally in the first years of life . . . [it] is the bedrock of human morality. . . . Almost every form of moral behavior is inconceivable without it" (Daniel & Herbert 1996, 54). Opal Whitely was a five-year-old girl who lived at the turn of the nineteenth century as the foster child of a poor logging family. Her remarkable ability to write gives us a rare glimpse into the nature of the child under six. Here she describes an encounter with a man who crossed her path one day:

> Today I saw a tramper coming on the tracks. This tramper walked steps on the ties in a slow tired way. When he was come more near I did have thinks he might have hungry feels. Most trampers do. I took the lid off my lunch pail. There was just a half piece of bread and butter left . . . I looked at the tramper. Then I did have little feels of the big hungry feels he might be having. I ran a quick run to catch up with him. He was glad for it. He ate it in two bites. (Whitely 1976, 29)

This young child's decision to share her bread was not the rational decision of a well-formed conscience. She allowed her "little feels" of his great hunger guide her. This is compassion. Compassion is at the root of the action of the Good Samaritan in the parable of Jesus. It is the root of Atticus Finch's advice to his daughter Scout to "Climb into someone else's skin and walk around in it for awhile" (Lee 1960, 87). It is the insight behind Simone Weil's statement, "The essential question of the moral life is 'What are you going through?'" (Weil 1996, 115). Compassion helps prepare the heart for moral action.

Finally, the heart is helped by an innate sense of union with all people and all things that is very strong in the child after age six. Using images from our faith tradition, the children express this unity in a far deeper and broader way than most adults. For example, we reflect together on the image of the True Vine about which Jesus said, "I am the vine, you are the branches" (John 15:5). When I ask, "Who are the branches of the True Vine?" the children invariably say, "Everyone." They include people of all countries, all religions, and all ages. They even include those who have died. Returning to the parable of the Good Shepherd, children under six first begin to understand that the sheep are people, connecting the sheep to their family members and friends. But after six, they say all people are the sheep of the shepherd, "the whole world." My own daughter, at the age of seven, came home one day and said, "I know who the sheep are; it's everything in creation the stars, the plants, the animals . . . And we (humans) are the "other sheep" being called to the flock of the Good Shepherd."

This sense of communion with creation explains why many children are deeply grieved about environmental abuses, killing animals for meat, wars, and other catastrophes that do not touch their lives directly. Why do they care? Because their empathy and sense of communion connect them to this pain. As adults our awareness of communion is renewed as we work with children. We then become much more careful not to draw lines among peoples and limit the children's area of concern to our town, our religion, or our people. Rather, we nurture children's universal sense of communion that will motivate their moral actions.

A Preparation of the Body

"Empathy is not enough. [Another] crucial building block of morality is self-discipline" (Daniel & Herbert 1996, 54). Coles (1986) wrote, "A well-developed conscience does not translate, necessarily, into a morally courageous life" (21). Guided by a sensitive conscience and inspired by a willing heart, many people are still unable to take moral action or refrain from immoral action. Their bodies are undisciplined and seem to be "out of control." And so we must also be attentive to the preparation of the body, self-discipline, in moral formation. Montessori believed that the only true discipline is self-discipline, and that it is developed through movement, not immobilization. She wrote, "Discipline must come through liberty (Montessori 1964, 86)." An artificially silenced and immobilized child has been annihilated rather than disciplined.

Children under six begin their work in a Montessori classroom with a series of exercises called "practical life." These are activities such as hand washing, sweeping, polishing, flower arranging, table scrubbing, pouring, and folding with materials that fit comfortably in the child's hand. They allow the children to be independent in caring for themselves and their environment. But they also build a firm connection between the mind's direction and the body's action. So the movement of the child gradually becomes self-controlled and purposeful: self-disciplined. Then the child can choose to run with joy and speed across a field, can choose to move small beads one by one in order to count and calculate, or choose to sit completely still to observe a bird feeding its young. Montessori said, "We call an individual disciplined when he is master of himself and can therefore regulate his own conduct" (Montessori 1964, 86).

How often today do we tolerate inappropriate behavior by saying, "He means well, but . . . " or, "She has a good heart but . . . " It seems that undisciplined children and adults abound, excused by labels or various disorders. But these diagnoses are not excuses. Even when the struggle is great and a difficulty identified, we can expect and help the child to achieve self-discipline. They cannot live a healthy and fruitful life without it.

Again Montessori (1964) wrote, "The task of the educator lies in seeing that the child does not confound good with immobility, and evil with activity ... because our aim is to discipline for activity, for work, for good; not for immobility, not for passivity, not for obedience" (93).

The young child focuses her work on her immediate world, her self, her home, and her classroom. The older child begins to want to work in the community as well. In our school the children over six participate eagerly in such projects as a community mural, planting a school garden, or raising money for a sister school in Uganda. Some of our nine-to-twelve-year old children directed their energy toward impoverished orphans in Haiti. These older children are learning, through their self-disciplined efforts, that they can make a positive difference in their world when given the opportunity for meaningful work. Truly "great and victorious" human work, Montessori (1964) notes that the child is not spurred by prizes or punishments but "stand upon the inner force" (24).

A Preparation of the Mind

Preparation of the mind is addressed directly after age six as the child's conscience begins to develop. Before age six, a child's understanding of right and wrong is based exclusively on the judgments of others, and the consequences of certain behavior. A child may have heard that it is "bad" to run into the street, and gets a time out or rebuke when she does so. She knows that it is "bad" to run into the street, but she hasn't made this judgment herself. It is her parent's judgment and the consequences of misbehavior that have convinced her. After age six the child begins to exercise her own moral judgment. She can think about running into the street and understand that it is "bad" not because running is bad, not because streets are bad, but because of the danger of moving vehicles.

We have two tools to support the development and exercise of the conscience: moral tales and general principles. Moral tales are stories in which two or more types of behavior are modeled and the children are invited to exercise their judgment about the behavior. In our setting these tales are taken from the parables of Jesus, such as the Good Samaritan and the Prodigal Son. The children are not at all involved in the story, and so are not threatened by the judgment. Their stance is distanced and objective. In their own good time, the children take the modeled behavior they have judged to be better and use it to guide their own actions.

General principles are also offered from one's faith tradition. In our case we first use the maxims of Jesus from the Gospels, such as, "Love your enemy," and "Do good to those who hate you." Later, we offer the Ten Commandments from the Hebrew Scriptures. These principles are often related to the lessons of the parables. In a world where all kinds of moral and immoral activities are modeled around children, to sort out the rules that could guide one's decisions is a great challenge. Offering them general principles from their beloved Good Shepherd is not a tedious prohibition or obligation but a gift to the children.

Finally, the conscience is supported by heroic role models. Not superheroes with powers children do not have, but real people who have made choices and lived lives that model and inspire moral actions. They are prophets, saints, and leaders such as Mahatma Gandhi or Martin Luther King. They are heroic children like Ruby Bridges, who at the age of six, walked through hostile crowds with a peaceful spirit, to integrate her public school in New Orleans (Coles 1986). These models are important, especially to nine-to-twelve-year-old children who are working hard to follow the guidelines and judgments of their conscience. Do not forget that we too are models for the children to follow, for good or bad. Every parent may be a hero, every teacher an inspiration, for one or many children. Our choices model for them how our own conscience is followed, compromised, or ignored on a daily basis.

Moral Formation and History

We have focused on moral formation as a preparation of the heart, mind, and body. But what is the purpose of the moral life? A moral person makes many choices each day and acts on those decisions. But a moral life also has a greater dimension. Awareness of one's life in the tide of history calls forth a moral vocation, a sense of working with God and humankind to contribute to the common good. We offer a vision of history from our faith that begins with creation and moves toward a time of universal peace, justice and union that the New Testament calls *"Parousia"* and the Hebrew Scriptures call *"Shalom"*. This movement is, first of all, God's work. But we are invited to collaborate with God. All of creation contributes to this work, but unconsciously. For example, trees and coral clean the air and water for the good of all the earth. But the cooperation of people is conscious and voluntary; it is a moral decision to make one's life work to move humankind closer to a time of universal wholeness, or *shalom* (Wolf, 1996).

Coles (1986) wrote, "I believe that the active idealism we see in some of our young takes place when a beckoning history offers, uncannily, a blend of memory and desire; a chance to struggle for a new situation that holds a large promise" (33). Buber spoke of our participation in this effort as well. "Creation—we participate in it, we encounter the creator, and offer ourselves as helpers and companions" (Buber 1970, 130).

Let's think about Kevin at the basketball game once again. Preparation of the heart motivated him to act on behalf of his friend. Preparation of the body enabled him to move to his friend's aid rather than watch, frozen, as he was threatened. Preparation of the mind enabled him to choose a path that defended his friend without violence toward the adult involved. A vision of the justice of *shalom* committed him to acting when he easily could have remained an observer.

With a complete preparation of the child, involving the heart, body, and mind, and a vision of their unique and necessary role in history, they can set their feet on a path of hope and love.

Implications for Adults

Too often religious life has become a matter of being "good," according to a complex formula of cultural, religious, and family norms. But children show us something far different. When we fully understand how deep and rich religious life can be before the age of six, with no moral implications whatsoever, we must ask ourselves, "What is at the heart of the spiritual life?" Children show us that this life is rooted in love, rather than morality. The moral life grows out of love for God, one another, and creation. It continues with the freedom to develop self-discipline, and a desire to be with God by collaborating with God to build the Kingdom of God.

References

Buber, M. 1970. *I and Thou*. New York: Scribner's Sons.
Cavalletti, Sofia. "God in Search of the Child". Unpublished.
———. 1984. Moral Formation. Lecture notes.
———. 1983. *The Religious Potential of the Child*. Chicago: Liturgy Training.
———. 1964. *Teaching Doctrine and Liturgy*. New York: Alba House.
Coles, Robert. 1986. *The Moral Life of Children*. Boston: Houghton Mifflin.
Daniel, M., and W. Herbert. 1996. "The Moral Child." US News and World Report, June 3.
Gilligan, C. 1982. *In a Different Voice*. Cambridge, MA: Harvard University Press.
Lee, Harper. 1960. *To Kill a Mockingbird*. New York: HarperCollins.
Montessori, Maria. 1996. *The Child in the Church*. St. Paul: Catechetical Guild Educational Society.
———. 1994. *From Childhood to Adolescence*. Oxford: Clio.
———. 1964. *The Montessori Method*. New York: Schocken.
———. 1966. *The Secret of Childhood*. Notre Dame: Fides.

Scharf, P. 1978. *Readings in Moral Education*. Minneapolis: Winston.
Thurman, Howard. 1976. *Jesus and the Disinherited*. Richmond: United.
Weil, Simone. 1951. *Waiting for God*. New York: Putnam's Sons.
Whitely, Opal. 1976. *Opal, the Journal of an Understanding Heart*. New York: Crown.
Wolf, Aline. 1996. *Nurturing the Spirit in Non-Sectarian Classrooms*. Hollidaysburg, PA: Parent Child.

Chapter 10

Nurturing the Infant Soul
Spiritual Formation and Very Young Children

—— Shirley K. Morgenthaler, ——
Jeffrey B. Keiser, &
Mimi L. Larson

Christians Are Made, Not Born

Teaching children, in the traditional sense, is viewed as a telling and listening experience, where information, skill, and attitude is transmitted from an experienced instructor to an inexperienced child. Within the local church, it is quite easy to find this instructional-training model where groups of children are broken down into similar ages with instruction that leans toward biblical knowledge, skills, and abilities (Boojamra 1989). While ultimately the act of coming to faith is the work of the Holy Spirit, this schooling-instructional model assumes that, at some point within this formal instruction, children will grasp the essence of the faith into which they were dedicated or baptized and become active followers of Jesus Christ (Westerhoff 1992).

While information transmission is important, John Westerhoff (2000) challenges this approach to Christian formation. Favoring a quote from Tertullian, "Christians...are made, not born" (as cited in Westerhoff 1992, 262), Westerhoff (2004) encourages a communal approach to faith formation: "If... children are to have Christian faith and live the Christian life, they will need to be nurtured in that faith and life. And that cannot be done adequately outside a community of faith" (1–2). It is the relational experience upon which the foundation of instruction and teaching is built. The key to deep, life-long learning is discovery and encouragement in experience. "Educators often identify learning as that which a person absorbs, accepts, relates to, or identifies with, out of his or her experiences. The experience is the key to what the person learns" (Nelson 1967, 163). This is where the family and the community of faith nurture and influence children. Every ritual, every corporate or intimate action, and every story within this context "in both word and deed" witnesses to the life of faith (Wilhoit 2008, 181).

Children are loved because they are God's fellow image-bearers. They, like any other person, have souls, a "unified body-mind-spirit" (Westerhoff 2000, 47) which is an individual's vital existence, created by God, which is always in relationship to him (Butler 1991). They are known by God before they are born (Jer 1:5), and their souls will extend beyond their earthly death (Luke 23:43). While it is real and authentic in its own unique way, the faith of the young child looks different from the faith of adolescence or adulthood, and nurturing children's souls requires an alternative approach as Jesus himself modeled. Children, created by God in his own image, are being drawn to him with authentic faith that is developmentally appropriate to them. So it is understandable that teaching, in the traditional sense, is not always the best option for young children. Rather, it is discovery, nurture, and formation, and the laying down of implicit memories that set the course for those "even infants" that Luke refers to in chapter 18 (Luke 18:15, ESV).

Exploring the Literature

Often times, in coming to a discussion on children's faith formation, the works of developmental theorists such as Piaget and Erikson or the faith theorist Fowler are used as a theoretical framework. But these theoretical frameworks are founded mostly in the cognitive realm. While we appreciate what these theorists contribute to our knowledge of child development, we have been frustrated by what we believe is a shallow understanding by them, as well as by many theologians, in regard to infants and toddlers and their faith formation. This is not to say that we do not appreciate developmental models. We do believe that anyone working with children should study and understand these models. But they do not satisfy us. We are left wanting more. As Westerhoff (2000) says, they are limited.

What does it mean to instruct, teach, or nurture an infant? How do they, in their unique development, actually learn? From recent research on implicit memory (Coe & Hall 2010; Thompson 2010), we understand that memories are laid down before the child has the language to identify the memory (Rofrano 2010; Rovee-Collier 1999). Later, when language is in place, a similar encounter can activate the implicit memory and move it into an explicit memory. Memory that can be thought about and talked about, and whose meanings can be explored, may have significant implications for the soul.

Implicit memories cover a wide range of experiences. Some of them we voice, but there are some, perhaps, that may never be recovered. Those implicit memories that have emotional content such as love, awe, wonder, or surprise will almost certainly be re-lived when a similar emotion connects itself to that long-ago memory (Coe & Hall 2010; Thompson 2010). For young children in the church, implicit memories are laid down through relational experiences as well as through instruction. These memories carry with them strong emotional content that will stay with the child throughout his or her life and may be transformed into explicit memories—memories that will shape faith formation and draw the child closer to Jesus Christ.

It is relational experiences, with both the implicit and explicit memories of those experiences, that forge the faith path for all of God's human creation. It is our belief that the strongest understandings of how faith is formed in earliest childhood come from two giants of the 20th century: John Westerhoff and Lev Vygotsky. The work of these two thinkers, to our knowledge, has never been examined together. Within the discussion of the learning and formation of infants and toddlers, we are challenging our understandings of how faithing (Westerhoff 2000) comes to be in the youngest among us, and how thought (Vygotsky 1986) comes to be laid down even before language is in place.

John Westerhoff and Intentional Communal Life

John Westerhoff believed that the community is foundational for a child's faith. The challenge for the faith community is to live an intentional communal life where faith is made visible in our daily actions for the edification of the entire community. As Scripture states:

> These commandments that I give you today are to be on your hearts. Impress them on your children. Talk about them when you sit at home and when you walk along the road, when you lie down and when you get up. Tie them as symbols on your hands and bind them on your foreheads. Write them on the doorframes of your houses and on your gates. (Deut 6:6–9, NIV)

This intentional integration of faith into our own daily lives acts as an incubator for a child's faith. As Westerhoff (2000) points out, "Persons learn first inactively through their experience, then by imaging (stories), and last of all through the use of signs (conceptual language)....The most significant and fundamental form of learning is experience" (61). According to Westerhoff, intentional experiential formation utilizes three different types of activities: incorporation, enculturation, and apprenticeship.

The faith community, first, intentionally incorporates the child, bringing him or her in, not as an isolated individual but as an equal participant in this Christian community. "We are corporate selves who have been created to relate with God and each other" (31). As a child is incorporated, the faith community also acculturates through the intentional development of environments for infants and toddlers. "God intends that the church be a unique witnessing community of faith, a converted, pilgrim people living under the judgment and inspiration of the Gospel, to the end that God's will is done and God's community comes" (40).

A faith community also enculturates through intentional relationships and experiences. The gospel story is not only a history; it is our story, our history—men, women, boys, and girls of all ages and colors. It is the linking of "'my story'" with the "'our story' of the church universal," as James Wilhoit (2008) writes, where we "understand that we are part of something far larger than ourselves" (117). It is through the use of story that we understand our world, which affects how we perceive it and how we engage it. As a community of change, our role is to "act with God in transforming the world into the community of our Lord and Savior Jesus Christ" (Westerhoff 2000, 41). The experiences a congregation shares together, the stories we tell and retell, the celebrations and actions in which we participate, all transmit, expand, and sustain faith. As Westerhoff contends, it is enculturation or "the processes of interaction in community between 'faithing' selves" where formation thrives (87).

Along with incorporation and enculturation, the faith community guides and mentors through apprenticeship. "Christian formation is the participation in and the practice of the Christian life of faith. We do that by identifying with a community, observing how persons in it live, and imitating them" (Westerhoff 1992, 267). For a child's faith, it is essential to interact with others who are striving to be Christian and to share experiences with these spiritual mentors. As Westerhoff (2000) also says,

> To live with others in Christian ways, to put our words into deeds and our deeds into words, to share life with another, to be open to influence as well as to influence, and to interact with other faithing selves in a community of Christian faith is to provide the necessary environment for experienced faith. (91)

A child must have a sense of belonging, for "all of us need to feel that we belong to a self-conscious community and that through our active participation we can make a contribution to its life" (91–92). This belonging and relational internalization of beliefs is essential for faith identity. It is in the intentional communal life and apprenticeship concepts of Westerhoff where we find kinship in the writings of Lev Vygotsky. While his writings are most often studied in colleges of education across the country, he also has much to say to the faithing community as visualized by Westerhoff.

Vygotsky and the Historically Childish

The Father holds the young with special regard. Children are to be considered full members of the community, not just immature creations that need time to become completely formed. In Luke 18, Jesus, in our opinion, sees the disciples' attempts to stop the little children from coming to see him as appalling as the moneychangers wrongly profiting from peoples' purchases of items for temple sacrifice (Luke 19).

Jesus sees young children as the Father sees them. In a powerful community moment, he blesses them in the presence of those who tried to keep this meeting from happening. It is no accident that Matthew, Mark, and Luke all recount Jesus' blessing of little children and infants. Only powerful and profound events in the life of Jesus are reported in three or more of the Gospels.

In reality, for many adults, childhood is a mystery, yet Christ knows that adults need to revere the time of childhood. Children receive the kingdom in ways that adults cannot or will not. This idea is deeply rooted in Scripture. There is a mystery of childlikeness that calls for the adult world to discover its secrets. Sociologists, psychologists, educators, poets, priests, pastors, parents, and politicians need to discover what Vygotsky (1986) calls "the 'historically childish'" (57). While the term *childish* can be viewed negatively in our culture, Vygotsky held it in regard, stating: "This stone that the builders rejected should be the cornerstone," referring to childhood and childishness (57).

What Vygotsky (1986) saw in childhood was something unmistakable that was a valuable addition to community life. Also, what is significant in these words is the clear reference to Psalm 118, but in this case what Vygotsky means is that it is the adult world that is rejecting what God sees as a cornerstone in the kingdom, a key to living abundantly in God's community—children and childishness. This cornerstone (childish, playful, awe-filled, delighting, filled-with-wonder, a place of unlimited possibility) is rejected by adult rationalism and logic because it is a light that pure rationalism and logic cannot understand. Without understanding this "historical childishness," adult rationalism and sensibilities cannot see or understand its value in community life.

A Comparison between Vygotsky and Westerhoff

We found significant similarities between the theories of Vygotsky and Westerhoff. Specifically, there are connections in terms of intersubjectivity and dialogical relationships, plus distancing and expanding faith. Further, Vygotsky's genetic law of cultural development and Westerhoff's idea of enculturation, along with Vygotsky's private speech and learning are powerful comparisons.

Intersubjectivity and Dialogical Relationships

We have found a similarity between Vygotsky's intersubjectivity and Westerhoff's understanding of dialogical relationships. Intersubjectivity (Berk & Winsler 1995) is the concept where children hold different understandings and, through interaction with others, come to a shared knowledge, a shared understanding. It is a sharing of purpose or an understanding of agreed purpose that involves a cognitive, a social, and, most importantly, an emotional interchange (Rogoff 1990). Similarly, Westerhoff believed that there is a dialogical relationship between equals. A community shares a common identity, common memory, traditions, understandings, and ways of life. They also have common goals and purpose. It is the individual who contributes to this common or community understanding. What one person brings to another is foundational in dialogical relationships. Part of this dialogical relationship incorporates reshaping. Through the dual process of individuation and the "concomitant process of searching for trustful intimacy with others," children are integrating their own understanding of faith while contributing to the community's tradition and reshaping it (Westerhoff 2000, 102).

Vygotsky's idea of intersubjectivity and Westerhoff's understanding of dialogical relationships have strong similarities. Both Vygotsky and Westerhoff emphasize the need for others to speak into our understandings and knowledge. The way children learn using intersubjectivity requires a dialogical relationship where another person reshapes what we understand as we reshape what they know and understand. This give-and-take is essential in learning. It takes a communal experience for a child to understand, to know, to feel, and to intuit.

Distancing and Expanding Faith

Distancing (Vygotsky 1986) is the concept of disassembling the scaffolding structure in learning. Adults and children practice this type of scaffolding in a collaborative process. When children need the adult, they are in close proximity, but when they do not need the help as much, the adult is still nearby. Children are willing to distance themselves to explore and discover. This idea of far-but-still-close facilitates children's thinking and encourages them to take on a little more responsibility each time they distance themselves from an adult. This is similar to the idea of a "secure base" within attachment, where children are willing to explore while the parent is close (Ainsworth 1979; Bowlby 1988). They will go and discover what toys or activities might be in a room while coming back for physical contact with the parent and then going out again to explore. Toddlers will attach, then distance themselves, and then reattach to their parents as they need.

Vygotsky's (1986) idea of distancing relates to Westerhoff's understanding of expanding faith. In his faith analogy of tree rings, an individual's faith can only be expanded in the proper environment and with the appropriate experiences and interactions with others (Westerhoff 2000). This happens both in early childhood and adulthood. "One seeks to act with other faithing selves in community and hence into new styles of faith, not so as to possess better or greater faith, but only to fulfill one's faith potential" (88). Westerhoff's idea of a questioning faith fits within this idea where adolescents need to distance themselves from the community and to gain their own understanding of faith in order to come back and embrace the community. Here, it is the adolescents who are practicing distancing in their faith formation, disassembling the scaffolding structure that has nurtured their spiritual development thus far. It takes a community and the ability to individuate from that community for a child to embrace his or her faith.

While Vygotsky's (1986) concept of distancing seems to connect to Westerhoff's understanding of searching faith that appears in adolescence, it also correlates to the idea of attachment and bonding that occurs in early childhood. Relational faith does not just happen in terms of our relationship with other people. Relational faith also describes how we relate to and understand God, no matter our age (infant, young child, adolescent, or adult). Just as a child-parent relationship is a relationship of attachment and bonding, so too is a relationship with God (Hall 2007a). This relationship is a spiritual attachment and a spiritual bond (Beck & McDonald 2004; Hall 2007a). Just like a child is attached to his or her mother and utilizes this secure base from which to explore (Ainsworth 1979; Bowlby 1988), God is seen as a secure base from which a child can theologically or spiritually explore (Beck 2006). Reimer and Furrow (2001) state: "Bonding... seemed to best represent the formalization of spiritual awareness in the child, especially where this was outwardly related, either to other people, or to natural surroundings" (20–21). While this is not explicitly stated by Westerhoff, this concept powerfully relates to experiencing faith (Westerhoff 2000). It is within these early years of childhood where attachment and bonding occur. What is significant is that the experience of faith formation (Westerhoff 2000) wraps around Ainsworth's (1979) concept of attachment and bonding. Distancing (Vygotsky 1986) happens throughout life, and expanding faith (Westerhoff 2000) does as well. The key connection between distancing and expanding faith is that both are built upon the foundation of experiencing faith at a very early age (early childhood).

Some research (Beck & McDonald 2004; McDonald et al. 2005) has proposed that these theories of religious attachment can be explained in terms of compensation, where attachment to God compensates for lack of a bond with a significant caregiver, or as correspondence, where attachment to God corresponds with a bond with a significant caregiver. Either way, in order for a spiritual bond to exist with God, God must be experienced as personal (Beck & McDonald 2004), and Hart, Limke, and Budd (2010) propose that secure attachment with a relational God equates to spiritual maturity. In this model of spiritual formation, God, paradoxically, can work closely, like Westerhoff argues, or at a distance, as Vygotsky suggests, to develop a strong and lifelong bond with the infant. The key to this paradox is the child's experience.

Genetic Law of Cultural Development and Enculturation

Vygotsky (1978) believed that understanding an individual meant understanding community. Within this genetic law of cultural development, there is first a social plane between people and then an individual plane. Social relationships genetically underlie an individual's higher function and interactions with others. In contrast, Piaget believes it is the individual who is first, with social interaction following. These differences are illustrated in how these two theorists view language and thought. Piaget (1959) believed that language came first, followed by thought. A child must first learn to speak before understanding and articulating that understanding. Vygotsky

(1986), in contrast, believed a child first thinks and then language follows. A child has the capability to understand. In time, language provides him or her the avenue to express this understanding.

This is significant for the church because whichever understanding we hold undergirds how we view children in the church. If we agree with Piaget's thinking, the church waits until a child has language capability before implementing any type of intentional faith formation. But if we adhere to Vygotsky, the church will embrace an idea closer to Westerhoff's understanding of enculturation. Enculturation is the process of interaction or relationship between and among a community of people. This community of all ages provides the interactive experience and environment for persons "to acquire, sustain, change, and transmit their understandings and ways" (Westerhoff 2000, 80). Here, within this interaction between "faithing selves," is where formation can thrive. Just as infants cannot survive without the society around them—someone to feed them, someone to care for them, and someone to hold them—the faith community with its intentionality and enculturation comes alongside pre-language children and nurtures them, sharing their faith through actions, through love, through daily life experiences where children experience theology through life-on-life living. Westerhoff's understanding of enculturation is deeply rooted in an understanding that the community and its social relationships underlie a child's ability to perceive the foundational beliefs of faith. Given all of this, it appears that a community's intentional loving relationships with children help them to come to understanding and experiencing faith, even in infancy.

Private Speech and Learning

Vygotsky believed private or inner speech to be an important part of how a child works on understanding (Berk & Winsler 1995). This is how children structure their thinking. Private speech is also how children "try on" a perspective or potential belief. By internalizing language, children share their understanding with others (expression), but eventually this understanding is turned inward, first to guide the self, and second to guide the child in and through complex social interactions. Experiences are shared and then personalized for children to understand who they individually are. The goal of private speech is not about others. It is for the individual and his or her self-regulation.

Children experience life and from that they develop images, which further develop into signs or conceptual language. For Westerhoff (2000), these three ideas—experiences, images and signs—are essential to how a child's faith is formed. Children learn through socialization or hidden curriculum, yet for an individual to come to an owned faith, he or she must go through a private wrestling of these ideas. This idea of "trying on" is illustrated in Westerhoff's second ring of affiliative faith. Here individuals incorporate the community's values and beliefs and then move to searching faith (the third ring) where they must decide whether or not they believe and accept the community's understanding of faith. The goal is owned faith, a faith that is personal and transformative. But an individual must go through this wrestling, this "trying on" of ideas in order for him or her to internalize faith into an owned personal belief.

For children and infants, there are multiple means of knowing. They can learn through story, which provides a narrative framework for interpreting meaning (Hall 2007b). Language is another means of knowing. According to Berk and Winsler (1995), Vygotsky describes learning through language as a transformation of the communicative language into inner speech, which is both an individual and social process, and it is this inner speech, which is an important part of how a child understands. Relationships with others also contribute to how a young child makes meaning since there is a connection between cognitive and social learning (Ainsworth 1969; Rogoff 1990).

Children also make meaning through everyday lived experiences, which can "shape a child's attitude and values and provide knowledge about many things" (Westerhoff 1987, 62). One common, everyday, lived experience for a child is play, which also enables him or her to make meaning (Yust 2004). Play provides a foundation for social awareness and skills (Elkind 2007; Harris 2007; Myers 1997), and David Elkind (2007) asserts that play is "the dominant and directing mode of learning" for early childhood (7). It is in play that a child has the opportunity to experience and "try out" new ideas that he or she is encountering without bearing any consequences (Eaude 2005). The experience of play provides the child a way to integrate these new ideas into family and community life (Paradise & Rogoff 2009).

This idea of private speech is crucial to a young child's faith formation. A child needs to use private speech or language to understand those difficult concepts in faith. From there, the child can decide whether or not to accept these beliefs as his or her own. Internalization of faith requires a shared experience as the foundation. Childhood faith becomes visible to others when a child can verbalize a prayer or a belief.

Learning within the Context of Community

For both Westerhoff and Vygotsky, it is within the context of community that learning occurs. It is the work of the apprentice with the somewhat-more-learned expert that creates learning for both apprentice and expert in that community. It is that scaffolding of learning from the known to the almost-known that requires the encouragement of community (Bodrova & Leong 1996). By scaffolding the almost-known, the expert supports the discovery of learning, whether that is reading or language or faith. And for Christians, the unfolding of faith as a relationship is the important phenomenon. For young children, it is essential.

Community embodies the power of the Spirit. This is why learning is a spiritual process with often-unpredictable patterns. Those patterns emerge from the influence of the community, the influence of the individual's interests and dispositions, and from the environment of love, learning, and acceptance that each young child experiences. The environment, an important influence in all learning, is the place where young children experience "faith-talk" among other people of faith (Lillard 2007; Montessori 1939).

The entity and quality of community affects the learning of the young child, which is further informed by an internal process, a spiritual process. And the community's actions are the result of the Spirit's direction for the good of the child, for protection, and for growth. The real responsibility of the church toward children is to provide a community where the Spirit can work and where children can begin to live out their creation (formation) through incorporation, enculturation, and apprenticeship.

The family environment also fosters formation. In that environment, the child's unique identity is shaped through apprenticeship to older siblings, parents, and even extended family by being incorporated into family activities through experiences and celebrations that make the individual story a part of the story of the family. Similarly, our Christian identity is formed through interaction with our Christian family, those believers with whom we and our families of origin live, worship, and experience life. Both our immediate family and our Christian family are comprised of people of varying ages, varying needs, varying gifts, varying weaknesses, varying interests and talents. It is that variety of a community that invites the child to learn where best and as best. In that environment, the Spirit of God works to nurture the faith and learning of each individual child.

Understanding the Infant Faith in Relationship to the Soul

The soul pervades and unites all existence. It is the overarching unity of who we are and informs all things including our development, behavior, cognitive abilities, emotions, choices, intellect, and consciousness. It is the soul that is in relationship to God and to others. A soul is the vital existence created for relationship and can be described as the essential life of a person (Butler 1991).

In light of this understanding of the soul, there is great value in studying Vygotsky and Westerhoff together, for neither really uncovered a concise understanding of infant development within cognitive and spiritual development. Yet, these ideas of intersubjectivity along with enculturation, individuation, and connectedness are essential for one's development of the soul, for becoming (Harter 1999). And what the soul specifically needs in infancy and early childhood is positive spiritual implicit and explicit memories, as well as an intentional spiritual communal life in which these memories are based.

Young children's experiences are the foundation for their learning, and creating early faith memories in infants and toddlers is essential to their faith formation. But how do we know that the memories we are building with them are being kept? How do we know that the experiences we are making with them matter? What differences are we making? What we know is that when we are engaging in activities and interactions that have the probability of being laid down as implicit memories, those memories that will influence and inform each young child's later understanding of the faith relationship with our great God (Senter 2004).

We build implicit memories from our birth (Coe & Hall 2010; Thompson 2010). Our understanding is that through our interaction as a faith community with young children in the church, we build implicit faith memories. Those memories are created before and without language and are stored in the soul of this young one (Vygotsky 1986). These memories are implicit memories that support "gut-level knowing" (Coe & Hall 2010, 237) where day after day, week after week, Sunday after Sunday, infants and young children are singing praises to our God (Ps 8:2) with the whole community of believers in the context of worship, of gathering, of greeting, of caring for one another, and of play. These memories are not verbal or captured in words, but instead are created in an entirely different way, "recorded in our emotions, perceptions, bodily sensations and our body's 'readiness' to respond in certain ways" (Coe & Hall 2010, 238). Those implicit memories ground the soul and scaffold its development, remaining stored implicitly—without labeling or specificity.

Implicit memories become explicit when they are needed, drawn from a deep well as cool water for one who thirsts. Language becomes the vehicle to express the memory; then, a caring "master" to whom the child (or even the adult) can apprentice for a time enters the story to lend additional life and meaning to the experience. This transforms the implicit to the explicit. At times, this transformation takes a large measure of courage. Not all implicit memories are happy or good. Memories of harshness, of cruelty, of abuse, of abandonment also are stored for later retrieval. However, in the context and support of a community, and through loving apprenticeship, those memories can become explicit when the time is right and the soul has the strength to see them and know them.

The question we are left with is how does the importance of building implicit memories affect and change the covenantal community? Vygotsky and Westerhoff provide good orderly direction for the building of implicit memory necessary for the betterment of our communities. It is the church's responsibility to provide a community of formation through incorporation, enculturation, and apprenticeship. It is through these communal experiences that a child encounters relational knowledge and begins to understand himself/herself as a creation and child of the Heavenly Father (Coe & Hall 2010). "Memories of relational experiences with emotionally significant people are etched in our souls and become filters that shape how we feel about ourselves, God, and others, and how we determine the meaning of events in our life" (239–40). Such an idea is not lost on Erikson (1963) who recognized that it is parental faith that nurtures trust in the infant. Such developed trust is based on a mutuality where each benefits. The infant relies on the parent for food, safety, and warmth. The parent receives maturity and exponential love, and, as a result, implicit memories are created for both. For the church, Erikson writes, "Trust born of care is, in fact, the touchstone of the *actuality* of a given religion" (250). It is critical for the church to understand the importance of infancy and early childhood as a place where these relational experiences occur, where implicit memories are created, where significant spiritual formation takes place.

These relational experiences are essential to a young child's structure of "self-in-relation (to God and human)" (Coe & Hall 2010, 236). Not only do children learn from these experiences, but it also provides the basis for secure attachment, which, in turn, solidifies their relationship with God. Children learn about God through emotionally significant relationships with other "faithing selves" in the faith community (Westerhoff, 2000). As Coe & Hall state, these experiences become etched into our souls, a "gut-level type of memory" that, when they are positive and healthy, play a significant role in a child's faith formation (260).

Our prayer is that ministry leaders recognize the significance of the spiritual formation of infants and toddlers as Jesus Christ did. These are not empty years, but a precious time of growth and development that is unique to their developmental stage. This is not about a formal education process but about life together where not only a child is shaped but we, as adults, are changed as well (Bonhoeffer 1993; Westerhoff 2000). In caring for children, playing with them, living life with them, the children are reminding us what it means to become like a little child and embrace the kingdom to which God is calling us.

References

Ainsworth, Mary D. Salter. 1969. "Object Relations, Dependency, and Attachment: A Theoretical Review of the Infant-Mother Relationship." *Child Development* 40, no. 4, pp. 969–1025.

———. 1979. "Infant-Mother Attachment." *American Psychologist* 34, no. 10, pp. 932–37.

Beck, Richard. 2006. "God as a Secure Base: Attachment to God and Theological Exploration." *Journal of Psychology and Theology* 34, no. 2, pp. 125–32.

Beck, Richard and Angie McDonald. 2004. "Attachment to God: The Attachment to God Inventory, Tests of Working Model Correspondence, and an Exploration of Faith Group Differences." *Journal of Psychology and Theology* 32, no. 2, pp. 92–103.

Berk, Laura E. and Adam Winsler. 1995. *Scaffolding Children's Learning: Vygotsky and Early Childhood Education*. Washington, DC: National Association for the Education of Young Children.

Bodrova, Elena and Deborah J. Leong. 1996. *Tools of the Mind: The Vygotskian Approach to Early Childhood Education*. Englewood Cliffs, NJ: Merrill.

Bonhoeffer, Dietrich. 1993. *Life Together*. San Francisco: HarperSanFrancisco.

Boojamra, John. 1989. *Foundations for Orthodox Christian Education*. Crestwood, NY: St. Vladimir's Seminary Press.

Bowlby, John. 1988. *A Secure Base: Parent-Child Attachment and Healthy Human Development*. New York: Basic.

Butler, Trent, ed. 1991. *Holman Bible Dictionary*. Nashville: Holman Bible.

Coe, John, and Todd Hall. *Psychology in the Spirit: Contours of a Transformational Psychology*. Downers Grove, IL: IVP Academic, 2010.

Eaude, Tony. 2005. "Strangely Familiar?—Teachers Making Sense of Young Children's Spiritual Development." *Early Years: Journal Of International Research & Development* 25, no. 3, pp. 237–48.

Elkind, David. 2007. *The Power of Play: Learning What Comes Naturally*. Philadelphia, PA: Da Capo.

Erikson, Erik. 1963. *Childhood and Society*. New York: Norton.

Hall, Todd. W. 2007. "Psychoanalysis, Attachment, and Spirituality Part I: The Emergence of Two Relational Traditions." *Journal of Psychology and Theology* 35, no. 1, pp. 14–28.

———. 2007. "Psychoanalysis, Attachment, and Spirituality Part II: The Spiritual Stories We Live By." *Journal of Psychology and Theology* 35, no. 1, pp. 29–42.

Harris, Kathleen. I. 2007. "Re-Conceptualizing Spirituality in the Light of Educating Young Children." *International Journal of Children's Spirituality* 12, no. 3, pp. 263–75.

Hart, Jonathan T., Alicia Limke, and Phillip R. Budd. 2010. "Attachment and Faith Development." *Journal of Psychology and Theology* 38, no. 2, pp. 122–28.

Harter, Susan. 1999. *The Construction of the Self: A Developmental Perspective*. New York: Guilford.

Lillard, Angeline S. 2007. *Montessori: The Science Behind the Genius*. New York: Oxford University Press.

McDonald, Angie, et al. 2005. "Attachment to God and Parents: Testing the Correspondence vs. Compensation Hypotheses." *Journal of Psychology and Christianity* 24, no. 1, pp. 21–28.

Montessori, Maria. 1939. *The Secret of Childhood*. New York: Stokes.

Myers, Barbara K. 1997. *Young Children and Spirituality*. New York: Routledge.

Nelson, C. Ellis. 1967. *Where Faith Begins*. Richmond, VA: Knox.

Paradise, Ruth and Barbara Rogoff. 2009. "Side by Side: Learning by Observing and Pitching In." *Ethos: Journal of the Society for Psychological Anthropology* 37, no. 1, pp. 102–38.

Piaget, Jean. 1959. *The Language and Thought of the Child*. 3rd ed. New York: Routledge.

Reimer, Kevin S., and James L. Furrow. 2001. "A Qualitative Exploration of Relational Consciousness in Christian Children." *International Journal of Children's Spirituality* 6, no. 1, pp. 7–23.

Rofrano, Frances J. 2010. "Affirming the Value of the Child: A Spiritual Curriculum for Infant/Toddler Education." *Encounter* 23, no. 2, pp. 39–44.

Rogoff, Barbara. 1990. *Apprenticeship in Thinking: Cognitive Development in Social Context*. New York: Oxford University Press.

Rovee-Collier, Carolyn. 1999. "The Development of Infant Memory." *Current Directions in Psychological Science* 8, no. 3, pp. 80.

Senter, Denise A. 2004. "Infancy: Faith Before Language." In *Human Development and Faith: Life-cycle Stages of Body, Mind and Soul*, edited by F. B. Kelcourse, 129–46. St. Louis: Chalice.

Thompson, Curt. 2010. *Anatomy of the Soul: Surprising Connections Between Neuroscience and Spiritual Practices That Can Transform Your Life and Relationships*. Carol Stream, IL: SaltRiver.

Vygotsky, Lev S. 1978. *Mind in Society: The Development of Higher Psychological Processes*. Edited by M. Coleet al. Cambridge, MA: Harvard University Press.

———. 1986. *Thought and language*. Cambridge, MA: MIT Press.

Westerhoff, John. 1987. "Formation, Education, and Instruction." *Religious Education* 82, no. 4, pp. 578–91.

———. 2000. *Will Our Children Have Faith?* Harrisburg, PA: Morehouse.

———. 2004. *Living the Faith Community*. New York: Church.

———. 1992. "Fashioning Christians in our Day." In *Schooling Christians: "Holy Experiments" in American Education*, edited by S. Hauerwas and J. H. Westerhoff III, pp. 262–81. Grand Rapids: Eerdmans.

Chapter 11

The Intersection of Intellectual Giftedness and Faith Development in Children

Amy Boone

In Matthew 18 (Matthew 18: 1–5, New International Version), Jesus' disciples question Him regarding who is the greatest in God's Kingdom. Jesus shockingly answers by saying whoever changes to be like a child is the greatest in the Kingdom of Heaven. In the following chapter, the disciples seem not to remember Jesus' earlier message and rebuke the people bringing children to Jesus. Jesus quickly reminds them again of the importance and value of children in God's social economy by saying, "Let the little children come to me, and do not hinder them, for the kingdom of heaven belongs to such as these" (Matthew 19:14, NIV). Azougaye (2013), a young Muslim student, says children and adults both have similar expectations of their religious traditions, but young people are seen as having a narrower perspective with regard to religion than adults. Jews read the words of Torah instructing the adults how to answer when the children ask questions (Exodus 12: 26, NIV). Jesus' words about children, the Muslim student's understanding that children experience religious traditions, and the words of the Torah indicating children will ask questions all identify children as their own spiritual agents with value and with characteristics adults should emulate. Who are these children? What qualities do children possess that adults should seek to imitate? What if a child is intellectually gifted?

Giftedness

Delisle (2006) contends that "giftedness is not something you do. Giftedness is something you are" (203). A child identified as gifted perceives the world through a lens of intensity and supersensitivity. This extreme sensitivity may affect gifted children more profoundly in their emotions than in their intellectual abilities. The intensity with which they live their lives seeps into every aspect of their being from their thinking to their emotions and to their soul (Deslile 2006).

The Columbus Group (1991) defined giftedness with the same attention to Delisle's (2006) assertion that giftedness is not an action tied to accomplishments, but rather part of the very essence of self. Their definition identified inner intensities and a heightened sense of awareness in gifted children that requires the adults in these gifted children's lives to understand that gifted children "not only think differently, they also feel differently" (Delisle 2006, 228).

Because giftedness affects every aspect of life, these intensities include thoughts, emotions, spirit, and soul (Delisle 2006). Parents and teachers who see giftedness as a unidimensional trait involving intellect do a disservice to gifted children by not engaging with them in the totality of their giftedness.

Gifted children experience asynchrony in their development physically, emotionally, and cognitively. Asynchrony involves development and awareness in these areas that is out of step with norms for a given age (Lovecky 1998). A gifted child might cognitively process a complex plan without the physical ability to carry out that plan. This child may ponder deep human suffering issues without having the emotional maturity to deal with the issues. Asynchrony, like the heightened intensities, demands that teachers, parents, and other adults understand and address the potential emotional vulnerability that asynchrony can create (Silverman 1995).

Cognitive and Moral Development

Gifted children develop asynchronously and move through various stages physically, cognitively, and emotionally at very different speeds than nongifted children. Research provides insights into the stages of psychological and moral development (Stonehouse 1998). Erikson (1985) describes fluid psychological stages correlated to age development while understanding that humans are not static creatures. These stages represent growth through common life stresses or traumas (Stonehouse 1998). Erikson labeled the eight stages with the negative and positive possibilities for each. For example, he named the first stage trust versus mistrust and the final stage integrity versus despair (Erickson 1985). Erikson believed that many of the adult societal problems could adequately be resolved with more consideration to childhood (Stonehouse 1998).

Piaget (1969) studied the moral development of children. Piaget concluded that children's thinking processes vary greatly from those of adults. Concerning cognitive development, children possess an innate drive to makes sense of their surroundings by exploration and play (May et al. 2005). Utilizing the work of Piaget, Kohlberg focused on moral development and the effect of children's cognitive sophistication on moral reasoning and choices (Stonehouse 1998).

Kohlberg, like Erikson, developed levels to categorize his research. Kohlberg's levels outline moral reasoning and address issues of authority, views on right and wrong, personal intentions, the ability to take another's perspective, and justice (Stonehouse 1998). Kohlberg's description of moral reasoning begins with self-centered motivation with an emphasis on personal consequences. It then moves toward societal norms and a simplified sense of equating right choices with goodness and poor choices with badness. Finally, the highest level of morality includes strong considerations of justice and value of all human life (Stonehouse 1998).

Psychologists have long believed adolescent psychology must include religious and spiritual development to be complete (Hall 1904). However, the research, data, and conclusions about spiritual and religious development of children and adolescents in the field of psychology remain scant (Stolzenberg, Blair-Loy, & Waite 1995).

Faith Development

Nye (2009) defines children's spirituality as "God's ways of being with children and children's ways of being with God" (5). Children innately try to make sense of their surroundings (Piaget 1969). They also consider any religious experiences or spiritual values they hold when attempting to make sense of life and their surroundings (Coles 1990). Capturing a plausible spiritual formation journey for children proves difficult. Children often lack the ability to remember spiritual experiences or the language to express those spiritual experiences (May et al. 2005). Informed by the work of previous theorists and researchers, Fowler developed a framework for faith development as an integral part of basic human development. Fowler begins with a definition that includes trust and loyalty as the centerpieces of a faith story (Stonehouse 1998). Through this lens, Fowler identified four stages of faith development in children (May et al. 2005). These stages move from the earliest ability to trust as a baby, through a ritualistic stage in which stories and values take shape to a more abstract ability to consider global and theological issues (May et al. 2005). Peterson and Seligman (2004) assert that these stages present some difficulty in determining whether children proceed through the stages fluidly and linearly. Children might skip a stage or move backward at some point. These authors contend that stages set up spirituality as a primarily cognitive process, eliminating the metaphysical nature of spirit.

In *Character Strengths and Virtues: A Handbook and Classification*, Peterson and Seligman (2004) identify strengths of character involving abstract areas of giftedness in people. One character strength focuses on transcendence. Transcendence includes spirituality, religiousness, and faith. People with a strength or giftedness in transcendence often exhibit fulfillment in their spiritual experiences, high morals, elevation of others, and traits of spiritual character. Peterson and Seligman (2004) argue that spiritual prodigies exist.

Another consideration within the discussion of faith development includes how spirituality exists and grows. As Tiger (1999) observed in historical moments that included religious importance, religiousness seems inheritable and biological. However, Geertz (1973) asserts, "religiousness is a cultural construct and that socialization is key in the transmission of religious beliefs and practices" (611).

Putting the Pieces Together

Asynchrony not only causes gifted children to think differently, it also causes them to feel differently (Delisle 2006). This asynchrony catapults children into thinking (and developing strong feelings) about many topics before they are emotionally or experientially ready. A young gifted child might inquire about matters of life and death without fully understanding the emotional depth of these topics (Lovecky 1998). Gifted children often ask questions of adults pertaining to difficult or weighty topics that adults are unable or unwilling to discuss with them due to the heavy content (Lovecky 1998). This lack of conversation leaves gifted children with even more anxiety since their eyes, brains, and hearts perceive the world with such great intensity and supersensitivity (Delisle 2006). If gifted children move through moral and cognitive stages quickly and with asynchrony, these same gifted children are likely to move through faith development stages faster, and again, with asynchrony. In the case of faith, gifted children may wrestle and contend with weighty matters of faith without the life experience to appropriately process and consider those matters (Matthews 1994).

A giftedness and faith discussion also involves current research showing correlations between intelligence and religious beliefs. An inverse or negative association exists between intelligence and belief in religion (McGreal 2014). Research concerning this correlation does not offer explanations to this inverse association nor does it make the mistake of equating correlation with causation. Rather, the research stands in isolation with only speculations about the negative association. Individuals often cannot make sense of tragedy or pain, causing them to turn away from religion (Pargament 1997). Because intelligent people may be more analytically driven, they may find formal religions in opposition to analytical data (Chamorro-Premuzic 2013). Another factor involves the personality traits of openness and non-conformity. These traits sit in opposition to formal religions. Chamorro-Premuzic (2013) contends that this specific trait of openness combined with intelligence could serve as the biggest predictor of religiosity or the lack of belief in religion or faith.

The American education system and religious education as operationalized in children's ministries, youth ministries, and religious schools, seems to follow two distinct schools of thought with regard to pedagogy. One teaches from a student-centered approach and the other teacher-centered. The teacher-centered approach views the adult as the expert, creating meaning for the child. The constructivist child-centered approach sees the adult's role as one of creating space and an environment in which the child discovers meaning. The teacher in a student-centered learning environment provides the framework for learning and meaning-making to occur (Hiltz 1994). Teacher-centered learning environments focus on answers, whereas student-centered environments encourage questions. Gifted children with pronounced intensities thrive on questions. Adults who teach and lead gifted students must allow, welcome, and engage with the questions whether easy answers are available or not (Delisle 2002). Piaget (2005) and Coles (1990) asserted that children seek to understand and make meaning of their environments whether considering new learning in a secular setting or a religious setting.

One German, gifted, Muslim student expressed frustration over the lack of explanations for her questions in her religious upbringing (Azougaye 2013). Due to the cognitive and spiritual asynchronous development of gifted children, these questions may frighten or intimidate the adults attempting to lead and teach gifted children (Lovecky 1998). A learning environment that encourages hard questions, stimulating deep thinking, actually deepens personal faith beliefs (Roehlkepartain 1993). However, many secular educational settings like public schools and religious education settings like churches default toward teacher or adult centered instruction in which the adult disseminates information and learning to the students. In both secular and religious settings, this pedagogical approach does not meet the needs of gifted learners or of any learners, for that matter.

Questions

This study seeks to explore the connection between intellect and religious beliefs. The study will also attempt to examine the asynchrony in cognitive, moral, and spiritual development that gifted children experience. The type of environment in which gifted children learn and grow affects their developing ideas and beliefs. Gifted students between the ages of 18–23 will be given open-ended survey questions about faith development. The researcher will also interview parents of gifted children in the same age bracket regarding their own child's faith development. Research questions for the study include:

1. Do gifted students experience more dissonance in their religious beliefs as they move through childhood and adolescence?

2. Does asynchronous development in gifted students affect their faith development?

3. Does the type of environment in which a gifted student's faith develops affect his or her beliefs?

Methodology

Questions emerged from the literature review that the researcher developed into an open-ended survey for students 18–23 years old. The researcher contacted the deans of the honors colleges at two private, Christian universities in West Texas and the gifted coordinator in a West Texas public school district about sending the survey to gifted students and honors students with whom they had contact. The sample of convenience (Walliman 2011) certainly could include some sampling bias, but for the purposes of seeking a broad first look at this topic, the accessibility to these students, because of the researcher's proximity to the deans and gifted coordinator, made the student sample one that could be most easily obtained. Participants completed a survey of open-ended questions (Walliman 2011) about faith development. The survey also included demographic questions about gender, age, the religious environment of the child, and the child's identification as gifted. 542 honors students at the two private, Christian universities in West Texas and individual gifted students at several other universities (within Texas) were invited to complete the survey. The researcher also used a structured interview (Walliman 2011) to interview the parents of several gifted college students, known personally to the researcher, who lived in the same town as the researcher. The survey respondents and interviewees overlapped in only one case.

Students submitted over 100 surveys, many of which were only partially completed. The vehicle used to create the survey included start times and finish times for the respondents. Many respondents answered the open-ended questions for up to an hour. 75 percent of the respondents answered that they had been identified as gifted in their schools. All responses were included in the results even though 25 percent were not technically identified as gifted through a school. All respondents were either identified gifted or accepted to a university honors program.

After the survey site closed, the researcher read through the transcripts of the responses looking for patterns. Once patterns emerged, the researcher coded the transcripts in order to draw conclusions. The researcher sought peer review (Walliman 2011) from a colleague to build credibility for the emerging patterns and subsequent conclusions.

Results

Three fourths of the respondents were female and one fourth male. Over 90 percent of the respondents identified their family as professing a faith belief and attending a place of worship regularly.

Over 90 percent of the students recalled asking difficult faith questions growing up. Some expressed satisfaction with the answers or reassurance from their parents, but many more expressed dissatisfaction and frustration with the answers they received to their faith questions. Adults often discouraged the questioning and the answers felt largely dissatisfying. Students questioned the contents of the Bible, the existence of God, good versus evil, and the nature of God as it pertains to heaven and hell. One respondent said he/she wondered if God existed and why He would allow terrible things to happen. This student asserts he/she was "encouraged to not think about things like that too much and just accept the way things are."

When asked about the focus of their church or religious teaching experience growing up prior to the age of twelve, 75 percent reported "information" as the key focus over emotion, experience, or personal awareness.

When asked the same question about the focus after they were twelve years old, the responses varied. Students responded that their youth group/teen experiences at church encompassed some information, along with emotion, experiences, and personal awareness. One student expressed that he/she felt youth groups "were more emotion and experience oriented, which is why they had camps and different events like that." This particular student said big, one-time experiences do not result in lasting change, so he/she generally avoided these experiences.

All of the respondents except one identified with at least one of Dabrowski's (1964) overexcitabilities. Of the five overexcitabilities (psychomotor, sensual, intellectual, imaginational, and emotional), the largest number of respondents identified themselves as having an intellectual overexcitability. One particular student revealed he/she often feels his/her brain does not shut down at night causing him/her to sleep very little. Another student stated that he/she, "has a hard time believing anything because there are too many questions that attempt to undermine my forming beliefs."

Over 90 percent of the students believed they had more questions than their peers about matters of faith. Their questioning often included doubts. They thought about faith differently than their peers. One student admitted he/she began questioning more once he/she began college away from home. This student's father, a pastor, believed questioning was the same as not having faith. Another respondent stated he/she had many friends who memorized books of the Bible and Bible trivia/facts, but that he/she wanted to know how a person can be sure those things are true. Similarly, another student said when he/she did ask questions, others told him/her to "just have faith," which was frustrating. One student identified her questions as "passionate extremes" that her peers did not seem to see.

When asked what specifically drew them to their faith tradition or religious beliefs, students identified four main categories: the people, the traditions of the church, the nature of God, and personal experience. Students repeated these same four major themes throughout the responses about positive experiences. However, when asked about what has turned them off within their faith tradition or religious beliefs, 60 percent identified people as the problem. Specifically, they listed people's hypocrisy, contradictions, inconsistencies, judgmental attitudes, and bad theology.

One question asked the students to consider whether thinking precedes action or action precedes thinking/belief. Of those who specified, 32 contended actions led to belief, but five saw it the other way. One student who confessed she has lost her ability to believe the Christian narrative said, "faith and spirituality are often a comforting womb, a safe haven that people will go out of their way to avoid losing, even resigning themselves to contradictory or hypocritical thinking." She went on to say, "it still rocks me silent sometimes when I think of losing that foundation." She confessed this loss feels heartbreaking at times, but that her life pushed her toward introspection and literature, changing her beliefs about faith and religion.

When asked from whom they sought answers to their questions, the respondents expressed many different answers. Many students asked parents, but several mentioned friends, the Bible or other reading material, or adults they knew. One student said, "For a while, I tried hard to seek answers, but I have stopped now and learned to keep things to myself. It is hard to find people who understand."

Students considered whether their religious education experiences were a good fit for them or not. Of the students who believed their experiences were a good fit, they stated their faith was strengthened, the leadership was passionate, and the experiences were challenging and loving. Of those who deemed their experiences less of a fit for them, they felt Christianity was made simpler than it actually is. They found the experiences to be shallow and insufficient for dealing with the real world. They also stated that rote memorization was emphasized without room for questions.

Students pondered some of the big topics of faith and spirituality: suffering and evil, hell, God's intervention in the world, and the reconciliation of science and religion. Of these large topics, students tended to identify with all of them. One student said he/she does not see evidence of God's working in the world. This student believes prayer is a placebo. Another student expressed frustration with the perceived nature of God. He/she questioned why God would pursue someone in life and then once that person dies, God suddenly stops that pursuit. One student finds the contradictions between science and faith frustrating and confusing. Another student acknowledged he/she wrestles with all of the big topics and also expressed confusion about Euthyphro's dilemma, homosexuality, free will versus determinism, universalism, and comparative religions.

All but nine of the students believed their giftedness affected their faith beliefs and religious development. Of those who said the effect was positive, they listed deep thinking, curiosity, and open-mindedness. Of the students suggesting their giftedness has negatively affected their faith development, the problem of finding spiritual peers surfaced. Students also mentioned the difficulty with accepting things at face value and asking questions that demanded proofs. One student said his/her giftedness "makes religion and spirituality much more exhausting." Another student believed that gifted people tend to be less religious because "blind belief is the opposite of rational thinking."

Within the parent interviews, the interviewees' children varied significantly in their personalities, particularly emotionalism. Those children who tended to be more emotional in all aspects of life, including two who had an emotional mental diagnosis, struggled the most growing up with faith questions and spiritual matters. Those children who saw life through a more black and white or concrete lens found faith easier to believe at face value.

Data Analysis

As Delisle (2006) asserted, gifted children think and feel differently. Throughout the survey responses, students repeatedly mentioned thinking about matters of faith differently and feeling different from their peers in their thinking. One student recalled adults encouraging her to not think about things like faith matters too much, and to simply accept what he/she was told.

Many of these gifted students found themselves asking questions of others and wrestling with extremely difficult topics. Respondents said adults very often discouraged their questions. Lovecky (1998) believes parents and other adults do not know how to respond to gifted children about matters of faith when the children's asynchronous contemplations stymie, frighten, and frustrate them. When a gifted child asks demanding questions of an adult, the grownup might hesitate engaging in conversation due to fear or their lack of personal consideration of the question. Students responding to the survey questions reported their questions were ignored or not answered. Adults suggested their confusion was due to mental or emotional problems. One respondent said his/her church was the least safe place for questions. As Lovecky (1998) also shows, a lack of engagement and conversation about difficult topics for gifted children leads to anxiety. Many respondents said they feel frustration, anger, and discouragement.

Another finding included the heavy emphasis on information in the early years of these students' faith development. The vast majority of the respondents noted their childhood religious experiences were predominantly informational. May et al. (2005) outline the pivotal work of Piaget in the 1930s in which Piaget contends children naturally seek to make sense of their world through exploration and play. Sisk and Torrence (2001) also believe children naturally seek to make sense of their world in spiritual terms, too. Gifted children's overexcitabilities only exaggerate this need to make sense of the world. Offering mostly informational experiences in the early years does not provide the best framework for asking questions in this teacher-centered environment.

Students spoke about high awareness of morality from a young age. As Stonehouse (1998) reminds, moral awareness identifies the highest level of morality. The students' memories of high morality and justice as children and teens further highlights the asynchronous elements existing in their spiritual development. Students frequently mentioned wrestling with the value of life, heaven and hell, justice, and the fairness of God. They contended with weighty topics earlier than other children as identified on Fowler's stages of development (May et al. 2005).

When children and teens experience asynchronous development, parents and other influential adults feel unprepared to deal with their questions (Delisle 2006). Because matters of faith hold such deep importance and significance, gifted children need adults willing to listen, discuss, and consider these most personal, intimate questions.

The little available research points to a slight connection between higher intelligence and less religiousness, but no clear reason for this seems apparent. Gifted people's minds often send them to seek analytical data on topics. One student responded in a survey question that he/she is now an atheist because there is no proof in the Bible. For students whose minds naturally lead them toward data and proofs, adults who tell them they should not think about these matters too hard certainly do not help in those students' spiritual development.

Galen and Kloet (2011) found that those who are not religious tend to be more open to experience than those who identify with religiosity and spiritual matters. Gifted individuals thirst for new learning and information. This trait of openness drives many gifted people to ask more challenging questions about matters of faith. When the adults in gifted students' lives do not encourage this curiosity and openness, spiritual development suffers. One student said, "I wondered if God really existed, why he allowed terrible things to happen, why he would make us imperfectly, etc. Adults in the church didn't really have good answers and I was mostly encouraged to not think about things like that too much and just accept the way things are." If a gifted student encounters this sort of response in a school classroom, that student feels stifled because his or her thinking is not welcome. How much more off-putting this approach must feel to a student who is pondering the deep meaning of life and of God.

Over 75 percent of the students reported the focus of their learning at a religious institution prior to twelve years old as information based. This emphasis on the lower levels of Bloom's (1956) taxonomy never satisfies the gifted child's mind. These children seek connections, applications, and analysis. Without this higher-level thinking, gifted students often disengage. They desperately need places to ask questions and not just receive information

(Starr 1994). Lovecky (1998) believes some adults might be afraid of challenging faith questions, which was confirmed by the students.

Conclusions

Although the scope of this study is limited, the data suggest that asynchrony in matters of faith is real and must be understood by adults guiding gifted children. Too many gifted children grow up with questions beyond those of their peers about matters of faith and receive unsatisfactory answers. Parents of gifted children who choose to raise their children in a context of faith must engage these children in questions about the weighty matters of life and God. Parents, as children's first spiritual example, must understand their gifted child's probable curiosity for answers and tendency toward openness. They must also meet their gifted child at a place for questions and seeking without fear. Children's ministers and youth ministers must educate themselves about the qualities of gifted children. Understanding the gifted child's expression of overexcitability and their intellectual ability would help children's ministers and youth ministers more adequately prepare for the inevitable questions of these bright children. A simple understanding of Bloom's Taxonomy (1956) would also benefit children's ministers as they seek to guide young children in faith. Allowing space for questioning and searching for truth would benefit gifted children. Religious institutions must create environments where questions are not only acceptable, but encouraged.

The almost nonexistent research about giftedness and faith development is frustrating, at best. However, the evidence of hurt, confusion, and frustration expressed by the students in the survey pulls the curtain back on a room full of possibilities. These gifted children whose beautiful and difficult minds and hearts sit waiting on the adults for guidance and wisdom may not know how to ask for what they need spiritually. Current experiences and practices of spiritual development are falling short for these brightest students. May this study about the relation between giftedness and spirituality spur further research, time, and thought.

References

Azougaye, Rukea. 2013. "Young, Gifted and Religious: What do We Expect from our Tradition and Our Society?" *European Judaism* 46, pp. 115–21.
Bloom, Benjamin S. and David R. Krathwohl. 1956. *Taxonomy of Educational Objectives: The Classification of Educational Goals, by a Committee of College and University Examiners.* Handbook 1: Cognitive domain. New York: Longmans.

Chamorro-Premuzic, Tomas. 2013. "Why are Religious People Generally Less Intelligent?" *Psychology Today*. https://www.psychologytoday.com/blog/mr-personality/201312/why-are-religious-people-generally-less-intelligent.
Coles, Robert. 1990. *The Spiritual Life of Children*. Boston: Houghton Mifflin.
Columbus Group. 1991. *Unpublished Manuscript of the meeting of the Columbus Group*. Columbus, OH.
Dabrowski, Kazimierz. 1964. *Positive Disintegration*. London: Little, Brown.
Deslisle, James. 2006. *Once upon a Mind: The Stories and Scholars of Gifted Child Education*. Mason, OH: Cengage Learning.
Erickson, Eric. 1985. *Childhood and Society*. New York: Norton.
Galen, Luke, and Jim Kloet. 2011. "Personality and Social Integration Factors Distinguishing Nonreligious from Religious Groups: The Importance of Controlling for Attendance and Demographics. *Archive for Psychology of Religion* 33, pp. 205–28.
Geertz, Clifford. 1973. *The Interpretation of Cultures*. New York: Basic.
Hiltz, Starr Roxanne. 1994. *The Virtual Classroom: Learning Without Limits via Computer Networks*. Wilmington, NC: Intellect.
Lovecky, Deirdre. 1998. "Spiritual Sensitivity in Gifted Children." *Roeper Review* 20, pp. 178–83.
Matthews, Gareth. 1994. *The Philosophy of Childhood*. Cambridge, MA: Harvard University Press.
May, Scottie, et al. 2005. *Children Matter: Celebrating Their Place in the Church, Family, and Community*. Grand Rapids: Eerdmans.
McGreal, Scott. 2014. "More Knowledge, Less Belief in Religion?" *Psychology Today*. https://www.psychologytoday.com/blog/unique-everybody-else/201401/more-knowledge-less-belief-in-religion.
Nye, Rebecca. 2009. *Children's Spirituality*. London: Church House.
Pargament, Ken. 1997. *The Psychology of Religion and Coping: Theory, Research, Practice*. New York: Guilford.
Peterson, Christopher, and Martin Seligman. 2004. *Character Strengths and Virtues: A Handbook and Classification*. Washington, DC: American Psychological Association.
Piaget, Jean. 1969. *The Psychology of the Child*. New York: Basic.
Roehlkepartain, Eugene. 1993. *The Teaching Church: Moving Christian Education to Center Stage*. Nashville: Search Institute.
Silverman, Linda. 1995. "The Many Faces of Asynchrony." *Keynote Address Presented at the Hollingsworth Center for Highly Gifted Children*. Cambridge, MA.
Sisk, Dorothy, and E. Paul Torrance. 2001. *Spiritual Intelligence: Developing Higher Consciousness*. Buffalo, NY: Creative Education Foundation.
Stolzenberg, Ross M., Mary Blair-Loy, and Linda J. Waite. 1995. "Religious participation in early adulthood: Age and family life cycle effects on church membership." *American Sociological Review* 60, pp. 84–103.
Stonehouse, Catherine. 1998. *Joining Children on the Spiritual Journey*. Grand Rapids: Bridge Point.
Tiger, Lionel. 1999. "The Past of an Illusion: How Optimism Brings us to God." *Free Inquiry* 19, pp. 28–29.
Walliman, Nicholas. 2011. *Research Methods: The Basics*. New York: Routledge.

Chapter 12

The Experience of Conversion in the Lives of Those Nurtured in Faith
A Phenomenological Study

— Edyta Jankiewicz —

THE SCRIPTURES DESCRIBE A tension between the need for nurturing children's faith (Deut. 6:5; Isa. 38:19; Prov. 22:6) and the need for conversion (John 3: 3,8). The Scriptures do not, however, describe *how* those nurtured in faith experience conversion. Consequently, most Protestant Christian denominations have adopted one of two approaches to children's ministry: either a "nurture" approach, which begins with infant baptism and is followed by nurture that does not expect a discernible conversion experience; or a "conversion" approach, which emphasizes personal sin and a distinctive point-in-time conversion, followed by believer's baptism (Estep 2002; May 1990).

In contrast, Kevin Lawson (2006) proposed a "combined approach" to children's faith formation (115), suggesting that both the conversion and nurture approaches have strengths that can be utilized and weaknesses that need to be addressed. A combined approach is practiced in the Seventh-day Adventist (SDA) denomination, which emphasizes the importance of *both* the spiritual nurture of children *and* a voluntary commitment to faith accompanied by a believer's baptism. While a memorable, point-in-time conversion is not generally expected, at some point in their Christian journey most second- and greater-generation SDA's are confronted with the need for being "born from above" (John 3:3,8). But how does one experience conversion if one has always been part of the family of God?

Contemporary research on conversion has considered this type of experience an outcome of "religious socialization" rather than "conversion," per se (Spilka et al. 1985, 210). As a result, the experiences of second- and greater-generation believers have not been included in conversion research (Paloutzian 2014; Paloutzian et al. 2013; Spilka et al. 1985), and are thus not well understood. Accordingly, the purpose of this study was to understand *how* those who have been nurtured in faith do experience conversion.

Methodology

A hermeneutic phenomenological approach to qualitative research was utilized in this study. While phenomenology seeks to *describe* the subjective experiences of individuals (Husserl 1900/1970; Merriam 2002), *hermeneutic* phenomenology attempts to situate experience in relation to the broader context of the individual's life (Lopez & Willis 2004; Wojnar & Swanson 2007). This study adopted a hermeneutic phenomenological approach based on the assumption that the experience of conversion in the lives of those nurtured in faith could best be understood within the broader context of their formative faith experiences.

Participants were selected through "criterion-based sampling," which involved selecting participants who had experienced the phenomenon under study; and "homogenous sampling," which involved selecting similar cases (Creswell 2007, 127). Accordingly, participants in this study were all SDA young adults (ages 25–40) who had grown up within an SDA context, who were at least third-generation SDA, and who continue to be members of SDA faith communities. Rather than pre-deciding on a certain number of participants, data collection was discontinued when new data no longer contributed new themes (Wolff 2002). The final number of participants in this study was fourteen.

The data for this research were collected through "intensive" or "in-depth" interviews (Charmaz 2006, 25). After obtaining informed consent, each participant was asked to verbally respond to the following questions: "Can you tell me what *faith* or *having faith* means to you? Beginning wherever you like, can you tell me about the experiences you think shaped your faith? Can you tell me what you understand by the word conversion? Have you experienced something that could be considered conversion? If so, can you describe that for me?" Interviews were recorded and transcribed verbatim.

Data analysis began with several readings of each interview transcript, followed by assigning a code to small portions of data. Throughout this process, analytic memos were also written. Coding methods were then implemented *across* the coded data, for the purpose of grouping similarly-coded data into categories. Categories were then woven together with the ideas generated through analytic memo writing, and organized into recurring themes (Saldana 2009). This process represents the goal of hermeneutic phenomenology, which is to generate an understanding of the phenomenon from a "blend of the researcher's understanding" and "participant-generated information" (Wojnar & Swanson 2007, 177).

Issues of trustworthiness were addressed by keeping a reflective journal in order to monitor subjective perspectives and biases; conducting in-depth interviews; searching for and discussing divergent findings; recursively checking interpretations against the data; and presenting findings humbly, in recognition of the subjective element within qualitative research.

Summary of Findings

Analysis of data resulted in four major shared themes that describe the *experience of conversion* in the lives of those nurtured in faith.

Process

The following descriptions of conversion are taken from research notes and are meant to give a picture of the conversations with the subjects in the study. Very few of the quotations from research notes were found in notes from all of the subjects. Each of the quotations included are meant to give a picture of the discussions between the researcher and the research subjects.

Conversion is not "a point in time" experience that includes "flashes of lightning or anything big;" rather, it is "a very slow" and "gradual process" that is facilitated by "a progression of experiences," which are like "multiple little 'aha' moments." For many, conversion is a relatively smooth process that involves "just filling in, building on the pattern" established early in life. For others, the process of conversion is more uneven, and includes times of "giv[ing] up" on faith or even "death of faith," followed by a long process of "rebuil[ding]" of faith; however, despite the uneven, "multi-level" nature of these experiences, conversion is still described as "definitely a process," facilitated by multiple "significant moments" or "turning points" rather than one "key moment that was, like, wow!" Furthermore, conversion is not a process with a definite beginning or ending, but rather, it is an ongoing process that is "still continuing" or "currently happening today." Conversion is "almost a daily thing," "a sort of daily experience" of "constant[ly] turning away from me to Christ" and "choosing [God] on a daily basis."

Integrates Intellectual Knowledge

Conversion integrates early childhood "understanding" of God with knowledge learned later in life. For many, learning during childhood centered on understanding "God's character;" on developing a "picture of who God is;" on learning that "God is real," "God is love," and God is "someone who cared for me and loved me." Those participants who considered their formative experiences to have given them a positive picture of God, as well as "enough knowledge" about Him, described the intellectual component of their conversion experience as a smooth process of ongoing cognitive assent to and/or gradual growth in childhood knowledge, resulting in belief becoming their "own."

In contrast, some described their childhood faith experiences as "limited" due to a lack of resources or parental guidance or as "very fundamentalist, very rigid and sectarian." These experiences resulted in either a deficient or distorted picture of God. Accordingly, conversion required a significant corrective component of augmenting childhood knowledge, as well as "un-learning" some elements of childhood understanding. This new learning resulted in a more biblical understanding of God, particularly "understanding the truth" of the Gospel, i.e., "really understand[ing], really, the work God does on our behalf" and "that Jesus is my Savior, you know, and that I can have joy and peace because it's His righteousness that God sees and not mine."

Integrates Affective Experiences

Conversion integrates childhood experiences of God with later experiences. Some participants described significant *personal* experiences with God during childhood, particularly "a very strong prayer life." For these participants, the experiential component of faith continued to be important to them; however, they did not describe their conversion in terms of significant change in the affective domain. In contrast, the majority of participants described *family* and/or *communal* faith experiences that included a positive affective component, but no significant *personal* experience with God during childhood. These participants described conversion in terms of significant growth in a *personal* experience with God, i.e., conversion was "the process of developing [a] relationship with God;" that "it was ever not there, but there was another step, [of understanding] that I would have a relationship with God." Through this process, faith became "felt" and "real" and "own[ed]."

Several participants, however, described childhood faith experiences that were negative in the affective domain, resulting in a faith that was "unfelt," and a picture of God as "distant" or "absent;" a God who "doesn't really care." For these participants, conversion began with significant affective experiences of recognizing "emptiness" or "something missing," resulting in "opening up to God." These participants described their conversion experiences in significantly more emotive terms, including "sobb[ing]" at baptism, as well as relating the "love" and "peace" and "joy" that knowing God had brought to their lives.

Transformational

Conversion is transformational as it leads to "making choices to turn from those things that are not helpful and turning to the things that [are]." This "turning" is the outcome of growth in both the intellectual and affective domains, i.e., as understanding of God grows, and as relationship with God develops, transformational "turning" in the behavioral domain follows. This transformational "turning" includes both *past* and *ongoing* experiences. *Past* experiences were described as "turning away" from time pursuits not congruent with faith commitments, "turning away" from relationships not supportive of faith, and "turning toward" vocational choices characterized by service to Christ and the furthering of His kingdom. *Ongoing* transformational experiences were described as "turning away" from sin and self, or "let[ting] go of self," which requires ongoing "repentance" and "re-conversion;" and "turning toward" God in "surrender," which is accompanied by a "desire to be more like Him" or "to have my character shaped more like God's character." It is through this *ongoing* transformational turning that conversion is "still continuing" or still "currently happening today."

The Essence of the Experience of Conversion

The participants in this study experienced conversion as a gradual, ongoing process, facilitated by multiple significant moments or events, which occurred across the course of their lives, rather than as a single turning point or even as a process with a definite beginning and ending. This process involves movement toward integration of childhood, adolescent and young adult experiences in both the intellectual and affective domains, respectively, resulting in both adequate intellectual understanding and a *personal* affective experience of faith. Only one participant described childhood faith experiences that integrated both adequate intellectual understanding of God and *personal* experience with God. All other participants described childhood faith experiences that were deficient in one of these; thus, the process of conversion could be seen as a movement toward rectifying these deficiencies.

Furthermore, some degree of integration in the intellectual and affective domains was necessary before the transformational "turning" normally equated with conversion could occur. This process of "turning" resulted in greater congruence between the intellectual, affective and behavioral domains of faith.

Discussion of Findings

Process

The New Testament describes conversion as a "definite and discernible turning" from a life without Christ to a life committed to Him (Knott 1982). Today, many Christian traditions continue to emphasize the need for identifying a definite "point of departure for the rest of Christian life" (Smith 2010, 18); however, Christians nurtured in faith often do not experience conversion in this way, and thus can "feel distant or alienated from their own experience because it does not fit the pattern of what they believe a conversion should look or feel like. This leads them to wonder whether their experience is legitimate" (3). As one participant in this study explained,

> I don't think there's ever been a point in my life when I think like, you know, I'm now converted. I kind of wish it would be that way. Seems like everyone else has that in their lives (laughs) . . . Maybe it's still coming.

Some authors recognize that conversion is "best understood if viewed as a complex process" (Packer, 1989, p. 22), or "a series of events—often a complex development over time, perhaps even several years" (Smith, 2010, p. 6). In contrast, while the participants of this study experienced conversion as a gradual process, they did not describe their conversion experiences in terms of a definite beginning and ending. Furthermore, rather than describing their conversion experiences in terms of the past, they considered conversion to be an ongoing process that was "still continuing." While the ongoing nature of conversion is not the emphasis in the New Testament or the earliest decades of the Christian Church, where the thought leaders were first-generation converts to Christianity who wrote primarily for first-generation Christian readers (Knott 1982), it does appear to be consistent with the Old Testament portrayal of conversion through the Hebrew verb *shubh*, which denotes an ongoing process of returning to a departure point, particularly in the sense of returning to an original relationship with God (Witherup 1994, 18). As one participant explained,

> I was filling in a survey just last week, and it asked about conversion, and I thought, I was probably converted again this morning, you know, in my devotional time, because it had been a, it had been an important devotional time for me that day, you know, and I came away refreshed . . . you know, it's almost a daily thing.

Integrates Heart and Mind

In the Old Testament, God's people are instructed to love Him with all their "heart" and "soul" and "strength" (Deut 6:4–9). Jesus reiterates this message when He states: "Love the Lord your God with all your heart and with all your soul and with all your mind" (Matt 22: 37–38). Evidently, God's ideal is a faith that integrates both heart and mind. But how does such a faith develop? Jonathan Kim asserts that the development of holistic faith requires both conceptual knowledge, which is "comprehended" rationally, and perceptual knowledge, which is "apprehended" relationally (Kim, 2010, p. 90). The participants in this study described their faith as "both cognitive and experiential," which reflected formational faith experiences that included intellectual knowledge about God, which they learned rationally, and affective knowledge of God, which they learned relationally.

Most participants, however, described formational experiences that were at least somewhat lop-sided or deficient in either the intellectual or affective domains, or both. Thus, it was growth in both intellectual understanding and affective experience that they experienced as conversion. As one participant explained,

> I understood that I was a sinner saved by grace and I always would be. And that Jesus is my Savior, you know, and that I can have joy and peace because it's His righteousness that God sees and not mine: fig-leafed, feeble, filthy-rag righteousness. (Laughs). I mean this is why we can be happy Christians. You can't be if you don't know that. And it's changed everything. I

feel so much better about everything than I ever have before. I can have joy and peace . . . [And] I love above anything the God who has given us all this . . . the fact that God would accept me on the basis of what Christ has done . . . I shouldn't be living! I shouldn't be breathing! . . . You want to know what faith means? (Laughs) . . . It means everything!

Gordon Smith (2001) asserts that a first-generation conversion, as described in the New Testament, includes both intellectual and affective elements. Thus, the integration of heart and mind described by the participants in this study is somewhat reflective of first-generation conversion; however, rather than being entirely new experiences, as is the case for first-generation Christians, the experiences of those nurtured in faith reflect an integration of childhood faith experiences with new faith experiences, resulting in a more holistic faith.

Transformational

The origin of the word "conversion" is the Latin word "convertere," which means to "turn altogether" or "turn around" (Oxford English Dictionary). Accordingly, in its theological sense, the term "conversion" signifies "an altogether turning around" from sin and ungodliness to righteousness and a godly life. This dramatic experience of turning, through repentance, is central to the experience of conversion in the New Testament (Smith 2001); however, having known the experience of repentance and forgiveness from childhood, the participants in this study did not experience repentance as a dramatic turning. Nevertheless, they still described experiences of transformational "turning," both *past* and *ongoing*, as part of their conversion.

Past experiences included "turning away" from specific behavioral choices that were not congruent with faith while simultaneously "turning toward" God, as well as "turning away" from secular pursuits and "turning toward" vocations that were more congruent with intellectual and affective faith commitments. These experiences are reflective of the New Testament concept of conversion portrayed through the Greek word *metanoia*, which implies "look[ing] at the past, at that from which [one] has turned" (Peace 1999, 348).

Ongoing experiences included "turning away" from sin and self through repentance and confession, as well as "turning toward" God by surrendering the will to His. This appears to be consistent with the Old Testament conception of conversion as "an *ongoing process*" (italics in text) of the "*re*turning" (italics in text) of God's covenant people "to what was formerly known," rather than a call to turn to "something totally new" (Witherup 1994, 18). Furthermore, the participants in this study described their *ongoing* experience of transformational "turning" in terms of an *ongoing* desire to grow in Christ-likeness, which is more traditionally considered part of sanctification rather than conversion.

Thus, in summary, the experience of conversion in the lives of those nurtured in faith can be understood as an ongoing process of integration between the intellectual, affective and behavioral domains. While most of the young adults in this study experienced faith formation in each of these domains to some degree, their conversion experiences complemented their formational experiences, resulting in a movement toward greater congruence among the three domains. However, as William R. Yount (2010) suggests, the "ideal," i.e., where "all three spheres [are] perfectly overlapped, forming a seamless, single whole," is found only in the life of Jesus (p. 336). Thus, the experience of conversion in the lives of those nurtured in faith can be considered somewhat reflective of the ongoing process of sanctification.

Final reflections

Articulating a conversion narrative, an important part of Christian experience that "heightens our appreciation" of God's presence and work in our lives (Smith 2010, 159), can be difficult for second- and greater-generation Christians. The results of this study appear to indicate that, for those who have grown up with faith, reflecting on childhood understanding and experience of God may be an appropriate starting point for thinking about conversion. Furthermore, examining later spiritual experiences within the framework of intellectual, affective and transformational elements may facilitate assurance of the legitimacy of one's experience. It may also identify any missing elements that need to be reflected on and addressed, which may, in turn, foster a more holistic faith experience. Accordingly, the results of this study not only confirm the importance of holistic Christian education in children's faith formation, but also suggest that a holistic, educational approach to ministry with third- and greater-generation adults may provide an environment in which the Holy Spirit can begin to address the deficiencies or distortions of our formational experiences, and thus to facilitate the "altogether turning around" of conversion.

Future Research

This study provides a preliminary framework for thinking about conversion in the lives of believers who have grown up with faith; however, due to the exploratory nature of this study, it leaves many questions unanswered: Do third- and greater-generation young adults within different denominational, socio-economic or cultural groups experience conversion similarly? How does understanding and experience of conversion in the lives of third- and greater-generation Christians change across the lifespan? Does the experience of second-generation believers differ significantly from the experience of third- and greater-generation believers? Further research is needed to address these questions.

References

Charmaz, Kevin. 2006. *Constructing Grounded Theory: A Practical Guide Through Qualitative Analysis.* Thousand Oaks, CA: Sage.

Creswell, John W. 2007. *Qualitative Inquiry and Research Design: Choosing among Five Approaches.* Thousand Oaks, CA: Sage.

Estep, James Riley. 2002. "Childhood Transformation: Toward an Educational Theology of Childhood Conversion and Spiritual Formation." *Stone-Campbell Journal* 5, pp. 183–206.

Husserl, Edmund. 1970. *Logical Investigations.* Translated by J. N. Findlay. 1900. New York: Humanities.

Kim, Jonathan. 2010. "Intellectual Development and Christian Formation." In *Christian Formation: Integrating Theology and Human Development*, edited by James Riley Estep and Jonathan H. Kim, 63–97. Nashville: B&H Academic.

Knott, B. 1982. "The Utility of a Metaphor: Examining the Relevance of 'Conversion' to Second-Generation Christians." Unpublished term paper, SDA Theological Seminary, Andrews University.

Lawson, Kevin E. 2005. "In Right Relationship with God: Childhood Conversion in Evangelical Christian Traditions." In *Nurturing Child and Adolescent Spirituality: Perspectives from the World's Religious Traditions*, edited by Karen-Marie Yust et al., 108–21. Lanham, MD: Rowman and Littlefield.

Lopez, Kay A., and Danny G. Willis. 2004. "Descriptive versus Interpretive Phenomenology: Their Contributions to Nursing Knowledge." *Qualitative Health Research* 14, pp. 726–35.

May, Scottie. 1990. *Conversion or Nurture of Children: A Survey and Analysis of Post-Bushnell, Popular Literature and Current Curriculum.* Unpublished document, Trinity Evangelical Divinity School, Deerfield, IL.

Merriam, Sharan B. 2002. "Phenomenological Research." In *Qualitative Research in Practice: Examples for Discussion and Analysis*, by Sharan B. Merriam and Associates, 93–95. San Francisco: Jossey-Bass.

Packer, J. I. 1989. "The Means of Conversion." *Crux* 25, pp. 14–22.

Paloutzian, Raymond F. 2014. "Psychology of Religious Conversion and Spiritual Transformation." In *The Oxford Handbook of Religious Conversion*, edited by Lewis R. Rambo and Charles E. Farhadian, 209–39. Oxford: Oxford University Press.

Paloutzian, Raymond. F., et al. 2013. "Conversion, Deconversion, and Spiritual Transformation: A Multilevel Interdisciplinary View." In *Handbook of the Psychology of Religion and Spirituality*, edited by Raymond F. Paloutzian and Crystal L. Park, 399–421. 2nd ed. New York: Guildford.

Peace, R. V. 1999. *Conversion in the New Testament: Paul and the Twelve*. Grand Rapids: Eerdmans.

Saldaña, Johnny. 2009. *The Coding Manual for Qualitative Researchers*. Los Angeles: Sage.

Smith, G. T. 2001. *Beginning Well: Christian Conversion and Authentic Transformation*. Downers Grove, IL: InterVarsity.

———. 2010. *Transforming Conversion: Rethinking the Language and Contours of Christian Initiation*. Grand Rapids: Baker Academic.

Spilka, B., et al. 2003. *The Psychology of Religion: An Empirical Approach*. 3rd ed. New York: Guildford.

Witherup, R. D. 1994. *Conversion in the New Testament*. Collegeville, MN: Liturgical.

Wojnar, D. M., and K. M. Swanson. 2007. "Phenomenology: An Exploration." *Journal of Holistic Nursing* 25, no. 3, pp. 172–80.

Wolff, Richard F. 2002. "Self-Reflection: An Essential Quality for Phenomenological Researchers." In *Qualitative Research in Practice: Examples for Discussion and Analysis*, edited by Sharan B. Merriam and Associates, 117–19. San Francisco: Jossey-Bass.

Yount, William R. 2010. *Created to Learn*. Nashville: B&H Academic.

Chapter 13

Communally Discerning the Legitimacy of Children's Revelatory Experiences with God

 Karissa Glanville ———

JULIE WAS PREPARING TO be a guest speaker at a church service. When she asked God what to speak on, she believed God told her to speak on love, and to ask her nine-year-old daughter, Bella. Prayer and hearing from God was a normal and natural part of Julie's family, even for the children. Bella was watching TV and had not planned to go with her mother to the service. When Julie asked Bella to pray regarding what Julie should speak about, Bella did so right away. Bella then told her mother that God said to speak about love. This confirmed what Julie believed God told her. However, Bella also saw a series of three vision-type pictures she believed were from God and were messages for the church. Bella's mother decided to have Bella come and share with the church as well. Little did they know that the series of three pictures perfectly represented two seasons in the past and the potential future directions of the church. They also didn't know the church was celebrating their 20th anniversary that day. The message Bella and her mother ended up sharing together with the church encouraged the congregation deeply. The first two pictures related to two distinct seasons representing the past 20 years of the church, and the third picture was an invitation and promise for a greater season to come.

At another church, 10-year-old Sarah was enrolled in a special class that trained children about the importance of character and how to participate in ministry of various kinds including using the gifts of the Holy Spirit, such as prophesying, giving words of knowledge, praying for healing, etc. Sarah went with her class on a field trip to the State Capitol building in order to bless the people who worked there. The children asked God to tell them about specific people and/or places to go and what to say. When Sarah prayed with her teacher and other students, she heard God tell her a basement room number and a message for someone who worked in that room. The teacher didn't even think there was a room with that number, but decided to take the risk with Sarah to go and find out. They found the room number in the basement, and a man working in it. Sarah was then able to give her message to the man who was incredibly encouraged.

At yet another church, a children's Sunday school class was invited to come on stage and was given the opportunity to bless or pray for the congregation if they wanted to. Nine-year-old James was scared and had absolutely no desire or intention to say anything. Yet when he got on the stage, he said he instantly had courage and wanted to bless the congregation. He said he knew it was God because, previously, he had been scared and had no desire to pray, and then he had courage. People in the congregation claimed to have been blessed by what he said and prayed.

These stories are just some of the ones that were recounted in four case studies done at four different charismatic/non-denominational churches in California in 2015 and 2016 as part of my PhD research (Glanville 2016). These four churches (Expression 58, Bethel Church, Blazing Fire Church, and Jesus Culture Sacramento) all have the foundational belief that God wants to and is capable of speaking to and ministering through children. In fact they all specifically train their children to hear from God and see it as a natural part of being a Christian. The children interviewed were ages 8–10. All of those interviewed (children and adults) were asked to share what it was that made them believe a child's specific revelatory experience was from God. From these case studies, a "Child-Community Discernment-Process Model" emerged (discussed further below). [For this study, I left it up to the communities to determine the definition of a "revelatory experience from/with God." For example, it could have been what the communities considered to be a God-inspired dream, hearing God's voice, encountering a non-human spirit being, being used by God to give a prophecy to someone, or being used by God through any revelatory gifts of the Spirit mentioned in 1 Cor 12:8–10.] This model reveals a holistic method of how children in certain communities are being trained to recognize and experience God within the context of community by creating and cultivating a context where children can learn to practice hearing from and experiencing God, and by being coached through the processes of discernment and application of perceived revelatory experiences.

Anticipations

Before the interviews commenced, I anticipated finding various theological and non-theological ways adults practiced discerning a child's experience. My preconceived idea of discernment within these communities could be described as a series of concentric circles as seen in Figure 1. I anticipated after a child had a revelatory experience with God of some kind, they would tell their parents (or in some cases their children's ministry leader first), who would then do their best to validate and/or discern whether the experience was from God or not. I did not consider the issue of whether much weight would be given to the child's opinion. If the parents were unsure in their discernment, I expected they might talk with others from their church with whom they had close relationships (fellow members or leaders they knew personally). If the source of the experience still could not be determined to the parents' satisfaction, and the possible implications of the experience seemed significant enough to the parents, I anticipated them reaching out more specifically to leaders within the church.

Figure 1. Relational Interactions

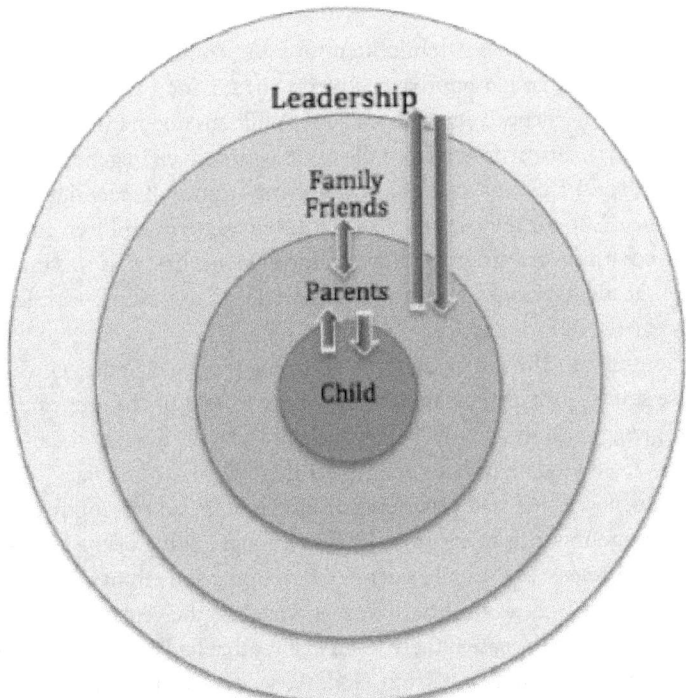

As Figure 1 shows, I expected the relationship between the child and parents to be more hierarchical, with the child relating the experience and the parent(s) passing judgment (two one-way arrows). I expected the interaction between the parents and the family friends as more equal and dialogical (represented by a two-way arrow). If the leadership of the church was brought in, I anticipated that too would tend to be more hierarchical (two one-way arrows), with the parents as the liaison between leaders and the child.

While reviewing current non-academic literature and resources from charismatic sources, my anticipated model was challenged through comments made by Becky Fischer. I had emailed her to ask if she had any curriculum that covered teaching children how to discern and/or parents and leaders how to discern whether their children's experiences were from God or not. Part of her reply was as follows.

> To answer your question, my curriculum *Hearing God's Voice* would address this in general by default. We teach the children how to recognize God's voice and how to spot counterfeits. There is one specific lesson on counterfeit voices and spiritual activity. But we have always felt by teaching them the real voice of God, and constantly encouraging them to read their Bibles, pray, etc., that they will learn to spot the counterfeit. (Fischer 2014b)

Further review of non-academic literature and training materials proved she was not alone in her approach (Toledo 2012; Lane 1998; Walters 1995; Baker ca. 1950; Harper 1999; Mapes 2009; Williams 2009; Fischer 2008; La Guardia 2007). Discernment from the top down, or even in general, was not addressed specifically, as much as was the importance of teaching children how to hear God for themselves. As the interviews of the children and those in their communities progressed, it became evident that what was taught in the non-academic books and training materials I examined, was actually largely carried out in practice.

Contrary to the anticipated discernment process (Figure 1), each of the case studies provided examples of the parents and/or children's ministry leaders giving great weight to whether the child actually thought their experience was from God or not. Sometimes, if there were no "red flags" in what the child believed they had experienced with God, the adults simply took the child's declaration of it being from God as enough. Some of the larger "red flags" would consist of the child saying or describing something related to the experience that went against Scripture and against the centrality of Christ. This was especially the case if there was a history that had proven to the adults that the child could not hear from God. As will be seen further below, the community's support before and after a child's experience helps to explain why so much trust could be placed in the child's ability to discern.

The discernment process in the communities could be seen to start significantly before the actual revelatory experience. As the children and their communities shared their stories, the processes that emerged were "Creating and Cultivating the Context," the actual perceived "revelatory experience," and the subsequent "Coaching through Follow-Up."

Creating and Cultivating the Context

In all of these churches, these children's revelatory experiences did not come completely unexpectedly. The parents and surrounding church community expected, facilitated, and attempted to prepare their children for it. In all of the communities, the following categories emerged relating specifically to creating and cultivating the context.

Children's ministry leaders and parents:

- Expected children to experience God and minister to others by the power of the Holy Spirit as a normal part of life.
- Specifically trained the children in ways they believed would teach the children how to hear from God.
- Included the children as part of the dialogue regarding growing in a relationship with God and hearing from him. This dialoguing included coaching, discussing, and praying together related to hearing from and experiencing God.
- Gave the children opportunities within the church and/or home to purposefully seek to experience God. as well as participate in ministry opportunities.

All of the parents interviewed:

- Were intentional about incorporating their relationship with God into their family life on a daily basis. They purposefully shared with their children about their own relationship with God, and attempted to live it out as an example for their children.
- Talked with or taught their children about stories from the Bible.

Children's ministry workers:

- Specifically trained the children how to prophesy over other people (peers and in some cases also adults).

The larger church community:

- Generally carried the supportive belief that children experiencing God and ministering to others by the power of the Holy Spirit was possible and could be expected.

All of these aspects emerged as common elements of the context that was created and cultivated in each of the communities.

A good example of creating and cultivating the context can be seen with Sarah, mentioned above. As well as enrolling Sarah in the special class at their church, Sarah's parents regularly shared with her and her siblings about their growing relationship with God and all they believed they were learning about how God speaks. Her parents also talked with them about what they believed to be identifying characteristics of the way God speaks, so the children would be able to potentially discern for themselves whether or not an experience was from God. The assumption and expectation from Sarah's family, from the children's classes at church, and from the congregation and leadership of the church at large, was that children could experience God, hear from him, and be used by him through the Holy Spirit.

The Revelatory Experience

Because revelatory experiences with God were seen as something that could be expected within these communities, the children were quite comfortable talking about their experiences among family members, with children's ministry workers, and with me. Some examples of the perceived revelatory experiences of the children in this study were:

- Dreams
- Receiving a revelatory message they believed God wanted them to tell someone else
- Seeing Jesus and feeling his presence powerfully
- Being given a revelatory or encouraging message, song or piece of artwork from God for the larger congregation.

Coaching Through Follow-Up

After the children were believed to have had a specific revelatory experience with God, coaching the child through follow-up was evident in all four of the communities. The following aspects of coaching through follow-up emerged among all of the churches and families:

1. Dialogue with the child regarding the child's perceived revelatory experience was present between the child and the children's ministry leader and/or parents. This dialogue could include discerning and praying together, helping the children learn from and/or apply what they'd experienced, or general encouragement. If the child needed help discerning whether their experience was from God, then the parents and/or children's ministry worker, were available to help the child discern.

2. Peers and/or siblings participated in listening to the child share their experience, and sometimes provided feedback on whether they thought the experience was from God. This was done in homes, churches and on 'field trips.'

3. The role which the whole church community took functioned as a generally supportive background, in that they did not find children having revelatory experiences with God out of the ordinary. The children were able to practice hearing from God with the support and encouragement of the larger church community.

All of this provided the potential for support on the back end of the children's revelatory experiences.

The Whole Discernment Process

The community discernment process that emerged as a whole, was one of continual motion as the child moved through the various parts of creating and cultivating the context, a perceived revelatory experience, and receiving coaching through follow-up. The child interacted with various community members as they played various roles at different times.

The size of the teardrops and subsequent crescent shapes do not necessarily represent the amount of participation or roles the members played in every situation in each community. The vicinity of the teardrops and crescents to the child depicts, rather, the general proximity and influence of those members in the life of the child on a general daily basis. At any given time, it may be the parents, peers, siblings, church at large, or the children's ministry leader who is creating and cultivating the context or coaching the child through follow-up. The parents may or may not be the first ones to engage with the child after their revelatory experience.

154 PART II: FORMATION

Figure 2. Child-Community Discernmvent Process Model with Tests

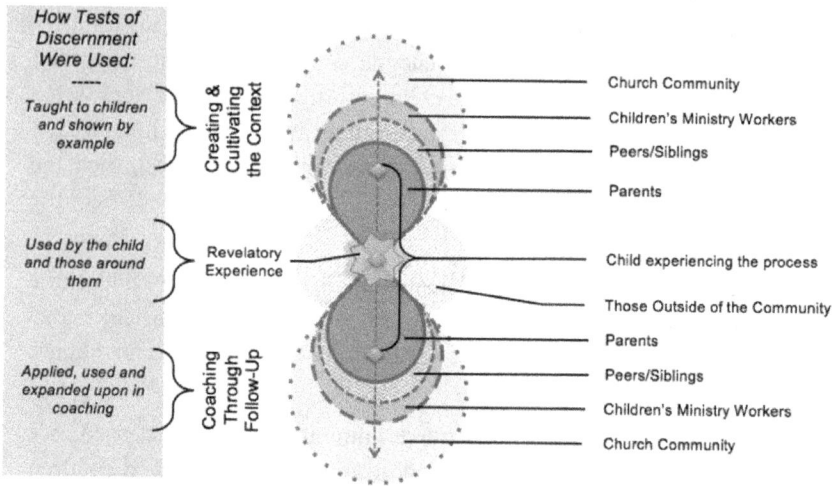

The lower half of the model, the "Coaching through Follow-Up" section *could* also be seen as part of creating and cultivating the context, in that it is part of continuing to provide or cultivate a (generally) safe zone where the children can continue to feel free to share about their experiences, and learn and grow through the discernment process. I have separated "Creating and Cultivating the Context" and "Coaching through Follow-Up" into two halves however, to highlight the timing, showing what was done before and after a child's particular revelatory experience.

Rose's story is a good example of seeing how the two ends of the "Child-Community Discernment Process Model" were evident in one community. I first heard ten-year-old Rose's story from, Rachel, the children's pastor at her church. During the worship times at their church services, Rachel is often up at the base of the stage, participating with the children in expressing worship through singing and dance. In her words, she helps "the kids engage in worship." One particular service, she looked over at Rose worshipping and found Rose with head raised, eyes closed, and appearing to be totally tuned in to something other than her surroundings. Rachel also said she strongly sensed the presence of God during that worship time and particularly on Rose. After their class was over that day, a beaming Rose came up to Rachel and told her she'd had her "first contact with Jesus" earlier during worship. Rose went on to tell how she had seen Jesus and was so drawn to him that she could think of wanting nothing else other than Jesus and worshipping him. Rose said that prior to this experience, she had never felt like she'd had a personal relationship with Jesus. That evening, however, she felt power when Jesus appeared to her. In Rose's own words, she elaborates how she felt afterward:

> I was listening to Rachel preach, I couldn't pay attention, and every single word was like, was like stale . . . except the word "Jesus." . . . I just felt a joy filling, filling me that entire evening . . . it was just . . . an incredible joy . . . I've never felt anything like it. It was like, you can be joyful if you just got an invitation to a party . . . but it isn't the same thing.

Rachel encouraged Rose to tell her parents about her experience, and Rose did when she got home. As Rose told me her account of the experience and what had followed, there were times she searched for descriptive words to use, or a clearer understanding of what had happened, or what the results of the experience meant for going forward in her life. As Rose shared, Rachel, and Rose's mother joined in the conversation, telling what they had previously discussed with Rose about what had happened and how they believed she could continue to cultivate this relationship with God. They continued to give input and discuss it further with Rose during the interview as well. It was obvious this was an ongoing discussion. The two women were honest and open about their relationships with God and what they believed God was doing in Rose's life through this experience, and yet they admitted they also didn't have all the answers. They let Rose know they were on the journey together with her to know and understand God and his ways. Rose's younger siblings sat or milled around the table where we were talking during the interview as well, evidence that the context of expectation and understanding how God works and speaks was being cultivated in their family as a whole, as well as in the context of the larger community.

When specifically asked about how the adults helped to mentor their children to learn to hear from God (create and cultivate the context), Rose's mother shared that as a family, they read the Bible "several times a week and talk about" it, they "play worship music . . . go to church pretty regularly . . . pray for each other" and

> More than anything, God is a natural part of our everyday life. There's nothing we do every day or even every week but we maintain relationships with God, and our kids see that and get invited to do the same. He's very real to us and is our biggest priority. Walking that out and making life decisions based on a Biblical mindset is something the kids see and hear us [the parents] doing.

Rachel was also asked how she believed their children's ministry helps mentor children into hearing God's voice. Her first answer was "consistency," that "almost every week" they

> provide a time during our corporate worship and preaching, for the kids to have personal interaction with Jesus . . . Many kids have powerful experiences with the Holy Spirit during these encounter moments. I often give them an opportunity to share what God is doing and that helps for me (and other teachers) to pastor them through the encounter. This also gives a chance for the other kids and teachers to be encouraged with what God is doing in our midst.

Rachel went on to say that they teach weekly lessons on related Bible stories, and they reinforce that the Bible "is the living Word of God". They also specifically train their kids to prophesy and pray by the power of the Holy Spirit.

Rose was supported on all sides by family, community, and peers who had an expectation that God could and would encounter children. The children at her church were given space to experience God as well as opportunities to minister to others. They are followed up with support, coaching, encouragement, and further teaching.

Using Follow-Up to Work Through Negative Community Impact

Though the majority of community input was supportive, there were also times when, unintentionally, it was not. Eight-year-old Jenna experienced some unintentional negative impact from her church community's response. However, her family was able to guide and coach her through the negative experiences. In one of their church services, the pastor had asked if anyone in the congregation had something from God to share with everyone. Jenna believed she did, so her parents let her go forward to share with the church. This showed that the entire community had created and was cultivating the context through welcoming child participation. After Jenna told the church what she believed God told her to share, members of the congregation were incredibly encouraging to her to the point that some of them were almost fawning over her. Because of this, Jenna decided to keep going forward each week to share something more with the congregation. She was enjoying all the attention. Her parents however, did not think that everything she was sharing was from God. Her father wanted to encourage Jenna and not shut her down from taking risks, but also wanted to help guide her. He asked her if she thought all of the things she had shared were from God. Jenna admitted she thought only some of them were from God, and the others she had made up. He helped Jenna come to her own conclusion to share only what she believed God had given her. The father trusted his daughter to be able to largely discern for herself. He also took the negative impact of the congregation and was able to coach her through making related decisions.

During the family's interview, Jenna also shared how she once took a picture she believed God had given her to draw, up on stage to show the congregation. The congregation had apparently laughed at her (because they thought she was so cute and precious, according to her parents), but she shared how she'd taken it as if they were making fun of her. She hadn't shared with the congregation since then. Upon realizing this during the interview, her parents gently helped Jenna to see the congregation had not been making fun of her. After that "coaching" discussion, Jenna showed renewed interest in sharing with the congregation once again.

It cannot be known if or how long it would have taken Jenna's parents to realize, under other circumstances, what had hurt Jenna's feelings and kept her from sharing since then. However, the coaching that occurred during the interview session became a firsthand glimpse into the community "coaching through follow-up" part of the process.

Conclusion

This research showed (and was backed by current non-academic literature), that the children in these selected charismatic churches were actually expected to be able to participate in the discernment process themselves. In anticipation that the children could and would have revelatory experiences with God, the community created and cultivated a context for this by teaching the children how to discern for themselves and providing opportunities for the children to practice hearing from God. After the children had revelatory experiences, the community coached the children through follow-up; creating space where the children could share about their experiences and be aided in discerning, understanding, and applying what they experienced.

References

Baker, H. A. 1950. *Visions beyond the Veil*. 12th English ed. Minneapolis: Osterhus.
Fischer, Becky. 2008. *Redefining Children's Ministry in the 21st Century: A Call for Radical Change*. Mandan, ND: Kids in Ministry.

Glanville, Karissa L. 2016. "Community Discernment: Discerning the Legitimacy of a Child's Revelatory Experience with God." PhD Dissertation, School of Intercultural Studies, Fuller Theological Seminary.

Harper, Mark. 1999. *Children of the Holy Spirit: How to Set Your Child's Heart on Fire for God*. Sauk Rapids MN: Mark Harper Ministries.

La Guardia, Lenny. 2007. *Releasing Children in Praise & Power: 1 of 6*. International House of Prayer.

Lane, Vann. 1998. *Children of Revival*. Shippensburg: Destiny Image.

Mapes, Patricia, and Greg Mapes. 2009. *Raising Spiritual Children: Cultivating a Revelatory Life*. Dayton, OH: Nexus Institute.

Robeck, Cecil M., Jr. 1994. "Discerning the Spirit in the Life of the Church." In *The Church in the Movement of the Spirit*, edited by W. R. Barr and R. M. Yocom, 29–49. Grand Rapids: Eerdmans.

Toledo, Jennifer. 2012. *Children and the Supernatural*. Lake Mary, FL: Charisma House.

Walters, David. 1995. *Children Aflame*. Macon, GA: Faith Printing.

Williams, Jeri. 2009. *Raising Prophetic Kids . . . Who Escort Heaven to Earth*. San Clemente, CA: Mashack.

Chapter 14

Spiritually Coping with the Bind between Trauma and Ambiguous Loss as Experienced by Foster Children

Ron Bruner &
Chase Thompson

Every year, thousands of foster children leave their families of origin following trauma experienced within their family. That trauma may take the shape of neglect, physical abuse, sexual abuse, exposure to a criminal or drug culture, or other life-threatening event. Whether a family causes trauma or inadequately protects children from it, safety for healing sometimes requires separation from family, at least for a time. Either the family or state authorities may place the children with foster families or in a residential childcare facility. Unfortunately, these post-traumatic stress disorders (PTSDs) lower children's level of functioning and slow their healing while in care. Some contend placement outside of the home is also traumatic and compounds the problem (Richardson 2012).

Although the symptoms look like those of trauma, we suggest that therapists and youth workers should not interpret the effect of familial separation to be episodic trauma, but instead to be ambiguous loss, a concept developed by Pauline Boss (1999). Distance from beloved family members—sometimes even the offender—creates a situation where loved ones are physically absent but persistently present in the child's mind. This reality creates a bind; the child needs distance from family to heal from trauma but, because familial separation causes ambiguous loss, the child experiences more deeply-reduced levels of functioning that further inhibit recovery, reconciliation, and reunification. Behavioral issues often worsen.

The family or community in which these children are placed should expect that such youth will test, occasionally severely, its hospitality—whether intentionally or not. Bruce Perry clarifies the problem:

> The responses of traumatized children are often misinterpreted. . . . Attempting to take control of what they believe is the inevitable return of chaos, they appear to 'provoke' it in order to make things feel more comfortable and predictable. Thus, the 'honeymoon' period in foster care will end as the child behaves defiantly and destructively in order to prompt familiar screaming and harsh discipline. . . . This response to trauma can often cause serious problems for children when it is misunderstood by their caretakers. (Perry and Szalavitz 2006, 55)

For the community, tests of safety are a call to remain vulnerable, to offer a balanced hospitality, and to give hurting youth treatment and resources that empower them to respond to their trauma and ambiguous loss (Bruner 2015).

Definition of Terms

In this chapter, we use the term "foster care" to include either placement with a foster family or a residential childcare facility. "Foster child" describes a minor in care outside the family of origin between infancy and eighteen years of age, regardless of their placement location. "Caregiver" describes an adult who cares for youth in foster contexts.

Because we build on Boss's theoretical constructs, we define several terms in ways coherent with her work. "Stress is defined as pressure on the status quo of a system" (Boss 2006, 35). For Boss, coping skills normally operate in the normal tension created by stress. When individuals or systems have the necessary resources to meet stress and attain "flexible equilibrium," that is resilience. Traumas break equilibrated tension by exceeding the individual's coping skills. "Coping skills are frozen; defense mechanisms fail" (35). This coheres with Serene Jones's characterization of trauma: "A traumatic event is one in which a person or persons perceive themselves or others as threatened by an external force that seeks to annihilate them and against which they are unable to resist and which overwhelms their capacity to cope" (2009, 13).

Ambiguous loss takes two shapes (Boss 1999). The first form includes individuals or families with a family member remaining physically present but psychically absent—an Alzheimer's patient, for one. The second type involves individuals or families with a family member physically absent but psychically present—a prisoner of war, for example. This second type also describes foster children. Boss connects ambiguous loss and the experience of a foster child, but does not discuss treatment issues specific to their situation (Boss 2006).

Although ambiguous loss is a subset of trauma, Boss differentiates ambiguous loss from episodic trauma by asserting that trauma is an internal emotional/physical, mind/body response to an overwhelming external threat; and that ambiguous loss has external relational causes. Where most trauma tends to be episodic, appropriately eliciting the narrative of the trauma event is key to the treatment plan (Ford & Cloitre 2009), ambiguous loss is an ongoing relational loss with no apparent ending or closure (Boss, 2006).

Boss details numerous ways ambiguous loss presents itself. Because of inherent uncertainty, children are "baffled and immobilized" (1999, 7). Immobilization compounds a low level of functioning. Existing relationships become "frozen" because the child cannot experience closure on lost relationships. Ambiguous loss may freeze out new, helpful relationships as well. The child experiences no communally supportive rituals (such as a funeral) because there has been no death. The "absurdity of ambiguous loss reminds people that life is not always rational and just," so bystanders often withdraw instead of offering support (8). Because ambiguous loss has no apparent ending, sufferers become physically and emotionally exhausted.

Treatment

Children entering foster care frequently suffer from PTSD and require appropriate therapy. The responsibility of caregivers is to provide a safe environment and resources to make normalcy possible, even if the child does not accept them. The therapist works with the child to address PTSD itself, which is a difficult process. Judith Herman describes it in this way:

> Recovery unfolds in three stages. The central task of the first stage is the establishment of safety. The central task of the second stage is remembrance and mourning. The central task of the third stage is reconnection with ordinary life. Like any abstract concept, these stages of recovery are a convenient fiction, not to be taken too literally. They are an attempt to impose simplicity and order upon a process that is inherently turbulent and complex. (155)

Unfortunately, the reduced level of functioning caused by ambiguous loss further inhibits the efforts of foster children to feel safe and to remember and mourn their trauma narrative. Children struggle to reconnect with ordinary life because they cannot imagine life away from their birth family as ordinary or normal.

Consequently, the distance necessary to empower safety and healing from PTSD often causes children to experience ambiguous loss, creating a bind between the PTSD and ambiguous loss diagnoses and complicating the therapist's search for healing. The therapist must work on two different but interrelated diagnoses at once: PTSD and ambiguous loss. Although therapists must maintain personal control of PTSD therapy, they can recruit the aid of caregivers in addressing ambiguous loss using relational methods within placement contexts that bring resiliency (Boss 2006). In sum, the child should have a unique therapeutic relationship with a licensed professional, but also work with a community of others who provide support and build resiliency. Boss calls this the psychological family.

Resiliency

Resilience is a complex concept connecting context (with negative and positive factors), processes (perception, reframing, changing environments, active coping) and internal resiliency factors (spiritual, cognitive, emotional, physical, and behavioral). Kumfer and Summerhays model a resilience framework that includes spiritual coping as a way for at-risk youth to adapt and reintegrate after stressors (2006). Researchers have also documented the effectiveness of spiritual coping in coping with loss and trauma, though some have noted that not all coping techniques are helpful (Pargament 2002). We assert that—as a part of culturally competent practice—caregivers and counselors can ethically assist children with positive spiritual coping techniques coherent with the child's cultural background and personal experience (Lum 2011). Many foster children possess a personal spirituality and emerge from a familial culture of spirituality that can empower coping with separation using spiritual practices. Accessing the work of Pargament and others (Pargament, Koenig, & Perez 2000), we will outline potential spiritual coping mechanisms that cohere with Boss's therapeutic goals for ambiguous loss and build skills for resilience after treatment.

Applying the Therapeutic Goals of Boss for Ambiguous Loss in Foster Care

According to Boss, coping skills normally operate within the normal tension created by stress. Traumas break that tension by exceeding the coping skills of the one experiencing trauma (2006). By working on coping skills, though, the therapist and child can both work toward the therapeutic goals of Boss and build virtuous habits out of these practices that will serve the child as he or she encounters stress. To improve coping skills and resiliency, Boss outlines six specific goals for those experiencing ambiguous loss: finding meaning, tempering mastery, reconstructing identity, normalizing ambivalence, revising attachment, and discovering hope. Identifying specific practices (listed below) within these categories and inserting them as goals within the plan of care for the child can lead to relief from ambiguous loss. We develop these concepts for children in foster care below.

Finding Meaning

Boss lists a number of ways for clients to find meaning (see Table 1: Comparison of the Categories of Boss & Pargament). Most of these practices are often, if not necessarily, connected with human spirituality. Most correspond with spiritual coping mechanisms described by Pargament, Koenig, and Perez (2000). Therapist and client do not need to use all of them; they need only access those positive methods that work for the client. Not all spiritual meaning-making approaches are effective.

Table 1. Comparison of the Categories of Boss and Pargament

Ways to Find Meaning Boss (2006, p. 83)	Religious Coping Strategies Pargament et al. (2000)
Naming the problem	
Dialectical thinking	
Religion and spirituality	Benevolent religious reappraisal +
	Punishing God reappraisal –
	Demonic reappraisal –
	Reappraisal of God's powers –

"+" indicates a positive coping method;
"–" indicates a negative or ineffective coping method

Forgiveness	Religious forgiving +
Small good works	Religious helping +
Rituals	
Positive attribution	
Sacrifice for a great good or love	Active religious surrender +
Hope	

"+" indicates a positive coping method;
"-" indicates a negative or ineffective coping method

We have observed that children who can describe their faith narrative in a more detailed way tend to lean more toward spirituality as a coping mechanism. "Grandmother always took me to church." Or, in contrast: "I only went to VBS every year for the cookies and Kool-Aid." In qualitative studies, though, researchers have found that adolescents struggle to tell their spiritual stories (Dean 2010; Sonnenberg, Visser-Vogel, & van Wijnen 2016). Perhaps this is because adults in many faith fellowships are inexperienced and inept at doing this (Bruner & Chancey 2013) and have not socialized their children in telling their own life narratives. Some youth experiencing at-risk circumstances tend not to care much about finding meaning or control, perhaps because their environment has been so chaotic it seems futile to seek either meaning or control.

For treating PTSD and ambiguous loss, the establishment of safety in the welcoming stage of treatment is fundamental. That safety empowers vulnerable youth to reveal their trauma narrative to their counselor in the second stage of PTSD counseling and allows the community to help make meaning of the larger-life narrative in building coping skills for ambiguous loss. Children will only tell that story if the community remains open to hear it and avoids minimizing or repressing it (Cohen, Mannarino, & Deblinger 2006). To encourage positive spiritual coping, the community can help the child through a "benevolent religious appraisal" (Pargament, Koenig, & Perez 2000).

Tempering Mastery

Mastery describes a person's sense of control over his or her own life (Boss 2006). Mastery is a powerful moderator of stress and an effective response to depression. It mitigates feelings of vulnerability in stressful settings and, because it can behave as a "self-fulfilling prophecy," empowering one to move forward (Boss 2006, 100). Boss asserts, though, that one can have too much or too little of it; too much and one can attempt fixing an impossible situation; too little and one might avoid action which could might be helpful. Our experience with young men in care is that they tend to the extremes; they either behave as if they have control of their situation when—in actuality—legal authorities do, or they resist making any attempt at control over circumstances or actions that might lessen stress or lead to healing and reconciliation. Learning to "temper" mastery would be a highly useful skill for them.

Boss proposes a number of strategies to temper mastery: recognizing that the world is not always just and fair, recognizing where views of mastery originate, externalizing the blame, decreasing self-blame, identifying past competencies, managing and making decisions, increasing success experiences, softening attribution, and accepting (sometimes) what will not change, having (sometimes) a sense of invincibility, knowing the exceptions, reconstructing rituals, and mastering one's internal self (2006). Therapists and clients must work together to choose strategies that are personally and contextually appropriate.

One spiritual coping skill we suggest to help temper mastery through Boss's strategies listed above is a practice that Pargament, Koenig, and Perez find to be positive: collaborative religious coping (2000). Those who used this skill tried to understand their situation with God's help, worked together with God toward a solution they perceived God to desire, or felt that God was already working with them to deal with their situation. At the same time, it is neither therapeutically helpful nor theologically accurate to assert that a youth's situation is a result of "God's will." This approach is a negative coping skill that constitutes "passive religious deferral" or "punishing God reappraisal" in the language of Pargament (2000). The therapist and the community must be prepared to help youth discern that not everything that happens in this world is God's will (Gen 4:1–16). Because humans have free will, they can choose paths that God would not choose (2 Kgs 13:16–19). This freedom does not diminish the sovereignty of God but highlights the God-given ability of humans to construct a meaningful narrative alongside this powerful Creator.

Reconstructing Identity

"Identity is defined here as knowing who one is and what roles one will play in relation to others in the family and community" (Boss 2006, 116). When removed from their family, ambiguous loss requires children to rethink identity questions involved with self-understanding and relational roles. Removal can eliminate one negative identity: scapegoating. Frequently for the identified patient in the family system, removal can empower the family to realize this child was not the source of their problems.

Reconstruction of identity for adolescents in care is complex. Adolescents are at a developmental stage where identity remains an open question; they may even be identity diffuse, a state lacking any real search for a commitment to identity (Marcia 1980). Adolescents experiment with various identities and risky behaviors to find a personal narrative and identity (Lightfoot 1997). Complicating progress are the adolescent's construction of multiple moral selves to deal with differing ethical demands of their social microsystems (O'Keefe 2014).

Robert Dykstra connects the effectiveness of the therapeutic environment for troubled youth with its ability to provide safety and hope to empower change (1999). Troubled adolescents struggle, though, to separate their self-image from that of their dysfunctional family system and discern between a true and false self-image, thus becoming "brittle" when facing change. If they unintentionally succeed in growing, they frequently subvert the new behavior and revert to old habits and identities. In their exercise of personal boundaries, two extremes dominate; either their self will be so porous that anyone can enter their life and flavor their conduct with outrageous behavior, or else their self will acquire an impenetrable shell restricting intimate conversation. "The boundaries of the disordered self seem opened entirely to invasion from another, or cordoned off by shame or rage from every intimate relation with another," asserts Dykstra (1999, 82).

Church camps, wilderness treks, and retreats empower spirituality as a means to positive identity reconstruction (Henderson & Bialeschki, 2008). Church camps often provide adolescents the environment, community, and time for serious consideration of identity. Youths can discard false identities and discover or rediscover positive identities by reconstructing their identities using spiritual relationships with God, with their peers, or with a congregation.

Normalizing Ambivalence and Revising Attachment

Religious faith does not necessarily better equip people to cope with ambivalence. Boss describes the problem.

> Therapists at my workshops frequently ask, "Isn't tolerance for ambiguity simply faith in God?" The answer is that yes, it is for

> some people, but the correlation between religious faith and tolerance for ambiguity is, in my experience, far from perfect. People with strong religious beliefs often show little tolerance for ambiguity; people with little religious faith may have a higher tolerance. . . . I pay less attention to specific religious beliefs and more attention to the more global beliefs and values that affect one's tolerance for ambiguity. (2006, 73)

Among the methods to normalize ambivalence, two methods connect strongly with the spiritual: reassessing and reconstructing the psychological family, and seeing the community as family (2006). "Theologians," Boss says, "deal with the reality of death, and psychologists and sociologists study ambiguity and ambivalence: We should come together" (155). When we understand death and ambiguity, it allows us to reconstruct a psychological family. People can remain important and present in our minds, even though they are physically absent, and we can cope with that ambivalence for a sustained period.

The church community or a segment of it—such as a foster family—can serve as an additional family in the life of a young person separated from the biological family. This move enacts Pargament's spiritual coping through comfort/intimacy with others and through closeness to God (2000). While the new family serves as a conduit of resources and relationships empowering survival and even flourishing, the young person becomes a functionally-necessary part of that body (Rom 12). It is essential that this newer family does not attempt to usurp the title or the unique significance of mother, father, or sibling in the family of origin. Regardless, church and foster families can remain significant to youth long after they have moved on to their adult life.

Revising attachments requires similar adjustments. In foster placements, close physical connection with family is not possible and closure of those relationships is not desirable. Boss explains that in such an ambiguous loss "the therapeutic goal is for a perceptual shift in the relationship—one that accepts the ambiguity and uncertainty of absence and presence" (2006, 164–65). For youth in foster care, the ambiguity is most often about how long the relationship is to remain suspended. As they see that their progress in healing brings the potential of reunification, they can—with more resilience—bear with temporary loss. For those for whom reunification is not legally possible, they must revise their attachment in view of their own need for safety and for their parent's need to change or to avoid incarceration.

Discovering Hope

For foster youth to discover hope, their caregivers must personally model it for those in their care. This is frequently challenging because, as Dykstra notes, "Troubled young people, after all, can pose an almost limitless range of potential tests of safety to those who would assist them, but from this intense and intricate relational dance is fashioned embryonic hope" (1997, 86).

Ultimately, Dykstra asserts, some youth experience such a depth of suffering that they can only begin to understand hope by looking backward from the resurrection brought by Jesus Christ. "The cross demands that ultimate hope must never be identified with wishful thinking or escapist behavior but instead be grounded in the suffering and shame of embodied human life. The resurrection, on the other hand, insists that . . . no abandonment in life or death will be able to separate God from God's creation" (89). To be truly therapeutic, though, youth and their therapeutic community must hope for more than some fond anticipation of an eternal heaven, but actively work alongside God to change the truth of current reality into a piece of that promised future. This concept relates to at least two coping concepts outlined by Pargament: "searching for comfort and reassurance through God's love and care," and "looking to religion for assistance in finding a new direction for living when the old one may no longer be viable" (Pargament et al. 2000, 524). Even spiritually attuned youth, though, often need assistance to see these as viable pathways to healing.

Conclusion

This chapter explains the powerful bind in which PTSD and ambiguous loss can overwhelm children in foster care. Removal from the home is sometimes necessary for the safety or benefit of the child, but this choice has side effects. Our work points to a deliberate course of action to untangle that consequential bind, using Boss's framework and the spiritual coping methods that cohere with it. Future work will continue exploration of potential methods for the therapist and community, enacting this methodology more broadly in the field, and working through emerging challenges.

References

Boss, Pauline. 1999. *Ambiguous Loss: Learning to Live with Unresolved Grief*. Cambridge, MA: Harvard University Press.

———. 2006. *Loss, Trauma, and Resilience: Therapeutic Work with Ambiguous Loss*. New York: Norton.

Bruner, Ron. 2015. "The Hospitable Community: A Trauma-Sensitive Environment for Children and Youth." *Journal of Child and Youth Care Work* 25, pp. 106–19.

Bruner, Ron, and Dudley Chancey. 2013. "Spiritual Health and Coping across Three Generations of Faith." National Council on Family Relations, San Antonio, TX.

Cohen, Judith A., Anthony P. Mannarino, and Esther Deblinger. 2006. *Treating Trauma and Traumatic Grief in Children and Adolescents.* New York: Guilford.

Dean, Kendra Creasy. 2010. *Almost Christian: What the Faith of our Teenagers is Telling Us About the American Church.* NewYork: Oxford University Press.

Dykstra, Robert C. 1997. *Counseling Troubled Youth.* Louisville: Westminster John Knox.

Ford, Julian. D., and Marylene Cloitre. 2009. "Best Practices in Psychotherapy for Children and Adolescents." In *Treating Complex Traumatic Stress Disorders: An Evidence-Based Guide,* edited by C. A. Courtois and J. D. Ford, 59–81. New York: Guilford.

Henderson, Karla A., and Deborah M. Bialeschki. 2008 "Spiritual Development and Camp Experiences." *New Directions for Youth Research: Theory, Practice, Research* 118, pp. 107–10.

Herman, Judith. 1992. *Trauma and Recovery: The Aftermath of Violence from Domestic Abuse to Political Terror.* New York: Basic.

Jones, Serene. 2009. *Trauma and Grace: Theology in a Ruptured World.* Louisville: Westminster John Knox.

Kumpfer, Karol L., and Julia F. Summerhays. 2006. "Prevention Approaches to Enhance Eesilience Among High-Risk Youth." *Annals of the New York Academy of Sciences* 1094, pp. 151–63.

Lightfoot, Cynthia. 1997. *The Culture of Adolescent Risk-Taking.* New York: Guilford.

Lum, Dorman. 2011. *Culturally Competent Practice: A Framework for Understanding Diverse Groups and Justice Issues.* 4th ed. Belmont, CA: Brooks/Cole.

Marcia, James E. 1980. "Identity in Adolescence." In *Handbook of Adolescent Psychology,* edited by J. Adelson, 159–87. New York: Wiley.

O'Keefe, Theresa. 2014. "Competing Value Worlds: The Felt Reality of Emerging Adults." Association of Youth Ministry Educators, Chicago, IL.

Pargament, Kenneth. 2002. "The Bitter and the Sweet: An Evaluation of the Costs and Benefits of Religiousness." *Psychological Inquiry* 13, pp. 168–81.

Pargament, Kenneth, Harold Koenig, and Lisa Perez. 2000 "The Many Methods of Religious Coping: Development and Initial Evaluation of the RCOPE." *Journal of Clinical Psychology* 56, pp. 519–43.

Perry, Bruce, and Maia Szalavitz. 2006. *The Boy Who Was Raised as a Dog: And Other Stories from a Child Psychiatrist's Notebook: What Traumatized Children Can Teach Us about Love, Loss, and Healing.* New York: Basic.

Richardson, Ralph. 2012. "Reconciling Youth in Residential Care to their Families." Christian Scholars' Conference, Lipscomb University, Nashville, TN.

Sonnenberg, Ronelle, Elsbeth Visser-Vogel, and Harmen van Wijnen. 2016. "Reconstructing Faith Narratives: Doing Research on the Faith of Adolescents." *Journal of Youth and Theology* 15, pp. 23–43.

Chapter 15

Nurturing Spirituality in Children Whose Parents Are Incarcerated

— Holly Allen, Carly Brandvold, —
Alana Lauck, & Erin Trageser

Zoey is an eleven-year-old girl who currently lives with people she refers to as her grandparents, though they are not biological relatives. Zoey's mom is in prison; her father died a year ago. Zoey's two younger sisters live with her, and she also has three half- or step-siblings who do not live in the house permanently, but have lived there from time to time. Zoey's uncle also lives in the house with them.

Serena is a ten-year-old girl whose mother is in prison. Serena has four siblings; she and her younger sister live with their aunt and two cousins. Serena's two older brothers live with another aunt, and her baby brother lives with her grandmother. Her father is not involved with her life at this time.

Cici is an eight-year-old girl who lives with her grandparents. Her mother is in prison and her two siblings are in foster care. Her father is not in her life at this time. Her grandmother is diabetic and is in a wheelchair; Cici likes to help her grandmother with jobs around the house.

In the fall of 2015, the five students in a children's spirituality course at Lipscomb University in Nashville, Tennessee spent ten hours with children whose parents are incarcerated. Zoey, Serena, and Cici (all pseudonyms) were among the five children in our study. Nurturing Spiritual Development in Children is an academic junior-level course that also functions as a "SALT" (serving and learning together) course, that is, a service-learning venture in which Lipscomb faculty and students work collaboratively with community partners. The community partner with whom we cooperated is Tennessee Prison Outreach Ministries (TPOM). TPOM offers in-prison services for incarcerated adults, re-entry services for returning citizens, and mentoring and summer camp programs for children whose parents are incarcerated.

Literature Review

More than 1.7 million children in the U.S. have an incarcerated parent in a state or federal prison (Glaze & Maruschak 2010). Approximately 120,000 incarcerated mothers and 1.1 million incarcerated fathers are parents with minor children ages 0–17 (The Pew Charitable Trusts 2010).

"There is no doubt that parental incarceration, in most contexts, represents a significant risk factor for children's antisocial behavior and adult offending," state the authors of a comprehensive cross-national analysis of effects of parent incarceration on children (Murray et al. 2014, 144). These authors clarify that a *risk factor* is something that yields increased risk for an outcome, but does not necessarily *cause* the outcome. Parental incarceration has been associated with depressive symptoms, aggression, delinquency, social exclusion, academic difficulty, lower cognitive functioning, and isolation as well as PTSD, abandonment, attachment, and anger issues (Johnson & Easterling 2012; Murray et al. 2014). In addition, parental incarceration increases the risk of children living in poverty and experiencing household instability (Phillips et al. 2006).

The children in our small study exhibited several of the difficulties outlined above; in the following brief literature review, we will offer insights regarding PTSD symptoms that may manifest as well as the shame and stigma that children of incarcerated parents may internalize. In addition, since all of the participants in our study had a mother who is in prison, we will explore the literature that examines risk factors for children whose mothers are in prison, rather than fathers.

Though the risks are evident, not all children whose parents are incarcerated exhibit academic difficulty, delinquency, depression, aggression or the other common outcomes listed above. Some display remarkable resiliency and become well-adjusted adults; key *protective* factors include "social support from non-family members, positive parent-child relationships, *religiosity*, a positive sense of self, and other external support systems that may reinforce a child's coping efforts" (emphasis ours; Nesmith & Ruhland 2008, 1121). In light of the focus of the course and our study, the last portion of the literature review will explore religiosity and spirituality as protective or mitigating factors for children whose parents are in prison.

PTSD in Children of Incarcerated Parents

Posttraumatic Stress Disorder (PTSD) is a "specific type of anxiety disorder that can occur after a horrifying traumatic event" (Grogan & Murphy 2011, 58). Common characteristics of PTSD can be re-playing or re-experiencing the trauma through vivid memories, nightmares or flashbacks, avoiding anything related to the trauma, emotional numbing, and hyperarousal, such as irritability, constant fear, or continual scanning for threats (Wethington et al., 2008).

Children whose parents have been incarcerated may develop PTSD after witnessing their parents commit a crime and/or be arrested. In one study of 192 incarcerated parents, 40 percent of parents reported that their children had been present at the arrest (Harm & Phillips 1998).

One reason this event may be traumatic to children (beyond actually being present during the arrest) would be that their parent was taken away with no explanation provided to them. Also, some children report "feeling as if they too were in trouble and under arrest because they [also] were taken away from their homes in police cars, held at police stations while waiting for someone to come get them, or detained in emergency shelters" (Phillips & Zhao 2010, 1246).

Long-term effects of PTSD from parental incarceration can include aggressive behavior, embarrassment that leads to poor social interactions, sleep disturbances, insomnia, and developmental delays such as immature speech or muteness especially in young children (Grogan & Murphy 2011).

Stigma and Shame Associated with Parental Incarceration

Keva Miller has been writing researching and writing about children whose parents are incarcerated for a decade (see e.g., Miller 2006; Miller 2007; Miller et al. 2017). Miller (2006) reports that children's caregivers tend to ignore the fact that the family member is incarcerated, and concludes that children's awareness of their caretakers' avoidance of discussing their parents' imprisonment contributes to children's understanding of society's stigma regarding criminal behavior and incarceration. Miller (2006) notes that 75 percent of the children they interviewed had "little or no emotional support to discuss their feelings and thoughts about their mother's incarceration" (477).

In their study with children whose parents are incarcerated, Nesmith and Ruhland (2008) came to similar conclusions; most of the children in this study said that they attempted to keep their family business private, explaining that the reason they did so was because it was the expectation of their caregivers.

Shame is an affective response to stigma; according to Condry (2007), shame is an "emotion at the core of stigma. It is . . . a key emotion felt by the stigmatized" (63). Miller (2006) found that children experienced intense shame and fear "that individuals may reject them because of their parent's actions . . . To protect themselves, children attempt to avoid rejection by withdrawing from meaningful relationships" (477).

Thus, the stigma and shame that these children feel may contribute to the isolation that is common in this population.

Effects of Mother's Incarceration

Though there are far more men in prison than women, and more fathers than mothers, it was the mother of each of the five children in our study who was in prison. This section of the literature review examines some of the unique issues that have surfaced in the case of a mother's incarceration compared to a father's incarceration.

A survey of incarcerated parents found that 9 out of 10 children whose fathers are in prison are living with their mothers, while almost half of the children whose mothers are incarcerated are living with a grandparent (Glaze & Maruschak 2010). Most children whose mothers go to prison were living with their mother before the incarceration; a few fathers become the primary caregiver, but because the mother often was not living with the father when she went prison, caregiver arrangements and home environments are likely to change—perhaps dramatically; some go to grandparents, other relatives, or close family friends. Some go into foster care.

"Attachment theory states that a child develops into a healthy, functioning adult in the context of a continuous relationship with and emotional attachment to a parent figure" (Hairston 2007, 18). Key years of growth and development for these children will occur apart from their mother, opening doors for abandonment and attachment issues to develop (Hairston 2007).

Religiosity and Spirituality as Protective Factors in Children

Though many children whose parents are in prison display problematic behaviors or attitudes, not all children do. Current research is examining what factors can encourage resilience in children who have faced adversity in their lives ranging from homelessness and economic disadvantage to survivors of war, terrorism, and disaster. Ann Masten's (2015) *Ordinary Magic: Resilience in Development* summarizes and synthesizes the best research on resilience in children and adolescents.

In her decades of research, Masten has constructed a list of "widely reported factors associated with resilience in young people" (2015, 148). Most of the factors on her list are ones that students in a one-semester course cannot influence or affect (e.g., intelligence, access to effective schools and neighborhoods); however, Masten describes one factor that can be addressed in a short-term setting: "Resilience is associated with hope, optimism, faith, and belief that life has meaning" (2015, 164).

Furthermore, Nesmith and Ruhland (2008) connect *religiosity* to resilience, noting that church and faith were important to many of the children in their study of children whose parents are incarcerated; "church offered an immediate support group while their faith helped them feel that their struggles had a deeper meaning" (1127). Prayer played a role as well: "I pray," says one interviewee. "It helps me calm down, because I have to talk sometimes and I say a prayer and it just goes away" (Nesmith & Ruhland 2008, 1127).

And last, the authors of the chapter "Resilience and Spirituality in Youth" indicate that multiple studies of resilience report faith and spiritual *support* as protective factors in children and youth who face overwhelming adversity (Crawford, Wright, & Masten 2006).

Because resilience research connects religiosity, faith, hope, belief, church, prayer, and spiritual support to resilience in children living in difficult circumstances, our class chose to seek ways to nurture spirituality in the children we worked with who have a parent in prison.

What Do We Mean by *Spirituality*?

A central process in the children's spirituality course—and for nurturing children spiritually in any setting—is constructing a working definition of children's spirituality. Because Lipscomb is a Christian university, TPOM is a Christian ministry, and the children we worked with have been part of TPOM's ministry in the past, we initially examined definitions of spirituality that are explicitly Christian. However, we wanted to construct a definition that can be used by those who work with children in governmental or other secular settings where a definition of children's spirituality from a Christian perspective would be problematic; it is being acknowledged, as noted above, that children, especially children from hard places, need every physical, intellectual, psychological, emotional, social, and *spiritual* resource available to them to survive and to thrive. Thus, a broad definition of children's spirituality usable by persons working with children in any setting is: *a quality present in every child from birth out of which children seek to establish relationship with self, others, world, and God (as they understand God)*. This definition offers a foundation from which to create opportunities to nurture the inherent human quality of spirituality that aids holistic well-being and survival.

The spirituality umbrella can also embrace the broad concepts of faith, belief, church, prayer, and hope that are referenced in the resilience studies above. Though we paid special attention to the children's relationship with themselves, others, and God, various questions and student-child activities tapped into the children's knowledge, feelings, and practices regarding church, faith, belief, prayer, and hope.

Methodology

We met with the five children in our study on four Saturdays from around 10:00 to 1:00 or so. The children were: Shoranda, age seven; Cici, age eight; Claire, age nine; Serena, age ten; and Zoey, age eleven. Shoranda and Serena are sisters; Claire and Zoey are sisters as well.

A TPOM advisory board member, Vickie Keen, who has worked with TPOM's summer camp program for children whose parents are incarcerated, selected the children and distributed the research permission forms to the participants' guardians. Each Saturday, Mrs. Keen picked up the girls in her mini-van and brought them to the Lipscomb University campus where we met in a classroom.

On the first Saturday, the Lipscomb students (also called mentors in this chapter) shared some of their own story along with pictures of their families and interests. We walked around the campus and showed the girls the campus fountain, the massive sports arena, various classrooms, and the cafeteria. We ate in the cafeteria (Lipscomb's College of Bible and Ministry had allotted funds to cover lunches for participants and the Lipscomb students). Over the course of the four Saturdays, as the students talked and listened to the girls, the children became more comfortable spending time and conversing with their mentors, making it very easy to experience a variety of relational activities. Over the four weeks, the student-child pairs

- Read books together

- Drew pictures of what they think God is like
- Participated in two Godly Play stories
- Wrote letters to God
- Asked questions
- Talked about God in swings on campus
- Ate together
- Prayed together
- Shared life stories
- Walked the labyrinth at Scarritt Bennett Center, an educational center near Vanderbilt University

Along the way, the Lipscomb students asked questions from an interview protocol. They also took careful notes each Saturday, recording what the children said, the stories they shared, the responses to the interview protocol, and the questions the children asked; the mentors also noted body language and other non-verbal signs they observed in the children. From these notes and observations, connections to the literature findings were made.

Results

As our class became familiar with the common difficulties associated with children whose parents are incarcerated, (e.g., depressive symptoms, aggression, delinquency, social exclusion, academic difficulty, lower cognitive functioning, and isolation; PTSD, abandonment, attachment, and anger issues; also, poverty and household instability), we began to see indications of some of these issues reflected in the girls in our study.

PTSD Symptoms

Several of the girls displayed some of the known PTSD symptoms. To our knowledge, none of the girls had been diagnosed with PTSD, nor did we attempt to treat or address the signs of PTSD we saw in the girls. Cici reported a repeated nightmare:

> In my dream. I am with my mom, and a dog is wanting to attack us. I keep yelling to my mom for her to run, but she won't. I yell, "Don't you care about me?" And she says, "I don't care if we get killed."

Cici says that she has this same dream very often and it is always the same. She always wakes after the dream and has trouble going back to sleep.

Three of the participants expressed fears of death. When Alana asked Serena what she prays for, Serena said, "I try to pray every night that I will wake up in the morning"; Shoranda, Serena's sister, expressed a similar fear. Zoey, the oldest of our participants, said, "I'm afraid to die and leave others." While this may stem from the recent death of her father, it also may correlate with her mom leaving the children for prison as well. In Zoey's case, her fear of death and loss is also intertwined with her concern for her sisters whom she would leave behind.

Stigma and Shame

The most obvious way we discerned that some of the girls felt the stigma and shame of having a parent in prison is that three of the girls never—not even once—indicated that their mother is in prison (Miller 2006; Nesmith & Ruhland 2008). We knew this information only because Mrs. Keen chose these children from those whom TPOM serves; we never knew the circumstances of the imprisonment, the prison location, the specific charges, or the sentences.

The only time Cici referred obliquely to her mother's absence was when she told Jessica (her Lipscomb mentor) that her dream vacation was to go to New York. Jessica asked her who she would go with, and Cici said, "I want to go with my momma, . . . but I know that won't ever happen." Jessica said that Cici seemed very downcast after this conversation.

Serena and Shoranda (sisters) were especially reticent regarding their family situation; they were quiet and reserved, opening up more toward the end of our time together, but clearly unwilling to speak about their mother's situation. When Shoranda drew her family, she showed her father living elsewhere, but she drew their mother with them—at their aunt's house.

In contrast, the other sisters, Zoey and Claire, were very open about their father's death, and the fact that their mother was in jail, and that they visited her only occasionally. They seemed unaware that others might find their circumstances troubling or stigmatic.

Effects of Mother's Incarceration (as vs. Father's Incarceration)

As noted earlier, none of the girls is living where they were before their mothers were imprisoned. Their lives were clearly disrupted; all five are living in a new setting, away from their mothers (as well as their fathers); also, all of them have siblings who do not live with them.

Erin noted that Claire has trouble dealing with the fact that her mother is away from her. One of the first conversations Claire and Erin had was about their favorite things. Erin shared a couple of her favorite things; Claire chose her mom. She said her favorite activities to do with her mom were jumping on the bed, running through fields, and snuggling in bed. Erin asked Claire how often she gets to see her mom, and with a wistful tone, she said, "Not often enough." Both Cici and Zoey referred to their mothers longingly, though neither Shoranda nor Serena mentioned their mom.

Nurturing Spirituality in the Participants

As we analyzed our data, some of the themes that emerged tapped into our definition of children's spirituality, specifically, the children's relationship with self, others, and God. Other themes related to spirituality also surfaced including belief, church, prayer, faith, and hope.

Nurturing the Child's Relationship with Self

All of the Lipscomb students reported conversations that revealed their children's understanding of themselves.

Zoey responded to the Good Shepherd Godly Play story in an unusual way; many children identify with the sheep in this story, connecting the Good Shepherd with a parent or with God, or with Jesus. However, as Zoey and her mentor, Carly, were de-briefing the story, Zoey said, "This story makes you think about what kind of shepherd you want to be;" Zoey went on to say that she wants to be "a shepherd that protects." Carly concluded in her final reflection paper that Zoey feels responsible for her sisters, and even her mother; Zoey articulated this self-appointed role in her family in identifying with the Good Shepherd.

Early in their time together, Serena told Alana that she loved science and math; Serena would sometimes show Alana her math homework, and Alana realized that Serena indeed possessed a keen understanding of the algebraic math she was completing. Over the four weeks, as the girls became familiar with the Lipscomb campus, Serena asked Alana several questions about going to college, and on the last day, Serena announced, "I think I could go to college." Nurturing this strong sense of self is a key piece in fostering spiritual development in children.

Others

Each of the girls revealed ways they relate to others, in their homes, at school, with friends, and at church. Claire has a best friend; Cici takes care of her grandmother when she needs help; Zoey feels responsible for her family; and both Serena and Shoranda disclosed their perception of how "church people" are supposed to act.

After participating in the Good Samaritan Godly Play story, Serena asked questions about the priest and Levite who passed by the injured man. Alana explained to her that they were "church people." Serena's immediate reaction was an incredulous: "They church people!?" It was clear that she believed the "church people" should have offered help.

God

Throughout the four Saturdays, there were multiple opportunities to gently unpack the God-child relationship, for example, during the letter to God, the drawing of God, the various forms of prayer, and the interview questions about God.

Jessica reported that initially Cici seemed reluctant to talk about God. During the first couple of weeks while they sat in the campus swings working through the interview protocol Cici hesitated before responding to some of the questions, and she shared no church experiences during their conversations. Jessica gathered from these observations that Cici's background included few formal faith experiences. In her final report, Jessica wrote, "It was quite touching on our last Saturday, that after we came out of the school cafeteria, [Cici] saw a swing on the campus, and she looked up at me and eagerly asked, 'Are we going to sit in the swing and talk about God?'"

Erin's conversations with Claire revealed Claire's complex relationship with God. Claire told Erin that she receives written notes from God and the devil: God writes positive notes in a rainbow-colored pen ("You passed your test! Here's your grades: all A's.") and the devil writes negative notes in a red pen ("You got all F's."). Very importantly, Claire said she has told other people about these notes, but everyone just seems to laugh it off. Erin listened intently.

Other religious/spiritual themes

One of the most interesting conversations of the semester was a dialogue with Shoranda as she responded to a few questions from the interview; this conversation tapped into all three relational themes as well as broader religious categories such as belief and faith mentioned by Masten (2015, p. 148).

Interviewer: Do you know anyone who knows God?

Shoranda: *Yeah, my friend Princess. She knows God.*

Interviewer: What makes you think Princess knows God?

Shoranda: *Well, she got baptized.*

Interviewer: So someone who gets baptized knows God?

Shoranda: *Well, I guess so, but I got another friend—her name is Paige—and she got baptized, but she don't act like it.*

Interviewer: What do you mean?

Shoranda: *She don't act like she's been baptized.*

Interviewer: How is someone who gets baptized supposed to act?

Shoranda: *Well, not like that!!*

There was a pause in the discussion.

Shoranda: *Do you know anyone who knows Jesus?*

Interviewer: Yes.

Shoranda: *Do you know Jesus?*

Interviewer: Yes, I know Jesus.

Shoranda: *Good, then I got some questions. Why do you think he is our king?*

Interviewer (responded with a few sentences): Do *you* know Jesus?

Shoranda: *Yes, but I don't always act like it either.*

Interviewer: How do you mean?

Shoranda: *Well, sometimes I don't act right.*

This multi-layered conversation with Shoranda took place during the third week of the study, before which Shoranda had been generally quite reserved about religious things. The conversation revealed several insights about Shoranda's religious and spiritual life: she switched the focus of the discussion from God to Jesus; she referenced baptism and the life change she thought it should bring; she evaluated her friends' behaviors—and her own; she asked her mentor a theological question.

Though this was a particularly rich discussion, insightful, even profound, spiritual conversations happened each time we gathered.

Discussion and Conclusion

One crucial point that has not been addressed in this chapter is that researchers in the field of children's spirituality have noted that children are "aware that there is a social taboo on speaking about spirituality" (Hay & Nye 2006, 132). In the Western secularized world, children's spirituality is usually suppressed, even repressed, and children become aware early on that expressed spirituality is inappropriate. Alana reports in her final reflection paper:

> I remember on the first day when we were just getting to know each other, I mentioned that Lipscomb is a Christian school, and this class was in a way a Bible class. On hearing this, Serena's facial expression was a mix of confusion and uneasiness. I believe that this was because she was not used to religious conversations. In our first two meetings, she continued her uneasiness whenever I addressed spiritual matters. She did not like to open up to me about her views on God. However, by our third meeting she seemed much more open to religious discussions. She told me about her prayer for safety and what she thinks God looks like ("He has big ears so he can hear everything").

Perhaps the most important thing that happened during the Saturdays the five Lipscomb students met with the five children is that conversations about spiritual things were welcomed and encouraged. Though there are few resources available for this neglected population (children whose parents are incarcerated), the government agencies that do provide psychological, financial, sociological, or other types of support do not typically offer opportunities for spiritual nurture.

If religiosity and spirituality can be connected to resiliency, as research indicates, creating opportunities for children in difficult circumstances to discuss with others their beliefs, their hopes, their faith, and their relationship with self, others, and God can foster that crucial protective factor of resiliency in these at-risk children.

In the fall of 2015, during four Saturdays on Lipscomb University's campus, five girls whose mothers are in prison spent ten hours of one-on-one time with caring college students who listened to them, prayed with them, encouraged them, and believed with them. As Shoranda, Cici, Claire, Serena, and Zoey peer into their futures, their experiences with prayer and contemplation along with open discussions about God, faith, hope, and belief can anchor them and contribute to their resilience despite their tenuous circumstances.

References

Allen, Holly Catterton. 2002. "A Qualitative Study Exploring the Similarities and Differences of the Spirituality in Children in Intergenerational and Non-Intergenerational Christian Contexts." PhD diss., Talbot School of Theology.

Braman, Donald. 2004. *Doing Time on the Outside: The Hidden Effects of Incarceration on Families and Communities.* Ann Arbor: University of Michigan Press.

Condry, Rachel. 2007. *Families Shamed: The Consequences of Crime for Relatives of Serious Offenders.* Cullompton: Willan.

Crawford, Emily, Margaret O. Dougherty Wright, and Ann S. Masten. 2006. "Resilience and Spirituality in Youth." In *The Handbook of Spirituality Development in Childhood and Adolescence,* edited by Eugene C. Roehlkepartain et al., 355–70. Thousand Oaks, CA: Sage.

Glaze, Lauren E., and Laura M. Maruschak. 2010. "Parents in Prison and Their Minor Children." Bureau of Justice Statistics Special Report. Washington: US Department of Justice.

Grogan, Sherry, and Kathleen Pace Murphy. 2011. "Anticipatory Stress Response in PTSD: Extreme Stress in Children." *Journal of Child and Adolescent Psychiatric Nursing* 24, pp. 58–71.

Hairston, Creasie F. 2007. "Focus on the Children with Incarcerated Parents: An Overview of the Research Literature." Annie E. Casey Foundation.

Harm, Nancy J., and Susan D. Phillips. 1998. "Helping Children Cope with the Trauma of Parental Arrest." *Interdisciplinary Report on At-Risk Children and Families* 1, pp. 35–36.

Hay, David, and Rebecca Nye. 2006. *The Spirit of the Child.* Rev. ed. London: Kingsley.

Johnson, Elizabeth I., and Beth Easterling. 2012. "Understanding Unique Effects of Parental Incarceration on Children: Challenges, Progress, and Recommendations." *Journal of Marriage and Family* 74, pp. 342–56.

Masten, Ann S. 2015. *Ordinary Magic: Resilience in Development.* New York: Guilford.

Miller, Keva M. 2006. "The Impact of Parental Incarceration on Children: An Emerging Need for Effective Interventions." *Child and Adolescent Social Work Journal* 23, pp. 472–86. doi:10.1007/s10560-006-0065-6

———. "Risk and Resilience Among African American Children of Incarcerated Parents." 2007. *Journal of Human Behavior in the Social Environment* 15, nos. 2–3, pp. 25–37. doi.org/10.1300/J137v15n02_03

Miller, Keva M., et al. 2017. "Variations in the Life Histories of Incarcerated Parents by Race and Ethnicity: Implications for Service Provision." *Smith College Studies in Social Work* 87, pp. 59–77.

Murray, Joseph, et al. 2014. *Effects of Parental Incarceration on Children: Cross-National Comparative Studies*. Psychology, Crime, and Justice Series. Washington, D.C.: American Psychological Association.

Nesmith, Andrea, and Ebony Ruhland. 2008. "Children of Incarcerated Parents: Challenges and Resiliency, in Their Own Words." *Children and Youth Services Review* 30, pp. 1119–30. doi:10.1016/j.childyouth.2008.02.006

Pew Charitable Trusts: Pew Center on the States. 2010. *Collateral Costs: Incarceration's Effect on Economic Mobility*. Washington, DC: Pew Charitable Trusts.

Phillips, Susan D., and Jian Zhao. 2010. "The Relationship Between Witnessing Arrests and Elevated Symptoms of Posttraumatic Stress: Findings from a National Study of Children Involved in the Child Welfare System." *Children and Youth Services Review*, 32, pp. 1246–54.

Phillips, Susan, et al. 2006. "Disentangling the Risks: Parent Criminal Justice Involvement and Children's Exposure to Family Risks." *Criminology and Public Policy* 5, pp. 677–702.

"Promoting Social and Emotional Well-Being for Children of Incarcerated Parents: A Product of the Federal Interagency Working Group for Children of Incarcerated Parents." 2013. Frederick: MD: Children of Incarcerated Parents Partnership, June.

Wethington, Holly R., et al. 2008. "The Effectiveness of Interventions to Reduce Psychological Harm from Traumatic Events among Children and Adolescents: A Systematic Review." *American Journal of Preventive Medicine* 35, no. 3, pp. 287–313.

Wilhoit, James. 2008. *Spiritual Formation as If the Church Mattered: Growing in Christ Through Community*. Grand Rapids: Baker Academic.

Yust, Karen M. 2003. "Toddler Spiritual Formation and the Faith Community." *International Journal of Children's Spirituality* 8, no. 2, pp. 133–49

Chapter 16

Intergenerational Community Service as a Means toward the Spiritual Formation of Children

 Joseph P. Conway ———

In recent decades, teen ministry leaders have sought to reverse age segregation trends and consumerist tendencies. Many approaches to spiritual formation had surrounded the teen with numerous activity options among peers but offered few opportunities to engage with more than a few token adults or regularly serve others. In recent years, "intergenerational" and "multigenerational" have become buzzwords, and teen ministries have drastically increased their emphasis on consistent community service and justice work. The results in teen ministry have been encouraging, and many have wondered about the ramifications for children's ministry as well as the church at large.

Youth Ministry as we know it, especially in Protestant circles, has long mimicked public education by separating kids from adults and teaching them at their level. Organizations like Young Life and Youth for Christ emphasized games, fun, and emotion in mostly age segregated atmospheres. While many came to know Christ in this setting, the emphasis on individualism and pop culture (leveraging cool) has offered diminished returns in recent years. Specifically, an increased theological shallowness accompanied by lower retention rates has brought alarm.

Research on Intergenerational Ministry and Spiritual Formation

In his *The Juvenilization of American Christianity*, Thomas Bergler speaks to these trends. While traditional teen ministry clearly rested on good intentions, Bergler calls out the "unintended consequences and unquestioned assumptions" (Bergler 2012, loc. 99). Instead of teens becoming like adults, it has led to the widespread embrace, by both adults and teens, of immature faith (Bergler 2012, 80). Bergler points to both consumerist trends bordering on spiritual narcissism as well as the widespread decline in biblical literacy and creedal awareness.

In similar fashion, Kenda Creasy Dean wrestles with the results of the influential National Study of Youth and Religion in her work *Almost Christian* (2010). In this groundbreaking study, researchers came to label the faith of many Christian teens and parents as Moralistic Therapeutic Deism (MTD), in contrast to orthodox Christianity. To reverse these trends, both Dean and Bergler point to the continued relevance of teen ministry while calling for significant changes in methodology and attitude. Bergler prophetically states, "Youth ministries will continue to serve as crucial laboratories of religious innovation" (Bergler 2012, loc. 2916). Wholeheartedly, I agree. The answer does not lie in discontinuing youth ministry. Rather, we must continue its strengths while addressing its weaknesses. As Dean says,

> "We have known for some time that youth groups do important things for teenagers, providing moral formation, learned competencies, and social and organizational ties. But they seem less effective as catalysts for consequential faith, which is far more likely to take root in the rich relational soil of families, congregations, and mentor relationships where young people can see what faithful lives look like, and encounter the people who love them enacting a larger story of divine care and hope" (2010, 11).

The message is clear. We must change the way we do youth ministry.

The church should not abandon teen ministry, but rather, find a way to spiritually form teens in the midst of a holistic ecclesiology. Teens need adults. The generations must be brought back together. As Bergler argues, "Only intergenerational communities of people devoted to mature Christianity can build seawalls high enough to hold back the tide of juvenilization that has now risen high enough to threaten all of us" (Bergler 2012, loc. 286). Of course, after years of age segregation, the implementation of intergenerational models proves intimidating. However, adults should be encouraged that teens desire this. As Dean reminds us, "The NSYR testifies to young people's willingness, even eagerness, to hang out with adults who support and encourage them" (Dean 2010, 121). Moreover, adults should be encouraged by studies that show measurable results. A Baylor University study on faith retention cited the highest faith retention rate among teens participating in ongoing community service and reflection alongside adults (Sherr et al., 2007).

I encountered many of these resources halfway through a decade of full time teen ministry (2000–2011). These insights meshed with my personal observations, and as I adopted a more intergenerational approach with an emphasis on service, I saw clear changes in both teens and parents. Consistent intergenerational community service creates depth and retention. The connection between beliefs and behavior comes out in challenging cultural moments of service. When one experiences the brokenness of this world in the midst of a community need, hard questions must be asked. This often spurs one on toward spiritual answers and resources, which leads to rich foundations of Scripture and doctrine. After making this shift, I observed spiritual formation the likes of which I had never seen in youth ministry. Together, teens and adults did more than just read the Scriptures, pray, and sing. With that foundation, they planned, executed, and reflected on concrete spiritual experiences of service. This allowed them to practice what they preached. Ideas previously seen as abstract doctrine became concrete practice. The Bible came alive. Theology became relevant. Faith deepened.

Having experienced this among middle and high school students, I began to wonder how far down one could apply intergenerational service. Would it offer similar results in children's ministry? Two things led me to this. First, I began having my own children and sought a more meaningful church experience and spiritual formation process for them. Second, I found myself as the sole minister at a small congregation with numerous children but no teenagers. This represents the story I want to tell.

Pursuing Spiritual Formation through Intergenerational Service

The Acklen Avenue Church of Christ is a small, revitalized congregation one-mile from downtown Nashville, Tennessee. After their facility flooded in the 2010 Flood, they experienced a year of displacement and discernment. When they returned in 2011, they brought a renewed commitment to community service and city engagement. A couple of months after their return, I became their preaching minister. Acklen possesses a unique demographic. At the time, our congregation of 100 had 40 children but no teenagers. It was common for children to equal or outnumber adults at services and events. The church voiced two main goals: serve the city and spiritually form the children.

At face value, those goals seemed in conflict. Urban ministry involves time, something many families of young children often lack. Urban ministry involves late nights, hard work, and situations that may not be safe or sanitized. Certainly, serving the city and forming the children would be separate goals. But they did not see it that way. Indicative of many small churches, they did not have a history of age-segregated ministry. Youth ministry trends, and the ensuing juvenilization, had never impacted them. Out of both necessity and conviction, they already practiced a level of intergenerational ecclesiology that exceeded most congregations.

Therefore, in a congregation that already embodied intergenerational habits, I sought to extend the emphasis on consistent intergenerational community service as a means of spiritual formation from teens to younger children, even preschool age. This small, urban congregation with a high percentage of young children asked how they could simultaneously serve the city while maintaining their commitment to intergenerational ecclesiology, thus reframing their desire for intergenerational service not as a problem to overcome but a tool toward spiritual formation. They sought to offer faith practicums for young families, where parents and children could prepare, execute, and reflect on service within the overall context of bible study and prayer.

From 2011–2016, the congregation applied understandings of intergenerational spiritual formation through community service in two main ways. First, the congregation accelerated their involvement with a local ministry, Room in the Inn. This local ministry connects the unhoused to churches offering hospitality every night from November 1 through March 31. Hundreds of churches in Nashville participate in this ministry. While Acklen had done this some before, they committed to a regular weekly night. More than just that, Acklen applied an intergenerational model to the ministry.

The children play a lead role in this hospitality ministry. On the first Sunday in November, when the overnight ministry begins, the children all come to the front during morning worship. They lay hands on all the pillows, which will be used by our guests. We pray that God will work through us and bless those who lay their heads in our space. We consistently reference the "least of these" of Matthew 25 as well as "entertaining angels" from Hebrews 13. In our evenings of hospitality, the kids help bring out the mattresses. Together, adults and kids make the beds. They set out our bins of toiletry kits and clean clothes. When our guests arrive, they sit at a common table with them. We all go around and introduce ourselves, and then, we join hands in prayer. On the nights when we host a family instead of singles, they play with the children. Afterwards, our kids participate in the clean-up process. All ages work together. The kids serve as an essential part of the team.

Beyond this ministry, Acklen pursued intergenerational spiritual formation through community service in a second way. Instead of a traditional, building-centered Vacation Bible School, the congregation implemented a Mission Week each summer, full of field trips and service opportunities. Each night of the week, families took their children out into the city for serving and learning experiences. Over the years, this has included short homeless immersion experiences, educational site visits, prayer walks, scavenger hunts, visitation, nature hikes, as well as numerous meals and supply deliveries. Every year, on the first night, we have a prayer service at our building and then hike up a hill overlooking Nashville. Everyone brings a picnic dinner as we look out on the city. We invoke the many "mountain" stories of the Bible and talk about the need to see the city so we can pray for and love the city.

Let me explain further some of our Mission Week experiences. One year, we did a Matthew 25 prayer drive. We loaded kids and adults up on two buses. Then, we drove to sites in the city representing the categories of Matthew 25: Hungry and Thirsty (soup kitchen), Stranger (homeless shelters and bus station), Naked (Goodwill), Sick (local hospitals), and Prison (city jail). As we drove by each site, we pulled over or circled while the kids prayed over the sites and people. Another year, we did a scavenger hunt through an area greatly impacted by poverty and immigration trends. Kids and parents had to find certain bus stops, ethnic grocery stores, houses of worship (both churches and mosques), immigration service offices, and Western Unions. In the car, families discussed trends in the neighborhood and prayed about how they could bless immigrants and those in poverty. The scavenger hunt ended with a shared meal at an ethnic restaurant indicative of the neighborhood. One year, we conducted what we called an Acklen World Tour. At our building, members from different countries decorated classrooms with mementos from their home countries. Kids rotated between Peru, Ukraine, Romania, and the United Kingdom. In each room, the host talked about their home culture, faith practices in their country, and shared snacks indicative of their culture. Families spent time in prayer for the global church, as well as those not in a relationship with Jesus. Lastly, one year, a street chaplain took adults and older kids/teens on a prayer walk through homeless camps and other sites indicative of the unhoused experience. In this brief immersion experience, they met and prayed with several individuals. All of these experiences offered time for parents to dialogue with their child beforehand and reflect afterward. We have found that the before and after conversations bring lasting power to the experience.

Most of these experiences connected with Acklen Partners. We reserve this designation for community ministries where someone in our body works full time, serves on the board, or has a long-standing relationship. At this time, Acklen Partners include local ministries focused on homelessness, healthcare, literacy, refugees, and educational opportunities for those behind bars. We contribute budgetary funds to them as well as consistent service. Therefore, all of our intergenerational service pursuits connect with a consistent ongoing relationship. We strive to avoid episodic relationships. Our church works with an Acklen Partner every month, so Mission Week represents a condensed highlight, not the totality of our intergenerational service.

Outcomes of Pursuit

From our increased involvement with Room in the Inn as well as Mission Week, the church experienced four main outcomes. First, we discovered what types of service work well for young children. As one might expect, projects involving manual labor, intense time commitments, and late evening hours did not work well. Also, overnight events as well as long drives present challenges for families with small children. We quickly crossed off things like Habitat for Humanity as well as anything involving leaving the city. Moreover, anything that takes intense adult focus, such as tutoring, proves difficult with kids.

However, we have excellent experiences with hospitality, field trips, visitation, collections, and deliveries. We feed groups in our building, and we often take food to other groups. Kids can help prepare, deliver, eat, and clean up from a meal. Also, we periodically take tours of ministries with which we regularly serve and contribute. Recently, we took a tour of Siloam Family Health Center. One of our members serves on the board, and our church makes an annual donation. Families came with supply donations, and we took a brief tour of their facility. In a similar manner, visiting and singing for the elderly works well for us. In addition, our families regularly make supply kits for city ministries. Children enjoy collecting supplies, putting them together, and understanding how they are used.

Of course, in our discovery process, we had several honest talks on safety. Not surprising, safety concerns represent one major reason why urban ministry and children's faith formation often exist as separate practices.

We assessed the safety of every ministry, and discerned ways to assuage concerns. For example, Room in the Inn does not screen out sex offenders. Likely, every child in our church has eaten a meal with a sex offender. At first hearing, that causes anxiety. We had to decide on safety measures. Our small facility and small number of guests (6) serve as an asset in this regard. It makes it much easier to keep an eye on our children at all times. Also, we rarely host the same guest twice, so familiarity never grows. Of course, we must strive to protect our children, but helicopter notions of protection can stifle faith formation. We have been steadfast in prayer and communal discernment at every step of the process. In summary, we collectively discovered what works well for us.

Second among outcomes, parents experienced clear signs of spiritual formation in their children. Many parents reported that children initiated conversations on poverty, prayed for the homeless on cold nights without prompting, and voluntarily contributed their money to help the poor. At our midweek prayer service, children regularly request that we pray for the homeless. These requests come up more in the winter, when we participate in Room in the Inn. This demonstrates the connected nature of practice and prayer. In both congregational prayer and family prayer at home, children regularly pray about recent experiences. In this way, our intergenerational service has significantly shaped how both the church and family pray together.

A couple of anecdotes demonstrate this further. One night, on the way home from our midweek service, I listened to kids from our church in the back of my van. One was my oldest daughter. The girls enthusiastically brainstormed on a comprehensive plan to end homelessness in Nashville. They were both seven years old at the time. They felt a sense of urgency and felt conviction that others would experience that same urgency. They firmly believed that poverty would end in the city if we all came together to tackle it. I cannot remember their whole plan, but I will just say the plan included them personally calling President Obama. Another story involves my middle daughter. This past winter, she had a stomach bug. One night, she leaned over the toilet as my wife pulled her hair back. Between bouts of sickness, she turned to my wife and asked, "What do the homeless do when they get sick? Who helps them?" Lastly, a friend shared this the other day. Over the past year, we have witnessed a lot of conversation concerning refugees. Our church hosts a community ministry that provides an afternoon reading program for refugee children. During this time, as a 4th grader seeking to process the rhetoric, she connected global events with the refugee children reading in our building. She and her parents had a long conversation about the Scriptures and refugees as they merged our congregation's community service to a global conversation. Our church regularly shares stories like this.

Third, teachers reported that children frequently mentioned these service experiences in bible class. As any teacher knows, the best illustrations center on shared experiences. Our congregation's intergenerational service has become the primary illustration for teaching. When our teachers conduct a lesson on the Good Samaritan or Great Commission, they appeal to recent shared experiences of service. Our class times have become centers of preparation for service and reflection afterwards. Class discussions often center on "How can we join God's mission in the world?" and "How did you see God's love for others when we _____?"

Fourth, early in the implementation of a more focused approach to intergenerational spiritual formation through service, I sought to measure results. A before and after survey (2013 and 2014) revealed key attitudinal changes among parents. I gave the adults a list of positive attributes to separately associate with Jesus, Acklen, and other congregations. After a focused year of strategic intergenerational service, they saw Acklen as more similar to Jesus. Those seeing Acklen as concerned with the poor went up from 86 percent to 94 percent. Also, those who characterized Acklen as "relevant" went up from 40 percent to 50 percent. Moreover, they saw Acklen as more concerned with the poor than other churches. I did not interpret this as judgment or hubris. Instead, I heard them expressing their shift to embrace service more fully than they did previously.

Besides attitudinal changes, I measured shifts in practices. In response to "I have friends who are poor," those marking true or mostly true went up from 36 percent to 41 percent. In response to "I have friends of a different ethnicity," those marking true or mostly true went up from 40 percent to 59 percent. In response to "I think about those who don't know Jesus," those marking quite often or very often went up from 40 percent to 63 percent. Those knowing the names of 8 or more people on their street went up 40 percent to 56 percent. In response to "I give money to non-profits that are not churches," those marking quite often or very often went up from 33 percent to 43 percent. Finally, I asked several questions related to number of times a person volunteered during the year, with and without the congregation. Volunteerism went up about 10 percent in all areas.

In conclusion, these represent exciting times in congregational ministry. Recent shifts to move away from age segregation and inward focused programs to an intergenerational embrace with a focus on outward service have proven effective. Positive trends of intergenerational spiritual formation through service can and should be extended from teens to younger children. While it remains too soon for our congregation to measure faith retention and depth of orthodoxy in contrast to MTD, we have seen clear signs of spiritual formation. Certainly, these renewed approaches present clear and tangible obstacles, but the results prove worth it. Kids should neither be confined to classrooms nor separated from adults. The whole body, full of all ages, should worship, study the Scriptures, and serve together. Kids are never too young to be a part of the body. Kids are never too young to serve others. Intergenerational groups of disciples serving in the name of the Father proves to be one of the main ways the Spirit makes us like the Son.

References

Bergler, Thomas. 2012. *The Juvenilization of American Christianity*. Grand Rapids: Eerdmans,

Dean, Kenda Creasy. 2010. *Almost Christian: What the Faith of our Teenagers is Telling the American Church*. New York: Oxford University Press.

Sherr, Michael, et al. 2007. "Community Service Develops Teens' Faith." Retrieved from www.baylor.edu/alumni/magazine/0503/news.php?action=story&story=45581.

PART III
Culture

Congregations, as do all organizations, have a culture. But like a painting, we see the paint, and forget the canvas on which it resides. Culture conveys the underlying assumptions, values, priorities, and purposes of a congregation, but this is often unspoken and assumed. Likewise, congregations reside within the broader cultural context of their society. In addition, there are more narrow ways in which culture shapes the ministries engaging childhood formation within the church itself.

This section explores the role of congregational culture in forming programs, ministries, and engagements with children. It also explores the broader societal influences, such as technology or children's secular education and the relation of the church's work to this. Similarly, this section explores the symbiotic relationship between the culture of the congregation and the ministries comprising it. The congregation both forms and is formed by the various ministries it implements and supports.

Readings throughout these chapters will bring you to a greater awareness of how culture shapes the church's ministry. You will also explore how culture forms and is formed by the ministry of the churches within its bounds. This exploration will lead you to an appreciation of the cultural context of your congregational and children's ministry.

We can talk of spirituality and both the congregation's and the culture's impact on the deepening of spirituality. That spirituality is a description of the child's relationship with God. Our next conversation then needs to be about ministry. It is ministry that responds to a concern about a child's relationship with God. It is ministry that comprises the activities and programs that grow out of your understanding of spirituality. It is ministry that impacts the spiritual lives of the children you serve as well as the lives of those serving the children.

Chapter 17

A Faith Worth Making

*Understanding the Cultural Nature of
Children's Theology—and Why it Matters*

David M. Csinos

I DIDN'T QUITE KNOW what to say when I heard it. As part of an ethnographic study into children's theological meaning-making and culture, I was getting ready to conduct a focus group with ministers and volunteer leaders at a predominantly white, suburban, middle-class congregation in the United Church of Canada. As we were waiting for other members of the group to arrive, the senior minister and I were chatting about how the project had been going so far. After telling her how grateful I was for her support in the study, she remarked that one person on the church board wondered why I wanted to include their congregation in research about children and inter-culturalism, since, in this person's estimation, their congregation had no culture.

This well-intentioned board member was naming a deep-rooted assumption among individuals and communities who are part of the dominant culture of North America: culture is other to us, we assume; it's something that people who are different from us have, whether because of race, ethnicity, country of origin, sexual orientation, religion, or another marker of human diversity. But, as I will discuss shortly, this simply isn't true. All people are participants in human cultures.

Within the field of children's spirituality and theology, researchers and theologians often neglect culture and cultural diversity. And even those who do give an eye toward culture tend to do so ways that inadequately address its complexity and overlook contexts of cultural diversity.

There are, in fact, four broad ways that scholars in the field address—or do not address—culture (Csinos 2017). First, without placing culture and diversity at the center of their gaze, some scholars speak of them in passing references and offer ideas that are situated within specific, although often unnamed, cultural contexts (Hay & Nye 2009; Westerhoff 2000). A second group of scholars give more concerted attention to culture by studying children's spirituality and theology within a particular cultural context (often a culture based on a shared national or regional context), rather than across different cultures and in contexts of cultural diversity (Dei 2002; Humphrey, Hughes, & Holmes 2008; Hwang 2005; Junker 2006; Kay & Ziebertz 2006; Mason, Singleton, & Webber 2007; Potgieter, van der Walt, & Wolhuter 2009; Savina 2001; Tolbert & Brownlee 2008; Ubani & Tirri 2006). Third, a few scholars address culture in research that explores the lives of children across multiple cultural contexts and amid contexts of cultural diversity (Bosacki & Ota 2000; Moore, Talwar, & Bosacki 2012; Nazar & Kouzekanani 2003; Search Institute 2008). Unfortunately, these studies do not often adequately consider culture as a variable in analyses of knowledge generated through research. The final grid on this landscape—and the one that is most sparsely populated—is made up of researchers who give critical attention to the importance of issues surrounding culture.

This brief overview of how scholars in children's spirituality and theology attend to (and overlook) culture makes it clear that there is a gap in the field. That is, there is a lack of scholarship that pays critical attention to culture and cultural diversity in children's spiritual experiences and theological meaning-making. To address this gap, I have conducted ethnographic theological research into how children make theological meaning in different cultural contexts.

Clarifying Culture

But what exactly is culture? Sociologist Carl James (2010) offers a definition of this term that I rely on because of its sheer breadth. Culture, he says, is

> a concept that refers to the way in which a given society, community, or group organizes and conducts itself as distinguished from that of other societies, communities, or groups. Culture consists of a dynamic and complex set of values, beliefs, norms, patterns of thinking, styles of communication, linguistic expressions, and ways of interpreting and interacting with the world that help people understand and thus survive their varied circumstances. (26)

Culture is anything and everything that combines together to make up the whole way of life of a people group. So even though some people assume culture is something only held by non-dominant members of a society, *we all have cultures*; we are all shaped by and we all shape the cultures in which we participate. We are all cultural participants. And Joyce Mercer (2005) has helpfully pointed out that children—and I would add all people—"exist in multiple cultures that vie for the right to be the dominant force of influence on their lives" (174).

James' definition frees culture from ethnicity, which many people assume to be synonymous terms. Culture certainly involves ethnicity, but it includes a vast number of ways that human beings identify and differentiate themselves from each other. So one can speak of Nigerian culture, Russian culture, and French-Canadian culture; these might be described as ethnic-based cultures. But one can also address Nashville culture, Evangelical Christian culture, Muslim culture, hip hop culture, LGBTQ culture, social media culture, and—most importantly for the research I conducted—congregational culture. Yes, congregations can, in and of themselves, be distinct cultural contexts, with particular sets of "values, beliefs, norms, patterns of thinking, styles of communication, linguistic expressions, and ways of interpreting and interacting with the world," to use James' definition again (2010, 26).

Even our theologies are cultural products. Theology does not exist apart from culture. All of our beliefs, understandings, and practices have been touched by the all-pervasive hands of culture. Theology consists, after all, of human phenomena created, sustained, and cast in stone by cultural beings in response to the particularities of time and place.

Armed with these assumptions, I set out to explore how children make theological meaning amid different cultural contexts. During 2013 and 2014, I engaged in ethnographic theological research at four diverse congregations in the United Church of Canada, each of which self-identified culturally in different ways. They were rural, urban, and suburban; wealthy and impoverished; small to mid-sized; struggling with declining numbers and experiencing ongoing growth; 200 years old and two decades old; white, Ghanaian, Aboriginal, and ethnically diverse. Within anywhere from a few months to a year and a half, I spent time at each of these congregations, participating in worship, helping with Sunday school and vacation Bible school, interviewing approximately five children from each faith community, and conducting focus groups with adult leaders.

Children, Theology, and Culture

At the broadest level, this sojourn has taught me that the ways that children make theological meaning are in many respects reflective of the culture of their broader congregation, especially its theological ethos. For example, at Messiah Methodist United Church, a congregation made up of immigrants from Ghana that blends its Ghanaian background with its contemporary Canadian context, I noticed that the children all freely interwove elements of many faith traditions, including Catholic prayers and aspects of African religions like ancestor worship. They tended to hold that elements of all religions are right in some ways and wrong in others. These assumptions colored the way they generated theology. And each one of these characteristics was central to the broader culture of their congregation. Their children, then, in each congregational setting, made theological meaning in a manner that reflected those of their broader faith community.

This is not to say, however, that the theologies of children were exact mirror images of those of their congregation. Rather, the broader culture of their faith community became a launching point, a place from which the children took their own theological excursions as they made meaning of their experiences, ideas, and contexts in ways that were all their own.

For many readers who have experience in research and ministerial practice with children's theology and spirituality, this may not seem like an earth-shattering assertion. Of course children's theologies are reflective of their broader congregation. But when we really stop to consider this idea, everything changes. When we actually put our presuppositions on hold and consider what these children teach us, — what these children taught me—our common means for researching and ministering with children are disrupted. No longer can we blindly rely on big-box curricula that are mass-produced with no eye for cultural context. Instead, we need to critically attend to the cultures in which we are working and not assume that if a particular program or approach worked well at a church down the road—or on another continent—it will be effective for our congregation, too. No longer can we assume that children are learning the exact theologies we are wanting to impart to them. No longer can we study children's spirituality and theology without attending to culture in intentional ways.

So while at one level, we all know what I learned from this research—children are unique individuals capable of incredibly rich theological thought—it's quite another thing to actually let this reality seep deep into our bones. To do so is to allow our current practices to be turned upside down and inside out. For the remainder of this chapter, I'll discuss how this study challenged me—as a researcher and as a practitioner—to rethink my assumptions and practices.

Rethinking Research

There are a number of challenges that the children in this study offer to those of us who conduct research into children's spiritual and theological lives. Here I will identify three major ways that they call us to rethink research. Yet since, as I believe, practitioners of children's ministry do well to take on the stance of a researcher at times, these challenges are not exclusive to scholars and academics (Csinos 2017).

Theological Products, Theological Processes

There is a significant amount of research in the field of children's spiritual and theology that opens windows into *what* children think. Yet the children who participated in this study call those of us who are researchers to also pay attention not only to the products of their theologies, but also to the process; we need to consider *how* they generate their theologies in the first place.

One of the most interesting dimensions of the processes of children's theology that I observed is that the meaning that they make and the processes by which they make such meaning may yield very different insights into their inner lives. Product and process do not always align in clear and consistent ways.

This was the case among the children at Burke Street United Church, a predominantly white, middle-class, suburban congregation. During my first visit to this congregation, I noticed that two children, Stephen and Rebecca, were Sunday school superstars. They were the ones their teacher could always count on to answer her questions and, for the most part, they could offer the responses she was looking for. Both children were willing to talk about their congregation and their theological ideas, and Stephen in particular displayed both eloquence and a degree of complexity as he shared with me. Yet when I pushed them to go deeper into their thinking rather than simply tell me what they have learned at church, both of them struggled to do so. While the *content* of their theological ideas seemed to showcase degrees of maturity and thoughtfulness, the *processes* by which they created their own theologies were weak and underdeveloped as compared to the ideas they articulated.

On the other hand, some children at Burke Street had a difficult time speaking about their theologies. Nicholas was anything but a Sunday school superstar. He disliked going to Sunday school and at times it was challenging for me to get him to talk about his theological ideas at any length—he seemed like the polar opposite of Stephen and Rebecca. Yet over half-way through our conversation, this boy began to tell me about the struggles he has to believe some of the things he hears about in Sunday school and worship services at this congregation. As I asked him to tell me more about why he believes some things that he hears but not others, he made meaning in ways that demonstrated a desire to engage in deep and rigorous theological thinking as he formed his own parameters for discerning the level of truth and reliability among biblical stories. The *content* of Nicholas' theological meaning-making may have been tenuous, but the *means* by which he generated meaning demonstrated a willingness to think deeply and wrestle with issues inherently wrapped in uncertainty, mystery, and wonder.

Individual Theology, Communal Theology

A second insight I learned from these children is that I cannot only conduct research that considers individual theology, but that I must also leave room for communal theology. Some studies into children's spirituality and theology rely on individualistic research methods, such as one-on-one interviews. In fact, I imagined my own study through interviews with individual children. Luckily, the minister at Parkdale United Church—a highly diverse congregation in terms of ethnicity, nationality, age, sexual orientation, and socio-economic status—required me to interview the children in pairs or small groups. Community is such a vital aspect of this intercultural church that it would have been inappropriate for the interviews to be carried out in individualistic ways.

From this experience, I learned that theological meaning-making can be an incredibly collaborative process. Those children whom I interviewed in pairs or small groups engaged in theological meaning-making through conversations with each other, at times affirming, challenging, and questioning one another's ideas and perspectives on issues such as God, sin, and creation.

This became particularly clear to me when I interviewed Jacob and Enoch. At one point, Enoch said that he once heard that, in his words, "whenever you lie a lightning bolt hits you that God throws at you which you can't really see." After Enoch said this, the other boy, Jacob, didn't seem to think that this matched his experiences. He's lied before, he admits. But he's never been hit by lightning. Instead of discounting Enoch's idea, Jacob demonstrated a willingness to expand his theological imagination in light of this conversation. As the boys continued to speak, Jacob wondered out loud: perhaps the reason he doesn't get struck by lightning when he lies is because he is already aware that he lied. Since he knows he lied, God doesn't need to bring it to his attention with a high-voltage warning. This young boy was demonstrating a willingness to engage in theological meaning that was made in conversation with others, to consider another's ideas and to allow another to engage with his own.

Those children whom I interviewed individually also generated theology through dialogue. Instead of talking with their peers, they created theology with me and my research assistants. In fact, this conversational approach to theology was the most frequent and obvious commonality among all participating children. They engaged in communal processes of theological meaning-making.

But the communal nature of theology among these children didn't stop here. They didn't just use conversation as a key means for theological thinking. At times I had a hunch that the meaning they generated was actually *communal* meaning, created and held collaboratively through discussion among one another. During my conversation three girls from Parkdale, all of them theologically riffed off of each other, finishing one another's thoughts and responding to questions I posed to their peers. Such a communal theological process did not simply involve the mining of individual ideas and experiences; it was a shared and communal practice that unfolded with one another in that very moment.

These young theologians challenge me to study children's theological meaning-making as a communal endeavor. Creating theology can not only be seen as a solo performance, but also as jazz improvisation, a highly relational enterprise. Each child brings her or his own particular ideas and questions and slants to the process of creating theology. And as they put their heads together, new sounds are formed that can't be heard fully apart from what their peers bring to the music.

Cultural Infusion

If, as my research taught me, children's theologies tend to reflect broader cultural contexts, then I had to attend to this at every stage of study. In particular, these children called me to critically attend to culture in the analysis and interpretation of my research. To do otherwise was to risk missing crucial meaning embedded in children's theologies by relying on either a de-contextualized analysis or one that is covertly rooted with the assumptions, norms, and epistemologies that I brought to it.

One of the congregations that I came to know through this project was Colkirk United Church, a small Aboriginal church on a rural First Nations reserve. All the children from this faith community who participated in this study possessed a narrative approach to theology, not only drawing on stories to make meaning, but also using narrative as a means of communicating their theology to me. As I reviewed transcripts of my conversations with these children, I had the sense that the stories they told me were more than just sources for generating and means for conveying theological insights. I wondered if perhaps the stories were the very stuff of their theology. Yet I struggled to make sense of this emerging interpretation, for my pre-existing assumptions surrounding theology caused me to see it as inherently propositional, that is, as something best expressed through arguments. If, for instance, someone asked me about what I learned from my research, I might respond by saying, "The theological meaning-making that children generate seems to be related in many ways to their congregational cultures." This is a fact that I can propose and debate based on the results of my ethnographic study.

The narrative nature of the theology of the children at Colkirk challenge this epistemological assumption. For these children, theology is inherently storied, and I needed to interpret it in a manner that aligned with this reality. Thus, to more fully and accurately make sense of the theologies of these children—and the children from every congregation—I had to attempt to interpret them not through my own epistemological views, but through those that they were offering to me. In this paradigm shift (which I am only partially able to make), my response to the question about my research might consist not in an argument or thesis statement, but in telling a story about my time among these children and their congregations. The story would not demand analysis or explanation. It wouldn't be just an example or description of a particular idea. The story itself would be the response, one left open to those receiving it to do with it what they must.

These children pushed me to attend to culture at every stage of research—from organizing a study to carrying out the fieldwork, from interpreting knowledge generated to communicating it to broader audiences. To more fully honor and more accurately hear the voices of the young people who participated in this research, it was incumbent on me to remain focused on culture and infuse it into every stage of research, piecing together interpretive lenses that reflected their broader cultural contexts. Yet such critical attention to culture is inherently fraught with difficulties, for the field of children's spirituality and theology grew out of and remains rooted in research and assumptions from western contexts. The theologies of these children challenge those of us who conduct research into young people's spiritual and theological lives to identify our presuppositions and explore the field through their eyes.

Disrupting Practice

These children did not only offer insights for those of us involved in research, they also gave clues for how the practice of faith formation can adapt to better engage children in theological meaning-making. Here I will share three ideas surrounding this.

Equipping for Theological Meaning-Making

These children challenge me to put primary emphasis on equipping young people to make their own theological meaning. In the world of children's ministry, there is a tendency for resources, programs, and curricula to focus on giving children particular nuggets of theological content. But the theological meaning-making of these young theologians push back against this instructional style of children's ministry. Each of them demonstrated that theology isn't simply something that children learn through what Paulo Freire (2007) names as a "banking" approach to education. Rather, they actively produce their own theology as they engage in and reflect on their congregations, their life experiences, and the theological ideas that are shared by the people in their lives.

At some of the congregations I studied, children's ministry seemed to focus on imparting specific points or facts to children, and within these churches children struggled to generate their own ideas. We who work with children in congregations and other ministry settings can move away from attempts to teach them particular facts or points and toward approaches that provide them with tools for, and practice in, active theological reflection. Such resources can include a wide variety of sources for theology (such as films, music, stories, etc.) and a number of different approaches for creating theology (such as storytelling and conversation).

Congregational Congruency

These children also called me to more closely examine curricula and models for children's ministry—whether Sunday school, VBS, or other initiatives—in light of broader congregational cultures. There were moments during the research process that I perceived congregations to be engaging in children's formation in a way that contradicted—or even undermined—the broader cultural ethos of their community.

This was most clearly evident at Burke Street United Church, where their model of Sunday school promoted a style of theology that was actually very different from that which the leaders espoused as vital to the wider congregation. While the minister at this church wants to help congregants engage with the stories of the faith for themselves and come to their own meaning, children's ministry focused on rote memorization and learning predetermined answers to specific questions. This lack of congruency between children's ministry and the broader congregational culture seems also to be correlated to the fact that, as I mentioned, some children in this church seemed like Sunday school superstars, but actually struggled to engage in deep theological thinking for themselves.

It is incumbent on leaders, especially within congregations that self-identify as part of the dominant surrounding culture, to become researchers in their own communities and study the multifaceted and complex culture of the entire congregation. Armed with a thick description of our churches, we can become better equipped to examine existing and proposed ministries with children and adapt them to better reflect their wider community. This isn't to say, of course, that this is a one-way street. Our congregations can—and should—be changed by the presence of children as well!

Something to Talk About

Finally, since a primary means through which children engaged in theological meaning-making was conversation, I've learned the importance of providing children with opportunities to talk about their views. Whether with one another or with me, being able to discuss their ideas and experiences gave the children space to reflect on and create theology for themselves. Unfortunately, however, several of the young participants in my study told me that they don't often speak about their deep theological ideas and experiences with others. And even among those who have shared with others, some said that their thoughts were not always taken seriously.

As we engage in conversational practices with children, we would do well to remember a few ground rules that emerge from my research. **First**, we must take children's thoughts seriously and be careful not to judge their theologies as more or less correct—or, worse yet—laugh at them! **Second**, we must be cautious to trust that, even if it's difficult to perceive, children will make their own theological connections and insights, so we don't need to push our own tendencies and assumptions onto them. We can trust the power of the Holy Spirit working in them. **Third**, sometimes children need a bit of encouragement to engage in a conversational approach to theology. They may not dive right in to the process of doing theology, but this might not be because it doesn't matter to them; they may simply need some time to become comfortable and build trust. None of us need seminary degrees or the best curricula to help children make theological meaning. All we need is a listening ear . . . and maybe a few questions to get the things rolling.

An Ethnographic Baptism

When I listened to the children who graciously and vulnerably guided me in this research process, I had the sense that holy moments were brewing. I resonate with Pierre Bourdieu's (1999) assertion that "the interview can be considered a sort of *spiritual exercise* that, through *forgetfulness of self*, aims at a true *conversion of the way we look at* other people in the ordinary circumstances of life" (614). I, too, have been converted by this process. Not only has my work as a researcher and practitioner been altered and challenged and strengthened and questioned, but so, too, has my faith. These children and their congregations have plunged me deep into the waters of their lives and I have arisen from them forever changed.

References

Beste, Jennifer. 2012. "Second Graders' Spirituality in the Context of the Sacrament of Reconciliation." In *Understanding Children's Spirituality: Theology, Research, and Practice*, edited by Kevin E. Lawson, 283–306. Eugene, OR: Cascade.

Bosacki, Sandra, and Cathy Ota. 2000. "Preadolescents' Voices: A Consideration of British and Canadian Children's Reflections on Religion, Spirituality, and their Sense of Self." *International Journal of Children's Spirituality* 5, pp. 203–19.

Bourdieu, Pierre. 1999. "Understanding." Translated by Priscilla Pankhurst Ferguson. In *The Weight of the World: Social Suffering in Contemporary Society*, by Pierre Bourdieu et al., 607–26. Stanford: Stanford University Press.

Couture, Pamela. 2007. *Child Poverty: Love, Justice, and Social Responsibility*. St. Louis: Chalice.

———. 2000. *Seeing Children, Seeing God: A Practical Theology of Children and Poverty*. Nashville: Abingdon.

Csinos, David M. 2018. "From the Ground Up: Cultural Considerations in Research into Children's Spirituality and Theology." *International Journal of Children's Spirituality* 23.1, pp. 53–66.

Dei, George J. Sefa. 2002. "Spirituality in African Education: Issues, Contentions, and Contestations from a Ghanaian Case Study." *International Journal of Children's Spirituality* 7, pp. 37–56.

Freire, Paulo. 2007. *Pedagogy of the Oppressed*. 30th anniversary ed. Translated by Myra Bergman Ramos. New York: Continuum.

Hay, David, with Rebecca Nye. 2006. *The Spirit of the Child*. Rev. ed. London: Kingsley.

Humphrey, Natalie, Honore Hughes, and Deserie Holmes. 2008. "Understanding of Prayer among African American Children: Preliminary Themes." *Journal of Black Psychology* 34, pp. 309–30.

Hwang, Mariana. 2005. "Understanding Korean-American Children's God-Concept in Relation to their Self-Concept Development." *Christian Education Journal* 2, no. 2, pp. 282–301.

James, Carl E. 2010. *Seeing Ourselves: Exploring Race, Ethnicity, and Culture*. 4th ed. Toronto: Thompson Educational.

Junker, Débora Barbosa Agra. 2006. "Resistance and Resilience: Cultivating Christian Spiritual Practices among Brazilian Children and Youth." In *Nurturing Child and Adolescent Spirituality: Perspectives from the World's Religious Traditions*, edited by Karen Marie Yust et al., 449–75. Lanham, MD: Rowman and Littlefield.

Kay, William K., and Hans-Georg Ziebertz. 2006. "A Nine-Country Survey of Youth in Europe: Selected Findings and Issues." *British Journal of Religious Education* 28, pp. 119–29.

Mason, Michael, Andrew Singleton, and Ruth Webber. 2007. "The Spirituality of Young Australians." *International Journal of Children's Spirituality* 12, pp. 149–63.

Mattis, Jacqueline S., et al. 2006. "Ethnicity, Culture, and Spiritual Development." In *The Handbook of Spiritual Development in Childhood and Adolescence*, edited by Eugene C. Roehlkepartain et al., 283–96. Thousand Oaks, CA: Sage.

Mercer, Joyce Ann. 2005. *Welcoming Children: A Practical Theology of Childhood*. St. Louis: Chalice.

Moore, Kelsey, Victoria Talwar, and Sandra Bosacki. 2012. "Canadian Children's Perceptions of Spirituality: Diverse Voices." *International Journal of Children's Spirituality* 17, pp. 217–34.

Nazar, Fatima, and Kamiar Kouzekanani. 2003. "A Cross-Cultural Study of Children's Perceptions of Selected Religious Concepts (Kuwait, the United States, and India)." *Alberta Journal of Education* 49, pp. 155–62.

Ovwigho, Pamela Caudill, and Arnold Cole. 2014. "Making Faith Their Own: Lessons for Children's Ministry from Kids' Reflections on Their Spiritual Lives." In *Exploring and Engaging Spirituality for Today's Children: A Holistic Approach*, edited by La Verne Tolbert, 158–69. Eugene, OR: Wipf and Stock.

Potgieter, Ferdinand J., Johannes L. van der Walt, and Charl C. Wolhuter. 2009. "The Divine Dreams of a Sample of South African Children: The Gateway to Their Spirituality." *International Journal of Children's Spirituality* 14, pp. 31–46.

Reynolds, Thomas E. 2008. "Improvising Together: Christian Solidarity and Hospitality as Jazz Performance." *Journal of Ecumenical Studies* 43, pp. 45–66.

Savina, Elena. 2001. "Soul: What Does It Mean for Russian Children?" *International Journal of Children's Spirituality* 6, pp. 55–65.

Search Institute. 2008. *With Their Own Voices: A Global Exploration of How Today's Young People Experience and Think about Spiritual Development*. Minneapolis: Center for Spiritual Development in Childhood and Adolescence.

Tanner, Kathryn. 1997. *Theories of Culture: A New Agenda for Theology.* Minneapolis: Augsburg Fortress.

Tolbert, La Verne, and Marilyn Brownlee. 2008. "The African American Church and its Role in Nurturing the Spiritual Development of Children." In *Nurturing Children's Spirituality: Christian Perspectives and Best Practices,* edited by Holly Catterton Allen, 320–38. Eugene, OR: Cascade.

Ubani, Martin, and Kirsi Tirri. 2006. "How do Finnish Pre-Adolescents Perceive Religion and Spirituality?" *International Journal of Children's Spirituality* 11, pp. 357–70.

Westerhoff, John H., III. 2000. *Will Our Children Have Faith?* Rev. ed. Harrisburg, PA: Morehouse.

Chapter 18

The Gentle Art of Moving Your Church's Family Ministry from Programs to Process

Trevecca Okholm

> Family ministry is not just a set of programs; it is a perspective, a set of 3-D glasses we put on to look at everything the church does. Ministering with families, then, does not mean simply developing a system of programs and support services but, instead, reviewing every aspect of congregational life to determine its impact on and support of families.—Diana Garland, 2012

Walking Away from Church

BEING A NORTH AMERICAN children's and family ministry practitioner in the last couple of decades of the twentieth century and into the dawning years of the twenty-first century, I found myself, alongside others in my field, wondering just when and how the church in my era had apparently gotten the focus wrong on how to form faithful Christ-followers who would remain in our churches and want to raise their own children there. The second half of the twentieth century was the era of flashy programs with cool theme-oriented meeting spaces and state-of-the-art curricula and resources. So, why, we asked ourselves, would so many young people who had gone through our programs now want to walk away from the church . . . and often walk away from their faith? These are the questions we started to ask even as we continued to buy into the ministry hype offered to us at a plethora of youth and children's ministry conferences and websites. After all, the best the church's cultural accommodation had to offer could not be wrong . . . right?

The point of this chapter and the questions I hope will begin to engage you as you read are: *What are the inherent dangers of primarily offering programs in our ministry?* and *What's the big deal about process?* Lutheran pastor, Tim Wright (2015) suggests a couple of other questions to engage our thinking. He asks that we stop right now in our frantic search for the next best advertised program we can try and ask ourselves. What is our ultimate call? Is it to create programs? Or is it to raise disciples (i.e., followers of Jesus committed to his church and his world)? And, just what might that calling to raise *churched* disciples look like? I can tell you, it looks more like the messy process of doing life together across our church members' ages and stages than it looks like programs and segregated spaces for youth, children, singles, and seniors to be ministered to by age and stage and affinity.

Historical Context

It is not enough to simply discuss the ways in which a process-based approach to ministry differs from a program-based approach without taking a brief look back at recent history of the church and the cultural influencers that affected the ministry from mid-twentieth century to today, primarily in the area of how to do ministry with youth and children. Timothy Paul Jones (2009) describes church administration of the twentieth century as being dominated by what he describes as a *segmented-programmatic* style of ministry that so enveloped the church's view of how to train children and youth in the Christian faith that many church members cannot imagine any other approach. In less than a two-century period, between the 1800s-2000s, this segmented-programmatic paradigm of ministry became, at least in most people's perceptions, "traditional." Why did this happen, what are the implications, and why is it so difficult to reverse this perceived "traditional" trend? The real issue is that over these past two centuries the church has slowly moved from being a *functional family* of members from all different ages and stages who never questioned if they would worship together, learn together, serve together, fellowship together, and support one another. Instead, it gradually moved toward more of an institutional church where people come to receive services. But perhaps the more crucial issue with offering slick programming is that the role of parents and grandparents, as well as other adults in the congregation has been undermined by the expectation of paid professionals taking the primary role in the discipleship of children and youth.

To really understand how this happened in our cultural setting, we need to go back and take a closer look at one key event in history—the post WWII era, when a convergence of events was taking place. Younger people returning from the war years were entering an era of increased affluence and mobility as well as burgeoning technological conveniences leading to increased privatization and more discretionary income. In addition, the family front porch was lost to inside environment controls (AC) and entertainment (TV). Sitting out on the front porch in view of neighbors thus went away. Sitting in the living room, together but not together, all facing the television set, became the after-supper story in families all across the nation.

There was an increased individualized mobility with people using cars instead of buses or trolleys. There was also the birth of a new demographic of adolescence (the term "teenager" was not coined until the early 1940s). Rather than walking to worship at the local community church, families were now free to drive to other locations and so could begin to pick and choose what other churches had to offer. Slinking in sideways into this scenario were various para-church organizations created to appeal to the hearts, minds, and entertainment tastes of teenagers. Churches soon found themselves not only in the position of competing for membership with the church across town which might offer slicker "programs," but also competing with evangelistic para-church organizations that offered cooler music with more entertainment as well as offering opportunities to "hang out" within programs designed just for them and for those in their age demographic. Thus, the advent of a relatively new phenomenon referred to as "consumer church" with professionalized church marketing and ministry programming. For more on this study of how the church changed during this era, Thomas Bergler's *The Juvenilization of American Christianity* (2012) is insightful.

Cultural Reality

Because the church in western culture has, for the most part, found itself in an uncomfortable position of either accommodating to or competing with an entertainment-saturated culture; the default mode is to offer programs that are easier to advertise, easier to carry out, more measurable, and more visually appealing to the *felt needs* and consumer ethos of our congregations. This particularly began to take place as churches began to offer more services—including training services in marriage, health, and parenting how-to. These services often became the essence of the church's ministry with families.

In the preface to his second edition of *Run With Horses*, Eugene Peterson (2009) says that "the most conspicuous response of the church at the loss of its 'market share' is to develop more sophisticated consumer approaches, more efficient management techniques. If people are not satisfied, we'll find a way to woo them back with better publicity and glossier advertising. We'll repackage church under fresh brand names" (9). This is the American way. After all, we in western culture have been formed under a consumerist worldview so that our response to the gospel is managed under consumerist terms. Yet, the huge irony is that the more we package the gospel in neat, advertisable programs, the more the consumers seem to be disappointed. "The gospel is not a consumer product; it does not satisfy what we think of as our 'needs'" (Peterson 2009, 10).

Frankly, creating an environment in which the processes of living faithfully together in an intergenerational community is just plain messy. And that is the heart of the issue: the processes of living faithfully together in an intergenerational community holds little *immediate gratification*. It is not perceived as *meeting my needs* and it is not a *fix-it* service for marriages and families, per se. The processes of living faithfully together within a varied-age-level community makes it hard to hold onto *consumer-driven* families that might find the program at the church down the street to be more appealing. So, basically, it is hard to *sell* process for ministry and ever so much easier to *sell* churches pre-packaged curricula or programs.

While the reality is that I cannot give you five easy steps to success, I can tell you that it is necessary to get messy in our ministries and in the processes of our ministries if we are going to form spiritually deep people and hold onto our children and youth who are wont to stray into the next best attraction. Rather than those five easy steps, process ministry is more along the lines of what Eugene Peterson (2000) refers to as "a long obedience in the same direction."

After taking a step back to look at the historical context as well as the cultural reality, it is important that we now take a step forward in this chapter and discuss the biblical and theological foundations of the Christian faith which mandate the *principles of* a process-focused ministry across the multiple generations of the church family.

Theological Foundation

One theological shift begins by addressing an attitude of family ministry *with* families instead of family ministry *to* or *for* families. Think about it, "to" or "for" reflects a consumerist vibe, while "with" reflects a sense of ownership and belonging. Furthermore, we need to ask what "family" is from a theological perspective and what the Scriptures teach us about how faith is formed. With that, this chapter hopes to end on a more encouraging, although still messy, note by leaving readers with some practical ideas on ways to begin to intentionally form a *Christian* worldview in our children and in their families, and with a final reminder of why the church *must* begin to look at *family* differently in order to be a witness *to* rather than a reflection *of* the secularist, consummeristic world in which we are situated.

One of the gurus of family ministry, Diana Garland, suggests that in the church we begin to use "family" as a verb rather than a noun—to "*family*" one another. She also reminds us that the essence of the Christian church is to give witness to a whole new social order, the Kingdom of God, not simply a repairing of the old (2012). By the invitation to be participants in the Kingdom of God in this world, the church is scripturally mandated to live in alternative theological reality. I address this scriptural mandate more fully in my book *Kingdom Family* (2012) by unpacking the worldview, habits, disciplines, stability and hospitality that have the potential of forming us into families who see the church community not as an institution that serves us, meets our needs, and makes us happy, but as messy places of belonging together as witness to commitment and fidelity. The Great Commandments of the New Testament—to love the Lord with all our hearts, souls, and minds and to love our neighbors as ourselves—are relational and process-oriented concepts rather than consumerist, program-oriented concepts. Many churches in the last half of the twentieth century missed that theological concept as they rushed to accommodate the culture and compete for their market-share.

In many of our churches today a successful family ministry is measured by the number of programs that have been implemented in any given year and on the number of attendees who showed up rather than by how lives have been reoriented toward God's Kingdom agenda. It is too often the case that churches are hiring a family pastor and developing a family ministry as a reaction to dismal retention statistics rather than as a strategy to carry out God's mission in the world. It has been repeatedly reported over the past few years that somewhere between 65 percent and 94 percent of churched youth drop out of church before their sophomore year of college. (Nelson & Jones, 2010) As a result, many congregations are shifting their ministry models, not because of convictions that have grown from a seedbed of sustained scriptural and theological study, but in order to increase the number of warm bodies.

Thus, in a tangible sense, family ministry is often reduced to attempts to meet *felt needs* of the families in their congregations by advertising and showing a film series on dealing with family themes such as marriage and parenting thus reducing life together with God's family to "how-to" training rather than giving space for the mystery of a people of God *as the family of God* to become integrated into what the church is about as a whole.

Even as far back as the 1980s, two Fuller professors, Dennis Guernsey and Ray Anderson (1985), defined the concept of family ministry as the church's ministry of empowering God's people to relate to one another as a family. Simply put, the process of family ministry is to *family one another* and invite children, youth, parents, grandparents, married and single folks to come together to worship, serve, learn, teach, care for, and get to know each other and so live into the Gospel reality while making a commitment to do this life together in community.

As an example, a more theological understanding of process-ministry might mean that instead of the church offering a series of parenting or marriage classes, older couples might invest time and energy in getting to know the young families (especially since in our mobile culture too many young families find themselves living far away from grandparents and other structural family members), inviting them over for a meal, offering to babysit on occasion, serving together on a mission trip, sitting beside wiggly children in worship services, and so on. If the older couple has teenagers in their home, this might also mean that those teens would connect in the same way, gaining the benefit of spending time with the younger couple, perhaps in a mentoring relationship, baby-sitting and just hanging out with younger kids.

A process-oriented ministry might mean that rather than offering a youth-only mission to build homes and run VBS in another state or country, the whole church and all ages and stages are invited to work and rub shoulders and do ministry together in a *familying* sort of way. In this way, they live out the church's mandate for unity such as expressed in Paul's group letter to the Ephesians or Jesus' prayer for the unity of the *whole* church family in order to bring glory to God.

Relation to Children's Spirituality

When ministry is reduced to programs, then our children lose several things in the effective formation of a mature faith. The major losses are a sense of belonging in community, personal ownership, and the knowledge that they are held accountable by the larger church family. While programs can offer lessons on life, the messier process of ministry offers the practice of life together. Another loss is that of mystery and wonder that comes not through teaching but rather through observation. The old adage that *our children are watching* is very much a process concept. At young ages or even as teenagers, they may not understand all that the adults do in "big" church worship and in the sacraments; however, they are watching and observing their elders' actions and attitudes. Giving them opportunities to be ushers, or to read scripture, or to listen to testimonies of their elders—as well as opportunity to share their own testimonies and be respected and listened to by adults—gives space to internalize the mysteries of faith. When parents and children (and old folks and youth) practice worship (or other aspects of life) together, it brings a consistent spirituality even more strongly into the field of belonging to something bigger than here and now. The practice of praying or meditating or sharing a ritual or ceremony together paves the pathway for a lifelong faith. As clinical psychologist, Dr. Lisa Miller (2015) points out, the pathway is permanent. "It will be there for both child and family in times of developmental change and challenge. We can invite our children into our space, whether we are meditating or praying, so they see our deliberate spiritual practice, participate in our spiritual rituals, and benefit from our purposeful creation of opportunity for spiritual insight, refocus, and growth."

A final word of warning from Bryan Nelson with Timothy Paul Jones (2010)

> *Family Ministry* is not the answer and before you make plans to launch a *family ministry* in your church, heed a few words of warning: *family ministry,* particularly a formal distinction in your overall church ministry, will not fix your church's problems, nor will it transform people's lives. The Gospel is what changes people—not programs or practices; not models or methods; but solely and only the Gospel of Jesus Christ. Why? Because gospel, by its very nature, is process . . . and not programs. (43)

Every local church should be concerned, first and foremost, about how the Gospel is presented, practiced and lived in community together. This includes considering how churches plan to teach on the subjects of marriage and parenting and how they encourage the ministry *of* families *with* families (not *to* families or *for* families). Healthy nuclear families should not be the goal. To place anything as the church's goal besides the glory of God experienced through the Gospel is to create an idol, and the idol of family ministry is an exercise in missing the point. Christian families are not the answer to humanity's problems. A people coming together and living out the glory of God together in worship, mission, and reconciliation is God's answer to humanity's problems. A congregational *process-focused* ministry with the whole family of God opens space for children of all ages to internalize and grow deeper in wonder and imagination, and to discover their "belonging space" within God's on-going Story.

References

Allen, Holly and Christing Ross. 2012. *Intergenerational Christian Formation: Bringing the Whole Church Together in Ministry, Community and Worship.* Downers Grove: InterVarsity.

Bergler, Thomas. 2012. *The Juvenilization of American Christianity.* Grand Rapids: Eerdmans.

Garland, Diana. 2012. *Family Ministry: A Comprehensive Guide.* Downers Grove: InterVarsity.

Guerensey, Dennis and Ray Anderson. 2012. *On Being Family: A Social Theology of the Family.* Pasadena: Fuller Seminary Press, 1985. Repr., Eugene, OR: Wipf and Stock.

Jones, Timothy Paul, ed. 2009. *Perspectives on Family Ministry: 3 Views.* Nashville: B&H Academic.

Jones, Timothy Paul, and Bryan Nelson. 2010. "The Problem and the Promise of Family Ministry." *Journal of Family Ministry* 1, no. 1, pp. 36–43.

Miller, Lisa. 2015. *The Spiritual Child: The New Science on Parenting for Health and Lifelong Thriving.* New York: Picador.

Okholm, Trevecca. 2012. *Kingdom Family: Re-Envisioning God's Plan for Marriage and Family.* Eugene, OR: Cascade.

Parsley, Ross. 2012. *Messy Church: A Multigenerational Mission for God's Family.* Colorado Springs: Cook.

Peterson, Eugene. 2000. *A Long Obedience in the Same Direction.* Downers Grove, IL: InterVarsity.

Peterson, Eugene. 2009. *Run with Horses: The Quest for Life at Its Best.* Downers Grove, IL: InterVarsity, 2nd ed.

Wright, Tim. 2015. *Sunday Schooling Our Kids Out of Church.* Amazon Digital Service, ebook.

Chapter 19

Embodied Faith Formation

Rebecca Chafee

WHAT WOULD IT LOOK like to reframe traditional Christian education as a lively, engaged, and embodied faith experience for all children of God? Instead of grouping children in age-based classes with intellectual learning goals, authentic experiences of worship, prayer, and spiritual formation could be offered in a multi-generational community. Children and adults could share a journey of faith that keeps faith relevant to daily living when faith formation is shifted from educational programming that teaches children *about* their faith to spiritual practices and worship experiences that help to *instill* faith in children.

The embodied faith formation model is grounded in spiritual-direction practices. It incorporates experiential, whole-body group activities for mixed ages, including *Godly Play*, Pretending Bible Stories, Praying in Color, Praying with the Body, and Dramatic Tableaux. This model grew out of the work I did over several years with a group of children and families at Pebble Hill Presbyterian Church in DeWitt, New York.

Reframing Children's Worship

For many years this church practiced a traditional model that offered Christian education to children and youth during the worship hour. Efforts made to include the children in worship were unsuccessful, as were efforts to maintain effective education in the traditional model. Teachers were reluctant to commit to missing worship every week, and rotating teachers meant inconsistent learning experiences and relationships. The children and youth learned little about weekly worship, and, when asked to age into the sanctuary, found both the format and the experience unfamiliar.

There is a real, reciprocal need: worshiping communities need children, and children need worshiping communities. When worshiping communities provide separate experiences to children, youth, families, and adults, they can lose their sense of the breadth of community and grow farther distant from concerns of younger people and families. A highly intellectual congregation may continue for decades in stasis, resisting what they perceive as dumbing down the worship experience to make it accessible to all members of their body and sacrificing children's authentic, albeit noisier and messier, worship experiences in the meantime. Young families whose children age out of classes find it too difficult to maintain active membership if youth feel marginalized, no longer part of education and not fully incorporated into the adult membership in a way that allows them to contribute and participate.

Worship Training for Children and Youth

Sensing the divide between Christian education and the congregation's worship, I began my ministry by offering the children worship training during their customary education time, concurrent with the adult worship hour. More than exposure to Bible stories, moral lessons, and ecological stewardship, the children needed to understand worship, sacraments, and prayer practices enough to participate as children of God with the broader church community.

To reinforce the change from Christian education to worship training, the program was named *Children's Worship*. The church followed a worship, coffee fellowship, then adult forum schedule, and so a *Children's Workshop* hour followed the coffee fellowship, offering children more hands-on work with the same material covered during *Children's Worship*. Standard curriculum provided content for the program, and we tailored the material to worship patterns during the first session and lively workshop activities following snacks and fellowship.

Children's Worship followed the flow and order of worship just as it was practiced in adult worship. Elements like prayer, music, word, and sacrament were comparable to those found in adult worship. In *Children's Workshop*, these familiar elements were embodied and expressed in noisier and messier ways. Children were offered leadership roles and asked to respond to the call of God expressed in the lessons of the day. Movement was not limited.

First Steps

I began with a copy of the congregation's standard worship bulletin in the reformed tradition, with four general movements: Gathering, the Word, Eucharist or Thanksgiving, and Sending. Children customarily began worship with their families, came up to the front steps for a children's message, and were released from worship to age-based classes for the remainder of the service. This release from worship signaled to the children that their worship was over, and they often raced down the aisle as if heading to the playground.

Maintaining the Fourfold Order of Worship meant that the children were simply moving to a different space to continue worship. They had experienced the Gathering and had begun to explore the Word in the sanctuary, so I crafted a new ritual to signify this continuity. Children typically served as acolytes, bearing light into the sanctuary at the start of worship to signify gathering in God's presence, and extinguishing the sanctuary light to carry it out into the world at the close of worship. With the pastor's help, we changed the children's message to reflect the scripture reading they were going to explore rather than offering a light version of the sermon. Following a brief prayer, acolytes lit their wands from the sanctuary candles and all the children formed a recessional leading to the *Children's Worship* space, where we used the sanctuary flame to light the children's candle.

Continuity of message and symbol made a real difference in the behavior of the children. They no longer raced and jostled down the aisle, and they maintained the same sense of wonder they had shared during the children's message. Replacing the typical object lesson related to the sermon with an introduction to the text the children would explore gave the pastor and adult congregation a connection with the children's program, as well as opening the dialogue with the Word that would continue in *Children's Worship*. No longer were the children serving as a prop for the adult sermon. Instead, adults were able to hear the Bible lesson that the children would work with. The children's message became a true dialogue between the children and the pastor, with other adults being offered the chance to listen in. Carrying God's light with us to light the candles in our own worship space not only modified the children's behavior, it empowered them to see themselves as equal members of the worshiping community.

Children's Worship Space

Space has a direct impact on experience. If at all possible, one must select a room that can be dedicated as a children's chapel and equip it for worship experiences rather than classroom learning. This chapel space must be in keeping with the church's sanctuary. Sanctuaries typically have thresholds or transition spaces as well as prominently displayed religious symbols that focus thoughts on God. In order to define a worship space in a ministry with shared space, I purchased a children's religious rug that featured a labyrinth pattern, rich colors, a symbol of a lighted lamp in the center, and a Bible verse printed around the border: "Thy word is a lamp unto my feet and a light unto my path" (Ps 119:105, KJV).

Our children's ministry was blessed with a custom-made stained glass rendering of Jesus and the Children as well as a hand-crafted ceramic cross decorated with lambs, fish, and other religious symbols. The Worship chairperson, gifted at sewing, made us cloths in liturgical colors to use on our worship table, which was complete with non-tip pillar candles, a plate, and a chalice. For several years we used a shared space and moved these items in and out of our worship room each Sunday, but these items provided our otherwise empty room with the aura of worship. We did not include tables and chairs in this space; instead, we set tables, chairs, and response materials in the other half of this classroom, behind an accordion room divider. When our worship was ended, the children enjoyed snacks in the adult coffee gathering and returned to the room with the accordion divider open, ready for response activities and games. The worship space remained intact for those who wished to continue exploring the worship themes.

Crossing the Threshold

Using a designated worship space and an acolyte procession to lead children from the sanctuary to this worship space each Sunday, we set about establishing worship routines. As the acolytes lit the candles on our worship table, children gathered in a circle on the rug. Adult leaders joined the children in the circle rather than sitting apart from it. An opening affirmation set the tone for worship and established children and adults as worship partners. A leader would begin this affirmation by saying, "Welcome to *Children's Worship* today. I'm [NAME], and I'm a child of God." Each child would announce his or her name in the same way. This affirmation served to set the tone and to build community. Regardless of background, denomination, or stage of faith, we could gladly affirm that each person present—child, adult, teen, and visitor—was a beloved Child of God.

Next came an opening prayer and liturgical call and response common to adult worship with our own added body movement. I would say to the children, "Peace be with you," while holding my hands out at my sides with palms facing them, just as the pastor does in worship. The children repeated this gesture toward me as they replied, "And also with you," signifying their offer of God's blessing to me in return.

Exploring God's Word

After this sequence, we continued to work with the Word portion of worship, recalling the introduction that the pastor provided in the Sanctuary. There were a number of interactive ways to explore the word, depending on the demographic on that day. I kept all children together, Pre-Kindergarten through fifth or sixth grades, in order to promote a multi-age community. With a large pageant-costume closet, we regularly dressed in costume and acted out the lesson. In *Children's Workshop* hour, we created some worship props that we could regularly use, like an Ark of the Covenant, candles, and banners. Embodying the lessons made them real to the children, and they were able to enter the story together and consider what it may have been like to experience it firsthand. Stories learned this way were not forgotten. And whether we read or acted out the Bible lesson, we always concluded, as worshipers in the Sanctuary did, with the leader proclaiming: "This is the word of the Lord" and the group responding "Thanks be to God."

Practicing Bible Skills

We also played hot-potato games and used wooden "books" to learn the books of the Bible, and over time our children were all able to read the scripture lesson of the day with the children's NRSV Bibles we supplied in this space. One immediate result of this practice was that we needed to lower the age at which we gave children Bibles. The custom had been to gift Bibles to third graders, but in the multi-age group at Pebble Hill, all children began asking to read a verse (haltingly, with help) by the second half of first grade. We moved the gift Bibles down to second grade. One parent spoke to me of his surprise at noticing his second-grader sitting in worship with him before the Time with Children; as the first lesson was read, his son pulled out a pew Bible, found the passage, and read along.

Practicing Prayer Skills

A written order of worship for each Sunday included prayers that I had found in the curriculum or written myself so that children began to lead prayers, as well. Children began arguing over whose turn it was to open or close in prayer. One day, when I had not prepared an opening prayer and the children were clamoring for a turn to pray, I invited anyone who would like to make up a prayer and welcome God to be with us today to lead the opening prayer. I had three takers, so each prayed spontaneously in turn. From that day on I prepared a prayer so that no volunteer need be too shy to lead, but I also regularly welcomed the children to make up their own prayers, and some did. Spontaneous group prayer was fairly rare among the adults in our congregation, but this led to children offering to bless meals the congregation shared. The children led the adults in this practice.

Pebble Hill's pastoral prayer custom is to open the floor for congregation members to share joys and concerns before bringing these requests to God in prayer. We echoed this in Children's Worship, too, along with some liturgical responses that are more typical for us during the Communion liturgy. Following a time of sharing together, a volunteer leader would open prayer with, "Let us give God thanks and praise," to which the group responded, "It is right to give our thanks and praise." The leader said, "Let us pray," and continued with the prepared prayer of the day, inviting the group to join in the Lord's Prayer at the end. The first closing benediction we initiated became such a popular ritual that we could not replace it. The children stood in a circle, putting one hand in a pile in the center as sports teams do, the leader said, "Go in peace," and the children flung their hands upwards as they replied, "to love and serve the Lord."

Worship Music

Music and hymns were included as they impacted the scripture. Many children did not enjoy singing hymns, so we focused on including simple responses that were often used in worship and using music videos that helped to explore the lesson. We used a set of hand chimes in worship to accompany ourselves in singing simple 2-chord rounds by setting out one chord on the left of the rug, the other on the right, and the steady tone included in both chords in the center. As leader, I could simply sing and point in the direction of the desired chord. Because this *Children's Worship* time was a 40-minute "hour," we did not attempt to "teach" songs, prayers, and worship skills. We simply experienced them, and then we practiced during the *Children's Workshop* hour.

Connecting Corporate and Children's Worship

As we embarked on this experiment in Reformed *Children's Worship*, our goal was to build connections between corporate worship in the Sanctuary and children's worship in our designated space. I made a practice of regularly narrating the worship elements as they were experienced in children's worship. By following the same order of worship and including many of the liturgical responses and prayers used in the Sanctuary, children became more equipped to participate fully in worship with their parents. I began building active roles for the children into corporate worship, intentionally planning for children to take leadership roles in corporate worship as they became accustomed to leading in children's worship. For example, one year we spent the season of Lent creating banners illustrating various names for Jesus. As each banner was completed, the children processed into the sanctuary holding the banner. Children led a short dedication liturgy using Bible verses and a prayer before mounting the banner on a stand in front of the church. During the week, the recently dedicated banner was moved to the side walls and the banner stand left empty for the new banner's dedication on the following Sunday.

Combined Worship That Speaks to All Ages

These worship practices continue today for children young enough to leave the Sanctuary for *Children's Worship*. The children who aged through this program into confirmation prefer to remain in the Sanctuary now unless they are needed to serve in the nursery or *Children's Worship*. We more regularly keep all children in worship to experience special music, Baptisms, Communion, Commissioning and Ordination of new officers, and other ceremonies of individual or congregational response. Corporate worship has grown to tolerate and then celebrate the middle school rock band playing and children serving as Liturgists without complaining that the services were being "dumbed down." Children's worship that acknowledged the spirituality of children grew into corporate worship that honors the spirituality of all persons.

Spiritual Practices for Life

Honoring the spirituality of others begins with spiritual practices that equip people for deeper relationship with God and others. Most spiritual practices that are meaningful for adults are also accessible to children, youth, and the differently-abled. These spiritual practices, when done alone, deepen personal relationships with God along the vertical axis of the cross-shaped life. Done in community, they deepen the faith-based aspects of our lives together along the horizontal axis of the cross-shaped life. Practices that appeal to all ages and can be done in community include *lectio divina*, praying with icons, liturgies and corporate prayers, listening prayers and meditation, and physical prayers like coloring or body movement prayers. Other practices are better done alone, including holy contemplative walks, daily *examen*, written prayers, and journals.

Embodied spirituality, or spiritual exercises that involve their whole selves, is especially important to children's faith development. Their less mature intellectual capacity gravitates to symbols, movements, rituals, images, and stories to give shape to ideas they are not yet able to articulate with the language available to them. Common rituals and symbols can draw people of any age closer to God and provide a transcendent experience. In faith communities, prayer, communion, liturgy, music, and visual symbols speak directly to the intuitive core of spirituality. Children can share equally with adults in spiritual encounters that transcend our cognitive understanding. Christian worship imitates patterns established early in Hebrew society, such as the story of David's city-wide celebration after the Ark of the Covenant was brought to Jerusalem, which included public prayers, offerings, blessings, singing, dancing, exhortation, feasting, and departing with joy (2 Sam 6). Jesus participated in Hebrew synagogue worship, and taught a specific pattern of prayer to his disciples (Luke 4:16; Matt. 6:5–15). Christian worship allows children, teens, and adults to share ritual, prayer, and worship.

The embodied spirituality that has moved Pebble Hill toward more inter-generational faith formation includes dramatic retellings of Scripture that invite children to immerse themselves in God's story, such as tableaux, dramatic readings, pretending Bible stories, and *Godly Play* storytelling. The following specific recommendations can enrich children's ministry and build inter-generational faith formation.

1. The spiritual practice of *Pretending Bible Stories* appeals to children and youth, but is also very effective in mixed-age gatherings (Guthrie 2013). Pretending Bible Stories is akin to *lectio divina*, with props and

costumes, in a playful community-building setting. It draws on dramatic improvisational skills and the interpretive practice of *midrash* to invite a group of players to immerse themselves in a scripture text and physically enact the story. A text is selected and the room outfitted with a selection of fabrics and props. Everyone plays—there are no spectators. The text is read once to understand the story, a second time to note characters and places to represent through play, and a third time the gathering dons costumes, sets the stage, and acts out the story. Following this embodied story play, discussion allows each player to share insights and new avenues for understanding opened up by this spiritual practice.

Sandy Eisenberg Sasso (2012) believes that while we read the same words of scripture, we hear those words differently based on our different contexts and backgrounds. Early Rabbis taught that one's understanding of Scripture derives not only from revelation from God, but also from interaction from our surrounding contexts. In *midrash*, God's revelation is more than the specific content of the text, but it is the beginning of a conversation with God in which we are participants (Sasso, 2012). In Pretending Bible Stories, each participant can feel the truth that through this type of play, God is talking directly to individuals. This method of experiencing God's stories invites people of all ages, languages, and backgrounds to dwell in the text and bring it to life, encountering God and continuing the conversation.

2. *Scripture in Tableaux* is an effective method of engaging young people in worship that builds on the practice of pretending Bible stories in a manner that is better suited to corporate worship services (Fairless 2000). Fairless (2000) offers wonderful examples of this embodied worship practice. Many different scripture readings can be presented in worship using this technique. All it requires is costuming, volunteers, a few props, and a bell or chime. The tableaux may be rehearsed in a short amount of time, as well. Ahead of time, read through the selected text and identify places that are well-suited to a visual display of emotion and action that is frozen in time. Indicate to the congregation that they are to close their eyes when they first hear the chime, keeping them closed during the reading, and then open them on the next chime to see the cast of characters frozen in place. Ring the chime and continue this practice through to the end of the text. The volunteers who act in this manner absorb the story, its emotions, and its message into their bodies. Those who listen and watch this retelling are similarly impacted.

3. *Godly Play* is another method for equipping children and youth to fully engage in their own faith development. Some of the language Jerome Berryman uses in recurring lessons invites young people to pay attention to their own spiritual experience and respect those of others around them. Instead of behavior modifying reminders like, "be quiet," *Godly Play* offers the reminder that we are quiet in this space because we do not want to disturb anyone else who may be talking to or listening to God in this place. After each storytelling session, children are invited into the story in more depth through wondering about its details, messages, and applications. Each story also requires a specific response activity that each child or young person undertakes through their own initiative, whether retelling the story, drawing or writing about it, or exploring another Bible story that calls to them. Equipping children with the building blocks of faith in this way requires that they engage with the material and make choices about the ways they will respond.

Cross-Generational Effects of this Approach

The resources offered by Caroline Fairless (2000) inspired my efforts to offer cross-generational worship experiences and leadership opportunities for children and youth. She offers an apt image in the subtitle of her book, *congregations in bloom*. *Children's Worship* and cross-generational worship efforts can result in congregations and worship services that bloom! Today that looks like colored pencils in every pew and a series of adult coloring images as bulletin covers. No longer are children offered a pew bag or a separate bulletin to color. People of all ages are enjoying the coloring sheets, saying that the practice gives them more auditory focus to better hear the sermon. All ages share their bulletin covers over fellowship following the service. And sometimes I hear that members have taken the bulletins home to color as a spiritual discipline and then bring them back to share on our bulletin board.

The surprise for the congregation is that worship need not be limited to silence, stillness, and cognitive thought. Movement, ritual, sound, and even noise is appropriate when it comes in response to the Word as it is spoken, read, preached, and sung. Children can perform in worship, but that is not worship. Children can follow directions, but again, that is not worship. Children can occupy themselves busily with crafts, games, and creative projects, but that is not worship. When children are prepared with the language, symbols, narratives, and rituals of faith, they can make appropriate response to God's call to worship and join the congregation in a full worship experience.

References

Fairless, Caroline. 2000. *Children at Worship: Congregations in Bloom*. New York: Church.

Guthrie, Suzanne. 2013. "Pretending Bible Stories." Class practicum. New York: General Theological Seminary, July.

Chapter 20

God and Digital Natives

How Tweens' High-Tech Habits Relate to Their Spiritual Lives

—— Pamela Caudill Ovwigho ——
& Arnold R. Cole

Today's tweens and teens are growing up surrounded by and immersed in digital technology. These "digital natives" make up the "iGeneration" and to most, the high-tech gadgets such as smartphones and iPads are simply the way things are done. Jane McGonigal (2010), in her TED Talk "Gaming can make a better world" notes:

> So, consider this really interesting statistic; it was recently published by a researcher at Carnegie Mellon University: The average young person today in a country with a strong gamer culture will have spent 10,000 hours playing online games by the age of 21. Now 10,000 hours is a really interesting number for two reasons. First of all, for children in the United States, 10,080 hours is the exact amount of time you will spend in school, from fifth grade to high school graduation, if you have perfect attendance. So, we have an entire parallel track of education going on, where young people are learning as much about what it takes to be a good gamer as they're learning about everything else in school. Some of you have probably read Malcolm Gladwell's new book "Outliers," so you would have heard of his theory of success, the "10,000 hours" theory of success. It's based on this great cognitive-science research that says that if we can master 10,000 hours of effortful study at anything by the age of 21, we will be virtuosos at it. We will be as good at whatever we do as the greatest people in the world.

And so, now what we're looking at is an entire generation of young people who are virtuoso gamers.

While McGonigal goes on to elucidate the positive aspects of video games, many researchers, educators, and child development experts voice concerns about how growing up in the digital age will ultimately impact children's physical (e.g., obesity), emotional (e.g., empathy), social (e.g., ability to hold conversations) and cognitive development (e.g., attention span). These concerns have contributed in part to the American Academy of Pediatrics (2016) issuing guidelines and recommendations about children and teen's digital media use.

Other than a few notable exceptions (Cole & Ovwigho 2015; Chapman & Pellicane 2014; Detweiler 2013; Hart & Frejd 2013; Leibovitz 2013) much less attention has focused on the spiritual implications of our high-tech habits. Yet, from a Christian perspective we strongly believe that all of life has a spiritual aspect. Anything that affects children's cognitive development may impact how they think about religious teachings, spiritual matters, and their faith. Similarly anything that influences children's social development has the potential to affect how they relate to God. Relationship is central to the Christian faith and private spiritual practices of communicating with God through prayer and scripture are usually encouraged.

In this chapter, we explore this spiritual aspect. Specifically we consider the intersection of children's high-tech habits, spiritual beliefs, and spiritual practices. The chapter begins by outlining theory linking children's faith development and technology usage. We then present a review of the latest research in this area, including data from a survey of 1,002 tweens (ages 8 to 12) about their spiritual beliefs and practices and video-game habits. The chapter closes with discussion of the implications of these findings for children's ministry practitioners.

Faith in the Context of Instant Messaging, Cyber Bullying, and Video-Game Narratives

Many early models of children's spiritual development drew parallels with their cognitive and emotional development. For example, Elkind (1997) contends that children's understanding of spiritual concepts grow and change as they move through Piaget's stages of cognitive development. Based on extensive interview data, Fowler (1981) proposed a model of faith development which can best be understood as a "meaning-making" process. That is, the individual strives to understand his or her own life, values and commitments.

More recently researchers utilized a theory-of-mind framework to understand how children's concepts of God grow and change over time and across cultures. These studies reveal that children generally do not associate limited beliefs, perspectives, and knowledge to God, as they do to humans (Barrett, Richert, & Dreisenga 2001; Barrett, Newman, & Richert 2003; Richert & Barrett 2005).

Another line of research has focused on how children perceive their relationship with God. Much of this work considers children's perceptions of God as loving, involved, distant or angry in the context of attachment theory and their relationships with their parents (Richert & Granqvist 2013).

Although we are making strides in understanding how children understand and experience concepts of God, the soul, and the afterlife, as well as how those relate to their moral attitudes and behaviors, there remains much work to be done. In particular, we still do not have a solid empirical understanding of how religious activities and practices (e.g., prayer, sacred texts, and rituals) impact children's religious, spiritual, and faith development.

There are several reasons to believe that children's involvement with digital technology may, in fact, impact their religious and faith development. One impact relates to children's comfort with and use of spiritual practices. Digital technology allows us to switch our focus and attention quickly and often. As a result, some contend the average attention span is getting shorter.

Research also documents that people with problematic video gaming habits tend to be high in escapism and experiential avoidance (Hilgard, Engelhardt, & Bartholow 2013). These two factors—a short attention span and a tendency to avoid internal experiences such as unpleasant memories and emotions—may impede private spiritual practices (e.g., prayer, meditation, and confession) that require cutting yourself off from external stimuli and focusing on inner thoughts and feelings.

Similarly, to the extent that digital technology impacts children's views and their ability to communicate and to empathize, it may also relate to how they relate to God, a key aspect of Christianity. This is the primary concern expressed by Chapman and Pellicane (2014). They argue that time in front of screens can erode a sense of togetherness and hinder a child's emotional and social development.

Finally, video games in particular present their own narratives. As Hayse (2009) notes: "On the surface, videogames may seem to teach values through an explicit curriculum of narrative arcs, textual messages, and graphical depictions. On a deeper level, videogames also teach values through the very procedures that constitute game play." Common elements in these narratives include the myth of redemptive violence, accumulation of objects and leveling up, and recurring death and "resurrection." Typically the player identifies with the main protagonist in the game. Most often this is a "messianic" figure who must save a virtual world. Just as the violence in video games may influence children's attitudes about it and their behavioral tendencies (American Psychological Association 2015), these narrative aspects could also affect their views on matters such as faith, God, death, and redemption.

Research Evidence for an Intersection of Video Games and Faith

While video games trace their history back to the 1950's, they've become part of the mainstream culture in only the last two decades. Today, children and adults alike have a wealth of gaming options from consoles, computers and arcades to social media platforms, mobile devices and handheld games. The types of games available has also expanded providing entertaining options for just about any interest.

In the United States, half of adults play video-games. Gaming is nearly universal among young adults, teens, and children. Worldwide, it's estimated that half a billion people spend at least an hour a day playing computer and video games.

It's important to consider that video games represent a modern form of play. In addition to providing entertainment and pleasure, play also supports children's intellectual and social development. Video games are fast-paced and often matched to our skill level to provide the right balance between challenge and achievement. Just like many pleasurable activities, they can relieve stress and give us a self-esteem boost when life is dragging us down. Playing with others, whether in person or virtually, helps us feel like we belong and are part of a larger community. The most popular games are frequently discussed in online forums, and YouTube is full of videos that provide game tips and strategies.

Several authors have explored the theoretical and theological relationship between digital media and spirituality (Chapman & Pellicane 2014; Detweiler 2013; Hart & Freijd 2013; Ovwigho & Cole 2015; Schut 2013). However, to date, empirical investigations have only considered how games may influence moral decision-making. Specifically, decades of research show that consuming high rates of violent media can increase aggression (see, for example, American Psychological Association 2015).

An emerging body of work suggests that media such as video games may be used to increase prosocial behaviors. For example, Jin (2011) showed that undergraduates who played a pro-social video game had higher empathy scores and tended to be more generous.

Technology Habits of "Church Kids"

In order to further explore the intersection of digital media and children's faith, we surveyed 1,013 children (age 8 to 12) from across the United States. Because our primary focus was on children being raised in the Christian faith, our sample was limited to those who attend church regularly (at least once a month).

To get a sense of tween's private spiritual practices, we asked how many days they had prayed, either alone or with their family, and how many days they read or listened to the Bible in the past week. Half of all tweens prayed and read the Bible one to three days each week (typically only one). Another 23 percent prayed but did not engage with scripture at all, and 12 percent did not engage in either spiritual practice. The remaining 15 percent are the most involved in private spiritual practices, praying and reading the Bible most days of the week.

We found that nearly all tweens who attend church regularly play video games for at least an hour during a typical week. Similar to what has been reported from other surveys, the children in our study spent an average of 12 ½ hours a week playing games, with boys playing for two more hours weekly than girls. The vast majority of kids said that their parents limited the number of hours they could spend on digital media (84 percent) and the types of games they could play (85 percent).

Although controversy still rages about game addiction as a psychological disorder (American Psychiatric Association, 2013), it's notable that 22 percent of boys and 11 percent of girls showed at least three signs of problematic gaming, such as fighting with others over time spent on games, neglecting other activities (e.g., chores or schoolwork), and playing games to avoid thinking about real life.

Consistent with other studies, we find that Problematic Gamers had higher experiential avoidance scores than tweens who weren't showing signs of Problematic Gaming. This tendency to avoid internal reflection correlates with their private spiritual practices as well. Tweens heavily involved with gaming prayed significantly less often than their peers (2.94 days vs 4.08

days, respectively). However, no differences were found in how often they read or listened to the Bible.

Our hypothesis of a relationship between video game habits and how tweens view God was also supported. We asked participants to rate on a 5-point scale (1 = not at all and 5 = very well) how well each descriptor fits their understanding of God. As the figure shows, problematic gamers gave significantly different ratings for 9 of the 11 descriptors. They view God as more angry, harsh and punishing than their peers. They also saw God as less loving, trustworthy, caring, present and powerful.

Figure 1. Tweens' Perceptions of God

Tweens' Perceptions of God

● Problematic Gamer ● Other Tweens

Angry**, Harsh***, Punishing***, Cares about me**, Forgiving, Loving**, Trustworthy***, Always there*, Cares about the world*, Involved, Powerful*

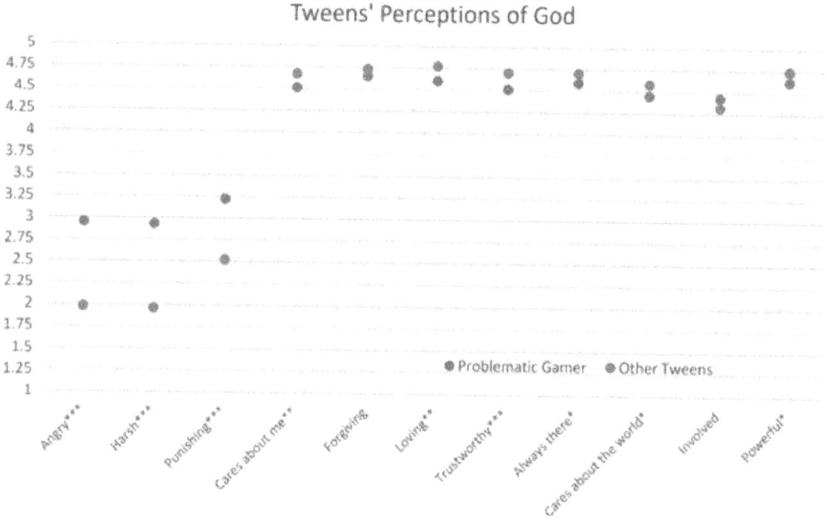

Ministering to Digital Natives

Emerging theory and data support the hypothesis that there is a relationship between tweens' high-tech habits and their spiritual lives. Specifically, children with high rates of involvement with video games are more likely to view God as angry and punishing. They are also less likely to see God as loving and caring toward them and toward the world. In addition, children heavily involved with video games avoid internal experiences (such as unpleasant memories) more than their peers and spend less time engaging in private spiritual practices.

It's important to note the limitations of these data. First, the results presented here are correlational and do not allow us to establish cause and effect.

Second, our sample consisted entirely of tweens living in the United States who attend church regularly. The results may not be generalizable to other cultures or to tweens with other religious views and practices. In addition, it's quite possible that the range on some of the perceptions of God is restricted precisely because of our focus on church attenders.

These limitations notwithstanding, we believe that these findings hold implications for both researchers and children's ministry practitioners. First, researchers and practitioners alike must consider how tweens high-tech habits may be impacting (and are impacted by) their faith and their understanding of the nature of God. Video games in particular present powerful narratives that function like curricula, likely influencing tweens' worldview. More research is needed to understand how children interact with and make sense of these game narratives, in the context of their faith and religious views.

We also suggest that "digital natives" may benefit from strategies to help them develop (and be comfortable with) private spiritual practices such as prayer and meditating on scripture. Digital media feed naturally into the brain's drive to seek out novelty. Their draw is so powerful that the average American checks his or her smartphone 46 times a day (Deloitte 2016). This habit of constantly seeking digital stimulation runs counter to the spiritual practices central to the Christian faith. Tweens and adults alike must train or retrain themselves to intentionally nurture their faith through prayer, meditation, and engaging with scripture.

Our third recommendation focuses on ministry approaches that embrace digital natives' reality. We encourage ministry professionals to creatively utilize game narratives to open spiritual discussions. For example, how does the crowd in Jesus' encounter with the woman caught in adultery parallel Minecraft mobs? Have they ever seen similar situations at school and how should they respond?

Playing games together provides a natural forum for these discussions. Qualitative studies show that tweens desire more honest spiritual discussions with their parents and church leaders. Experiencing game narratives may open the door for helping them draw parallels to spiritual ideas and grow in their faith.

References

American Academy of Pediatrics. 2016. "Media and Young Minds." *Pediatrics* 138, pp. 1–6.

American Psychiatric Association. 2013. "Internet Gaming Disorder Fact Sheet." *Diagnostic and Statistical Manual of Mental Disorders*. 5th ed. Arlington VA: American Psychiatric.

American Psychological Association. 2015. *Technical Report on the Review of the Violent Video Game Literature*. http://www.apa.org/pi/families/review-video-games.pdf

Cole, Arnold. and Ovwigho, Pamela. 2015. *Managing your family's high tech habits*. Uhrichsville OH: Barbour.

Chapman, Gary and Arlene Pellicane. 2014. *Growing Up Social: Raising Relational Kids in a Screen-Driven World*. Chicago IL: Northfield.

Deloitte. 2016. global mobile consumer survey: US edition, 2016. https://www2.deloitte.com/us/en/pages/technology-media-and-telecommunications/articles/global-mobile-consumer-survey-us-edition.html

Detweiler, Craig. 2013. *iGods: How Technology Shapes our Spiritual and Social Lives*. Grand Rapids: Brazos.

Hart, Archibald, and Sylvia H. Frejd. 2013. *The Digital Invasion: How Technology is Shaping You and Your Relationships*. Grand Rapids: Baker.

Leibovitz, Liel. 2013. *God in the Machine: Video Games as Spiritual Pursuit*. West Conshohocken PA: Templeton.

Hayse, Mark. 2009. "Redeeming Videogames: Examining the Implicit Theological Curriculum of a Procedural Medium." Presented at the Association of Youth Ministry Educators, Louisville KY.

Hilgard, Joseph, Christopher R. Engelhardt, and Bruce Bartholow. 2013. "Individual Differences in Motives, Preferences, and Pathology in Video Games: The Gaming Attitudes, Motives, and Experiences Scales (GAMES)." *Frontiers in Psychology* 4, p. 608.

McGonigal, Jane. 2010. *Gaming Can Make a Better World*. Video file. http://www.ted.com/talks/jane_mcgonigal_gaming_can_make_a_better_world?language=en.

Richert, Rebekah, and Pehr Granqvist. 2013. "Religious and Spiritual Development in Childhood." In *Handbook of the psychology of religion and spirituality* edited by Raymond F. Paloutzian and Crystal L. Park, 165–82. New York: Guildford.

Schut, Kevin. 2013. *Of Games and God: A Christian Exploration of Video Games*. Grand Rapids: Brazos.

Chapter 21

What do Kindergarteners' Spiritual Experiences and Expressions look like in a Secular Classroom?

Jennifer Mata-McMahon

SPIRITUALITY IS FREQUENTLY AVOIDED in the public school and secular classrooms in an attempt to prevent possible controversy. However, by ignoring, preventing, or discounting spirituality, educators can also inhibit children's spiritual growth. Based on findings from a phenomenological qualitative research study conducted through observations and interactions with both children and their significant adults, it is argued that educators should be responsible for addressing children's spirituality in the classroom and for re-introducing these topics into early childhood education.

This chapter will begin by exploring the literature on children's spirituality, looking at the different approaches to definitions of spirituality: as human nature (Elkins 1998; Hart 2003; Hay 1987; Kessler 1999, McCreery 1994; Palmer 1999; Scott 2001, 2003), as something *other* (Bosacki 2001; Myers & Myers 1999), as a combination of human nature and otherness (Champagne 2001; DeMarco 2000, in Stutts & Schloemann 2002), and lastly as essence, consciousness, and direct sensory awareness (McCreery 1994; Hay & Nye 2006; Johnson 2006; Miller 2000; Reimer & Furrow 2001). To then share the definition I put forth, understanding spirituality as "an innate human characteristic, a potential we are all born with, which allows us to connect with something beyond us (transcendence or divine), feel part of the greater universe, and be connected to otherness. Spirituality encompasses the individual capacity and the essence of life, providing humans with a window to greater consciousness and more profound understanding of being, meaning, and purpose" (Mata 2015, 18).

Following, a review of the scarce research studies that collect empirical data directly from children will be presented (Champagne 2003; Coles 1990; Hay & Nye 2006). We will then discuss the conceptual framework used encompassing Hart's (2003) five spiritual components of children's spirituality, Elkins's (1998) eight paths for spiritual development, and Hay and Nye's (2006) operationalization of their term relational consciousness in the three categories of spiritual sensitivity and awareness. This framework anchors the completion of a phenomenological qualitative study (Creswell 2007) venturing into a kindergarten classroom, to focus on the phenomenon of *children's spiritual experiences and expressions* for four amazing kindergarteners, within their classroom environment.

The study conducted will be explained and some of the data, collected through direct observations, and through informal conversations with parents and teachers serving as informants (Genishi 1981), and organized into thick descriptions (Merriam 1998) as well as individual profiles for each of the four focal children will be shared. We will posit connections between the findings arrived at and the proposed definition for spirituality. We will look at possible relationships between how children express their spirituality in a classroom environment, how they make connections with the *Other* beyond themselves, how they develop an understanding of being and life purpose.

The findings identified as spiritual experiences for children in the classroom were joy, concern for others, relationships, and imagination. Both internal prompting and external situations or events seemed to be triggers for children to express freely their spirituality and their spiritual self. Based on these findings, recommendations for early childhood practitioners and teachers as to how to begin incorporating strategies for spiritual support in the classroom will be offered, as well as a call for teacher education programs to incorporate into their program curricula spaces for discussion and study of children's spirituality (Miller 2006). Recommendations for further empirical research studies with children will also be made, as well as the need to look into interdisciplinary studies with a *pluricultural* perspective of children's spirituality (Mata-McMahon 2016). From all of the above, this chapter will hopefully be relevant and useful for practitioners working directly with children, and teacher educators working to best prepare future teachers; as well as scholars and researchers conducting studies in the field of children's spirituality.

Defining Spirituality

The term spirituality is an elusive one, one that has been quite difficult to define, given the ethereal nature of this phenomenon. Spirituality, pertaining to the spiritual realm, constitutes a challenge for anyone attempting to define it in the material, rational realm. Scholars have debated what spirituality means, and it seems as though it is possible for the term to be defined differently depending on the individual attempting to do so, because spirituality can and tends to encompass types of experiences that can vary from person to person.

Nevertheless, in my search for common ground on defining the term spirituality, I found three salient categories into which I could group the different definitions I encountered. These categories are: spirituality understood as human nature, spirituality seen as a process of unifying with "something other," and spirituality as essence, consciousness, and a direct sensory awareness.

Spirituality as Human Nature

Scholars who define spiritualty as human nature tend to understand it as a characteristic shared by all humans, and not just a few (Elkins 1998; Hart 2003; Hay 1987; Kessler 1999, McCreery 1994; Palmer 1999; Scott 2001, 2003). They consider spirituality as pertinent to being human, and explain it as a "universal human phenomenon found in all cultures and in every age" (Elkins 1998, 5). Some go so far as to base their research work into children's spirituality on the assumption that all humans are spiritual and have spiritual experiences, regardless of whether they might mediate these experiences through religious doctrines or other types of frameworks.

In exploring children's spirituality as spiritual development, Benson, Roehlkepartian, and Rude (2003) explain that it consists of growth in the intrinsic capacity for self-transcendence. Boyatzis (2008) proposes a more universal approach to Benson et al.'s natural inclination to spirituality, or what Boyatzis explains others have termed the "biological argument" (Hay, Reich, & Uysch 2006). Boyatzis proposes a social-ecological model based on Brofenbrenner's (1979) theory, through which the many influences on children's spiritual development can be studied, taking into consideration and analyzing the different social, and I would add cultural, contexts of growth. Boyatzis (2008) also warns, and I highly agree, that understanding and studying children's spiritual development as a process of growth needs to move beyond the common stage theory used to study development. He argues that "our understanding of spiritual development has been impeded by a reliance on stage models," and argues that this reliance has distorted our understanding of the cognitive limitations and assumptions of maturity of children depending upon their age, as well as imposing an "implicit notion that development entails 'forward progress'" (53).

Moving from this traditional stage-theory understanding of development, and particularly spiritual development, spirituality is understood by some as an intrinsic capacity, or, how I view it, an innate potential. Scott (2003) further explains that once spirituality was accepted as a category of human development and health by the United Nations Convention on the Rights of the Child in 1991, the view of spirituality as a distinct aspect of human experience, not contained by categories of moral, mental, or social development, was supported. Spirituality since then has been considered a category in and of itself, different from other developmental areas, related to human nature.

Spirituality as Unifying with *Something Other*

Other scholars understand spirituality as a consequence of a connection or a phenomenon that originates outside the human being, nevertheless having a great impact on the human's inner core (Bosacki 2001; Myers & Myers 1999). Scholars, who view spirituality as unifying with something other refer to it as an intimate and direct influence of the divine in people's lives. Myers and Myers (1999), explain that this connection with something other represents a construction of meaning that informs the way we engage in the process of transcendence.

Allen (2008), in her review of different definitions of spirituality explains that there are two common themes found: self-transcendence and relationality—meaning the relationship with self, others, the world and the transcendence. Lewis (2000) also speaks of spirituality as an orientation toward ourselves and our relations with all other things, while de Souza (2004) speaks of a movement toward the Ultimate Unity, explaining that at the deepest levels of connectedness an individual may experience unity with the Other (Austin 2000; Newberg et al. 2001; Hyde 2008a).

Still, other scholars combine the understanding of spirituality as human nature with the conviction that it is a result of unifying with something other (Champagne 2001; DeMarco 2000, as cited in Stutts & Schloemann 2002). Champagne (2001), explains that "spirituality cannot be disassociated either from the human or from what is beyond the human, in transcend [sic] and in immanence" (83).

Spirituality as Essence, Consciousness and a Direct Sensory Awareness

Lastly, there is a third category under which definitions of spirituality can be found; definitions pertaining to spirituality as essence, consciousness, and direct sensory awareness (McCreery 1994; Hay & Nye 2006; Johnson 2006; Miller 2000; Reimer & Furrow 2001). These scholars define spirituality as dynamic, using terms regarding being active, energetic, vibrant, vigorous and vital.

Miller (2000) speaks of spirituality in terms of essence and consciousness and explains that to become truly spiritual means "to change radically one's personality, and with such change the realization that this material world is only one part of the total existence" (39). Using this lens, spirituality can be understood as a human connection with divinity, which goes beyond the individual to connect to the essence of life, providing us with a greater consciousness and/or understanding of life and our purpose in it.

After studying and investigating the different views on defining spirituality, I ventured to put forth a definition of my own, the definition that guided the study that I share in this chapter. I understand spirituality as,

> an innate human characteristic, a potential we are all born with, which allows us to connect with something beyond us (transcendence or divine), feel part of the greater universe, and be connected to otherness. Spirituality encompasses the individual capacity and the essence of life, providing humans with a window to greater consciousness and more profound understanding of being, meaning, and purpose. (Mata 2015, 18)

Reviewing the Empirical Research on Children's Spirituality

Recently, I conducted a review of the research looking specifically at empirical data-driven studies published between 2005 and 2015, covering ten years of studies conducted directly with children (Mata-McMahon 2016). Having difficulties in finding studies completed within the age range of my interest (birth to age 8), I expanded my search to include studies done with older children or young adolescents. I found studies looking at children's spirituality, which included children as their research participants, fell under three main categories regarding the topic of study. These categories were, studies looking at: (1) spiritual meaning-making and relationships to/with God, studies on (2) children's spirituality in education, and studies looking into (3) identity formation and sense of self.

Spiritual Meaning-Making and Relationship to/with God

Under this category I found the study conducted by Hay and Nye (1998/2006) in which 38 children between ages of 6 and 11 were interviewed. Through their analysis they established three main categories of spiritual sensitivity reflecting the different realms in which children can have spiritual interactions, that included both making meaning and relating to God. Also, a study by Moore et al. (2011) in which 32 participants ages 7 to 11 and their parents were interviewed and surveyed, regarding the role of spirituality in their lives, finding that prayer and God's ability to help them as a result of prayer, were the most salient themes.

Other studies in this category also point to how children make meaning of the spiritual realm and how their relationship with God informs this meaning-making endeavor (Fisher 2015; Mitchell, Silver, & Ross 2012; Moore, Talwar, & Bosacki 2012). From reviewing these studies it can be gathered that regardless of the faith belief or non-belief of children, God and the child's relationship to God tends to have a strong presence in the early childhood years, as a means of comfort as well as a means for improving children's well-being.

Children's Spirituality in Education

In this category I primarily found studies looking at how teachers understand spirituality, as well as how they see it being incorporated into the curriculum and facilitated in the overall educational experience (Fisher 2007; Fraser 2007; Helm, Berg, & Scranton 2008; Hyde 2008c; Jacobs 2012; Kennedy & Duncan 2006; Mata 2012, 2013, 2014; Tan & Wong 2012).

I found only a few studies looking into explaining children's spirituality in relation to education, looking specifically at children as participants. The study I conducted (Mata 2015), which will be explained in more detail in section V. is one of them. Bone (2005) also put forth a study exploring three different early childhood settings, including the voices of children, teachers, and parents, in her data. She found that the preparation and sharing of food provided for appreciation and social interaction and opportunities for spiritual renewal.

Hyde (2008b), Mountain (2007), and Wills (2011) also conducted studies in school environments, observing and interviewing primary-aged children. The contribution that these studies make to the field of early childhood education is primarily in the call they all make to revise the quality of the experiences children are having in schools in order to allow for children to be happier, to take children's spiritual characteristics into consideration, honor the spirit of the child, and engage in creative arts within religious and spiritual education curricula.

Identity Formation and Sense of Self

Regarding the formation of identity and the sense of self, the studies I found emphasized the importance of spirituality in children's worldview and identity formation (Moriarty 2011), and presented spirituality as a mechanism for increasing happiness (Holder, Coleman, & Wallace 2008).

Interestingly, in comparing studies from different religious doctrines, I found that while working with a Western population, faith and prayer were considered pillars for resilience during crisis (Gunnestad & Thwala 2011), while Buddhist youth did not see the divine properties of religion as determinative. They more so understood the responsibility of taking ownership for their own lives as a result of the law-like effects of religion (Yeung & Chow 2010). This juxtaposition in findings seems to highlight the need for further study and thinking about the differences within religious practices and spiritual beliefs, and how those differences frame children's understanding of themselves, their connections to others, and the meaning and purpose they allocate to life.

Conceptual Framework

Regarding the conceptual framework I used in order to both frame and then interpret the findings from the study I conducted, I focused on Hart's (2003) five spiritual components of children's spirituality, proposed as: wisdom, wonder, connections, wondering, and the invisible. Through a retrospective approach to findings, Hart conducted interviews with adults regarding their spiritual experiences as children. He collected a number of anecdotal accounts both from adults' recollections of their experiences as children, and their recollection of their children's experiences. From these anecdotal testimonies on spiritual experiences, Hart found that these five categories were the most repeated ones in the stories that were shared with him.

Hart explains, Wisdom as a way of knowing and being that emerges through an opening of mind and heart. Children demonstrated wisdom through an understanding that life is about love, and were reported to offer simple yet deep propositions to comfort and counsel others. Wonder was found in moments in which boundaries blurred and consisted of experiences that involved feelings of awe, connection, joy, insight, and a deep sense of reverence and love. Wonder, like wisdom, is also non-rational, it involves a direct knowing, that occurs beyond our control. Hart (2003), noted that children seem to have a willingness and an ability to surrender that welcomes wonder. Connections, or what Hart (2003) called Between You and Me, was way in which children experienced spirituality through the close, loving relationships they held. Voluntary demonstrations of compassion, communion, empathetic resonance, giving thanks, and forgiveness were evidence of relational spirituality in children. Wondering was seen when children demonstrated their intuitive capacity to pose deep questions in search of meaning regarding the purpose of life. And finally, Seeing the Invisible, the fifth category of children's spirituality found by Hart, comprises all the inexplicable experiences children recount involving dreams, angels, invisible friends, and other occurrences that happen in altered states of mind, like out-of-body and near-death experiences. Hart (2003) explains that children tune in to more subtle levels of reality in which they see visions, hear voices, feel energy, know things at a distance, and find insight and inspiration.

Elkins (1998) offered an interesting perspective on spirituality and how it is lived, which also informed the framework used to complete this study. His proposed eight paths for spiritual development also offered guidance into understanding how children could potentially experience and express their spirituality. Even though Elkins studied adolescents and young adults, the eight paths he proposed helped guide my understanding of what I was observing in the children, as well as opened the possibility, quite concretely, of other ways and paths of being spiritual, other than the traditional and common religious path. Elkins' proposed eight paths for spiritual growth and development are: the feminine, the arts, the body, nature, psychology, mythology, relationships, and the dark nights of the soul. Even though some of these paths would not necessarily be ones children would take to experience and expand on their spirituality, paths like relationships, the arts, and nature seem to be ones to which I have observed children to be naturally drawn.

Both Hart (2003) and Elkins's (1998) contributions to my conceptual framework are summarized in the following image:

Figure 1: Elkins' Spiritual Paths and Hart's Spiritual Components

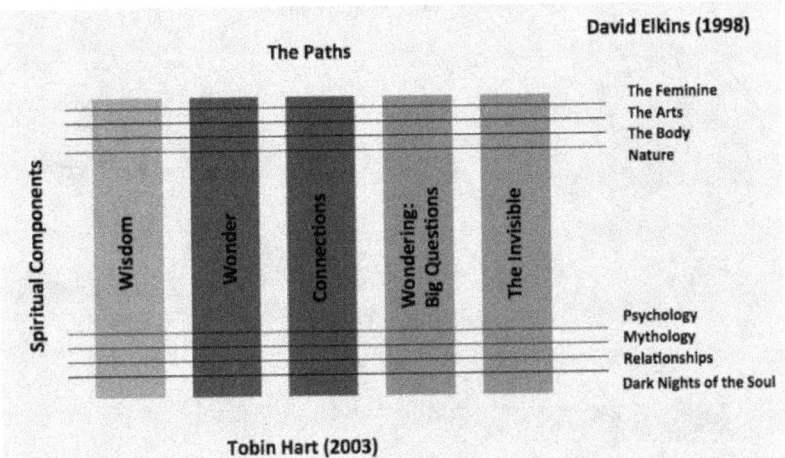

Finally, Hay and Nye's (2006) operationalization of their term relational consciousness into three categories of spiritual sensitivity and awareness, as awareness-sensing, mystery-sensing, and value-sensing, also helped interpret my findings. Nye (2013) defines relational consciousness as an initially natural capacity for awareness of the sacred quality of life experiences. She explains that this awareness can be conscious or unconscious and in childhood, she says that spirituality is particularly about relating to others more than oneself, in order to create a deeper inner sense of Self.

Within the proposed relational consciousness, Hay and Nye (2006) found three distinctive categories of spiritual sensitivity, related to how children experienced their spirituality. The category of awareness-sensing relates to paying close attention and being present and in tune with the activity at hand. Within this category, Hay and Nye (2006) found subcategories of here-and-now, tuning, flow, and focusing. The second category, mystery-sensing, relates to the awareness of aspects of life experiences that in principle are incomprehensible. Subcategories of mystery-sensing encompass wonder and awe, and imagination. The third and last category found was value-sensing, which relates to what is valued in life, associated with profound emotions and a search for life's purpose. The subcategories proposed for value-sensing are delight and despair, ultimate goodness, and meaning.

Interconnections between the three theories used as a conceptual framework for the work I completed can be summarized in the image below, in which it can be observed that there are some overlaps within what each of these scholars proposed, in order to better understand children's spirituality.

Figure 2: Interconnections between Hart, Elkins and Hay and Nye's Theories

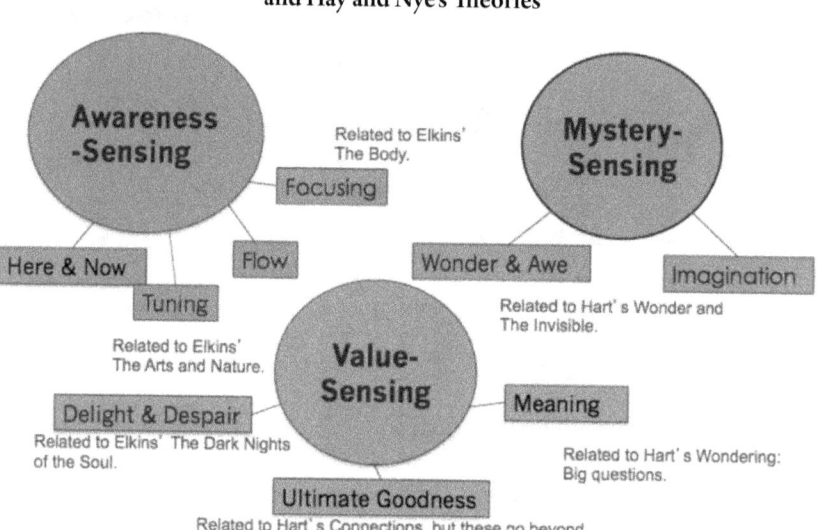

This conceptual framework set the stage for what I might be able to observe in the study I set to carry out. I went into the kindergarten classroom, hoping to see whether Hart's (2003) characteristics were observable in the children with whom I was working. I also wanted to see which other aspects of spirituality were observable within these children's experiences and expressions. Elkins's (1998) paths, offered a framework to understand that secular avenues toward spirituality, other that religious practices and beliefs, were possible. If these eight paths were an option for adolescents, then perhaps there might also be other options for children. Lastly, Hay and Nye's (2006) relational consciousness and different proposed awarenesses to explain children's spirituality, set the stage for what to observe when in the classroom with the participating children.

Phenomenological Qualitative Study

When I approached the study of children's spirituality, because of the scarcity of studies published on this topic, I decided that an exploratory study, looking into directly observing children in order to be able to describe the phenomena, was the pertinent approach. Thus I embarked in a phenomenological qualitative study (Creswell 2007) venturing into a kindergarten classroom in a private, secular school in New York City. My focus was the study of the phenomenon of children's spiritual experiences and expressions, focusing on four kindergarteners between the ages of five and six, to be observed within their classroom environment, while in their day-to-day school experiences.

The four children I focused on came from diverse ethnical, racial and cultural backgrounds. They (Anna, Mark, Ellen, and Matt) were White, African-America, Asian, and Mixed race (White and Asian). These children were selected without regard to their religious affiliation, yet this was noted as demographic information. The participating children were selected through opportunistic purposive sampling (Patton 1990), taking advantage of new leads, which came up during the initial fieldwork and preliminary observations. The criteria of selection were based on preliminary observations conducted in the kindergarten classroom in a two-week period. Children were selected based upon their willingness to interact with me, diversity in race and gender, information provided by the teachers, and the parent's consent to have their child participate in the study. The number of children selected was chosen because it seemed as a manageable number to work with, as I was the only researcher collecting and analyzing data.

I conducted many hours of in-class observations, as a participatory observer using a reactive entry strategy (Corsaro 1981). I carried out one-on-one activities with each of the children, and also facilitated a whole-group activity with all four children during after school hours, for which I carefully designed semi-structured protocols. Furthermore, I asked the children's teachers and parents to participate as informants (Genishi 1981) in order to attain background information on the children's spiritual experiences, as well as to guide my observations. After collecting data for several months, organizing and analyzing it using grounded theory methods, I compiled the findings for each of the four children into rich descriptive profiles, as individual cases (Merriam 1998), highlighting each child's uniqueness and individuality in expressing and experiencing spirituality. I then looked across the four children, completing an inter-profile analysis (Merriam 1998), to establish commonalities.

Findings and Discussion

From the study conducted and explained in the previous section, findings seemed to reflect that a spiritual experience, for the four children I observed, was any experience through which they could express (1) joy, (2) compassion and kindness, (3) a sense of relating to others, and/or their (4) creative and imaginative self. Expressions within these four categories were observed in situations or events in which children freely expressed their spirituality and their spiritual selves, without direct prompting from an adult. This led me to realize that at this age, children are still uninhibited by cultural and social constraints, and can express their spiritual selves freely and openly, and not necessarily secretively, as Hart (2003) had proposed. It seemed as though children were able to be kind, care for others, connect to their surroundings, enjoy a favorite activity, be helpful, and be concerned, without the permission of, or even prompting from, their teachers.

In looking at what prompted these types of expressions illustrating children's spiritual experiences, I found that these could be both inwardly and outwardly triggered. Sometimes an internal emotion or thought seemed to be prompting the children to express themselves spiritually, and might provoke pondering and searching through inner thought and conversations. Other times an event around them, which the children witnessed, was the main trigger point for them to act upon spiritually. They might have observed another child in need of help picking up a workstation, or a teacher needing help holding the door for others, and they voluntarily offered support, expressing both their concern for others and their empathy in noticing others having a need that they were able to identify.

In looking at possible relationships between how children express their spirituality in a classroom environment and how they make connections with others beyond themselves, I thought it would be interesting to also seek understanding of how they consider, if not make sense of, their self-being and life purpose. Analyzing the findings in this light would help me make connections between the proposed definition for spirituality I offered previously, and what I was able to observe in the kindergarteners. In this sense I observed that there were some unique qualities in how these four children expressed themselves spiritually. For Anna, for example, relationships and being there for others whom she cared for deeply, was very important, and came up frequently as a theme in the notes on the observations I completed for her. In her case, her emerging purpose seemed to be of service to others. It seemed as though being empathetic and acting upon that, by being helpful was what gave meaning to her sense of self, and thus could potentially be a component of her life purpose. Of course, this is not to say that Anna would have been able to verbalize this in so many words, as she was only five years old at the time, and probably had not figured out what her life purpose was, as many of us adults have not either. Yet, in realizing the trend in her expressions within the classroom experiences, and connecting those with the information provided by her parents and teachers, Anna seemed to be a very compassionate and giving girl, who was moved, some could say by Spirit, to be of service to others; thus her spiritual path could be identified as a path of Service.

In contrast, in looking at Mark's profile, based on the hours of observing him in the classroom, it seemed evident that for him Joy was the most common expression of spirituality. Mark rejoiced in happiness, in engaging in activities that would bring him joy and/or would provide a shared joy with others. Mark would spontaneously dance when music was playing in the background while children with immersed in classwork, he would sing his favorite songs and make up song beats while he played. He would also tell children jokes and remind them of funny events they had lived together, to prompt them to smile and laugh. Mark seemed to be on a mission to be happy and make others happy too. It seemed that delighting in the joys of life, and helping others do so as well, was Mark's calling. Again, I would be hard-pressed to say that Mark could verbalize this if asked, yet from an observer's perspective, one looking at children's spiritual expressions, I would say Mark's path to spiritual growth and development is through Happiness.

In looking for commonalities among the children I observed in my study, I was able to identify these four main ways in which children express their spirituality, as (1) joy, (2) compassion and kindness, (3) a sense of relating to others, and/or their (4) creative and imaginative self. These add to the categories proposed by Hart (2003), and Hay and Nye (2006) thus helping expand our knowledge base on what children's spirituality might look like.

In considering specifically and individually each child, as a unique human being, with preferences and likes, it was easy to identify certain paths, similar to those proposed by Elkins (1998) for adolescent and adults. For Anna, it was a path of Service, while Mark seemed to prefer a path of Happiness. We need to continue looking at children and observing them in their natural environment, in order to continue to identify ways in which we can best support them in finding and following their spiritual paths, whatever they may be, in order to help nourish their spiritual development.

Recommendations for Early Childhood Practitioners, Teacher Educators, and Researchers, along with Conclusions

Based on these findings, recommendations for early childhood practitioners and teachers as to how to begin incorporating strategies for spiritual support in the classroom seems important. The more children are able to freely express themselves in their classroom and school environment, the more we will be able to support them in finding their path, their calling, and ultimately discovering their life purpose and meaning. Children, like Anna and Mark, could identify what seems to make them tic, from a spiritual perspective, what allows them to connect with the otherness around them, and ultimately what permits them to express and further develop this innate potential they have of being spiritual.

The call is not for teachers to completely redesign their curricula, more so to allow for time and space in their daily schedules and routines for children to connect with others, express their inner desires, and find a fertile ground to pose their questions and test their answers. Finding our life purpose or the meaning of being alive, here, with those around us, is not an easy task. Yet it could be made easier if adults working with and around children allowed for them to freely experience and express themselves spiritually in a supportive environment. I found through my study that children will express their spiritual selves regardless of an adult prompt, yet in order to see this side of children flourish, grow, and not dissipate with age, it seems important that teachers nurture spirituality, as much as any other developmental area for the children under their charge.

Teacher-education programs also need to rethink how they prepare teachers to work with children. These programs need to incorporate into their development, theory, and methods courses aspects related to children's spirituality, in order to support teachers in nourishing this aspect of children's development. Teachers, ultimately, will have the highest level of responsibility, as they are the ones working directly with children. Teacher educators need to best prepare them to do so.

Lastly, scholars and researchers need to continue to further explore this field of study. More is needed in regard to empirical research completed directly with children, in order to better understand the different ways in which children express themselves spiritually, and to identify common paths children might be taking to develop this area of themselves. Also, it is interesting to identify what teachers and parents might be doing that is hindering this growth for children. More interdisciplinary studies need to be completed, also taking into account differences in cultural backgrounds, and as I suggested before, using a *Pluricultural* lens (Mata-McMahon 2016) to make connections and distinctions between experiences and expressions from different paradigms and frameworks for life in both the material and spiritual realms.

References

Allen, Holly Catterton. 2008. "Exploring Children's Spirituality from a Christian Perpective." In *Nurturing Children's Spirituality: Christian Perspectives and Best Practices*, edited by Holly Catterton Allen, 5–20. Eugene, OR: Cascade.

Austin, J. 2000. "Consciousness Evolves When Self Dissolves." In *Cognitive Models and Spiritual Maps: Interdisciplinary Explorations of Religious Experience*, edited by J Andresen and R Forman, 209–30. Thorverton, UK: Imprint Academic.

Benson, P. L., E. C. Roehlkepartian, and S. P. Rude. 2003. "Spiritual Development in Childhood and Adolescence: Toward a Field of Inquiry." *Applied Developmental Science* 7, pp. 205–13.

Bone, Jane. 2005 "Breaking Bread: Spirituality, Food and Early Childhood Education." *International Journal of Children's Spirituality* 10, pp. 307–17.

Bosacki, Sandra Leanne. 2001. "Theory of Mind or Theory of the Soul? The Role of Spirituality in Children's Understanding of Mind and Emotions." In *Spiritual Education: Cultural, Religious, and Social Differences: New Perspectives for the 21st Century*, edited by Jane Erricker, Cathy Ota, and Clive Erricker, pp. 156–69. Brighton: Sussex Academic.

Boyatzis, Chris J. 2008. "Children's Spiritual Development: Advancing the Field in Definition, Measurement, and Theory." In *Nurturing Children's Spirituality: Christian Perspectives and Best Practices*, edited by Holly Catterton Allen, 43–57. Eugene, OR: Cascade.

Bronfenbrenner, Urie. 1997. *The Ecology of Human Development*. Cambridge, MA: Harvard University Press.

Champagne, Elaine. 2003. "Being a Child, a Spiritual Child." *International Journal of Children's Spirituality* 8, pp. 43–53.

———. 2001. "Listening to . . . Listening for . . . : A Theological Reflection on Spirituality in Early Childhood." In *Spiritual Education: Cultural, Religious and Social Differences: New Perspectives for the 21st Century*, edited by Jane Erricker, Cathy Ota, and Clive Erricker, pp. 76–87. Brighton: Sussex Academic.

Coles, Robert. 1990. *The Spiritual Life of Children*. Boston: Houghton Mifflin.

Corsaro, William A. 1981. "Entering the Child's World: Research Strategies for Field Entry and Data Collection in a Preschool Setting." In *Ethnography and Language in Educational Settings*, edited by J. Green and C. Wallat, 117–46. Norwood, NJ: Ablex.

Creswell, John W. 2007. *Qualitative Inquiry and Research Design: Choosing among Five Approaches* 2nd ed. Thousand Oaks, CA: Sage.

de Souza, Marian. 2004. "Teaching Effective Learning in Religious Education: A Discusion of the Perceiving, Thinking, Feeling and Intuitive Elements in the Learning Process." *Journal of Religious Education*. 52, no. 2, pp. 22–30.

Elkins, David N. 1998. *Beyond Religion*. Wheaton, IL: Quest Books Theosophical.

Fisher, John W. 2015. "God Counts for Children's Spiritual Well-Being." *International Journal of Children's Spirituality* 20, pp. 191–203.

———. 2007. "It's Time to Wake up and Stem the Decline in Spiritual Well-Being in Victorian Schools." *International Journal of Children's Spirituality* 12, pp. 165–77.

Fraser, Deborah. 2007. "State Education, Spirituality, and Culture: Teacher's Personal and Professional Stories of Negotiating the Nexus." *International Journal of Children's Spirituality* 12, pp. 289–305.

Genishi, Celia. 1981. "Codeswitching in Chicano Six-Year-Olds." In *Latino Language and Communicative Behavior*, edited by R. P. Duran, 133–52. Norwood, NJ: Ablex.

Gunnestad, Arve, and S'lungile Thwala. 2011. "Resilience and Religion in Children and Youth in Southern Africa." *International Journal of Children's Spirituality* 16, pp. 169–85.

Hart, Tobin. 2003. *The Secret Spiritual World of Children*. Makawao, HI: Inner Ocean.

Hay, David. 1987. *Exploring Inner Space*. London: Mowbray.

Hay, David, and Rebecca Nye. 2006. *The Spirit of the Child*. Rev. ed. London: Kingsley.

Hay, David, K. H. Reich, and M. Utsch. 2006. "Spiritual Development: Intersections and Divergence with Religious Development." In *The Handbook of Spiritual Development in Childhood and Adolescence.*, edited by E. C. Roehlkepartian et al, pp. 46–59. Thousand Oaks, CA: Sage.

Helm, Judy Harris, Stacy Berg, and Pam Scranton. 2008. "Documenting Children's Spiritual Development in a Preschool Program." In *Nurturing Children's Spirituality: Christian Perspectives and Best Practices*, edited by Holly Catterton Allen, 214–29. Eugene, OR: Cascade.

Holder, Mark D., Ben Coleman, & Judi M. Wallace. 2008. "Spirituality, Religiousness, and Happiness in Children Aged 8-12 Years." *Journal of Happiness Studies* 11.2, pp. 131–50.

Hyde, Brendan. 2008. "I Wonder What You Think Really, Really Matters? Spiritual Questing and Religious Education." *Religious Education* 103, pp. 32–47.

———. 2008. "The Identification of Four Characteristics of Children's Spirituality in Australian Catholic Primary Schools." *International Journal of Children's Spirituality* 13, pp. 117–27.

———. 2008. "Weaving the Threads of Meaning: A Characteristic of Children's Spirituality and Its Implications for Religious Education." *British Journal of Religious Education* 30, pp. 235–45.

Jacobs, Anne C. 2012. "South African Teachers' Views on the Inclusion of Spirituality Education in the Subject Life Orientation." *International Journal of Children's Spirituality* 17, pp. 235–53.

Johnson, H. 2006. "Difference, Exploration, Certainty and Terror: A View from a Londoner about the Formation of Children's Spirituality as Relational Consciousness." *International Journal of Children's Spirituality* 11, pp. 57–70.

Kennedy, Anne, and Judith Duncan. 2006. "New Zealand Children's Spirituality in Catholic Schools: Teacher's Perspectives." *International Journal of Children's Spirituality* 11, pp. 281–92.

Kessler, Rachael. 1998/99. "Nourishing Students in Secular Schools." *Educational Leadership* 49, pp. 49–52.

Lewis, J. 2000. "Spiritual Education as the Cultivation of Qualities of the Heart and Mind: A Reply to Blake and Carr." *Oxford Review of Education* 26, pp. 263–83.

Mata, Jennifer. 2013. "Meditation: Using It in the Classroom." In *Spirituality in the 21st Century: Journeys Beyond Entrenched Boundaries*, edited by W. Van Moer, D. A. Celik, and J. L. Hochheimer, 109–19. Oxford: Inter-Disciplinary.

———. 2012. "Nurturing Spirituality in Early Childhood Classrooms: The Teacher's View." In *Spirituality: Theory, Praxis and Pedagogy*, edited by M. Fowler, J. D. Martin, and J. L. Hochheimer, 239–48. Oxford: Inter-Disciplinary.

———. 2014. "Sharing My Journey and Opening Spaces: Spirituality in the Classroom." *International Journal of Children's Spirituality* 19, pp. 112–22.

———. 2015. *Spiritual Experiences in Early Childhood Education: Four Kindergarteners, One Classroom*. New York: Routledge.

Mata-McMahon, Jennifer. 2016. "Reviewing the Research in Children's Spirituality (2005-2015): Proposing a Pluricultural Approach." *International Journal of Children's Spirituality* 21, no. 2, pp. 140–52.

McCreery, Elaine. "Towards an Understanding of the Notion of the Spiritual in Education." *Early Child Development and Care* 100, pp. 93–99.

Merriam, Sharan B. 1998. *Qualitative Research and Case Study Applications in Education*. San Francisco: Jossey-Bass.

Miller, John P. 2006. *Educating for Wisdom and Compassion: Cretaing Conditions for Timeless Learning*. Thousand Oaks: Corwin.

Miller, Judith S. 2000. *Direct Connection: Transformation of Consciousness*. Danbury: Rutledge.

Mitchell, Monique B., Christopher F. Silver, and Christopher J. Ross. 2012. "My Hero, My Friend: Exploring Honduran Youths' Lived Experience of the God-Individual Relationship." *International Journal Of Children's Spirituality* 17, pp. 137–51.

Moore, Kelsey, Victoria Talwar, and Sandra Bosacki. 2012. "Canadian Children's Perceptions of Spirituality: Diverse Voices." *International Journal Of Children's Spirituality* 17, pp. 217–34.

Moore, Kelsey, et al. 2011. "Diverse Voices: Children's Perceptions of Spirituality." *Alberta Journal of Educational Research* 57, pp. 107–10.

Moriarty, Micheline Wyn. 2011. "A Conceptualization of Children's Spirituality Arising out of Recent Research." *International Journal of Children's Spirituality* 16, pp. 271–85.

Mountain, Vivienne. 2007. "Educational Contexts for the Development of Children's Spirituality: Exploring the Use of Imagination." *International Journal of Children's Spirituality* 12, pp. 191–205.

Myers, Barbara Kimes, and Michal Elaine Myers. 1999. "Engaging Children's Spirit and Spirituality through Literature." *Childhood Education* 76, pp. 28–32.

Newberg, Andrew, Eugene D'Aquili, and Vince Rause. 2001. *Why God Won't Go Away: Brain Science and the Biology of Belief*. New York: Ballantine.

Palmer, Parker J. 1998/99. "Evoking the Spirit in Public Education." *Educational Leadership* 6, pp. 6–12.

Patton, M. Q. 1990. *Qualitative Evaluation and Research Methods*. 2nd ed. Newbury Park, CA: Sage.

Reimer, K., & J. Furrow. 2001. "A Qualitative Exploration of Relational Consciousness in Christian Children." *International Journal of Children's Spirituality* 6, pp. 7–23.

Scott, Daniel. 2001. "Storytelling, Voice and Qualitative Research: Spirituality as a Site of Ambiguity and Difficulty." In *Spiritual Education: Cultural, Religious, and Social Differences: New Perspectives for the 21st Century*, edited by Jane Erricker, Cathy Ota, and Clive Erricker, pp. 118–29. Brighton: Sussex Academic.

Scott, Daniel G. 2003. "Spirituality in Child and Youth Care: Considering Spiritual Development and "Relational Consciousness"." *Child & Youth Care Forum* 32, pp. 117–31.

Stutts, A., and J. Schloemann. 2002. "Life-Sustaining Support: Ethical, Cultural and Spiritual Conflicts Part I: Family Support—a Neonatal Case Study." *Neonatal Network* 21, pp. 23–29.

Tan, Charlene, and Yew-Leong Wong. 2012. "Promoting Spiritual Ideals through Design Thinking in Public Schools." *International Journal of Children's Spirituality* 17, pp. 25–37.

Wills, Ruth. 2011. "The Magic of Music: A Study into the Promotion of Children's Well-Being through Singing." *International Journal of Children's Spirituality* 16, pp. 37–46.

Yeung, Gustav K. K., and Wai-yin Chow. 2010. "'To Take up Your Own Responsibility': The Religiosity of Buddhist Adolescents in Hong Kong." *International Journal of Children's Spirituality* 15, pp. 5–23.

Chapter 22

Religious and Spiritual Struggles Among Adolescents

Implications for Youth Workers and for Research

STEFFANY J. HOMOLKA,
JULIE J. EXLINE,
JOSHUA A. WILT,
& KENNETH I. PARGAMENT

RELIGIOSITY AND SPIRITUALITY (R/S) have been linked to better mental and physical health, more health-promoting behaviors, less risky behaviors, and can be indicators of personal thriving among adolescents (King et al. 2013). However, researchers know little about the potentially challenging aspects of r/s among youth nor its potential implications for scholarly and ministry work. Experiences of conflict, strain, or distress around r/s are known as *r/s struggles* (Exline 2013). This chapter briefly reviews adult-r/s-struggle research and the status of adolescent-r/s-struggle research. It then examines results of a study with adolescents and their r/s-struggle experiences, focusing on the implications that this study and related studies have for adolescents and those who research and work with them.

Adult Struggle Research

In comparison to adolescent-struggle research, r/s struggles have been studied more thoroughly among adults (Exline 2013; Exline & Rose 2013). Researchers have identified different types of r/s struggles (Exline et al. 2014), including divine (e.g., anger toward God), demonic (e.g., feeling attacked by the devil), interpersonal (e.g., feeling mistreated by religious people), moral (e.g., guilt about moral failures), ultimate meaning (e.g., existential crises), and doubt (e.g., feeling troubled by religious questions). Studies have consistently linked adults' r/s struggles to indicators of poor well-being, including depression, anxiety, anger, and physical health (Abu-Raiya et al. 2015; Exline 2013). Furthermore, these studies reveal that many adults confirm experiencing r/s struggles at some point in their lives, though often at low levels. Some studies (Ai et al. 2011) also suggest that struggles are associated with long-term r/s growth; though, this research is mixed (Pargament et al. 2006).

Furthermore, researchers (Exline & Grubbs 2011; Wilt et al. 2016) have investigated how adults cope with struggles. They found that people who told another person about their anger with God experienced greater spiritual engagement if they received supportive responses. However, those who received negative feedback (e.g., indications that anger at God was wrong or they were made to feel guilty, ashamed, or judged) were more likely to experience greater struggles. Furthermore, participants who thought experiencing anger toward God was wrong were less likely to tell others about their struggle, were more likely to feel distant from God, and were more likely to experience further struggles and engage in substance use.

Overall, the aforementioned research indicates that r/s struggles play an important role in many adults' lives. Such research also carries potential implications for adolescents. From a developmental standpoint, the adult research prompts questions regarding whether r/s struggle experiences begin prior to adulthood. If so, what are the characteristics of adolescents' struggles and their relationships to other areas of youths' lives? Research suggests connections between adolescent r/s and well-being. For instance, r/s has been consistently linked to lower depressive (Pössel et al. 2011) and anxiety symptoms (Davis et al. 2003) as well as better academic performance (Regnerus & Elder 2003). Furthermore, r/s may help protect against the effects of exposure to violence and trauma (Laufer & Solomon 2011) and reduce the likelihood of risky and antisocial behaviors (Resnick et al. 2004). R/s may also function as a protective factor against suicidality (Nkansah-Amankra 2013)and generalized estimating equations were used to assess individual and contextual characteristics predicting suicidal behaviors in adolescence and in young adulthood. Distinct trajectories of suicide ideation and suicide attempt were identified for the total sample and for the gender groups. Results showed marked gender differences in the trajectory of suicide ideation and attempt patterns. Religiosity effects on suicidality were prominent in adolescence but not in young adulthood. Analysis showed that an important window of opportunity for preventing the escalation of suicidality exists during the early adolescent period, an opportunity that should be emphasized in interventions on adolescence suicide prevention." However, this research is only just beginning to delve into aspects of r/s that may be more challenging or distressing for adolescents (ages 13–18, excluding college students).

Adolescent Struggle Research

In regard to adolescents' r/s struggles, several studies (Hunsberger et al. 2001; Puffer et al. 2008) found differences in current r/s doubting (a form of r/s struggle) based on adolescents' identity development two years prior. Adolescents who endorsed no identity commitment as well as those reporting identity achievement reported greater r/s doubts than those in identity foreclosure and those with a diffuse identity. Other studies (Carpenter et al. 2012; Cotton et al. 2013) found that greater r/s struggles were linked to more anxiety, depression, and poorer health. These studies used the Brief RCOPE (Pargament et al. 2000) including potentially helpful and harmful religious expressions. The RCOPE was tested on a large sample of college students who were coping with a significant negative life event. Factor analysis of the RCOPE in the college sample yielded factors largely consistent with the conceptualization and construction of the subscales. Confirmatory factor analysis of the RCOPE in a large sample of hospitalized elderly patients was moderately supportive of the initial factor structure. Results of regression analyses showed that religious coping accounted for significant unique variance in measures of adjustment (stress-related growth, religious outcome, physical health, mental health, and emotional distress, which frames r/s struggle in terms of negative religious coping with a particular stressor and emphasizes struggles focused on God. Additionally, a recent review of youth r/s research (Homolka & Exline 2016) revealed that several youth measures contain items that tap into struggles and results from these studies suggest that greater struggle is associated with poor mental and physical health and well-being. Given these initial adolescent findings and the results from adult-struggle studies, it is important to examine adolescents' r/s struggles more in depth and to use this information to better understand and help adolescents with their struggles. The next section presents a study (Homolka 2016) intended to help researchers and youth-care workers with this task.

Study of R/S Struggles among High School Students

Participants and Procedures

A study was conducted with students (N = 319) ages 14 to 17 (M_{age} = 15.6, SD = 1.1) from three U.S. preparatory high schools (one secular, n = 70; one coeducational Roman Catholic, n = 91; one all-girls Roman Catholic, n = 158) in the Great Lakes region. The sample largely identified with at least one religion (n = 264), with 257 endorsing at least some belief in God and 233 endorsing Christian beliefs exclusively, 181 of which were Catholic. A few other religions were also represented, though minimally, including Judaism, Islam, and Hinduism (total n = 10). Since one school was an all-girls school, the sample was largely female (n = 252). Most participants were White (n = 244) and heterosexual (n = 273).

Participants completed a survey indicating the level to which they experienced various struggles, as measured by the 26-item Religious and Spiritual Struggles (RSS) Scale (Exline et al. 2014) adapted for adolescents and the 14-item RSS Adolescent (RSS-A) supplementary subscales (Homolka 2016). The RSS and RSS-A assess overall struggle and eight specific forms of struggle: Divine, Demonic, General Interpersonal, Moral, Doubt, Ultimate Meaning, Parents/Family (e.g., conflict with parents over religious behaviors), and Friends/Peers (e.g., religious identity conflict with friends/peers). Although primarily validated among U.S. adults in predominantly Christian samples, the RSS has also undergone some validation in Muslim (Abu-Raiya et al. 2015), Jewish (Abu-Raiya et al. 2016), and nonbeliever (Stauner et al. 2016) samples. The RSS-A items were developed from college students' and adolescents' (non-college 13—18 year olds) descriptions of struggles they experienced as adolescents. Participants also completed standardized measures of anxiety, depression, anger, bullying and victimization, hassles, self-esteem, disordered eating, body image, insomnia, insecure attachment to parents, and positive and negative mood. The survey gathered relevant demographic data as well, along with measures of religious comfort and commitment. All of the aforementioned measures, including the newly adapted RSS and the new RSS-A, demonstrated good reliability and validity in this adolescent sample (Homolka 2016).

Key Results

Types and Frequency of Struggles. Students' responses indicated that most experienced some form of r/s struggle, though typically at low levels (see

Table 1). Moral, Ultimate Meaning, and Doubt Struggles received the most endorsement, although still at modest levels (between "a little bit" and "somewhat," on average). Only 16 students reported no r/s struggles.

Table 1. R/S Struggle Means and Percentage of Students Endorsing at Least Some Struggle

Struggle Types	Scale Range	Mean	SD	Minimum Mean	Maximum Mean	Student Endorsement
Divine	1–5	1.50	0.80	1	5	54.1 percent
Demonic	1–5	1.21	0.58	1	5	22.3 percent
Interpersonal	1–5	1.59	0.74	1	5	65.9 percent
Moral	1–5	2.06	0.97	1	5	83.3 percent
Ultimate Meaning	1–5	1.99	1.11	1	5	70.1 percent
Doubt	1–5	1.94	0.98	1	4.75	72.2 percent
Parents/Family	1–5	1.48	0.82	1	5	54.5 percent
Friends/Peers	1–5	1.23	0.43	1	3.83	42.9 percent
All Struggles	1–5	1.58	0.53	1	3.43	95 percent

Note. Scale Range = 1 to 5; Scale: 1 = Not at all, 2 = A little bit, 3 = Somewhat, 4 = Quite a bit, 5 = A great deal. Mode for all scales was 1. SD = Standard Deviation; Minimum Mean = The lowest average among students; Maximum Mean = the highest mean among students; Student Endorsement = Percentage of students who endorsed experiencing at least one struggle item as "a little bit" or greater.

Demographic Differences. Statistical analysis using ANOVA with Bonferroni comparisons and t-tests, as relevant, were conducted to examine differences in struggle experience based on demographics (see Tables 2 and 3). Struggles examined by age in years revealed that younger youth tended to report lower overall r/s struggle than older youth, $F(3, 315) = 3.94$, $p = .01$, $\eta^2 = .04$—a difference that was most noticeable when comparing 14- to 16-year-olds, $t(142) = -3.14$, $p = .02$, with 17-year-olds, $t(158) = -3.32$, $p = .01$. Specifically, older youth reported more overall struggle, including General Interpersonal, Moral, Ultimate Meaning, and Doubt Struggles, than those who were younger. Interestingly, 15-year-olds reported the most Friends/Peers r/s struggle.

No differences in overall struggle were found between male and female youth nor between White and racial/ethnic minority students. However, females reported significantly greater Moral, $t(134.5) = -2.98, p = .02, \eta^2 = .02$, and Ultimate Meaning struggles, $t(313) = -1.98, p = .05, \eta^2 = .01$, than males. Furthermore, the 29 non-heterosexual participants reported more r/s struggle overall, $t(300) = -4.87, p < .01, \eta^2 = .04$, including more General Interpersonal, $t(30.3) = -3.15, p < .01, \eta^2 = .03$, Ultimate Meaning, $t(32) = -5.28, p < .01, \eta^2 = .05$, Doubt, $t(298) = -3.37, p < .01, \eta^2 = .05$, and Parents/Family struggles, $t(30.4) = -2.99, p < .01, \eta^2 = .01$. Of note, the aforementioned struggles are closely tied to personal and r/s identity and interactions with adults.

The 59 agnostic and atheistic youth reported significantly more struggle overall, $t(76.6) = 2.21, p = .03, \eta^2 = .02$, than those who endorsed at least some belief in God, including more General Interpersonal, $t(69.9) = 4.44, p < .01, \eta^2 = .10$, Ultimate Meaning, $t(74.6) = 3.07, p < .01, \eta^2 = .04$, and Parents/Family struggles, $t(68.9) = 2.65, p = .01, \eta2 = .04$. However, they reported less moral struggle in comparison, $t(104.9) = -3.15, p < .01, \eta^2 = .02$. Similarly, the 31 who identified with a minority reported greater r/s struggle overall, $t(251) = -2.04, p = .04, \eta2 = .02$, than those reporting Christian beliefs, including Ultimate Meaning struggles, $t(250) = -2.20, p = .03, \eta2 = .02$.

Additionally, among youth endorsing at least some belief in God, participants with parents who placed "a lot" of emphasis on r/s experienced greater overall struggle than those who had parents who placed "none" to "quite a bit" of emphasis on r/s, $F(4, 251) = 2.85, p = .02, \eta^2 = .04$, with a statistically significant difference between "a lot" and "quite a bit" of parent r/s emphasis, $t(74) = -3.12, p < .01$. Youth also differed in terms of Parents/Family struggle based on parental r/s emphasis, $F(4, 251) = 5.33, p < .01, \eta^2 = .08$. Such youth whose parents placed "a lot" of importance on r/s beliefs and practices experienced significantly more Parents/Family r/s struggles than similar youth whose parents placed "a little," $t(58.5) = 3.45, p < .01$, "moderate," $t(69) = -2.26, p = .03$, or "quite a bit," $t(59.6) = 2.69, p < .01$, of importance on r/s.

Among youth who endorsed agnostic and atheistic beliefs regarding God, youth significantly differed based on overall struggle as well, $F(4, 54) = 10.24, p < .01, \eta^2 = .43$; greater struggle overall was reported for those whose parents placed a "moderate" ($t_{mod\ vs.\ none}(29) = 4.04, p < .01; t_{mod\ vs\ little}(24) = 4.67, p < .01$) or "quite a bit" ($t_{qab\ vs.\ none}(29) = 4.23, p < .01; t_{qab\ vs\ little}(24) = 5.21, p < .01$) of importance on r/s in comparison to youth whose parents placed "none" to "a little" importance on r/s. Upon closer examination, a pattern emerged for those who endorsed atheistic and agnostic beliefs in God where youth of parents who placed "moderate (medium or average)" to "quite a bit" of importance on r/s tended to report significantly greater Divine, Moral, Doubt, Parents/Family, Friends/Peers, and overall r/s struggles in comparison to youth whose parents placed little to no importance on it.

In comparison to youth from secular schools, those attending Catholic schools reported more religious commitment, (M_{Cath} = 2.4, SD = 0.9 vs. M_{sec} = 1.7, SD = 0.7; $t(151.0)$ = 6.06, $p < .01$, $\eta^2 = .08$), and comfort (M_{Cath} = 2.7, SD = 0.9 vs. M_{sec} = 2.0, SD = 0.9; $t(313)$ = 5.81, $p < .01$, $\eta^2 = .10$), but also more r/s struggle overall, $t(171.2)$ = 2.88, $p < .01$, $\eta^2 = .02$, particularly Divine, Moral, Doubt, and Parents/Family struggles, suggesting a higher level of engagement with r/s overall (including both its comforting and difficult aspects). Consistent with this reasoning, both Catholic schools had more students who endorsed being Christian (n_{Cath} = 203, 84 percent vs n_{sec} = 30, 42 percent, $\chi^2(1)$ = 50.00, $p < .01$), believing in God (n_{Cath} = 214, 87 percent vs n_{sec} =43, 61 percent, $\chi^2(1)$ = 26.01, $p < .01$), and having parents who were Christian (n_{Cath} = 217, 89 percent vs n_{sec} =38, 54 percent, $\chi^2(1)$ = 46.10, $p < .01$) and placed substantial importance on r/s (M_{Cath} = 3.5, SD = 1.1 vs M_{sec} =2.4, SD = 1.2; $t(315)$ = 7.03, $p < .01$, $\eta^2 = .14$). Small associations were found between higher overall struggles and lower religious commitment ($r = -.18$, $p < .01$) and religious comfort ($r = -.28$, $p < .01$). Several forms of struggle ($r = -.16$ to $-.32$, $p < .01$) also demonstrated this relationship (see Table 4).

Table 4. Pearson Correlations between R/S Struggles and Indicators of Poor Well-Being and R/S

	Div.	Dem.	Int.	Moral	Mng.	Doubt	Par/Fam	Friends	Overall
Depression	.45**	.15**	.37**	.41**	.69**	.41**	.30**	.22**	.58**
Anxiety	.35**	.22**	.33**	.40**	.47**	.35**	.24**	.24**	.48
Anger	.48**	.22**	.39**	.49**	.52**	.42**	.29**	.25**	.57**
Bullying	.04	.33**	.21**	.23**	.17**	.12*	.09	.13*	.22**
Victim.	.30**	.27**	.30**	.27**	.26**	.21**	.12*	.30**	.36**
Hassles-Par.	.37**	.22**	.25**	.40**	.43**	.32**	.45**	.22**	.52**
Hass.-Friends	.30**	.11*	.27**	.31**	.38**	.30**	.14*	.24**	.37**

	Div.	Dem.	Int.	Moral	Mng.	Doubt	Par/Fam	Friends	Overall
Poor B. I.	.24**	.07	.22**	.37**	.41**	.34**	.19**	.18**	.39**
N. Com. Beh.	.29**	.06	.28**	.29**	.32**	.33**	.21**	.22**	.38**
Neg. Mood	.45**	.25**	.34**	.44**	.60**	.37**	.23**	.21**	.54**
Anx. Attach.	.38**	.26**	.15*	.17**	.25**	.17**	.28**	.11†	.34**
Avd. Attach	.32**	.20**	.21**	.27**	.34**	.25**	.36**	.21**	.42**
Insomnia	.33**	.11*	.29**	.38**	.50**	.36**	.26**	.21**	.47**
Health	-.21**	-.10†	-.24**	-.28**	-.40**	-.34**	-.23**	-.24**	-.39**
Pos. Mood	-.27**	-.16**	-.22**	-.25**	-.45**	-.28**	-.19**	-.14*	-.37**
Self-Esteem	-.41**	-.17**	-.31**	-.39**	-.63**	-.34**	-.27**	-.17**	-.51**
School Sat.	-.29**	-.07	-.24**	-.18**	-.28**	-.24**	-.21**	-.19**	-.33**
GPA	-.15**	-.11†	.03	-.06	-.08	-.02	-.16**	-.02	-.12*
R. Comm.	-.06	.02	-.19**	.05	-.24**	-.16**	-.18**	-.07	-.18**
R. Comfort	-.17**	-.03	-.29**	.05	-.32**	-.23**	-.24**	-.15**	-.28**

*$p \leq .05$, **$p \leq .01$, †$p \leq .10$

Note. Div. = Divine R/S Struggles; Dem. = Demonic R/S Struggles; Int. = Interpersonal R/S Struggles; Moral = Moral R/S Struggles; Doubt = R/S Doubt Struggles; Par/Fam = Parents/Family R/S Struggles; Friends = Friends/Peers R/S Struggles; Overall = Overall R/S Struggles; Hassle-Par = Hassles with Parents; Hass.-Friends = Hassles with Friends; Poor B.I. = Poor Body Image; Neg. Mood = Negative Mood; Anx. Attach. = Anxious Attachment to Parents; Avd. Attach. = Avoidant Attachment to Parents; Pos. Mood = Positive Mood; Self-Esteem = Positive Self-Esteem; School Sat. = Satisfaction with School; GPA = Grade Point Average; R. Comm. = Religious Commitment; R. Comfort = Religious Comfort

Links to Well-Being. This study also investigated the relationship between adolescent struggles and well-being. We found that all 8 forms of struggle were associated with indicators of poor well-being (see Table 4). Using guidelines for effect sizes suggested by Gignac and Szodorai (2016), total r/s struggle was strongly associated with higher anger, greater hassles with parents, poorer self-esteem, greater negative mood, and more depressive symptoms. Moderate associations were found with insomnia, anxiety, dissatisfaction with their school, self-reported poor physical health, and avoidant attachment to parents. Smaller associations were found between overall struggles and hassles with friends, poor body image, more negative compensatory behaviors for self-perceived overeating, less positive mood, anxious attachment to parents, lower grades and satisfaction with grades, and greater frequency of bullying others and being the victim of bullying. In sum, r/s struggles were associated with many indicators of distress and difficulty.

Table 2. R/S Struggles Experiences: Between-Participant Comparisons based on Demographics

Demographic Groups	n	Overall Struggles	Divine	Demonic	Inter-personal	Moral	Ultimate Meaning	Doubt	Parents/Family	Friends/Peers
		**			*	**	**	**		**
Age										
14	66	1.4 (.5)ab	1.4 (.7)	1.2 (.6)	1.4 (.8)c	1.8 (.7)d	1.6 (.9)e	1.6 (.7)g	1.4 (.7)	1.1 (.2)h
15	81	1.6 (.6)	1.6 (.9)	1.3 (.6)	1.5 (.6)	2.0 (.9)	1.9 (1.1)f	1.8 (.8)	1.5 (.9)	1.3 (.6)h
16	78	1.7 (.5)a	1.5 (.8)	1.3 (.7)	1.7 (.7)	2.2 (1.1)	2.4 (1.2)ef	2.0 (1.0)	1.5 (.9)	1.2 (.4)
17	94	1.7 (.5)b	1.5 (.8)	1.2 (.4)	1.8 (.8)c	2.3 (1.0)d	2.0 (1.1)	2.2 (1.1)g	1.5 (.8)	1.3 (.4)
Gender						*	*			
Male	64	1.5 (.5)	1.4 (.6)	1.2 (.6)	1.6 (.8)	1.8 (.7)	1.7 (1.0)	1.8 (.9)	1.5 (.8)	1.2 (.5)

PART III: CULTURE

Demographic Groups	n	R/S Struggle Types Mean (SD)								
		Overall Struggles	Divine	Demonic	Inter-personal	Moral	Ultimate Meaning	Doubt	Parents/Family	Friends/Peers
Female	252	1.6 (.5)	1.5 (.8)	1.2 (.6)	1.6 (.7)	2.1 (1.0)	2.0 (1.1)	2.0 (1.0)	1.5 (.8)	1.2 (.4)
Sexual Orientation			*		**		**	**	**	
Hetero.	273	1.5 (0.5)	1.5 (.8)	1.2 (.5)	1.5 (0.7)	2.0 (1.0)	1.9 (1.0)	1.9 (1.0)	1.4 (0.8)	1.2 (.4)
LGBQ	29	2.0 (0.6)	1.7 (1.0)	1.3 (.9)	2.2 (1.1)	2.2 (1.1)	3.1 (1.3)	2.5 (1.1)	2.1 (1.2)	1.3 (.5)
Belief in God			*		**	**	**		**	
Believer	257	1.5 (.5)	1.5 (.8)	1.2 (.6)	1.5 (.6)	2.1 (1.0)	1.9 (1.0)	1.9 (1.0)	1.4 (.7)	1.2 (.4)
Ag/Ath	59	1.7 (.6)	1.4 (.8)	1.1 (.4)	2.1 (1.0)	1.8 (.8)	2.4 (1.3)	2.1 (1.1)	1.8 (1.1)	1.3 (.6)
Faith		*					*			
Christian	221	1.5 (.5)	1.5 (.8)	1.2 (.6)	1.5 (.6)	2.2 (1.0)	1.8 (1.0)	1.9 (.9)	1.4 (.7)	1.2 (.4)
R/S Min.	31	1.7 (.6)	1.7 (1.0)	1.1 (.5)	1.8 (.8)	2.0 (1.0)	2.3 (1.2)	2.3 (1.3)	1.7 (.8)	1.3 (.4)
School		**	**		**		*	**		
Catholic	245	1.6 (.6)	1.6 (.8)	1.2 (.6)	1.6 (.8)	2.2 (1.0)	2.0 (1.1)	2.0 (1.0)	1.5 (.9)	1.2 (.5)
Secular	74	1.5 (.4)	1.3 (.6)	1.2 (.6)	1.5 (.7)	1.8 (.8)	2.1 (1.2)	1.7 (.8)	1.3 (.5)	1.2 (.4)

$^* p \leq .05$, $^{**} p \leq .01$.

Note. ANOVAs using Bonferroni correction or *t* tests, as relevant, were conducted to identify struggle differences between demographic groups. Asterisks indicate when such a test was significant. For Age, means with shared subscripts differ at p < .05 using the Bonferroni correction. No significant differences found between races or parent r/s. Ag/Ath = Agnostic/Atheist; R/S Min.= R/S Minority

Table 3. R/S Struggles Experiences: Between-Participant Comparisons based on Parents' Emphasis on R/S

		Struggle Types *Mean* (SD)								
Parent R/S Emphasis	n	Overall Struggles	Divine	Demonic	Inter-personal	Moral	Ultimate Meaning	Doubt	Parents/Family	Friends/Peers
Believers		*					**		**	
None	8	1.3 (0.2)	1.1 (0.2)	1.0 (0.0)	1.2 (0.3)	1.6 (0.7)	1.3 (0.5)	1.8 (1.0)	1.2 (0.3)	1.1 (0.2)
A Little	46	1.6 (0.6)	1.6 (0.9)	1.3 (0.9)	1.6 (0.7)	2.3 (1.0)	2.0 (1.1)	2.1 (1.0)	1.2 (0.4)b	1.2 (0.5)
Moderate	75	1.6 (0.6)	1.6 (0.9)	1.3 (0.6)	1.4 (0.6)	2.1 (1.0)	2.1 (1.1)	1.9 (1.0)	1.4 (0.7)c	1.2 (0.5)
Quite a Bit	78	1.4 (0.4)a	1.3 (0.5)	1.2 (0.5)	1.4 (0.5)	2.1 (0.9)	1.6 (0.8)	1.8 (0.8)	1.2 (0.5)d	1.1 (0.3)
A Lot	49	1.7 (0.6)a	1.6 (0.9)	1.2 (0.4)	1.6 (0.7)	2.3 (1.0)	2.0 (1.1)	2.0 (1.0)	1.8 (1.1)bcd	1.2 (0.4)
Agnostics and Atheists		**	*			**		**	**	*
None	22	1.5 (0.5)ef	1.2 (0.5)	1.2 (0.6)	1.9 (0.8)	1.5 (0.7)i	2.0 (1.3)	1.8 (1.0)k	1.2 (0.5)no	1.3 (.6)

Struggle Types Mean (SD)

Parent R/S Emphasis	n	Overall Struggles	Divine	Demonic	Inter-personal	Moral	Ultimate Meaning	Doubt	Parents/Family	Friends/Peers
A Little	17	1.4 (0.4)gh	1.2 (0.4)	1.0 (0.0)	1.8 (1.0)	1.5 (0.5)j	2.4 (1.4)	1.5 (0.5)lm	1.2 (0.4)pm	1.1 (0.2)q
Moderate	9	2.3 (0.6)eg	2.0 (1.4)	1.1 (0.2)	2.6 (1.1)	2.5 (1.2)ij	3.1 (1.2)	2.9 (1.2)kl	2.7 (1.4)np	1.9 (0.8)q
Quite a Bit	9	2.3 (0.5)fh	2.0 (1.4)	1.3 (0.6)	2.4 (1.0)	2.1 (0.5)	3.2 (1.1)	2.8 (1.1)m	3.2 (1.2)om	1.3 (0.6)
A Lot	2	2.0 (0.1)	1.0 (0.0)	1.0 (0.0)	2.4 (1.1)	1.9 (0.5)	1.6 (0.9)	3.3 (0.7)	2.6 (0.9)	1.5 (0.2)

$^* p \leq .05, ^{**} p \leq .01$.

Note. ANOVAs using Bonferroni correction were conducted to identify struggle differences based on parental r/s emphasis. Means with shared subscripts differ at p < .05 using the Bonferroni correction. Asterisks indicate when an ANOVA test was significant. Believers include all youth who endorsed believing in God at least sometimes. Atheists and agnostic youth did not significantly differ on any struggles except Doubt where the atheistic youth did not demonstrate significant differences but the agnostic youth did and drove the above findings for Doubt. Scale: 1 = None, 5 = A Great Deal.

Qualitative Descriptions of Adolescent Struggles. To identify struggles not assessed by the RSS and RSS-A, participants were also asked to write down any other personal r/s struggle experiences. Several youth described r/s identity development struggles. For instance, one adolescent wrote, "I struggled with finding who I was spiritually and what religion I wanted to follow. I felt out of place..." while another noted, "I've had trouble trying to figure out what I personally believe in versus what my family/friends believe in quite a bit

. . . It's hard for me to be convinced about what I believe in when everyone around me doesn't share those beliefs." A youth in the throes of a conflictual process of religious identity development wrote, "I've only started questioning my religion since I entered high school. In elementary school, however, I wasn't feeling the need to think about my choice to change my religion yet. Now, I've felt as if I'm being possessed and going against God even though I don't want to deep inside my heart."

Other students' descriptions of r/s identity development struggles included the role their parents played in this process, particularly when their parents were not perceived as supportive: "In eighth grade I began to question my faith and my mother pushed it to the side, telling me that I was just lazy and didn't want to attend church every Sunday. What I really needed was her support to tell me that I should expand my knowledge on other religions and find out what fits me best," and "Lately I have begun to see my family's religion differently and I do not agree with all of the church's beliefs. My parents have confronted me about this issue, and have told me that they wish for me to find a religion that I spiritually connect with, but they do not seem supportive."

Still other youth expressed struggles with sexuality, including gender roles (e.g., "My parents greatly believe in modesty. They take the Bible and completely flip it to mean I can't wear tank tops and skinny jeans. Their beliefs are based on that men can act how they want, that it is up to the women to change how they look and act so they are not tempted. This happens daily and has permanently damaged our relationship") and sexual behaviors (e.g., "I also have had a problem with the decision of premarital sex. My partner is of the same religion and though we both know it is wrong, we both consent. I tend to worry if God will punish me for this later in my lifetime"). Sexual orientation in conflict with r/s was also a source of struggle for some. For example, one participant noted, "My best friend is gay and my parents don't let me participate in things such as the gay parade to show that I support him and his lifestyle due to their beliefs." Another reported, "I struggle with my personal beliefs on matters such as abortion, and gay marriage, versus the Church's teachings on these subjects or subjects similar to these. I also struggle picturing what I would do if I were in one of these situations, or felt/did something I wanted that was against the Church. I have also had strong conflicting ideals with the Church and its teachings on sexuality and chastity. These feelings have led me to have strong opposing feelings against the Catholic Church, and have heavily considered leaving the Catholic Church when I am older"). Others expressed r/s struggles with their sexual identity (e.g., "Being bisexual and Christian is very difficult").

Youth in the Catholic schools also expressed struggles associated with the r/s component of their schools. Sometimes these struggles were about feeling pressured and mistreated for minority beliefs (e.g., "I also feel pressured by my Catholic School to conform and scorned for my beliefs"). In other cases, youth were frustrated with the lack of r/s exposure (e.g., "I have had a Catholic education my whole life so I have doubts about whether or not I have been brainwashed into believing my religion. It has been hard to separate what I truly believe from what has been taught to me . . . " and "I often question my childhood because I have learned so much religion in classes but I still know so little"). Some felt that they had to outwardly endorse certain beliefs at school in order to get good grades (e.g., "At school I often have to pretend to believe in certain things or act a certain way in order to succeed academically"), while others felt less motivated at school due to the r/s component (e.g., "I don't believe what they are teaching in many religion classes and that makes it hard for me to learn those things. I don't feel motivated to study if I will disregard the information later"). Finally, one youth expressed concern that it might stunt her r/s identity development (e.g., "I have been going to Private Catholic school since age five, so all of my friends and family have the same religion as me . . . Now a particular set of beliefs have been instilled in me for so long, I do not know if I can ever challenge myself to think beyond what I do now about God-related matters").

Adults' Concerns about Adolescents' Struggles. It should be noted that over 70 public and private schools and school districts were contacted during the recruitment phase. It was challenging to find schools who were willing to allow their students to complete this type of survey. Two schools voluntarily dropped out of the study, citing concerns that the survey would cause students to experience r/s struggles or give students the impression that religion was "bad." Likewise, a few parents expressed concerns similar to those Catholic schools that chose not to participate; however, a majority of parents' comments were positive.

Implications

This study carries several important implications for researchers and for individuals who work with youth, particularly within r/s settings. First, it is important to understand and assess adolescents' r/s-struggle experiences, in addition to their positive-r/s experiences, beliefs, practices, and contexts. Prior research has provided tools to assess the positive and neutral aspects of r/s. Now, with the preliminary validation of the adapted RSS and new RSS-A, researchers and youth workers have the ability to quantitatively assess adolescents' struggles. Furthermore, as demonstrated, adolescents' struggles include areas that are not directly assessed by quantitative measures. Thus, it is also important that researchers and youth workers ask open-ended questions that encourage youth to describe their r/s struggles.

Second, students at both the Catholic and secular schools certified struggles (especially of the interpersonal and r/s identity development forms), though often at low levels. Thus, it is highly likely that most youth experience at least some form of r/s struggle, regardless of their context, making struggles a normal experience for adolescents. Studies suggest that struggles are associated not only with indicators of poor well-being, but they may also carry the potential for spiritual growth (Desai & Pargament 2015; Exline et al. 2016). Furthermore, adult research (Exline & Grubbs 2011; Exline et al. 2012) indicates that it is important to foster a supportive, non-judgmental environment where individuals can express their struggles, since some people may believe that it is wrong to do so. The need for support of adolescents experiencing struggles may be challenging for some parents and schools. Reinforcing this point, some parents and non-participating schools voiced such concerns regarding the current study (Homolka 2016). Non-supportive responses to disclosures of r/s struggle have been linked to adults feeling distant from God, experiencing more struggles but expressing them less, and possibly even walking away from faith (Exline & Grubbs 2011). While such research has yet to be conducted with adolescents, it is reasonable to hypothesize that adolescents experience similar issues.

Perhaps the link between parents' greater importance of r/s and youth's greater r/s struggles noted in the current results might be weakened if parents were to realize that their children's struggles are a normal part of life. Their children may be able to resolve their struggles more easily (with possibly a greater likelihood of remaining in the parents' faith) if met with acceptance and support. More research is needed to evaluate this possibility. At this stage, though, it seems reasonable to suggest that youth care workers attempt to normalize adolescent r/s struggles for youth, their caregivers, and their religious and academic institutions. Additionally, given the frequency of r/s struggles among youth and their connections with distress, it would be valuable for researchers to include struggle questions in their assessment of youth r/s.

Third, although it is important to address all adolescents' struggles, youth workers should pay particular attention to older adolescents, as they are likely to experience significantly more struggles. Further research is needed to determine why this is so. Studies (Krause et al., in press) among adults indicate that younger adults experience greater struggles. Taken altogether, perhaps struggles are particularly pronounced in late adolescence and early adulthood. Older adolescence and young adulthood is likely a pivotal time in r/s identity development when many are determining their personal r/s identities separate from their families and r/s contexts.

Furthermore, youth care workers and researchers should also give close attention to LGBTQ youth, non-r/s youth, and non-Christian youth, since they are more likely to experience r/s struggles, especially of the interpersonal form. Research has consistently shown that r/s minorities, non-r/s people, and LGBTQ individuals experience significantly more discrimination and mistreatment at the hands of the r/s, Christian, and/or heterosexual majority (Doehring, 2013; Stahl et al., 2016). Thus, it is not surprising that such adolescents experience struggles stemming from their r/s interactions with others. Hence, these youth need supportive people with whom they can feel safe to talk about their struggles and minority status. Youth workers should also be alert to situations in which such youth may experience greater struggles due to their minority status. More research is needed to determine the consequences of such youth receiving judgmental responses regarding their struggles.

Fourth, youth workers and researchers should recognize that religious environments, even while offering the benefits of r/s community and education, may also create additional opportunities for r/s struggles to occur. Though causality cannot be implied, this study's Catholic school students experienced significantly more struggles and described struggles resulting from their religious school context. To address this, r/s youth workers can incorporate teachings on struggles drawn from sacred texts and religious history to help normalize struggles for youth. Nearly all faiths include stories of r/s struggles. Within Judaism and Christianity, Sarah, Hannah, Martha, Moses, Job, King David, and Saul/Paul are just a few such examples. Additionally, it is important to not base student evaluations on their r/s beliefs or endorsements of specific beliefs (note that some students within this study described experiencing this). Requiring such introduces the possibility that youth who believe differently will experience greater r/s struggles, which may serve to further alienate them from their r/s community and its beliefs.

Fifth, those who do research and/or work with youth should recognize that struggles are normal but also distressing; there is a dark side to youths' r/s lives. Struggles may affect or be affected by youths' well-being. They are also likely intertwined with adolescent identity development. Therefore, the integration of struggles into work and research with adolescents is crucial to understanding and serving them well. Empathy and sensitivity to youths' struggles may go a long way to helping youth to feel heard and to find r/s stability within the often tumultuous r/s identity development process.

Limitations

While this study presents a number of important implications, such implications are also limited. First, given that the sample was largely White, Catholic, middle to upper class, private-school educated, and Midwestern, we cannot be certain that results presented here will generalize beyond these groups. Furthermore, school environments have been shown to shape adolescents' r/s (Barrett et al. 2007; Cohen-Malayev et al. 2014), suggesting that the r/s environments of the schools may have influenced participants' struggle experiences and the degree to which they reported these struggles. Finally, the survey's self-report format and the schools' voluntary choice to participate (or not) may have allowed biased responding and inflation of correlations due to common-method variance. Future studies should survey key figures in adolescents' lives (e.g., parents) to address this problem. Despite these limitations, the current findings are consistent with those found among adults. They also suggest the value in further study of struggles that may be more particular to youth, such as identity-development issues and disagreements with parents and peers about r/s issues.

References

Abu-Raiya, Hisham, et al. 2015. "Prevalence, Predictors, and Implications of Religious/Spiritual Struggles among Muslims." *Journal for the Scientific Study of Religion* 54, pp. 631–48.

Abu-Raiya, Hisham, et al. 2015. "Robust Links between Religious/Spiritual Struggles, Psychological Distress, and Well-Being in a National Sample of American Adults. *American Journal of Orthopsychiatry* 85, pp. 565–75.

Abu-Raiya, Hisham, et al. 2016. "An Empirical Examination of Religious/Spiritual Struggle among Israeli Jews." *The International Journal for the Psychology of Religion* 26, pp. 61–79.

Ai, Amy L., et al. 2011. "Modeling the Post-9/11 Meaning-Laden Paradox: From Deep Connection and Deep Struggle to Posttraumatic Stress and Growth." *Archive for the Psychology of Religion* 33, pp. 173–204.

Barrett, Jennifer B., et al. 2007. "Adolescent Religiosity and School Contexts." *Social Science Quarterly* 88, pp. 1024–37.

Carpenter, Thomas P., et al. 2012. "Religious Coping, Stress, and Depressive Symptoms among Adolescents: A Prospective Study." *Psychology of Religion and Spirituality* 4, pp. 19–30.

Cohen-Malayev, Maya, et al. 2014. "Teachers and the Religious Socialization of Adolescents: Facilitation of Meaningful Religious Identity Formation

Processes." *Journal of Adolescence* 37, pp. 205–14. http://doi.org/10.1016/j.adolescence.2013.12.004.

Cotton, Sian, et al. 2013. "Spiritual Struggles, Health-Related Quality of Life, and Mental Health Outcomes in Urban Adolescents with Asthma." *Research in the Social Scientific Study of Religion* 24, pp. 259–80.

Davis, Timothy L., et al. 2003. "Meaning, Purpose, and Religiosity in At-Risk Youth: The Relationship between Anxiety and Spirituality." *Journal of Psychology and Theology* 31, pp. 356–65.

Desai, K. M., and Kenneth I. Pargament. 2015. "Predictors of Growth and Decline Following Spiritual Struggles." *International Journal for the Psychology of Religion* 25, pp. 45–56.

Doehring, Carrie. 2013. "An Applied Integerative Approach to Exploring How Religion and Spirituality Contribute to or Counteract Prejudice and Discrimination." In *APA handbook of Psychology, Religion, and Spirituality*, edited by Kenneth I. Pargament, 2:389–403. Washington, DC: American Psychological Association. http://doi.org/10.1037/14046-020.

Exline, Julie J. 2013. "Religious and Spiritual Struggles." In *APA Handbook of Psychology, Religion, and Spirituality*, edited by Kenneth I. Pargament et al., 1:459–75. Washington, DC: American Psychological Association.

Exline, Julie J., and Joshua B. Grubbs. 2011. "'If I Tell Others about My Anger toward God, How Will They Respond?' Predictors, Associated Behaviors, and Outcomes in an Adult Sample." *Journal of Psychology and Theology* 39, pp. 304–15.

Exline, Julie J., et al. 2016. "Predictors of Growth from Spiritual Struggle among Christian Undergraduates: Religious Coping and Perceptions of Helpful Action by God are Both Important." *Journal of Positive Psychology* 12.5, 501–8.

Exline, Julie J., et al. 2012. "Anger, Exit, and Assertion: Do People See Protest toward God as Morally Acceptable?" *Psychology of Religion and Spirituality* 4, pp. 264–77.

Exline, Julie J., et al. 2014. "The Religious and Spiritual Struggles Scale: Development and Initial Validation." *Psychology of Religion and Spirituality* 6, pp. 208–22.

Exline, Julie J., and Eric D. Rose. 2013. "Religious and Spiritual Struggles." In *Handbook of the Psychology of Religion and Spirituality*, edited by Ralph F. Paloutzian and Crystal L. Park, 380–98. New York: Guilford. http://doi.org/10.1080/14766086.2011.582684.

Homolka, Steffany J. 2016. "Validation of Religious and Spiritual Struggles Scales for Adolescents." PhD diss., Case Western Reserve University.

Gignac, Gilles E., and Eva T. Szodorai. 2016. "Effect Size Guidelines for Individual Differences Researchers." *Personality and Individual Differences* 102, pp. 74–78.

Homolka, Steffany J., and Julie J. Exline. 2016. "The Existence and Nature of Religious and Spiritual Struggles Among Children and Adolescents: A Review of Research on Youth and Religiosity/Spirituality." Manuscript in preparation.

Hunsberger, Bruce, et al. 2001. "Adolescent Identity Formation: Religious Exploration and Commitment." *Identity* 1, pp. 365–86.

King, Pamela E., et al. 2013. "Search for the Sacred: Religion, Spirituality, and Adolescent Development." In *APA Handbook of Psychology, Religion, and Spirituality*, edited by Kenneth I. Pargament et al., 1:513–28. Washington, DC: American Psychological Association.

Krause, Neal, et al. forthcoming. "Exploring the Relationships among Age, Spiritual Struggles, and Health. *Journal of Religion, Spirituality, and Aging* (in press).

Laufer, Avital, and Zahava Solomon. 2011. "The Role of Religious Orientations in Youth's Posttraumatic Symptoms after Exposure to Terror." *Journal of Religion and Health* 50, pp. 687–99.

Nkansah-Amankra, Stephen. 2013. "Adolescent Suicidal Trajectories through Young Adulthood: Prospective Assessment of Religiosity and Psychosocial Factors among a Population-Based Sample in the United States." *Suicide and Life-Threatening Behavior* 43, pp. 439–59.

Pargament, Kenneth I., et al. 2006. "Spirituality: A Pathway to Posttraumatic Growth or Decline?" In *Handbook of Posttraumatic Growth: Research & Practice*, edited by Lawrence G. Calhoun and Richard G. Tedeschi, 121–37. Mahwah, NH: Erlbaum.

Pargament, Kenneth I., et al. 2000. "The Many Methods of Religious Coping: Development and Initial Validation of the RCOPE." *Journal of Clinical Psychology* 56, pp. 519–43.

Pössel, Patrick, et al. 2011. "Bidirectional Relations of Religious Orientation and Depressive Symptoms in Adolescents: A Short-Term Longitudinal Study." *Psychology of Religion and Spirituality* 3, pp. 24–38. http://doi.org/10.1037/a0019125.

Puffer, Keith A., et al. 2008. "Religious Doubt and Identity Formation: Salient Predictors of Adolescent Religious Doubt." *Journal of Psychology and Theology* 36, pp. 270–84.

Regnerus, Mark D., and Glen H. Elder. 2003. "Staying on Track in School: Religious Influences in High- and Low-Risk Settings." *Journal for the Scientific Study of Religion* 42, pp. 633–49.

Resnick, Michael D., et al. 2004. "Youth Violence Perpetration: What Protects? What Predicts? Findings from the National Longitudinal Study of Adolescent Health." *Journal of Adolescent Health* 35, pp. 1–10.

Stahl, Michelle A., et al. 2016. "Adolescence: The Issue of Lesbian, Gay, Bisexual, and Transgender." *International Journal of Child and Adolescent Health* 9, pp. 313–25.

Stauner, Nicholas., et al. 2016. "Bifactor Models of Religious and Spiritual Struggles: Distinct from Religiousness and Distress." *Religions* 7, pp. 68.

Wilt, Joshua A., et al. 2016. "Personality, Religious and Spiritual Struggles, and Well-Being." *Psychology of Religion and Spirituality* 8, pp. 341–51.

Chapter 23

Connecting Children with God through Nature
Why We Should and how we Can

—— Beverly J. Christian ——

Spirituality is a fragile yet strong component of human life, especially in children. Writers focusing on children's spirituality acknowledge that despite multiple ways in which God is viewed, an overarching belief in a personal relationship with something or someone outside of themselves is widely acknowledged by children (Allen & Ross 2012; Barrett 2012; Louv 2008). From a Christian perspective, spirituality involves the development of a mindful relationship with God as Father, Son and Holy Spirit and an ongoing response to that relationship within the context of a community of believers. In order to flourish spiritually, children need reference points that direct them toward God and help them build a relationship with Him. This chapter explores how the natural world can offer a reference point that supports the Bible and the faith communities espousing the Bible in nurturing children's spirituality, and how this may be facilitated by parents and teachers in a home, church or school context.

Goodwin (2009) makes the observation that the early chapters of Genesis establish a symbiotic relationship between humanity and the natural world. The issue of why nature needs humanity is worthy of its own discussion (Ray 2006), but is not the topic of conversation for this chapter. While Christianity often takes a stewardship approach to the natural world, this chapter focuses on the less-explored experiential approach and the issue of why nature is important to faith formation in children.

The World in Which Today's Children Live

The twenty-first century is characterized by rapid change, and this has become obvious both in how we live and where we live. Patterns of human behavior are changing and children are falling victim to overstimulation and hurry sickness in a fast-paced society (Fishbaugh 2011; Louv 2012). They are transported from event to event, and sometimes parent to parent, after school and on weekends in an attempt to juggle family life, work, hobbies, and sport. Many childhood activities are highly structured and controlled by adults. Few children enjoy the extended hours of free play in the outside natural world that their parents and grandparents experienced while growing up (Louv 2008). Instead, technological devices are contributing to a disconnect with nature (Bauer 2009; Burdette &Whitaker 2005; Louv 2012; Wilson 2012). Even when today's children are allowed the freedom to choose their play mode, more often than not they reach for a technological device that keeps them indoors. If the "screenagers" (Rushkoff 2008) of today experience the natural world at all, it is increasingly through virtual reality, applications for which are growing at an escalating rate (Louv 2012). Add to this the changing patterns of place, which include the spreading built environment and the concomitant shrinking natural environment, and it becomes apparent that even if many children chose to go outside, they would struggle to find the canyons and streams, forests and fields that featured in their parents' childhood activities. Urbanization is continually on the rise as the world's inhabitants increasingly abandon the wide open spaces in search of employment and financial security. As Knight (2013) notes, "before the urbanization of the nineteenth century it was not necessary to create formal links between education and the outdoor environment" (2), but that is not the case in the twenty-first century.

This world of virtual nature experiences (Burdette & Whitaker 2005; Louv 2012), overstimulation (Fishbaugh 2011), and the shrinking of children's play spaces to the family home or apartment in urban areas (Louv 2008), is increasingly limiting the time children spend in nature (Bauer 2009). This is resulting in what Louv (2008) calls "Nature-Deficit Disorder" (11). In response to these changes, a rising number of educators, social commentators and environmentalists are calling for nature to again become an important part of every child's life (Erickson & Ernst 2011; Louv 2008; Wilson 2012).

Reconnecting Children with Nature
—A Global Perspective

The global movement to reconnect children with nature is largely motivated by a desire to foster the wellbeing of children. Historically, there have always been champions of the child/nature connection. Reggio Emelia pre-schools, the Steiner approach to education and the philosophies of Pestalozzi and Froebel all emphasize the importance of play in the outdoors. Others promoting the nature/child connection include Hahn's Outward Bound model, Baden-Powell's scouting clubs and a variety of church and community organizations that spawned the summer camp movement (Paris 2008). Today, an increasing number of organizations promote sustained and regular time outside in nature. Though varying in their philosophical, physiological and psychological approach to the benefits of nature, these organizations have a common goal; to enhance the wellbeing of the whole child.

One organization focused on well-being is the Forest School movement, based on a Scandinavian model and growing rapidly in the United Kingdom and further afield. This program is described as "an inspirational process that offers all learners regular opportunity to achieve, as well as to develop confidence and self-esteem, through hands-on learning experiences in a local woodland or natural environment with trees" (Knight 2013, 16). The aims of Forest schools include support for the child/nature nexus, holistic development, the fostering of resilience, independence, confidence, creativity and community building (Warden 2015). Also listed as a goal is the development of "spiritual aspects of the learner" (Knight 2013, 17). Many mainstream schools are also recognizing the benefits of intentional outdoor connections, and are experimenting with custom-designed play grounds where children can interact with nature (Alaniz 2015).

The idea of connecting children to nature is not limited to formal education. When Louv (2008) published his national bestseller, "Last Child in the Woods", he was elaborating on a renewed interest in connecting children with the natural world (Kellert 2005; Kessler 2000; Warden 2007; Young & Elliot 2003). An increasing number of authors are promoting the benefits of connecting children of all ages to nature; citing health benefits, the development of creativity, problem-solving, self-esteem, communication skills, empathy, social-emotional and cognitive development as some of the positive outcomes of spending time outdoors (Burdette & Whitaker 2005; Erickson & Ernst 2011; Kessler 2000; Louv 2008; Ward 2009; Warden 2007; Wilson 2012). These benefits alone are enough for Christian parents, teachers and pastors to justify the fostering of a child/nature nexus, but there is an additional reason. The natural environment also offers opportunities for faith development and a platform for nurturing spirituality.

Many authors and organizations promoting nature education for children acknowledge a heightened sense of spirituality. Although they use the term spirituality in the broadest sense of the definition, such as Kessler's something "larger and more meaningful than day-to-day existence" (2000, 29), or Wilsons's "sense of transcendence" (69), none however, focus on developing an encounter with God as creator, and most disassociate the spiritual from any form of organized religion, preferring instead to defer to values and moral development (Kellert 2005). There is mounting evidence, however, to support a connection between nature and spirituality. Barrett (2012) offers evidence that children begin life with sense-making brains. He posits that they see purpose and function in nature and automatically search for the designer. Such a notion is consistent with Louv's (2012) suggestion that the ability to sense a higher power is accelerated when all senses are fully engaged, as when immersed in nature.

A Christian worldview, however, moves beyond a vague sense of spirituality. Instead, it positions God as creator and sustainer of the natural world, humanity included (Ps 8:3-4; Ps 139:13-14; Rev 4:11). The implications of this stance determine the relationship between individuals and the natural world; and therefore offer a framework for extending the innate beliefs that young children hold of God.

A Christian Perspective on Connecting with Nature

Although the literature is generous in its acknowledgement of the benefits derived from connecting children with the natural world (Burdette & Whitaker 2005; Erickson & Ernst 2011; Louv 2008; Warden 2007; Young & Elliot 2003), there is less evidence that Christian educators are fully recognizing the value of nature experiences in connecting children with God. While society, schools, churches, and families may share some common goals when fostering nature awareness in children, Christian educators can add a further reference point. The natural world adds another dimension to build on children's natural propensities toward God; that of exploring their innate sense of God, and more importantly, experiencing the presence of God. Therefore, nature may play an important role in the developing spirituality and faith of children. Referred to by some as God's second book (Bailey 2009; Goodwin 2009, White 2000), but in reality God's original book, the natural world confirms the supremacy of God as creator and illuminates the character of God (Christian 2017).

Those who have explored spiritual growth through nature acknowledge several components of faith formation. Among these are understanding, experiencing and sharing, that is, understanding of the Holy Scriptures, experiencing God in everyday life and sharing with community one's own experience of God (Foster 2012; Jonker 2015). Learning in the natural world has the potential to enhance all three areas of faith formation. Children learn about God's law of selfless love as they explore the wonders of the natural environment. Children experience God through their senses when immersed in nature. Children, in solitude, celebrate their delight and awe of God's creation, and then share it with their parents, peers and teachers. God can be experienced in a variety of ways, including Bible reading, family rituals, and belonging to a faith community that intentionally creates an environment where children enjoy the presence of God (Allen & Ross 2012; de Roos 2006; Fischer 2014; Moriarty 2011; Mountain 2011; Thompson 2010). The wonder and majesty of nature also has potential to create spiritual reference points that help children connect the dots in their relationship with God (Christian 2010; National Institute of Christian Education 2015; Stankard 2003). Despite this support for nature experiences, children still do most of their learning about God within four walls.

Experiencing the God of Creation

Does it matter if Christian parents and educators teach about God without stepping outside? I believe it does. The natural world provides a reference point for children to learn about who God is and how God acts. The Bible itself claims that "ever since the creation of the world, His invisible attributes, His eternal power and divine nature, have been clearly seen, being understood through what has been made" (Rom 1:20 NASB). Jennings (2013) puts it this way, "God's nature of love is seen in creation because all nature, all life is built, designed, constructed to operate on the template of God's love" (24). Many attributes of God's character are revealed through the natural world. Graham (2009) reasons that "the intricacy and diversity of creation could only have been developed with an infinite mind, capable of making every diverse dimension of the creation fit and work with every other dimension" (51). That God values diversity is apparent with a simple nature walk or visit to a zoo. But it is not only diversity that testifies to a creator. The building materials of nature, such as spider silks and abalone shells, have properties that surpass equivalent man-made materials, supporting a case for intelligent design (Dovich 2009). That God is a master of order is also evident in nature. From the Fibonacci pattern of a pine cone to the fractal spirals of the nautilus shell, design and order are visible everywhere. Paralleling that order is beauty. The intricate loveliness of a lyrebird's plumage, the iridescent scales of coral reef fish and the delicate pattern of a snowflake all speak of a God who values beauty. Yet, although nature reveals much about God, much also remains a mystery. This engenders a sense of awe. The secrets of bird migration patterns or the caribou as they begin their annual trek across the tundra are examples of these mysteries of nature and are a testament to the God who is above and beyond humanity.

Yet there is an anomaly in nature. Not everything is perfect, and amazing opportunities to explore God's redemptive acts may be lost if parents and teachers ignore the ugly and destructive side of nature. Nature offers evidence of a breach in humanity's face-to-face communion with God. While we cannot be certain how the natural world changed after the fall of humanity, we can observe object lessons in nature that point to both the long-term effects of sin, and the endurance of selfless love, through which the healing of the breach can occur (Jennings 2013). As such, the natural world supports the belief that undergirds the epic story of salvation, and therefore an experience in nature may enhance a child's understanding of salvation, for it is in nature that the dichotomy of decay with regeneration, death with life, and taking with giving becomes evident. This may occur without adult intervention, or through guided discussions with adults who honor a biblical worldview. The selfless, amazing, inspiring and awesome become visible. This experience, this sense of transcendence, focuses on a creator God who also recreates through everlasting love.

Nature provides ample opportunities for children to catch glimpses of God's everlasting love for His children. "God is love" (1 John 4:8), and evidence of this love is found in the natural world. Natural laws testify to the selfless love of God and all nature is a living object lesson of a selfless love that restores and renews. The caterpillar gives up its life in order to emerge as a resplendent butterfly, the pine cone gives up its seeds to regenerate the forest. The log, rotting on the forest floor, enriches the soil so new life can flourish, and the imperfection planted in an oyster is transformed by giving in to a perfect pearl. These examples demonstrate that God's eternal law of unselfish love runs deep in the natural laws that govern life. The law of selfless love also provides evidence that God sustains. The turning seasons offer an example that the cycle of life is sustained. The cycle that keeps water in motion is a prime example of the law of giving. Water stagnates if withdrawn from this cycle. If the cycle is interrupted, life is impacted. Both selfishness and its antithesis, selflessness, can be observed in the natural world.

With so many opportunities to learn about the character and actions of God, and to experience the presence of God without distraction, the natural environment can offer a truly sensory and spiritual experience for children. Immersion in the natural world arouses all the senses and creates an atmosphere of responsiveness to God. Connecting children with nature may be an important way of helping them encounter God in a world where the sounds of humanity may otherwise drown out the creator's voice.

Re-Establishing the Connection

Three ways in which Christian educators can facilitate a connection with God through nature are the use of intentional nature experiences, free-play immersion in natural environments and serendipitous moments.

Intentional Nature Experiences

Intentional nature experiences fall into two categories: taking children to nature, and bringing nature to children. An intentional nature experience involves a purpose and an outcome, and guides children toward a new understanding. An important part of the guiding process involves intentional questioning. For teaching examples, see Table 1.

Table 1. Examples of Intentional Outdoor Nature Activities

Goal	Purpose	Activity
To recognize that all people are God's children, loved by Him.	Makes connections between diversity in leaves and diversity in people. Discovers examples of diversity in nature.	Children collect a variety of leaves. Examine them with magnifying glasses. Sort them and create categories. Question children about their diversity. What does this tell them about God? Make a comparison to people. Ask what this tells them about God. Ask children to look around for other examples of diversity.
To teach the concept of selfless giving.	Articulates that selfless giving involves giving up something so that something else may flourish. Links selfless giving in nature to the sacrifice of Jesus Christ.	Examine a rotting log. Feel the breakdown of the wood. Search for evidence that new life is growing from the log. Question children about what the tree has to give up in order for fungi and new plants to sprout and grow. Ask what this tells them about God. (Guide through questioning to the sacrifice of Jesus Christ.) Ask children to look around for other examples where death enables new life.

Although the ideal is to take children out into nature frequently, this is not always possible. Children can still connect with nature in their homes, churches or classrooms when nature is brought to the children (Wilson 2012). Those responsible for teaching children and teens in church settings can bring nature objects into their Bible lessons that encourage the children to reflect on God's character and ways. Table 2 provides suggestions for bringing nature into the classroom.

Table 2. Examples of Intentional Inside Nature Activities

Purpose	Outcomes	Guided Activity
To explore design in relation to purpose and a designer	Reflects on the design of a feather	Provide a variety of feathers, some soft and downy, some wing feathers that interlock. Use magnifying glasses, explore the shafts and how they appear. Question children about differences and similarities and the purpose of the feathers.
To explore the concept of a new life after conversion	Reflects on a metaphor of conversion: a tree shedding bark	Find a photograph of a tree that is shedding its bark. Bring some of the bark into the classroom. Compare the color and texture of the shed bark to the new bark. Ask, "How is conversion like a tree shedding bark?"

Gardens, whether in pots or plots, also provide an ongoing source of nature experiences, and encourage children to nurture and value growing plants. Gardens also provide opportunities to observe and to hold extended conversations over time about life cycles and growth (Warden 2015). This can be done within a Christian context. Once children become aware of how nature demonstrates the character and actions of God, they will be able to find their own examples and share them.

A popular way to bring nature into the classroom is through technology. Carefully selected nature documentaries and virtual field studies may be useful tools. They can teach children about the natural world and God's creative power, but they are limited when it comes to children encountering God. Since children learn and experience life through their senses and technology restricts sensory input (Aitken et al. 2012), relying on technology alone is not adequate in connecting children with nature and, therefore, with God. The sight and sound of a cascading waterfall in nature is enhanced by the smell of wet leaves and fine spray on one's face, something not experienced on a screen. The silence of the natural world that allows thought processing is not available with the ongoing commentary that accompanies a nature documentary. Therefore, virtual nature experiences should be supplemented where possible with real nature experiences.

Free-Play Immersion

Not all nature experiences need to be intentional. Some of the best moments occur when children are allowed to immerse themselves in the natural environment with no agenda (Wilson 2012). It is claimed that play is essential to both learning (Robinson & Aronica 2015) and spirituality (Mountain 2011). Play in natural environments increases learning potential. Just merely being in the natural environment is therapeutic, and some also advocate for times of silence in nature, times to listen to the gentle chirping of crickets, the rustling of branches, or the intensity of a thunderclap or waterfall. McDaniel (2006) calls this "deep listening" (30) and purports that "when there is no listening, God is absent" (29). Langdoc (2013) also supports the value of quiet times to enhance children's experiences with God. If quiet, reflective times are combined with a peaceful, outdoor setting, the encounter with God will be even more powerful. Sitting on a sand dune listening to the waves crash on the beach is a spiritual experience in itself that needs no explanation. Lying on a mattress of pine needles and watching the forest giants sway overhead in the wind develops a sense of God's majesty that may surpass a sermon. Watching leaves in their autumnal glory flutter earthwards in the morning sunlight may connect a child to God in ways not possible in a more conventional setting.

Serendipitous Moments

Finally, there are serendipitous moments where children connect to God in a profound way. Serendipitous moments may occur inside or outside, during intentional nature experiences or during unstructured exploration or play. These moments cannot be planned, and intuitive Christian teachers and parents will recognize the moment when a child makes a spiritual discovery, and celebrate with the child. The adult's role in this process may involve a joint voyage of discovery with a child, or it may involve remaining silent until asked to join the conversation.

God-Encounter Conversations

The investigative approach adopted to teach children scientific ways of looking at the world can be adapted to help a child develop their understanding of God. The role of the adult in conversations about God will vary depending on the type of nature experience. Warden sees the adult role in nature experiences as ranging from explicit teaching to "the calm supportive structure of an almost silent presence" (2015, xiii). Aitken et al. highlight the importance of "honoring a child's sense of wonder" (2012, 22) and encourage teachers to adopt "an attitude of excited discovery" (25). This occurs when adults cultivate their own sense of wonder and join their students in their awe of God's created world. This results in a God-encounter conversation. God-encounter conversations take place during an experience with the natural world. They involve an adult and child coming together in a sense of awe and wonder. Sometimes this awe may have to be nurtured; other times the adult simply joins the child in their attitude of excitement and wonder. The child is encouraged to observe, marvel, and share observations while the adult engages, facilitates, and questions where appropriate. Intentional questions to ask may include the following: *What are our senses telling us? What does this tell us about God? What can we learn from this? What more do we want to learn?* These questions are important in gently directing the child's mind toward God.

As children explore the colors, textures, sights and sounds of God's creation, the teacher who is attuned to their wonderment will recognize when the time is right to instigate a conversation with God. Simple questions giving children the option to tell God about what they have just discovered will guide the young learner into prayers of thanksgiving and praise. These may take the form of songs, dances, monologues or artworks along with the more traditional forms of prayer. Time to reflect and write may also provide opportunities for older children to converse with the creator God and help develop a meaningful relationship with Him.

Conclusion

In addition to the cognitive, social-emotional and physical benefits touted by the global back-to-nature movement, the natural world provides opportunity for spiritual development. More specifically, it provides opportunities for children to experience God through a multi-sensory approach. Children immersed in the natural world may find a reference point through which they can further develop their understanding of God's creative and sustaining power, character of love, and the law of love on which the universe operates. The natural world can open children's eyes to the consequences of sin and the wonders of salvation. It can also open their hearts to the work of the Holy Spirit. In an often confusing and complicated world, the natural environment offers another set of coordinates to guide children's incipient spirituality and faith development.

References

Aitken, Jenny, et al. 2012. *A Sense of Wonder: Science in Early Childhood Education.* Albert Park: Teaching Solutions.

Alaniz, Vanessa. 2015. "The Magic of Nature Play." *Class Ideas K-3* 75, pp. 6–7.

Allen, Holly C., and Christine L. Ross. 2012. *Intergenerational Christian Formation.* Downers Grove, IL: InterVarsity.

Bailey, Rosemary. 2009. "The Need for Nature." *Journal of Adventist Education* 71, pp. 4–8.

Barrett, Justin. 2012. *Born Believers: The Science of Children's Religious Belief.* New York: Free.

Bauer, Stephen. 2009. "Go Ask the Ants: Using Nature to Teach Moral Values." *Journal of Adventist Education* 71, pp. 14–17.

Burdette, Hilary L., and Robert C. Whitaker. 2005. "Resurrecting free play in young children: Looking beyond fitness and fatness to attention, affiliation and affect." *Journal of the American Medical Association* 159, pp. 46–50.

Christian, Beverly J. 2010. "Children and learning." In *Developing a Faith-Based Education: A Teacher's Manual*, edited by Barbara J. Fisher, 29–43. Terrigal: Barlow.

Christian, Beverly J. 2017. "Nature-Based Learning in Christian Schools: Essential Element or Optional Extra?" *Teach Journal of Christian Education* 11, pp. 21–27.

De Roos, Simone A. 2006. "Young Children's God Concepts: Influences of Attachment and Religious Socialization in a Family and School Context." *Religious Education: The Official Journal of the Religious Education Association*, 10, pp. 84–103.

Dovich, Laurel. 2009. "Integrating Faith and Learning in an Engineering Classroom." *Journal of Adventist Education* 71, pp. 36–39.

Erickson, Deanna M., and Julie Athman Ernst. 2011. "The Real Benefits of Nature Play Every Day." *Wonder* 260, pp. 97–99.

Fishbaugh, Angela. 2011. *Celebrate Nature: Activities for Every Season.* St. Paul: Redleaf.

Fischer, Becky. 2014. *Redefining Children's Ministry in the 21st Century: A Call for Radical Change.* Mandan: Kids in Ministry.

Foster, Charles R. 2012. *From Generation to Generation: The Adaptive Challenge of Mainline Protestant Education in Forming Faith.* Eugene, OR: Cascade.

Graham, Donovan I. 2009. *Teaching Redemptively: Bringing Grace and Truth into your Classroom.* 2nd ed. Colorado Springs: Purposeful Design.

Goodwin, H. Thomas. 2009. "Repairing the Breach: Reconnecting Students with Nature," *The Journal of Adventist Education* 71, pp. 9–13.

Jennings, Timothy R. 2013. *The God Shaped Brain: How Changing your View of God Transforms your Life.* Downers Grove, IL: InterVarsity.

Jonker, Laura. 2015. "Experiencing God: The History and Philosophy of 'Children and Worship.'" *Christian Education Journal Series* 3, no. 12, pp. 291–313.

Kellert, Stephen R. 2005. *Building for Life: Designing and Understanding the Human-Nature Connection*. Washington DC: Island.

Kessler, Rachael. 2000. *The Soul of Education*. Alexandria: Association for Supervision and Curriculum Development.

Knight, Sara. 2013. *Forest School and Outdoor Learning in the Early Years*. 2nd ed. London: Sage.

Langdoc, Bryan. 2013. "Quiet, Please! Turning down the Volume in Children's Spiritual Formation." *Liturgy* 28, no. 51–59. DOI: 10.1080/0458063X.2013.774885.

Louv, Richard. 2008. *Last Child in the Woods: Saving our Children from Nature-Deficit Disorder*. 2nd ed. Chapel Hill: Algonquin.

Louv, Richard. 2012. *The Nature Principle: Connecting with Life in a Virtual Age*. Chapel Hill: Algonquin.

McDaniel, Jay. 2006. "In the Beginning is the Listening." In *Ecology, Economy and God: Theology that Matters*, edited by Darby K. Ray, 26–41. Minneapolis: Ausburg Fortress.

Moriarty, Micheline W. 2011. "A Conceptualization of Children's Spirituality Arising out of Recent Research." *International Journal of Children's Spirituality* 16, pp. 271–85.

Mountain, Vivienne. 2011. "Four Links between Child Theology and Children's Spirituality." *International Journal of Children's Spirituality* 16, pp. 261–69.

National Institute for Christian Education. *Transformation by Design: A Curriculum Development Resource for Christian Schools*. Penrith: National Institute for Christian Education, 2015.

Paris, Leslie. 2008. *Children's Nature: The Rise of the American Summer Camp*. New York: New York University Press.

Ray, Darby. K. 2006. "Prologue." In *Ecology, Economy and God: Theology that Matters*, edited by Darby K. Ray, 1–8. Minneapolis: Ausburg Fortress.

Robinson, Ken, and Lou Aronica. 2015. *Creative Schools: The Grassroots Revolution that's Transforming Education*. New York: Viking.

Rushkoff, Douglas. 2008. *Screenagers: Lessons in Chaos from Digital Kids*. New York: Hampton.

Stankard, Bernadette. 2003. *How Each Child Learns: Using Multiple Intelligence in Faith Formation*. Mystic: Twenty-Third.

Thompson, Kristin. 2010. "With Jesus in the Family: How Early Childhood Attachment Styles Influence Later Relationships, both with God and in the Workplace." *Teach Journal of Christian Education* 4, pp. 26–32.

Ward, Jennifer. 2009. *Let's Go Outside: Outdoor Activities and Projects to Get You and Your Kids Closer to Nature*. Boston: Trumpeter.

Warden, Claire. 2007. *Nurture through Nature: Working with Children under Three in Outdoor Environments*. Auchterarder: Mindstretchers.

Warden, Claire. 2015. *Learning with Nature: Embedding Outdoor Practice*. London: Sage.

White, Ellen G. 2000. *True Education: An Adaptation of Education by Ellen G. White*. Edited by B. Russell Holt. Nampa: Pacific.

Wilson, Ruth. 2012. *Nature and Young Children: Encouraging Creative Play and Learning in Natural Environments*. 2nd ed. New York: Routledge.

Young, Tracy, and Sue Elliot. 2003. *Just Investigate: Science and Technology Experiences for Young Children*. Croydon: Pearson.

Chapter 24

The Building Blocks of Faith

A Model for Integrating Children's Ministry into the Congregation's Vision for Faith Formation

Robert J. Keeley
& Laura Keeley

LAST YEAR, LAURA ATTENDED a gathering of pastors, elders and deacons and described her position in faith formation ministries. During a dinner break, she walked by a pastor she knew who recently moved to a new church. Laura asked about his new congregation and he replied that he was really impressed with the congregation and their emphasis on faith formation. He continued to say that they had an excellent Sunday school program with plenty of volunteers. There were many things, though, that he didn't talk about. He didn't mention the adult involvement in the community, the teen's relationships with the adults or how worship is transforming lives. For this pastor, faith formation was just a new term for Sunday School, or perhaps more broadly, Church Education.

In contrast, this past semester, Robert was teaching a seminary class on Discipleship and Teaching and asked students to think together about what the point of Church Education is. The students did a great job of talking in groups about the question and, when they reported their conversation to the class, they saw faith formation in almost everything the church did! This very broad response was just the opposite of the narrow interpretation that Laura had had in her conversation.

These two interactions highlighted one of the difficulties encountered when having conversations about faith formation; people really don't have a robust definition of what it is, how to address the issue or even what language to use. For a congregation, the conversation is both too broad and too narrow.

Faith formation is part of everything we do: worship, church education, outreach, fellowship, service, etc. At the same time faith formation is about how each and every one of us is forming our faith. The Building Blocks of Faith model can address both the broad vision of the church as well as give a narrower look at the individual needs of the people of all ages in the congregation by using the same concept with a common language.

The real power of the Building Blocks Model is in how it can help a congregation think about their faith-formation ministries. Building Blocks can be used to give a unifying structure to ministries in a church for members of all ages, including children. By using the same framework for children, teens, adults and seniors, the church is better able to assess, evaluate and respond. There isn't a separate vision for children. There may be different programs and ways to meet the vision for children but everyone in the congregation is moving in the same direction and embracing the same vision.

What are the Building Blocks of Faith?

The Building Blocks of Faith are these four statements which apply to all people regardless of age:

- I belong
- I know
- I have hope
- I am called and equipped

These four statements are echoed in Scripture, including the passage where Jesus meets the two travelers on the road to Emmaus in Luke 24. Lesli Van Milligan (2017) points out that Jesus joins the two discouraged travelers, enters their conversation and shares their sorrow, making it clear to them that they *belong*. The travelers pour out their hearts to him, building on the foundation of belonging. Jesus then reframes the narrative from discouragement into the larger narrative of God's faithfulness. They *know* and hear the story of God. The travelers reach Emmaus and invite Jesus into their home where Jesus gives thanks, breaks bread and gives it to them. Their eyes are opened and their *hope* is restored. Energized by this hope the disciples leave to share this good news. Hope *equips* them to take on their *calling*.

We also see echoes of these four ideas in Psalm 34:1–7 we read that how good it is to *belong* to God. The passage continues with "Taste and see (*Know*) that God is good" in verses 8—10. In verses 11–16 the author then references our being *called and equipped* when he writes "How good to turn from my selfish heart and to do good for my Father who hears my every cry." The Psalm ends with the *hope* that our Father hears us and redeems our lives.

Description of the Building Blocks

"*I belong*" is the first of the four building blocks. People of all ages need to know that we belong first and foremost to God. Research by George Barna suggest that 93 percent of young people consider themselves to be Christian by the age of 13 (2003, 33). While Barna goes on to define what a real Christian is from his perspective, the point for our work is that, for the overwhelming majority of children who grow up in a faith community, they, to a greater or lesser extent, have lived their way into faith. Don Richter writes that "for almost everyone, faith begins in practice rather than belief" (2010, 24). Damascus Road experiences are not the way everyone comes to faith. In many cases, teens have thought about their faith about as much as someone has thought about breathing. They just are Christians—people of faith, like their parents.

When we belong to Christ we also belong to the community of believers. Craig Dykstra puts it well in *Growing in the Life of Faith*: "The life of faith is deeply personal, but it is not individual or isolated. Only because both faith and the life of faith are communal and historic realities can they belong to us as individuals" (2005, 19). This sense of belonging, which is vital to faith growth, is embedded in community. It is often through belonging to this community of faith that we come to know that we belong to Jesus.

Kevin Lawson, quoted in *Children's Ministry* Magazine, says "Most of us have experienced this in our own growing up. We were glad to be a part of the church or some other group we were in long before we really understood why the group believed what it did. It's important that we allow kids to do this in our churches, but in the process, begin to teach them the whys behind what we believe and do" (Editors, 2014). This also matches what James Fowler (1981) suggests in his theory of faith development. He theorized that children tend to mirror the faith of their parents.

While this feeling of belonging is important to children as they first come to understand Christianity, it is also important for all of us, even as we grow older. The Heidelberg Catechism begins with the question, "What is your only comfort in life and in death?" The answer is all about belonging: "That I am not my own but belong body and soul, in life and in death, to my faithful Savior Jesus Christ." The importance of belonging does not disappear as we get older. Older members need to be reminded that they belong as much as younger ones do.

But belonging is not sufficient for faith. We need to know God, his stories and the stories of his people. The building block, *I know* refers to our desire to know more about God, how he worked in the lives of people in the past and how he is working in our lives and in our world today.

We have four children, all of whom are married. Our relationship with our sons-in-law and daughter-in-law are based on two things. First of all, we love them and welcome them into our family simply because they are married to our children. But, while that is an important part of our relationship, it is not the only part. As we have come to know them we have come to love *them*, not just as our sons- and daughter-in-law, but also as people. Before we knew them well we were ready to accept them but now that we know them, we actually have a relationship with them. Through that relationship we come to know who they are and what is important to them. That's similar to our relationship with God. In order to really love him we need to know him. The way to know him is through his Word, the Bible. Knowledge of who God is and what he has done shows us what is important to God and is crucial to a faith that is growing.

Christian Smith and Melinda Denton (2005, 162) were the first to coin the phrase "Moralistic Therapeutic Deism" (MTD) to signify the somewhat empty beliefs that many young people—and older adults—believe in at this point in our cultural history. Since that time, a number of others have written about the cause of this malady, including Powell, Mulder and Griffin, who cite it, along with the "Golden Rule Gospel" as being responsible for many young people having a weak faith (2016, 130). This MTD is a classic example of what happens when we know the idea of God but not the actual God of the Bible. Without actually knowing the Scriptures we reduce the grand story of God's revelation to "do unto others." It becomes merely an exchange of good deeds on our part with insurance against hell on God's part. Actually knowing who God is and what he has done is important.

The building block *I have hope* is a concept that can be difficult to define in contemporary culture. Hope has often been confused with the idea of "wish." When one says "I hope my team wins" what they're really expressing is a wish that their team will win. Hope in God is more than that. Our lives are caught up in our culture, and we can be easily made despondent by the havoc that sin has brought to our world. But that is not all there is. We live today in the hope that this world can be redeemed. We live in both the now and in the not yet. Hope keeps us looking up and looking ahead.

People of all ages, including children, need hope to grow in their faith. Hope gives our faith a forward posture. What we read and hear about in scripture happened in the past. But hope points us in the other direction. Hope is the assurance that God is up to something big. God has a grand plan to restore the earth and to bring his kingdom here. This has been a common theme in Christendom for ages and continues today. U2 named one of their recent albums *No Line on the Horizon*, looking forward to that time when God's kingdom will arrive in all its fullness. Brian Keepers (2016) puts it this way: "Most simply, hope is faith applied to the future. It is the bold and courageous act to trust that the future is in God's hands and these are good hands. Hope does not guarantee that things will turn out the way we want; instead, it insists that no matter what happens, God's word and promises will prevail."

Hope is well connected to the building block, "I am *called and equipped*." As we look to the future, we see that God not only has a grand kingdom project that he is engaged in but that we have a place in that project. God has called us to do his work and has equipped us to have a role. This calling can be as all-encompassing as a vocation but it can also be a smaller role, like being hospitable by talking to a person at church. These callings are sometimes for a season and for other times longer. Robert spent the first twenty years of his career teaching math to middle and high school students before feeling that he was called to work with college students teaching education and curriculum. God equipped him to do both of those tasks but he was called to do them at different times in his life.

Whether this calling is for a short time or for twenty years we all need to know that God has called us to a task (or tasks) for which he has gifted or equipped us. Early in his life, David was called and equipped to be a shepherd. David was later called and equipped to face giants. The same skill he needed as a shepherd facing down lions and bears with his sling were the skills needed to bring down Goliath. God's call for David to face the enemy of Israel was received in the context of years of equipping.

In developing the Building Blocks model, we are building on the work of Karen-Marie Yust, who suggests six themes related to children's spirituality (2004) and Kenda Creasy Dean, who notes four theological accents that she found in her observation of the faith of teens (2010).

Scottie May (n.d.) notes a list of six characteristics that she says are "necessary for the nurture and formation of children. The following is not a list to be read linearly but characteristics that interact with one another in encounters with God at the hub:

> Encounters with God
> Leading to
> Developing a sense of awe and wonder
> Leading to
> Knowing his character and actions
> Leading to
> Knowing and being formed in the character of God's people
> Leading to
> Owning an identity as part of the people of God
> Leading to
> Engaging in service and mission." (68)

It is easy to find the four building blocks embedded in May's idea; being formed and owning an identity map to "belong," knowing God's character maps to "know," a sense of awe and wonder is similar to "hope" and engaging in service and mission connects to "calling and equipping."

Using Building Blocks

The next step is asking if our churches are meeting the needs expressed in all four building blocks for the members of our congregations. One way to do that is by using a chart similar to the one in Appendix A. The four Building Blocks are listed along the left edge and the top row of the chart is differentiated by age groups. Your leadership team should complete the chart by entering the ministries that address the building block in each square for the designated age group. For example, the box at the intersection of Belong and Children may be filled in with Sunday school, Children's worship, and nursery programs. One area of ministry can address a number of building blocks. Worship, for example, could be a source of *hope* as well as a source of *knowing*.

After completing the chart, look at each box and ask questions like:

- Are the programs in the box sufficient for the people in the group?
- What are we missing?
- Is there an area in which we need to refocus?

As you fill in the chart, you can also add the many interactions that happen in church that are not part of the programs. For example, in our church most of the adults gather for coffee and fellowship after our worship service. This time at church is an important part for members to feel like they belong. Even though this isn't an official church program, it is an important part of our ministry. Add these informal ministries to the chart so you have a more complete view of your church's work.

The conversations about faith that happen when filling in the chart will provide your team with a way to talk about and to look at how the congregation is meeting the needs for the faith of all the people in your church. For example, perhaps many adults do not stay for coffee and fellowship. The team looking at the chart might want to talk about if there are other ways the adults who leave immediately after worship receive their feeling of belonging.

The chart in Figure 1 is just one example of ways that churches have used Building Blocks to evaluate and plan their ministries. The chart can be changed to meet your needs by changing the top row to represent many different ways of thinking about the people in your congregation. You could differentiate them by location or by how engaged they are in the life of your church. A Children's Ministry Director might actually put the names of some of the people in his or her care along the top. By changing the top row, your team can think about each group (or person) and ask, "How are we, as a church, addressing this particular building block for this group (or person)?"

Figure 1. The Building Blocks of Faith

	Children	Teens	Young Adults	Middle Adults	Elders Seniors
I Belong					
I Know / Understand					
I Have Hope					
I Am Called and Equipped					

A congregation can choose to use the Building Blocks Assessment (see Figure 2) to assess where their congregation is strong and which areas could be improved. This assessment takes an individual about 10 minutes or less to complete and is easy to score. This tool was designed to get information very quickly from either a leadership team or an entire congregation. Each of the twenty statements gets a response of either 0 (not at all), 1 (yes, sometimes) or 2 (Yes, most of the time.) Each Building Block has five statements. The scores can be added together to get a score for each of the Building Blocks. The scores for each Building Block or for each question can be considered as a church begins to have conversations about what is working well and what needs additional attention. The data from this assessment gives a congregation a snapshot of how they are meeting the faith needs of the people.

Figure 2. The Building Blocks Assessment

This assessment is based on the Apgar scoring method used to describe the health of newborns right after birth. It is meant to be a quick, first-impression look at how the four Building Blocks of Faith are evident in your congregation. Don't overthink your responses—go with your initial reaction to each item.

Based on your experience in this church **in the past three months**, write a number (0, 1, or 2, described as follows) in front of each of the statements below.

        0 (Not at all)   1 (Yes, sometimes)   2 (Yes, most of the time)

I Belong
- _____ I know that I belong to God.
- _____ This community is a warm, welcoming place.
- _____ I feel welcomed and embraced by this community.
- _____ We treat one another with respect and care about our relationships with each other.
- _____ I have a place or way to contribute to this community.

I Know and Understand
- _____ We encourage each other to know God and God's stories.
- _____ I frequently learn new things about God.
- _____ A Bible study or prayer group is available for me.
- _____ I hear stories of how God is working in the lives of people in this church.
- _____ I read the Bible and pray regularly.

I Have Hope
- _____ We listen to each other, telling and hearing faith stories.
- _____ I am confident in the expectation that God will renew this world.
- _____ Our actions show and reinforce the hope that our congregation has in Christ.
- _____ I am sure enough of the hope I have in Christ that my life decisions are based on it.
- _____ Our congregation works in our community to show Christ's love in concrete ways.

I Am Called and Equipped
- _____ I am encouraged by this congregation to discern my gifts and my calling.
- _____ I am affirmed in my calling by this congregation.
- _____ There are opportunities to serve God in a variety of ways in this congregation.
- _____ Our congregation responds to needs in our church, our community, and our world.
- _____ I encourage others in the use of their gifts.

While we have some data from the churches who have piloted the assessment we don't have enough to give average scores for each question (or even each category) but we have found that discussing the results as a leadership team has been helpful as churches look at what they have discovered for their congregation. One of the most valuable things to do with the results is to look at them by age group. A church with which we worked discovered that their oldest members scored higher than their other groups in the area of hope. Now the church has the opportunity to talk about using a great resource in their most senior members that they did not realize they had.

Building Blocks of Faith can help a congregation make changes on how to grow faith in the people with whom they are working. It has been used in more than a dozen churches in the United States and Canada and those churches have found new ways of using the Building Blocks in their ministries. Here are some examples.

- A church in Michigan asked their elders to use the four building blocks as a template for discussions on home visits to congregation members.
- A church in Minnesota has had a potluck sponsored by each ministry program in their church. During the last 10 minutes of the event the sponsoring program shares how their program is working with all four building blocks.
- A church in Washington found the four Building Blocks in Psalm 34 and used the Psalm and Building Blocks as a way to structure a Sunday-School teacher's prayer meeting.
- In Ontario, the high school youth listed Bible verses for each Building Block. They used that work as the framework for their meetings for the year.
- A church in Detroit, MI developed a mentoring program based on the Building Blocks.
- Resources for churches to use this model have been developed and collected by the Faith Formation Ministries of the Christian Reformed Church and can be found in the "Building Blocks of Faith Toolkit." Examples of the resources there include
  - Children's sermons that illustrate the Building Blocks.
  - Biblical texts with Building Blocks embedded in them: Luke 24, Genesis 3, Isaiah 43, and the book of Ezekiel.
  - Small group discussion guide about how to strengthen their current programs and create a vision for the future.
  - Family Devotions.

Since the Building Blocks of Faith model is appropriate for all ages, children and children's programming are not isolated but benefit by being part of the same vision for faith as the rest of the church. Children's program directors and volunteers can be part of broader discussions about faith since everyone is working from the same perspective toward the same goal. The model is also flexible enough that it can be used in just one ministry in a church, like the children's ministries, without conflicting with other ministries. The faith statements are so basic that they will coordinate with other vision statements.

We have found that the four-part Building Blocks model has allowed congregations to have good conversations about their faith-formation ministries. It is easy to explain and to use, while at the same time giving people in the congregation a common language to begin talking about faith formation.

References

Barna, George. 2003. *Transforming Children into Spiritual Champions*. Ventura, CA: Regal.
Burke, Lynda. 2017. *Psalm 34, Building Blocks of Faith Toolkit*. Christian Reformed Church, 12 Aug. 2016. 03 Feb.
"The Building Blocks of Faith Toolkit." 2017. *Christian Reformed Church*. n.p., 04 Jan. 2017. 25 Jan. https://www.crcna.org/FaithFormation/toolkits/building-blocks-faith-toolkit.
Dean, Kenda Creasy. 2010. *Almost Christian: What the Faith of Our Teenagers is Telling the American Church*. Oxford: Oxford University Press.
Dykstra, Craig. 2005. *Growing in the Life of Faith: Education and Christian Practices*. 2nd ed. Louisville: Westminster John Knox.
Editors. 2014. "The Future of Children's Ministry." *Children's Ministry*. http://childrensministry.com/articles/the-future-of-childrens-ministry/.
Fowler, James W. 1981. *Stages of Faith*. San Francisco: HarperSanFrancisco.
Heidelberg Catechism. 1563. http://www.crcna.org/welcome/beliefs/confessions/heidelberg8catechism.
Keeley, Laura, and Robert J. Keeley. 2014. "Building Blocks of Faith." *Lifelong Faith*, pp. 2–12.
Keepers, Brian. 2016. "Dangerous Hope." *The Twelve*. N.p., 19 Dec. Accessed Jan. 2017. https://blog.perspectivesjournal.org/2016/12/19/dangerous-hope/.
May, Scottie. 2007. "The Contemplative-Reflective Model." *Perspectives on Children's Spiritual Formation: Four Views*, edited by Michael J Anthony, pp. 45–102. Nashville: Boardman and Holman.
Powell, Kara Eckmann, Jake Mulder, and Brad Griffin. 2016. *Growing Young: Six Essential Strategies to Help Young People Discover and Love Your Church*. Grand Rapids: Baker.
Richter, Don C. 2010. "Embodied Wisdom: Faith Formation Through Practices." In *Shaped By God: Twelve Essentials for Nurturing Faith Formation in Children, Youth, and Adults*, edited by Robert J. Keeley, pp. 23–36. Grand Rapids: Faith Alive Christian Resources.
Smith, Christian, and Melinda Lundquist. Denton. 2005. *Soul Searching: The Religious and Spiritual Lives of American Teenagers*. Oxford: Oxford University Press.

Van Milligan, Lesli. 2017. "Luke 24: Emmaus Road." *Building Blocks of Faith Toolkit*. Christian Reformed Church, 12 Aug. 03 Feb. https://www.crcna.org/FaithFormation/toolkits/building-blocks-faith/luke-24-emmaus-road.

Yust, Karen-Marie. 2004. *Real Kids, Real Faith: Practices for Nurturing Children's Spiritual Lives*. San Francisco, CA: Jossey-Bass.

Chapter 25

What's God Got to Do with It?
Nurturing Spirituality and the Ability to Thrive

Pamela Ebstyne King

> "Be still. God has roused himself from his holy dwelling."
>
> —Zechariah 2:1–6, 10–11, 13

"GOD HAS ROUSED HIMSELF from his holy dwelling." The early Jews understood God to dwell and reside in the Holy of Holies within the temple. But no longer! Zechariah says, "Be still. God has roused himself from his holy dwelling" (2:13). God is on the loose, moving in this world. We know from the Bible that God's way in the world is one of creating, redeeming, and perfecting, and God invites us into that work. He is not a still God—a God stuck in a temple. Not a God in a tabernacle. Not God in a box. God is on the move and he invites us as his people into his movement and work. We are called to participate in God's ongoing work in the world. As children's pastors and youth pastors, that is exactly what we do—our work is a participation in God's ongoing work in the world as we nurture faith in the young people we serve.

As I have studied thriving empirically (King, Carr, & Boitor 2011; King & Clardy 2014) and written on theological perspectives of thriving (King 2016; King & Whitney 2015), I am more and more convinced that at the heart of thriving is an invitation. This invitation comes from the living God—and an invitation invokes a response. There is a two-way dynamic. There is a reciprocating interaction of invitation and response between Creator and created.

We see the first movement in this two-way dynamic of invitation and response in the reality that Zechariah describes. God is on the move and invites us into his work of creating, redeeming, and perfecting. Christian educators and pastors play a crucial part in extending God's invitation to the children and families we work with. In a sense, you are like an invitation platform. Just like people use Evite or Paperless Post to extend invitations to many, God uses children's and youth pastors to reach out and extend invitations to young people to know God and to join God in his ongoing work in the world.

In the church we often give much attention to our salvation in Jesus Christ. In doing so, the church has often emphasized what Jesus has *saved us from*—sin and death—and not so much what Jesus *saved us for*: for participating in his ongoing redemption and repair of this world. In other words, for thriving.

From this perspective, it is important to point out that thriving is not a destination. One can never attain the status of thriving. Thriving is not static or fixed. It is inherently dynamic. Thus, no fixed benchmarks of thriving exist. In my work, when dialoguing with youth about indicators of thriving, they have said things like, "Please don't give us another test to be measured or judged by. We don't want an SAT of Thriving"

Thriving is not a benchmark or a set of benchmarks. Thriving does not consist of attaining a certain GPA, a certain salary, and certain type of purpose, or even a certain level of joy. It is not a destination. It is not even memorizing the Bible verses assigned by a Sunday school teacher. We will never hear from WAZE or a navigational app, "You have reached your destination! Thriving is just ahead on your right." At least this side of eternity, this is something we will never hear.

Although thriving is not a destination, thriving does have a direction.

Transformation toward *Telos*

This divine invitation to thrive is a journey of transformation *toward* a destination, even though it is *not* the destination. Thriving leads somewhere. It has a direction and purpose. As I have taught and written on human development as a Christian over the years, I have asked the following questions: What are humans developing toward or evolving toward? What is God's purpose for humanity? From a very practical perspective, I have asked, What is the goal of parenting? What is the ultimate goal of my teaching and research? Is the point to nurture or promote happy, successful, competent children? Or is it something other than that?

When asking these questions about God's intention for humankind, I have found the social sciences wanting for answers to these questions about ultimacy. At these moments, I am grateful to be bi-disciplinary and able to draw on theology as a source for beginning to understand God's goal or hope for humankind. Specifically, the Greek word, *telos*, which means purpose, goal, or fulfillment, has been helpful in addressing my questions about God's purposes for humankind.

Theological understandings of *telos* give insight into what God's intention for humans may be and thus inform my understanding of human development. This concept of *telos* or goal provides the direction toward which human development aims. So although thriving (this side of eternity) is not a destination, it has a direction. We are headed toward a *telos*—toward what God created each of us for, toward God's purposes for humankind. From this perspective, the invitation to thrive is an invitation toward a specific *telos*. I understand this goal for humankind in three ways: We are to be conformed to the image of God in Christ, as we are and become our unique selves, and as we are related to God, others, and creation.

Conformity to Christ

First, as Christians we affirm that we are made in the image of God. The Bible tells us that Christ is the perfect image of God (Col 1:15). Thus, becoming like Christ is part of our *telos* (see figure 1). Being conformed to the likeness of the image of God in Christ is a shared *telos* among humans. We take on the ways of Christ and grow toward the character of Christ (King & Whitney 2015). From this perspective, our ministry involves nurturing children and youth through our teaching, discipleship, and modeling to become more like Christ. We promote the virtues that Christ embodied, such as love, hope, patience, and forgiveness. We teach on the ways of Jesus, so that young people can pattern their lives after the life of Jesus.

Figure 1. *Telos* of the Reciprocating Self

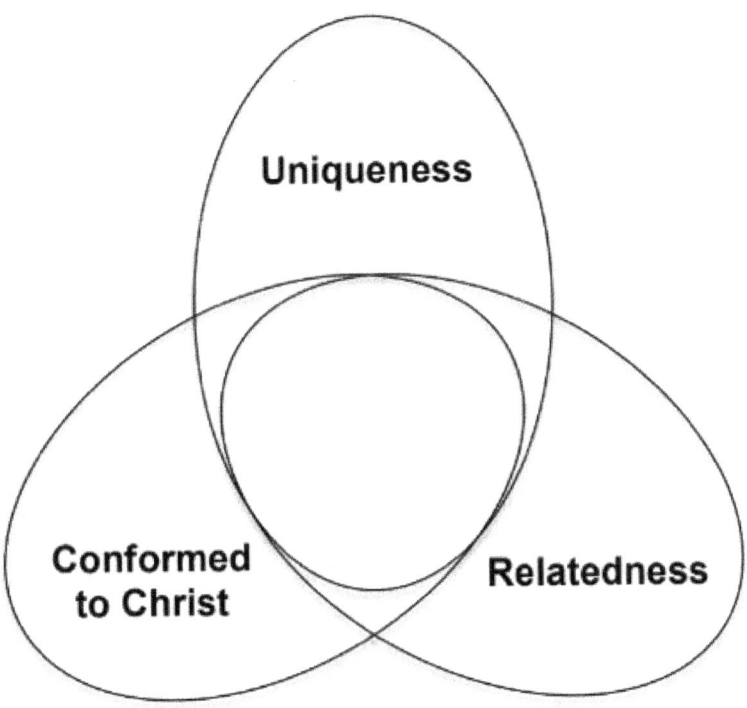

Uniqueness

Second, although we are called to conformity to the image of God in Christ, that does not mean uniformity with Christ. An element of our *telos* is to be and become more fully the unique person that God created us to be (Figure 1). Drawing on trinitarian theological interpretations of the image of God, we recognize the uniqueness of the three persons of the Godhead: Father, Son, and Spirit. Although as humans we cannot apprehend the inner workings of the Trinity, based on biblical interpretation we garner that God exists in simultaneous uniqueness and unity (Balswick, King, & Reimer 2016; King 2016; King & Whitney 2015). So although our *telos* is to become more like the image of God in Christ, we each image God uniquely, with our own particular identity, giftedness, and passions.

This is so important to our work in child and youth ministry. Each of the children and youth you work with are uniquely created, even that young person who drives you crazy in Sunday school or at youth group. The psalmist tells us that each of those kids was fearfully and wonderfully made (Ps 139:14)—even the little rascal in my mind! Part of our role in ministry is to enable these young ones entrusted to our care to become more fully the persons God created each of them to be.

Relatedness

As much as we celebrate human uniqueness, we must always remember that thriving is a dynamic. As such, it insists on relatedness. God created humankind to be in relationship—with God, with other people, and with his creation. While the Trinity is comprised of the three unique persons, God exists in perfect unity. One of my favorite theology professors, the late Ray Anderson, liked to say "God is a being in community." Similarly, humans are created to live in community, in relationship. We are not created to just live with or among people, but called to live in reciprocating relationships with people. One way of understanding our *telos* comes from the concept of becoming *reciprocating selves* (Balswick, King, & Reimer 2016; King 2016). We are created to be in mutual relationships with God, with one another, and with creation. We are created for connections.

This relationality extends beyond our personal relationships. We are also called to relate and tend to others and to the creation around us. Theologians also emphasize God's mandate to humankind to have dominion as covenant partners and caretakers of all of God's people and God's creation (Balswick, King, & Reimer 2016; King 2016; King & Whitney 2016; Mouw 2012). From this standpoint, as children and youth workers, we can understand ourselves as God's ambassadors here on earth. In other words, God is making his appeal through us (2 Cor 5:20) to the children and youth we serve. As such, we are to nurture the youth we serve to be fully formed or forming to become individuals in full relationship with God, people, and creation.

God created us to be reciprocating selves, not renegade selves. I think this is an important point of contrast with contemporary culture, which emphasizes individuality. Even the growing movement of positive psychology promotes the concept of "flourishing," which emphasizes developing to one's fullest potential, experiencing life satisfaction, having a sense of meaning and living with consistency to that sense of meaning. In this concept of flourishing, there is no obligation or responsibility to another. This is not biblical. This is not our *telos*. We do not thrive and move toward our *telos* without regard to another. Thriving is not individualism run amuck. It is not unbridled humanism. It's not about "me, me, me . . ." In fact, it's the turning "me" on its head to find "we" (Figure 2).

Figure 2. Me Thrives, When We Thrive.

Our *telos* involves understanding our fit with the people and world around us. Our ongoing relatedness to God, others, and the world leads us to a deepening discovery of our places of contribution. As such, a distinguishing aspect of thriving is contribution to the greater good. We enable youth to thrive and define their purpose. We nurture their gifts, so they can help others thrive. Thriving is not just doing well. It is not just living up to one's own potential; it is also giving back as we are conformed to Christ.

Our *telos* is to become reciprocating selves, individuals who live as differentiated selves in mutual, respectful relationship with God, with other people, and with the broader world around us. Our hope for ourselves—and the youth we work with—is to grow in uniqueness as we discover our places of contribution in the broader world and become more like Christ. How does this occur? Thriving is not only a journey of transformation toward the capacity for reciprocating relationships; it also *occurs* through reciprocity.

Thriving is a journey of transformation toward our *telos*—being conformed to the image of God in Christ, as our unique selves, as we discover and live out our fit and contribution to the people and the world around us. This is a dynamic process that occurs as young people work out who they are in relationship with the world.

Development through Relationships

Development occurs through relationships. It occurs through the give and take between young persons and their family, their friends—and broader relationships like the economy and the values of the day. The dominant theories in developmental psychology are systems theories (Overton 2013). These focus on the relationships between individuals and the many different systems in which they live. For example, we understand how a child develops in the context of their family, their school, their ethnicity, and so on. A late mentor of mine, Peter Benson, understood this. He was known for saying, "Relationships are central to thriving and the oxygen of life."

I imagine that if you think back on your own journey of development, you can identify many individuals who came alongside you and nurtured your personal uniqueness—your interests, your sense of purpose. These individuals enabled you to be more like Jesus, and helped you find your way in making contributions to the world around you. Perhaps these people challenged you to live with more compassion, encouraged you to lead in your church youth group, or invited you on a mission trip.

A few years back, I had the opportunity to study highly spiritual youth around the world (King, Clardy, & Ramos 2014). These were young people nominated or recognized for living with profound spirituality. The narratives of these young people's recounting of their faith formation revealed that their spiritual commitments were less the result of profound mystical experiences and more due to social interactions with ordinary people in their lives. These findings suggest that faith formation is often forged in the ongoing ordinary social interactions in teens' lives and that spirituality is often shaped through the ebb and flow of life (King, Abo-Zena, & Weber 2017). Specifically, their stories describe that everyday interactions of offering support and encouragement, discussing beliefs or moral dilemmas, teaching, and serving as role models have the potential to shape and influence a young person's spiritual commitments. Additionally, the findings suggest that intentional gatherings such as religious youth groups, camps, retreats, and prayer groups can be seminal, occasional, or ongoing reinforcements.

As much as scripture, beliefs, rituals, and practices are vital, this study demonstrates that these religious elements are often amplified by relationships. It is almost like relationships activate beliefs and rituals—they make them real and make them meaningful to young people.

Thriving occurs through relationships. Thriving is not an individual proposition. It is a corporate endeavor, a relational pursuit. We cannot thrive on our own. Over the years, my work in psychology and theology has focused on a particular kind of relatedness, particularly how youth relate to God. I have been curious about the concept and experience of transcendence.

Research has demonstrated that not all relationships and not all interactions are the same. Interactions marked by transcendence or the sacred have the potential to be very powerful—for good or for bad. In the study of the teen spiritual exemplars mentioned above, we found that experiences of transcendence informed meaning and changed the way these youth understand the world and themselves. When young people experience the love and grace of God, they not only gain clarity of their beliefs, but their relationship with God fuels devotion and commitment. These beliefs and values then shape how they live out their lives in the world.

For these exemplary youth, this sense of transcendence was not merely a lofty feeling, but an experience of being connected and being known—of encountering and being encountered by God, by the sacred. As Christians, we are not surprised by this research finding. We know that an encounter with the loving God transforms people. We know that when we encounter grace and love, we are altered. We know that when the Holy Spirit is involved (even I, as a Presbyterian, know), we are altered. We believe in the subjective act of salvation through the death and resurrection of Jesus Christ. When we realize that through Christ we are forgiven, we are not only released from the fear of death, but we are also released to lead a life of love and fullness—a life of thriving.

For the youth in the study, mature spirituality or faith was dynamic. It was not merely a feeling or a sense of connection to something beyond the self, not a list of beliefs or doctrines, not a résumé of appropriate and impressive behaviors. No, their lives were lived as a response to their encounters with the transcendent. Specifically, the Christians in the study lived their lives in response to an ongoing encounter with the living God.

If at the heart of thriving lies an invitation, for these highly spiritual youth, their lives declared an enthusiastic RSVP, a living RSVP. They experienced something sacred, beyond themselves, that changed the way they understood themselves and the world and influenced how they lived their lives. Their experience of transcendence—for some it was God, for others Allah, for others being a part of the Covenant people of God—this encounter was an invitation that evoked, required, a response. The response transformed their beliefs and values, goals, purpose, and commitments—and actions. They lived their lives differently because of their experience and their understanding of the sacred.

This is an important point about thriving; remember the concept of human *telos* proposed at the beginning of this chapter? The *telos* of the children and youth we serve is to become like the image of God in Christ, as their unique selves, but also as they make meaningful contributions to those around them. For some young people their contribution is to their families, for others it is to their friends, for others, their contribution to those less fortunate in their community, or for yet others their contribution is to the broader world.

Transcendence fuels or propels this commitment to contribution. In fact, it is our encounter with the living God that sustains our ministry and work. (I know it's not the salaries in children's and youth ministry that keep you there!) Our understanding of ourselves as part of God's greater work in this world keeps us ministering to others.

Thriving is ignited and fueled from transcendence. When young people experience themselves as God's beloved daughters and sons, to the extent that this encounter shapes their sense of identity, understanding of the world, and responsibility to participate in God's ongoing work in the world, they are on the trajectory of thriving.

Transcendent Coordinates

People, especially in the broader academy, often ask me, why religion? Why is religion so helpful for kids to thrive? Among the several ways I might respond, I point to the concept of the transformative power of transcendence discussed above. Religion offers encounters with God that are so meaningful and profound that they propel change in the way in which kids understand themselves and their place in the world.

Second, I suggest that religion not only offers an encounter with the divine, but also provides an embodied belief system. Religious traditions exist in a real community of people offering defined ideals, values, and beliefs, as well as actual examples of how to live them out. In this way religion provides a community of coordinates, and each young person needs coordinates to locate oneself. Young people are not ultimately intelligible apart from the family and community within which they exist. Furthermore, people are not intelligible without reference to the transcendent horizon within which they exist and to which their deepest longings point.

Coordinates are necessary to locate oneself in the world. To illustrate this point, I draw on a favorite game during my childhood. I used to love to play Battleship with my brothers, and now I like to play it with my kids. Do you remember how you find a boat? The players take turns calling out coordinates, "C4 ... B6 ... A9 ..." The boats are located and found by coordinates. Youth need coordinates to locate themselves—to form an identity.

They need reference points to know their course. Navigating the waters of adolescence is no easy task. There are abundant opportunities, but there are also turbulent waters and deep waters, with sharks along the way.

As youth today work out their lives—their sense of self, their identity, their purpose, their "sparks"—they have so many options through which to discover and explore all of this.

They have so many outlets that it's dizzying. A multitude of allegiances compete for their attention and time. These are not just activities, but so many options to follow—Facebook, Instagram, other social media. Kids are invited to follow, to like, to belong. It's hard to know who you are and to whom you belong when you are following so much. These are all different stories that youth are literally following. How does anyone make sense out of all that?

Religion provides an alternative: a grand story to follow and to which to belong. It gives a set of coordinates in which young people can find themselves. When youth know what story they are part of, they can begin to find and understand their role in that story: whether it is the gospel narrative of being a follower of Jesus, aligning oneself with the Jewish notion of *tikkun olam*—of being a part of God's covenant people in the repair of the world—or understanding oneself as a contributing citizen of a democracy.

When you know the story to which you belong, and when you know your role in that story, you gain a profound sense of purpose. That is what we are invited into: the ultimate story of God's ongoing work in this world. When we find ourselves contributing to a greater story, we thrive.

If we understand thriving in this light, then we understand the invitation is not simply to accept what God has done through the cross, but also to accept and embrace our part in God's ongoing and unfolding story of faithfulness. Our invitation to thrive is then understood as an invitation to a new order, one set forth and defined by the pattern—the *logos*—of Christ. We understand that when Jesus says "Follow me," he's not referring to Instagram or Facebook; he is referring to a way of life and participation in his ongoing ministry here on earth. We remember that when he left this earth as a physical man, he gave us his Spirit to empower us and to continue his work on this planet.

Now that's a set of coordinates.

So then how do we extend this invitation to children and youth? How do we serve as God's agents of transformation and thriving on earth? As a youth pastor, Sunday school teacher, or volunteer, you are often a young person's coordinates. In fact, you are professionally trained coordinates—your lives and work provide reference points. Your teaching tells the story. Your ministry efforts can connect them to the story. And your lives—lived out in front of them—model and exemplify God's story of love and grace (no pressure here!).

As you serve as coordinates, I ask, How do you enable youth to become more Christ-like? To understand who they are as God's unique creations with particular gifts, passions, and sparks? How do you encourage their understanding of how they fit into and contribute to God's greater story?

No doubt, when we ourselves are deeply connected to God's love, we will be compelled by this love to extend God's invitation to thrive on to God's children. I offer a blessing to you in your ministry as one in which you both simultaneously encounter the love of Christ and extend God's invitation to thrive, and then nurture young people on their way toward God's *telos* for them.

References

Balswick, Jack, Pamela Ebstyne King, and Kevin S. Reimer. 2016. *The Reciprocating Self: A Theological Perspective of Development*. Rev. 2nd ed. Downers Grove, IL: IVP Academic.

King, Pamela Ebstyne. "The Reciprocating Self: Trinitarian and Christological Anthropologies of Being and Becoming." *Journal of Christianity and Psychology* 35, pp. 215–32.

King, Pamela Ebstyne, Mona M. Abo-Zena, M, and Jonathan D. Weber. 2017. "Varieties of Social Experience: The Religious Cultural Context of Diverse Spiritual Exemplars." *British Journal of Developmental Psychology* 35.1, pp. 127–41.

King, Pamela Ebstyne, Drew Carr, and Ciprian Boitor. 2011. "Religion, Spirituality, Positive Youth Development, and Thriving." *Advances in Child Development and Behavior* 41, pp. 161–95.

King, Pamela Ebstyne, and Casey E. Clardy. 2014. "Prevention and the Promotion of Thriving in Children and Adolescents." In *Christianity and Developmental Psychopathology: Theory and Application for Working with Youth*, edited by Kelly S. Flanagan and Sarah E. Hall, 179–202. Naperville, IL: InterVarsity.

King, Pamela Ebstyne, Casey E. Clardy, and Jenel Sánchez Ramos. 2014. "Adolescent Spiritual Exemplars: Exploring Spirituality in the Lives of Diverse Youth." *Journal of Adolescent Research* 29, pp. 186–212.

King, Pamela Ebstyne, and William B. Whitney. 2015. "What's the "Positive" in Positive Psychology? Teleological Considerations Based on Creation and Imago Doctrines." *Journal of Psychology and Theology* 43, pp. 47–59.

Mouw, Richard. 2012. "The Imago Dei and Philosophical Anthropology." *Christian Scholar's Review* 41, pp. 253–66.

Overton, Willis F. 2013. "A New Paradigm for Developmental Science: Relationism and Relational-Developmental-Systems." *Applied Developmental Science* 17, pp. 94–107.

Contributors

Dr. Holly Catterton Allen is Professor of Family Science and Christian Ministries at Lipscomb University in Nashville, TN. She teaches undergraduate courses such as Nurturing Spiritual Development in Children and Family Ministry. Her recent books include *InterGenerate: How Churches Can Become More Intentionally Intergenerational in Outlook and Practice* (Abilene Christian University Press, 2018) and *Intergenerational Christian Formation: Bringing the Whole Church Together in Ministry, Community, and Worship* (with Christine Ross, InterVarsity Press, 2012).

Amy Boone, MEd, is a teaching and learning specialist who works with faculty at Abilene Christian University in course design and professional development. She also teaches as an adjunct at Hardin Simmons University. Amy's research on intellectual giftedness and faith development has been published in Children's Ministry Magazine and will be presented at the Council for Christian Colleges and Universities Conference in 2018.

Carly Brandvold graduated from Lipscomb University in Nashville, TN with a degree in Leadership Communications in 2016. She is currently pursuing her Masters in Divinity from Lipscomb with plans to graduate in May of 2018. Originally from Jacksonville, FL, Carly considers the beach her second home. Passionate about spiritual development and Jesus' love for children, Carly has found her niche working in children's ministry. Carly now lives in Nashville, TN, where she works as the Kids Pastor at Ethos Church.

CONTRIBUTORS

Ron Bruner (DMin, Abilene Christian University) has served as the executive director of Westview Boys' Home in Hollis, Oklahoma, since 1999. His scholarly interests include the theology of children, adolescent spiritual formation, and care of youth experiencing at-risk circumstances. Bruner is co-editor of *Along the Way: Conversations about Children and Faith* with Dana Kennamer Pemberton, and *Owning Faith: Rethinking the Role of Church and Family in the Faith Journey of Teenagers* with Dudley Chancey.

Rev. Rebecca Chaffee has a special interest in children's spirituality and ministry practices that nurture lasting faith connections among children and congregations. She earned her MDiv with a concentration in Spiritual Formation from Northeastern Seminary and is working on her DMin at University of Dubuque Theological Seminary. Chaffee currently serves as pastor, First Presbyterian Church in Caledonia, New York, following eight years in Family Ministries at Pebble Hill Presbyterian Church in Dewitt, New York.

Beverly J. Christian lectures at Avondale College of Higher Education in Cooranbong, Australia, and is active in the Christian Education Research Centre of that institution. Her research interests include the culture and ethos of Christian schools, nature-based learning, and best pedagogy practice. Her aim as a lecturer is to help pre-service teachers develop their God given potential as caring and innovative classroom practitioners.

Taryn Cleaves has ministered to children and their families for over six years and is currently the Children's Pastor at Bettendorf Christian Church in the Quad City area of Iowa. She completed her Masters of Children's and Family Ministry at Bethel Seminary (St. Paul). In her spare time (what's spare time?) she enjoys reading, writing, baseball, photography, hanging out with her 3 cats (Jonas, Phoebe, and Theo), and enjoying a cold Dr. Pepper.

Arnold Cole, EdD, is Chief Executive Officer of Back to the Bible, an international media ministry headquartered in Lincoln, Nebraska. His research focuses on developing methodologies, processes, and best practices to instill significant behavioral change. He received his BA & MA in Psychology, and his EdD in Institutional Management from Pepperdine University. His publications include *Unstuck* and *Tempted. Tested. True.*

J. P. Conway serves as the minister at the Acklen Avenue Church of Christ in Nashville, Tennessee and teaches part time at Lipscomb University. He has degrees from Abilene Christian University, Gordon-Conwell Theological

Seminary, and Fuller Theological Seminary. He and his wife are the proud parents of three daughters.

Julie Exline, PhD, is a Professor in the Department of Psychological Sciences at Case Western Reserve University. She is a licensed psychologist and a certified spiritual director.

Barbara Fisher, recently retired from the School of Education at Avondale College of Higher Education (Australia), has researched and lectured in religious education for over 30 years. She has taught in New Zealand, Australia, and studied and taught in the United States of America. She is the lead author of the textbook Developing a faith-based education: A teacher's manual (2010) and is passionate about promoting an interactive and engaging transformational approach to studying biblical narratives.

Karissa Glanville, PhD, writes novels and children's books (under the name KL Glanville) as well as non-fiction. She is also a business owner and speaker. Her doctoral work looked at the community discernment process that occurred in various Christian communities when children claimed to have a revelatory experience from God. She enjoys traveling and teaching, hanging out with friends old and new, crafting miniatures, and dreaming up stories that inspire.

Steffany J. Homolka, PhD, is assistant professor of psychology at Angelo State University in San Angelo Texas. She earned her PhD from Case Western Reserve University.

Marva Hoopes, EdD, serves as Christian Education Specialist in the department of Bible, Theology, and Ministry at Malone University in Canton, Ohio where she teaches courses in ministry, missions, and theology. She has also held the position of Children's Pastor for 26 years in the Evangelical Friends denomination, has served as a curriculum consultant and writer, as well as participated in leadership on the regional and national Christian education boards of Evangelical Friends Church.

Edyta Jankiewicz currently works as assistant professor of discipleship and religious education at the SDA theological seminary at Andrews university in Berrien Springs, MI. Her passion and interest in faith formation and spiritual growth have been shaped by her experiences as a wife, mother and missionary.

Laura Keeley is a Regional Catalyzer in Faith Formation Ministries for the Christian Reformed Church in North America and Director of Children's Ministries for 14th St Christian Reformed Church in Holland, MI. She is the author of articles, book chapters and *The Staff Ministry Handbook* and co-author of *Celebrating the Milestones of Faith*.

Robert J. Keeley is Professor of Education at Calvin College and Visiting Professor of Discipleship and Faith Formation at Calvin Theological Seminary. He is author of a number of articles and book chapters as well as author of *Helping Our Children Grow in Faith* and editor of *Shaped by God*.

Jeffrey B. Keiser, MEd, is currently an Adjunct Professor of Education. He holds a B.S. in Sociology from Arizona State University, and a Master's degree in Education from Concordia University Chicago. He lectures and consults with schools, churches, and ministries.

Pamela Ebstyne King, PhD joined Fuller as assistant professor of marital and family studies in 2008, after serving the School of Psychology for eight years as an adjunct and research professor. In 2014 she was named Peter L. Benson Associate Professor of Applied Developmental Science. Dr. King works with the Thrive Center for Human Development and is actively engaged with the Fuller Youth institute.

Alana Lauck graduated summa cum laude from Lipscomb University, in Nashville, TN, with a Bachelor of Arts in Psychology and Spanish in the Spring of 2016. She has been employed at Lipscomb University since August of 2016 as a Financial Aid Loan Counselor. Currently she lives in her hometown of Nashville, TN with her husband, K. J. Lauck. Alana plans to attend graduate school to receive her Master's in Marriage and Family Therapy at Lipscomb University. She hopes to continue to contribute to psychological research in the coming years.

Mimi L. Larson, PhD, is Visiting Assistant Professor of Christian Formation and Ministry at Wheaton College and adjunct Professor of Educational Studies at Trinity Evangelical Divinity School. Her research specialty is in the area of young children's faith formation. Having served in practical church ministry for over 25 years, Mimi also serves as the Children's Ministry Catalyzer for Faith Formation Ministries, a ministry of the Christian Reformed Church in North America.

CONTRIBUTORS

Sandra M. Ludlow, BEd (EC), is Course Convenor at Avondale College of Higher Education Cooranbong NSW Australia. Her current research interests include co-constructed curriculum and nurturing preschooler's spiritual awareness, biblical knowledge and faith formation.

Catherine Maresca is the founder and director of the Center for Children and Theology in Washington DC (www.cctheo.org). She has been working with children and adults in the Catechesis of the Good Shepherd since 1982 as a catechist and trainer. Her book, *DoubleClose, the Young Child's Knowledge of God*, explores how young children do theology, and some of their insights into God, the Kingdom of God, incarnation and resurrection.

Dr. Jennifer Mata-McMahon is an early childhood educator, working in the field since 1995, with an EdD from Teachers College, Columbia University (2010). She is the coauthor of *Ambiente en Acción* (Environment in Action) (Unimet, 2006), author of *Spiritual Experiences in Early Childhood Education* (Routledge, 2015), and coeditor of *Spirituality: An Interdisciplinary View* (Inter-Disciplinary Press, 2016), as well as the author of several book chapters and journal articles related to children's spirituality.

Erin Minta Maxfield-Steele is an Episcopal priest from the Shenandoah Valley in Virginia. Erin was raised in the Mennonite tradition and unschooled until age thirteen. She and her partner, Allyn Maxfield-Steele, met while attending Vanderbilt Divinity School in Nashville. Erin and Allyn live in rural North Carolina with their sweet dog, Johann.

Shirley K. Morgenthaler, PhD is Distinguished Professor of Education at Concordia University-Chicago. With a ministry spanning over 50 years, she has developed early childhood academic programs at the both the undergraduate and post graduate levels as well as developed an early childhood lab school. She has authored *Right From the Start: A Parent's Guide to the Young Child's Faith Formation* and *Children and Worship: Lessons from Research*, as well as edited *Exploring Children's Spiritual Formation: Foundational Issues*. She is also the current editor of the *Lutheran Education Journal*.

Trevecca Okholm, MA is an adjunct professor in Practical Theology at Azusa Pacific University with an emphasis in family ministry and teaching in the church. She is a Certified Christian Educator in the Presbyterian Church/USA. She currently serves the church as a family ministry consultant, a speaker for parent groups and women's retreats, and unofficial trainer/facilitator for Godly Play/Children and Worship.

Pamela Caudill Ovwigho, PhD, is the Executive Director of the Center for Bible Engagement, Lincoln, Nebraska. Throughout her career she has researched a variety of topics from welfare policy to family violence to spirituality. Currently she focuses on scripture engagement, spiritual growth, and church health. Her publications include *Managing Your Family's High Tech Habits* and *Better Relationships, Better Life*.

Kenneth I. Pargament, PhD, is Professor Emeritus of Psychology at Bowling Green State University in Bowling Green, Ohio. His nationally and internationally known research addresses religious beliefs and health. His current research program addresses how elderly people who struggle with their religious beliefs and hold negative perceptions about their relationships with God and life meaning have an increased risk of death, even after controlling for physical and mental health and demographic characteristics.

Chase Thompson (MS, Cameron University) has counseled with the residents of Westview Boys' Home in Hollis, Oklahoma, since 2010. A licensed professional counselor (LPC), he is also a TBRI® (Trust Based Relational Intervention®) practitioner and an EAGALA® (Equine Assisted Growth and Learning Association®) certified member. Thompson has extensive experience in counseling with parents, treatment of autistic youth, and therapy with violent offenders.

Erin Trageser, a Chattanooga, Tennessee native, is a 2017 graduate of Lipscomb University with a BA in Family Relations. She focused her research on PTSD in children whose parents are incarcerated. Following the conclusion of Holly Allen's class, Erin pursued an internship with Tennessee Prison Outreach Ministry (TPOM) where she worked on a Christmas gift giveaway for children like those they worked with whose parents were incarcerated.

Joshua Wilt is a postdoctoral fellow in the department of psychological sciences at Case Western Reserve University. He received his PhD in personality psychology from Northwestern University in 2014, where he was an active member of the Foley Center for the Study of Lives. His research is broadly concerned with investigating affective, behavioral, cognitive, and desire (ABCD) components that are relevant to personality structure and function.

www.ingramcontent.com/pod-product-compliance
Lightning Source LLC
Chambersburg PA
CBHW052147300426
44115CB00011B/1555